John Jamieson

Sermons on the Heart

John Jamieson

Sermons on the Heart

ISBN/EAN: 9783744734820

Printed in Europe, USA, Canada, Australia, Japan

Cover: Foto ©Thomas Meinert / pixelio.de

More available books at **www.hansebooks.com**

SERMONS

ON THE

HEART:

IN TWO VOLUMES.

BY

JOHN JAMIESON, M.A.

MINISTER OF THE GOSPEL, FORFAR.

VOL. I.

As in water face answereth to face: so the heart of man to man.
PROV. xxvii. 19.

EDINBURGH:

PRINTED BY NEILL AND COMPANY;
SOLD by C. DILLY; J. MATTHEWS; C. ELLIOT, and T. KAY; BELLAMY
and ROBARTS; London; M. GRAY, C. ELLIOT, and W. LAING,
Edinburgh; J. DUNCAN, and R. FARIE, Glasgow.

M,DCC,LXXXIX.

ENTERED IN STATIONERS HALL.

ADVERTISEMENT.

SOME, it may be feared, from the very title of this Work, may condemn it without a trial. Men are naturally disposed to think well of their own hearts, to boast of their goodness, and to palliate even the worst actions by claiming integrity of design; as if all their transgressions were owing to the surprise of temptation, some pitiable weakness, or unaccountable fatality. So powerful is the principle of self-love, especially with respect to the heart, that he who dares to arraign it, is in danger of being viewed by the bulk of mankind as an enemy to human nature. Those who extol the powers of man in his fallen state, who either deny or draw a veil over the fatal effects of the first transgression, are supposed to discover the goodness of their own hearts, and their love to others; nay, to represent their beneficent Creator in a more amiable point of view, than that in which he appears as the Redeemer of lost man. Many are so prepossessed by these notions, that they will not even attempt to exercise their boasted reason in a fair investigation of truth. The cry of " Fanaticism" and " Enthusiasm," is deemed a sufficient reply to all that can be offered on the other side. But men of reason ought to blush at this conduct. *It is not the manner of* their *law to condemn any man without hearing him.* Both parties profess to adhere to one supreme standard, how much soever they may vary as to the mode of interpretation: and to this we are willing to refer the decision of the cause. *To the Law, and to the Testimony, if* we *speak not according to this word, it is because there is no light in* us.

The design of the proposed Work is candidly to represent the Heart of Man, as far as possible, according to the just and striking likeness exhibited on the table of Divine Revelation. If the picture given shall, on a fair comparison with the great original, be found unjust, then let it be condemned. If otherwise, let every man who views it, remember that it is his own. For, *as in water face answereth to face, so the heart of man to man.* In this Work it hath been the Author's aim to treat the subject all along in a practical manner, and to appeal for the truth of what is asserted, not only to the testimony of Scripture, but to man's inward feelings. Many of the proofs of natural depravity, here exhibited, are so obvious, that even carnal men cannot deny them without giving the lie to their own consciousness and experience. They must, therefore, either bring forward some cause equally adequate to the production of effects so various and astonishing, and at least equally agreeable

able to the scriptural account; or stand *convicted* and condemned *by their own conscience.* For Example must be acknowledged, even by themselves, entirely insufficient; as, if they be not singularly successful in blinding their minds, they cannot but be sensible of many secret workings of iniquity in their hearts, the patterns of which they have never received from others; because they are no less secret in them.

To many it may appear that a great deal too much is offered on one general head. But it hath been a principal object to hold up the Heart of Man in various points of light, and at the same time to avoid repetition as far as the nature of the subject will allow. And to every one who is but a little acquainted with his own Heart, after all it will appear that *the one half hath not been told.* For *who can know it?* It must also be remembered, that the whole of Divine Revelation naturally divides itself into two great branches;— the description of man's Ruin by the breach of the first covenant, and that of his Restoration by the second. If the former be not really believed and well understood, one can neither have a genuine faith, nor a just apprehension of the latter. The doctrine of human depravity is a key indispensably necessary for unlocking the precious treasures of the Word. While this depravity itself, as enthroned in the heart, is the great cause of the denial and contempt of the genuine doctrine of salvation in its contrivance, purchase and application; ignorance of the reality or extent of the disease may be viewed as next in energy, in producing rejection of the remedy. For *they that be whole need not a physician.* Men may have a sort of doctrinal notion of the corruption of nature, which hath no influence on their hearts. Thence they receive other doctrines, diametrically opposite; and deny those which are inseparably connected with this. Whatever be their profession, they do not *believe* it *with the heart;* else they would not be so eager to build up with the one hand, what they pull down with the other; or to burn *incense* to the *drag* of corrupt nature, as an atonement for the dishonour done to it, in charging it with corruption; by framing such a system of human ability, in spiritual respects, as could only be true, if the heart were entirely pure. But disbelief or ignorance of this doctrine, is, indeed, the copious fountain of almost every error that hath defiled the Church of Christ.

These considerations are in themselves so important, as in some degree to entitle a work on this subject to a serious and attentive perusal by those into whose hands it may fall. Whatever the Author might plead from the solicitations of some who heard these discourses, and whose opinion he highly respects; or from any usefulness ascribed to them by others, who, he trusts, are now in that place where there is no occasion for

the

the feeble *light of a candle*; the considerations above-mentioned had far more weight in determining him to submit them to the eye of the Public. A variety of discourses might have been presented, which would have been far less obnoxious to the generality of readers, and less irritating to the corruption of any. But there seemed to be more occasion for something on this subject, than on the peculiar doctrines of the Gospel; as there are innumerable discourses on the latter, unspeakably superior to any thing that the Author could offer, already in the hands of the Public; while few writers have enlarged on the former. The generality of those also who have treated this subject, have done so, perhaps rather too much for the bulk of readers, in an abstract and systematical manner. As all these Sermons, except one or two, were delivered in an ordinary course of preaching; this plan was adopted, only in consequence of finding little fruit from the former. Evidences brought from experience and facts, especially when supported by the authority of Scripture, are, as means, more likely to be useful to the greatest part of mankind, than abstract reasoning; how necessary soever this be, at times, in disputing with the wise of this world: although neither can have any saving effect, without the gracious operation of the holy Spirit. A great part of Scripture, indeed, seems to be designed for the very purpose of proving the depravation of our nature, in the manner mentioned. It appears to be a primary intention of the Spirit of inspiration, to strike the imagination, conscience and affections of man, with a progressive display of human wickedness, from the very entrance of sin; and thus to demonstrate, in the most cogent manner, its abominable nature, universal extent, and fatal effects: as many of the judgments there recorded, were originally meant to bring down this doctrine, in some sort, to the very level of the senses.

The Author is sensible that there are innumerable defects in this Work, both as to matter and style. With respect to the latter, it hath been his principal aim to render himself intelligible to every reader. It is feared, that few will have patience to peruse it, to whom this would be the leading objection. Were the Public entertained with romantic ideas of life, a description of feelings which were never realized, or a history of the heart from characters that never had an existence, save in the warm imaginations of writers; far more attention might be expected. The attempt might be applauded, as throwing light on the important study of Man. But can a portrait of the Heart be more unworthy of attention, because it is originally drawn by the finger of God? Can characters afford no instruction or entertainment, merely because they are real? Or, is the history of Human Nature less valuable, because

it

it does not derive its authorities from the dreams of a glowing fancy, or from the peculiar manners of one country; but from the annals of the Church, for near four thousand years, and from a Book, which, with the greatest minuteness and fidelity, describes the manners of men, in characters that apply to every nation, and to every age? Is a description of the diseases that infect and ravage the heart, the worse that it is accurate, faithful and unerring? Or, is it the less worthy of our regard, that it does not resemble those of human physicians, with respect to the uncertainty of cure, or the impropriety of applications; but is connected with the prescription of a Remedy, infinite in value, unfailing in efficacy, and freely offered to all? Whatever mistakes the Author may be chargeable with; he is conscious, that, to the utmost of his power, he hath endeavoured to derive the description here given of the heart, from the infallible testimony of that God, who *searcheth all hearts, and understandeth all the imaginations of the thoughts;* without either wishing to exaggerate the account, or daring to pervert or conceal any thing that seemed to bear the awful impress of Divine authority.

Various modes of expression, here used, may appear antiquated, and unsuitable to the refined taste of this age. But they will bear the greater resemblance to the sentiments they convey. Many, in our time, have laid aside such terms as were formerly used on religious subjects; because, as they pretend, they have been prostituted by some, as the engines of Hypocrisy or Enthusiasm. But it is certainly safest to *speak, not in the words which man's wisdom teacheth, but which the holy Ghost teacheth.* For *the words of the Lord are pure words; as silver tried in a furnace of earth, purified seven times:* while we know that, in every age, the introduction of new terms hath either prepared the way, or been meant as a covert to error. Those, who are not ashamed of old doctrines, need not be ashamed of old expressions, or go back to the schools of heathenism to borrow new ones. While they still retain the sacred stamp of inspiration, there is no more reason for rejecting them, because they may have been sometimes abused, than for wishing for a new Bible, because every heretic, however much he despises or tortures its language, palms his errors on the one we have.

It is, and through grace, will be the earnest desire and prayer of the Author, that He, who hath the hearts of all in his hand, may bless this Work as a mean of acquainting some with their own Hearts, who yet walk in darkness, and *know not at what they stumble;* and of increasing this important knowledge in others, in whom *the day* of grace hath already *dawned.*

CONTENTS
OF THE FIRST VOLUME.

	Page
SER. I. On the Evil of Sin,	1

Jer. ii. 19. *Know therefore and see, that it is an evil thing and bitter, that thou hast forsaken the Lord thy God.*

SER. II. On the Bitterness of Sin, — 16

Jer. ii. 19.—*Know therefore and see, that it is an evil thing and bitter, that thou hast forsaken the Lord thy God.*

SER. III. On the Plague of the Heart, — 49

1 Kings, viii. 38.—*Who shall know every man the plague of his own heart.—*

SER. IV. On knowing the Plague of the Heart, 70

1 Kings, viii. 38.—*Who shall know every man the plague of his own heart.—*

SER. V. On the Necessity of Knowing the Plague of the Heart, — 88

1 Kings, viii. 38.—*Who shall know every man the plague of his own heart.—*

SER. VI. The same subject continued, — 107

SER. VII. On Heart-knowledge as connected with National Reformation and Deliverance, — 125

1 Kings, viii. 38.—*Who shall know every man the plague of his own heart.—*

SER. VIII. On the Atheism of the Heart, — 154

Psal. xiv. 1. *The fool hath said in his heart, There is no God.*

SER. IX. On the Evidences of Heart-Atheism, 166

Psal. xiv. 1. *The fool hath said in his heart, There is no God.*

SER. X. On the Consequences of the Atheism of the Heart, — 182

Psal. xiv. 1. *The fool hath said in his heart, There is no God.*

SER. XI. On the Deceitfulness of the Heart, 201

Jer. xvii. 9. *The heart is deceitful above all things.*

SER. XII. On the Deceitfulness of the Heart, with regard to the Commission of Sin, — 220

Psal. xxxvi. 2. *He flattereth himself in his own eyes, until his iniquities be found to be hateful.*

SER. XIII. The same subject continued, — 235

CONTENTS.

SER. XIV. On the Deceitfulness of the Heart, in stifling Convictions, — — 251
Jer. viii. 5. *They hold fast deceit, they refuse to return.*

SER. XV. On the Deceitfulness of the Heart, in embracing false grounds of Confidence, — 276
Isa. xliv. 20. *He feedeth of ashes; a deceived heart hath turned him aside, that he cannot deliver his soul, nor say, Is there not a lie in my right hand?*

SER. XVI. The same subject continued, — 292

SER. XVII. The same subject continued, — 310

SER. XVIII. On the Deceitfulness of the Heart, with respect to the Performance of Duty, — 326
Psal. lxxviii. 56, 57.—*And kept not his testimonies; but turned back, and dealt unfaithfully, like their fathers: they were turned aside like a deceitful bow.*

SER. XIX. On the Deceitfulness of the Heart, with respect to the Omission of Duty, — — 353
Psal. lxxviii. 56, 57.—*And kept not his testimonies; but turned back, and dealt unfaithfully, like their fathers: they were turned aside like a deceitful bow.*

SER. XX. On the Deceitfulness of the Heart, as influencing the Conduct in Life, — — 372
Jam. i. 22. *But be ye doers of the word, and not hearers only, deceiving your ownselves.*

SER. XXI. On the Deceitfulness of the Heart, in the Abuse of Prosperity, — — 393
Jer. xlix. 16. *Thy terribleness hath deceived thee, and the pride of thine heart.*

SER. XXII. On the Deceitfulness of the Heart, with respect to Adversity, — — 410
Isa. lvii. 17. *I smote him; I hid me, and was wroth, and he went on frowardly in the way of his heart.*

SER. XXIII. On the Deceitfulness of the Heart, in disregarding Providential Dispensations in general, 430
Psal. lxxviii. 7. 8.—*And not forget the works of God;— and might not be as their fathers; a generation that set not their heart aright, and whose spirit was not stedfast with God.*

SER. XXIV. The same subject continued, — 451

SERMON I.

On the Evil of Sin.

Jer. ii. 19.

Know therefore and see, that it is an evil thing and bitter, that thou hast forsaken the Lord thy God.

SALVATION by Christ is the sum and substance of the holy Scriptures. In this, as their centre, all the lines of divine revelation meet. To this, all the histories and prophecies, types and ceremonies, precepts, promises and exhortations, contained in the word, either immediately or ultimately relate. They all point out Jesus as *the end of the law for righteousness.* But as sinners must know their disease, before they can see the necessity of improving the remedy, there are many calls, commands and expostulations addressed to them, declaring the evil and danger of sin. These may be thought unnecessary, because every man has some notion of his being a sinner; intimations of which we have even among the most unenlightened nations. But although this is a truth that every man pretends to believe, there are few who believe it in a right manner. So unjust, partial and unaffecting are the apprehensions, which the generality entertain of sin, that it plainly appears they know not what it is. They reckon deliverance from it so easy a matter, as to despise the salvation purchased by Christ at such infinite expence, as if it were a thing of naught. But, to declare the real nature of sin, the necessity of a saving apprehension of it, the importance of the work of redemption, and to leave every hearer of the gospel without excuse, the Lord addresses himself in this manner to sinners, whether they will hear, or whether they will forbear: *Know therefore and see, that it is an evil thing and bitter, that thou hast forsaken the Lord thy God.*

We learn from the connection, that the Lord, by the Prophet, is here immediately pleading with his ancient people, as to that sin with which they were eminently chargeable, the worship of false gods. But we may justly understand his language, as containing a description of the nature of sin, extensively considered. For the idea conveyed by this expression, *Thou hast forsaken the Lord*, and the characters of *evil* and *bitter*, are applicable to sin in general. The words immediately in view are introduced with a sentence, the truth of which is found by every sinner, sooner or later: *Thine own wickedness shall correct thee, and thy backslidings shall reprove thee.* Was this awful denunciation accomplished by God with regard to his ancient people, when, in his providence, their attachment to idolatry proved the source of their national correction in the Babylonish captivity? And is it not as really verified, either in a temporal or spiritual respect, in the experience of every sinner who *goes on in his trespasses?* Sin often carries its own punishment along with it. Thus, *the wickedness of the sinner corrects him*, when he feels the dreadful stings of conscience on account of sin, that sometimes attend the very perpetration of it, and which, unless the conscience be awfully seared, are its inevitable consequences. These stings are often so keen, that all the pleasures and blandishments of life cannot assuage the pain, or remove the poison. Nay, these very pleasures are embittered in the enjoyment; and life itself, how pleasing soever in a natural point of view, becomes a torment. The *wickedness of the sinner corrects him*, when it not only wounds the peace of his mind, but so impairs his health, and spirits, and worldly circumstances, that himself and every thing around him are constant memorials of his extreme folly. But alas!

to the impenitent sinner, this correction is severest in the end, compared with which, all his former sufferings are only *the beginning of sorrows.*

In opening these words, we propose,

I. To make some introductory observations;
II. To speak of the *evil* of sin;
III. To consider its *bitterness;*
IV. To show by what proofs sinners may *know and see,* that it is *evil and bitter.*

It is *first* proposed to offer a few observations.

1. It may be observed, that men in general *think lightly* of *sin.* They consider it rather as a failure or infirmity of nature, than as positive transgression, guilt or vileness. Nay, some are so abandoned as to account sin no evil at all; at least, they pretend to do so. Therefore, it is said, that *fools make a mock of sin**. When they read or hear of its evil and wickedness, they ridicule all such representations. They laugh at its nature and consequences. Some even go so far as to glory in their iniquity. The more that the drunkard debases himself below the brute-creation, the more he boasts. The debauchee triumphs, not only in the frequency of his abominable prostitution, but in his success in seducing others to iniquity. The profane sinner exults in the fruitfulness of his invention, in the language of blasphemy. These are the persons whom the Spirit of God describes as placing their *glory in their shame* †, and *declaring their sin as Sodom* ‡. Men will often confess they are sinners, and pretend to pray for the pardon of sin; when, perhaps, they have not one affecting thought with respect to its evil, and are nowise serious in their pretended prayers. They will patiently hear ministers preach against sin, and enlarge on its evil; but give themselves no further trouble about

* Prov. xiv. 9.   † Phil. iii. 19.   ‡ Isai. iii. 9.

about it: becaufe they confider it juft as their bufinefs to fpeak evil of fin; as if the Holy One had not declared that HE *cannot look upon it.*

2. THE great reafon why men think fo lightly of fin is, that they *think lightly* of *God.* Our judgment of any thing is always in proportion to our efteem or difefteem of its oppofite. God and fin are two contraries; and we will unavoidably form our eftimate of fin, according to that which we form of effential holinefs. Many profefs to believe the being of God, but are deftitute of any concern for his glory. They acknowledge their dependence on him: yet they act as if they were unaccountable. They are regardlefs of fin, becaufe they have no fear of God. Therefore, it is added in the verfe,—*and that my fear is not in thee, faith the Lord of Hofts.*

3. THERE is an *infinite* evil in fin. This may appear impoffible, becaufe man, its fubject, is a finite being. But although viewed in man, or in any creature as its fubject, it can be only finite; with refpect to God, the object againft whom it is directed, it is infinitely evil: for it is an affront to his infinite perfections. Men themfelves judge of the evil of crimes, not fo much by the perfon who commits them, as by the object againft whom they are committed; and according to the ftation or dignity of the injured party, they are viewed as greater or lefs. Thus, that which is only felony, when affecting a fellow-fubject, becomes high treafon, when committed againft the Sovereign. In forming an eftimate of the evil of fin, we are not fo much to judge of it by the relation it bears to ourfelves, or to fociety, as by that which it bears to the great God, who is principally offended. The evil of fin, as committed againft him, appears fo enhanced, that notwithftanding its fatal effects with regard to ourfelves or others, we may fpeak of every tranfgreffion in the language of David in his penitential pfalm: *Againft thee, thee only have I finned, and done this evil in thy fight* *. Every fin ftrikes againft God, as peculiarly

* Pfal. li. 4.

culiarly and directly, as if no other were either affected or offended by it, or even privy to the commiſſion. Had there not been an infinite evil in ſin objectively conſidered, it would not have required infinite ſatisfaction. *It was not poſſible that the blood of bulls and goats could take away ſin.* It indeed required the *ſhedding of blood*: but this blood muſt be of infinite value. That of the ſinner himſelf could not ſuffice. Therefore *God muſt purchaſe the Church with his own blood* *. For without this there could have been no ſalvation. It was neceſſary that the ranſom ſhould be infinitely precious;—not becauſe of the multitude of ſinners to be redeemed; for they, being finite, could never, by reaſon of their number, require infinite ſatisfaction:—not merely becauſe of the multitude of ſins from which they were to be redeemed, which, in a certain ſenſe, as exceeding all human calculation, may be called infinite †; for theſe were all known to him, and he could have exacted the ranſom, without exceeding in the leaſt:—but by reaſon of the evil of ſin, which required that infinite ſatisfaction ſhould be given to Divine Juſtice. This is the great reaſon why the ſufferings of hell are eternal. For as the ſinner, on account of his finite nature, cannot give that infinite ſatisfaction which the juſtice of God demands, or, in other words, ſuſtain the whole of divine wrath at once, it is neceſſary that it be continued for ever, that what he cannot ſuſtain in its full extent, may be meaſured out in endleſs duration. This, we ſay, is the great reaſon, for it is not the only one. Their continuance in ſin would, of itſelf, ſubject them to continuance in ſuffering.

4. *All* ſin has an infinite evil in it. As it hath been proved, that this is an attribute of ſin in general, as being committed againſt a God of infinite perfection; it muſt be aſcribed to *every* ſin. For the evil of its nature ariſing, not from that degree of guilt which belongs to any particular tranſgreſſion, or the peculiar atrocity attending it, but from its oppoſition to the nature

---

* Acts xx. 28.   † Job xxii. 5.

nature of God, as will be more fully declared afterwards; *every* sin must partake of this evil nature. Some sins indeed are more aggravated, and attended with more atrocious circumstances than others. But it will not thence follow, that some sins are infinitely evil, and that others are not. Is it objected, " That if " this be a property essential to sin, no one offence " can be greater than another, that the least trans- " greffion is, in a comparative point of view, as hei- " nous as the greatest, because, that which is *infinite* " admitting of no degrees, it cannot be said that one " sin is *less*, and another *more* infinitely evil, as this " would be a denial of the infinite evil of sin altoge- " ther ?" But although every sin be infinitely evil, it must be remembered, that it is only so *objectively*, as terminating on God, and not *subjectively*, as committed by the creature. Were it afferted, which could not be done without the greatest absurdity, that all sin is infinitely evil in the strict and proper sense of the expression, in reference not only to its object, but to its subject: even then it would not follow, that there were no difference in the acts of sin. Thus in the Divine Nature, which, in the full and proper sense of the word, is the only *Infinite*, although infinitude necessarily belongs to all its perfections, yet there is a very great difference with respect to the displays and effects of these. Infinite wisdom, power and goodness are displayed in the works of creation and providence ; but all these are displayed in a more striking manner in the work of redemption. The exertions are all infinite, and so admit of no degrees. But the expressions and effects are different. There is no more infinite wisdom, power, or goodness, put forth in any one work, in which these perfections are exerted, than in another ; but there is a more illustrious manifestation of these in some works than in others.

THEREFORE, we must distinguish between the *nature* and *acts* of sin. Although every sin is infinitely evil, yet in some particular acts, there is a greater display of this evil than in others. This is agreeable

to

to the doctrine of our catechisms. " Some sins in
" themselves, and by reason of several aggravations,
" are more heinous in the sight of God than others *."
Some sins *in themselves* are so, as being more immediately opposed to the Divine Being, and containing a
greater degree of virulence and enmity against his glorious perfections, as being committed against the first,
rather than the second table of his holy law. Atheism
and blasphemy are greater sins than theft or covetousness. It is an higher offence against God, to murder our neighbour, than to hurt his reputation only.
Thus we read of some *abominations greater than others* †; of *greater sin* ‡; of *sin which is unto death;*
and *sin which is not unto death* §. Some sins are also
more heinous than others, because of their *aggravations*. Sin derives its aggravations " from the per-
" sons offending; from the parties offended; from
" the nature and qualities of the offence; and from
" the circumstances of time and place."—Therefore,
in urging this consideration, we do not mean to insinuate, that a man, because he is already a sinner, may indulge himself in the commission of the
greatest sins, thinking that he can become no worse;
for we have seen, that there are different degrees
in the evil, and, therefore, in the guilt and pollution of sin. But we urge it, to warn sinners of the folly of being unconcerned about what they call *little*
sins, because these same little sins will as certainly insure them of eternal punishment, if they continue under the guilt of them, as the *greatest*. Can any sin be
little, which offends and injures a God of infinite majesty and perfection? Can any sin be little, which has
so much guilt as to expose the subject of it to everlasting condemnation? The guilt of one sin, yea the guilt
of the least sin, comparatively viewed, as really exposes
to eternal wrath, as that of the greatest, or of all our
sins accumulated. The *least* sin implies in it ingratitude, unbelief, rebellion, and atheism. And what
more

---

* Larger Cat. q. 150. † Ezek. viii. 6. 13. 15.
‡ John xix. 11. § 1 John v. 16.

more can be said of the *greatest*, save that these ingredients exist in a greater degree; as arising from the means enjoyed, the mercies received, and its immediate tendency, which subject the transgressor to an higher degree of guilt, deformity and pollution? The law saith; *Cursed is every one that continueth not in* ALL *things, which are written in the book of the law to do them* *. Christ, who came not to destroy the law, but to fulfil, further declares; *Whosoever shall break* ONE *of these* LEAST *commandments,—shall be called the least in the kingdom of heaven* †. It was

II. Proposed to speak of the *evil* of Sin.

Sin is said to be *an evil thing*,—

1. BECAUSE it is contrary to the *nature* of God. This is the supreme standard of truth and righteousness. Every thing is *good*, just as it is like God, or *evil*, as it is unlike him. There can be no good in the world, but that which is a resemblance of his nature, and an emanation from himself; and disconformity to him is that which alone constitutes the essence of evil. Now, sin being unlike God, must, of necessity, be *evil*. Men may talk as they will of moral rectitude, and the fitness of things. But these are terms without meaning, unless we understand them as relating to the perfections of the Divine Nature; for there can be no notion of rectitude, fitness, or propriety, abstracted from the nature of God. This is the standard of right and wrong which is in every man's breast. How unjust and deficient soever the apprehensions he may entertain of these, through his own disconformity to God, he naturally reduces all his ideas to this standard, and when attempting to deviate from it, he acts in opposition to the dictates of conscience, which knows no other. It is impossible it can know any other: for this is the test of right and wrong, the umpire and witness that God hath implanted within us, and however weak and imperfect its representations, they still refer

to

---

* Gal. iii. 10.   † Mat. v. 19

to the nature of God; however hardened and feared the conscience itself, as it can never be altogether erased, if it has any motions at all, they are still directed to this quarter. Even Heathens themselves, amidst all their ignorance and corruption of the means which they enjoyed, had some remaining sense of the Divine Nature, as the only standard of truth or moral rectitude. Their laborious, although unsuccessful, investigations into the origin of moral evil, were a demonstrative evidence of this. For notwithstanding the gross and impious representations that the Poets gave of their Deities, their Philosophers, knowing, from the dictates of conscience, that the Divine Nature must be infinitely removed from sin, were extremely at a loss to account for its entrance into the world. Being destitute of Revelation, and having all their traditions so corrupted, that they could learn nothing certain from them; they adopted innumerable theories for explaining this undeniable fact, which however false and fruitless, plainly discovered their sense of the nature of God as the standard of truth, and their sense of sin as being his opposite. To this purpose speaks the Apostle: *For when the Gentiles, which have not the law, do by nature the things contained in the law; these, having not the law, are a law unto themselves: which shew the work of the law written in their hearts, their conscience also bearing witness, and their thoughts the meanwhile accusing, or else excusing one another* [*].

2. BECAUSE it is contrary to his holy *law*. This is the exact transcript of his nature. He hath delineated his own likeness in the commands and threatenings of the law. These are especially declarations of his holiness and justice, those perfections by which he cannot but hate sin, and cannot but punish it. He hath manifested great kindness to man, by revealing his will in the written word; because man discovers by this means what God requires, and what he forbids. It is a beacon constantly deterring him from sin, and prompt-

---

[*] Rom. ii. 14, 15.

ing him to duty. We are not called to form our apprehensions of these from the nature of God, abstractly and essentially considered, but from that striking representation of it impressed on his law; because otherwise we can have no just apprehension of them. Now, the strict and proper idea of sin is, "the want of conformity to, or transgression of the law of God." We are not to consider these as two distinct ingredients in sin; for they cannot be viewed separately. Wherever there is a want of conformity to the law, there must be a transgression of it: for *sin is the transgression of the law;* John iii. 4. There may be such a transgression, where no act of sin is openly committed, as in that which is secret; nay, where there is no actual sin chargeable, as in children who are *transgressors from the womb.* But there can be no want of conformity to the law, that does not immediately and necessarily imply transgression. For this very want is a disposition of the mind directly opposing the law, which requires holiness in heart and nature, as well as in life. Sin can never be viewed as a bare defect; for wherever there is this want of conformity, it is inseparably attended by depravity, and a principle of opposition. This is the very meaning of the word used by the Apostle John, which is rendered *transgression of the law.* It means *unlawfulness,* such a deviation from the law as implies contrariety to it. It signifies a removal from that integrity which the law requires, not only the want of original righteousness, but a propensity to all sin; yea, it is applied to the commission of the greatest sins, as in Matth. vii. 23. *Depart from me, ye workers of iniquity.* So also Rom. vi. 19. *Ye have yielded your members servants to uncleanness, and to iniquity, unto iniquity.* The formal idea of sin is said to consist in this, of its being a transgression of the law, because *where no law is, there is no transgression**. This notion of sin is usually illustrated by the situation of a person under a *bodily* disease, who, not only labours under the want of a proper temperament of humours, but hath a positive disorder

---

* Rom. iv. 15.

disorder among them. So sin, which is a *moral* disease, a malady of the soul, not only implies a want of proper conformity to the law, but a real opposition to it. But it ought to be observed, that men are chargeable with sin, even when destitute of the written word; because they have the remains of the law upon their hearts.

3. It is an attempt against the *moral government* of God in the world. This is the necessary result of its being a transgression of the law. For God, as the Creator of the universe, hath an undoubted right to act as its Supreme Ruler; and the way in which he governs his intelligent subjects is by *a law*, suited to the nature he hath given them. Now, when this law is broken, God's moral government is denied and rejected. The sinner thus does all in his power to dethrone God. Every sin is a denial of all the Divine perfections. Therefore is sin so often described in the holy Scripture as *rebellion*. *I have nourished and brought up children; and they have rebelled against me* *. *This is a rebellious people, lying children, that will not hear the law of the Lord* †. *They rebelled and vexed his holy Spirit* ‡. In the same manner speaks the Prophet Daniel in his confession of sins: *We have sinned and committed iniquity, and have done wickedly, and have rebelled by departing from thy precepts, and from thy judgments* §. Thus a departure from God's precepts is accounted rebellion by God himself, and by all who have a due sense of the evil of sin.

4. Sin appears to be *evil*, because it is *abominable* to God. This is the unavoidable consequence of its opposition to his nature, law, and moral government. Being contrary to his nature, it must also be the object of his abhorrence. Sin is the very reverse of God's holiness, and therefore he must hate it. For God, being infinitely and absolutely perfect, must be the object of his own love; and therefore, sin being contrary to his own perfection, must be the object of his hatred.

* Isa. i. 2. † Isa. xxx. 9. ‡ Isa. lxiii. 10. § Dan. ix. 5.

hatred. Could God ceafe to hate fin, he would ceafe to be God; for then he would ceafe to love himfelf, he would ceafe to be holy. But, in the word, he conftantly declares his unchangeable hatred of fin. It is called *that abominable thing which* God *hateth;* Jer. xliv. 4. *Oh! do not this abominable thing that I hate.* Sin is not here particularly mentioned; but it is defcribed much more emphatically. It is called *the abominable thing.* It is thus defcribed by way of eminence, as denoting that it is abominable in fuch a fenfe, as to admit of no parallel; fo very abominable, that although the thing itfelf be not fpecified, there is no danger of any thing elfe in the world being miftaken for it. Yea, it is that abominable thing *that God hates.* The hatefulnefs of fin is thus doubly expreffed. It is reprefented as abominable in its nature, and abominable to God. It is fo abominable, that nothing elfe in the univerfe is the object of Divine hatred, or nothing elfe but on account of fin. As if it were not enough, that fin is called *the abominable thing,* and that which God *hates;* it is elfewhere fpoken of as that which *his foul hateth.* Pfal. xi. 5. *Him that loveth violence his foul hateth.* God speaks of his foul after the manner of man; not as if he had a foul, like man; but as the foul of man is that by which he wills and acts, fo alfo God hath in himfelf a faculty of willing and acting; but of fo fuperlative a nature, that it is the fountain of all being, willing and acting to his creatures. The fame word is fometimes rendered his *foul,* and at other times his *life.* When his *foul* is faid to hate fin or wickednefs; the meaning therefore is, that he hath the moft perfect abhorrence of it; that he hates it abfolutely and effentially; that he cannot but hate it; that it is as neceffary for him to hate it, as it is for him to *live* as the felf-exiftent God; that he hates it with all the power and energy of his infinite, eternal, and neceffary *life.* When God hates with his foul or life, it denotes the moft abfolute and unalterable hatred; as when he fwears by his life, to exprefs the moft abfolute certainty*.

IT

---

* Ifa. xlix. 18.

It is the character of mankind in general, that *they do abominable works* *. Man, because of his sin, is represented as abominable to God; Job xv. 16. *How much more abominable and filthy is man, who drinketh up iniquity like water?* There is a *how much more* introduced here, an argument from the less to the greater. If *he putteth no trust in his saints*, if *the heavens are not clean in his sight*, if his holy angels and heavenly hosts, which are here meant, are not clean, not in respect of any positive defilement, but because of their natural imperfection, as being only derivatively holy; if they are not worthy of confidence, as being destitute of necessary perfection;—how unspeakably vile must man appear, who, not only in his best estate, is less perfect than they; but in his depraved condition, is positively defiled by sin, and so attached to iniquity, that he greedily drinketh it up, as a thirsty person drinketh water? To declare the essential holiness of God, and the great evil of sin, it is said, that *he is of purer eyes than to behold evil, and that he cannot look on iniquity;* Hab. i. 13. This is a metaphor taken from a person, who has such a thorough abhorrence of any object, that he cannot look upon it, that the very appearance or apprehension of it makes his nature shudder. The strongest metaphors that nature can afford, are heaped on each other, to declare the abominable nature of sin to the holy God: which expressions are by no means to be confined to idolatry, as only denoting God's hatred of *it*, but to be extended to *all* sin whatsoever. *Their vine is of the vine of Sodom, and of the fields of Gomorrah: Their grapes are grapes of gall, their clusters are bitter. Their wine is the poison of dragons, and the cruel venom of asps* †. As the *guilt* of sin refers to the justice of God, and is the obligation of the sinner to punishment, because of the transgression of the law; so the *filth* of sin respects his holiness, and is that which renders the sinner abominable in the eyes of Infinite Purity.

5. That

---

* Psal. xiv. 1.   † Deut. xxxii. 33, 34.

5. That sin is *an evil thing*, is evident from that *malignity* which is in its nature. Does the Justice of God proclaim the *guilt* of sin? Do we learn its *filth* from its contrariety to Divine holiness? Its *malignity* also appears by its opposition to the alluring perfection of love. The first sin of man included this in it. For it was a rebellion not only against the just and holy God, but against that God who had eminently manifested his goodness and liberality to man, in giving him every thing that could tend to his temporal comfort, and that could encourage and enable him to secure his eternal happiness by obedience; especially in entering into a federal transaction with his own creature, in delivering his law in the form of a covenant containing a promise of life, when he might have simply revealed his will in the form of a law, guarded by the penalty of death. The great and unmerited goodness of God towards his creature, appeared in making him a party with himself, in coming under an obligation to the work of his own hands, for the gift of that which it was of his own free love to bestow. Therefore there was great malignity in the sin of Adam, as committed against such ineffable goodness. But the wickedness that is in sin is greatly increased by reason of the revelation of grace to lost mankind. The love of God was, indeed, displayed to innocent man. But it was not displayed with such lustre, at so great an expence, and in a manner so infinitely transcendent, as in the promulgation of eternal life through the Son of God. Divine love to innocent man was undeserved; but love to fallen man is opposed to the greatest demerit. As it is the contrariety of sin to infinite holiness that constitutes its essence; opposition to infinite love constitutes its highest aggravation. The *evil* of sin surpasses comprehension in all, but it is of such a superlative nature in gospel-hearers, that it cannot be surpassed. Sin against the law of nature, although it has the essence of sin, being committed against law, is yet comparatively no sin, when put in the balance with that which is committed against the light and love of the gospel.

gospel. Therefore saith our Lord of the Jews: *If I had not come and spoken unto them, they had not had sin**. To represent this malignity which belongs to sin, it is declared, that *the carnal mind is enmity against God*†. Therefore is sin in Scripture so often described under the notion of wickedness; not as if that sin only were meant, which is open and enormous, as some apprehend; but to intimate that wickedness which is essential to every sin, as committed against a God of love and mercy.

6. BECAUSE it makes man the *slave* of *Satan*. By the law of his creation, he is the subject of God. To him he owes his service, and to him only. From this argument, the Psalmist encourages others to worship God. *Know ye, that the Lord is God; it is he that hath made us, and not we ourselves; we are his people, and the sheep of his pasture* ‡. His innumerable mercies of a temporal nature, in feeding, clothing, and protecting us, are additional motives enforcing our subjection to him. *In him we live and move, and have our being.* And if we live by him, we certainly ought to live to his glory. His grace in the work of redemption is a superadded tie to his service, strongly enforcing every other.—But sin alienates us from the service of God, and engages us in that of Satan his enemy. *For he that committeth sin is of the devil, for the devil sinneth from the beginning* §. Man, as *dead in trespasses and sins, walks according to the course of this world, according to the prince of the power of the air, the spirit that now worketh in the children of disobedience;* Eph. ii. 1. 2. Here the Apostle, in a beautiful and striking manner, connects two ideas, that in themselves directly oppose each other, but perfectly harmonize in man as unregenerate. These are *death* and *life*. He describes the spiritual *death* of man, as consisting in a *life* of sin and subjection to Satan, in *walking according to the course*, or, as the expression might well be rendered, *according to the* LIFE *of this world.* And indeed, *the life of this world* is at best nothing more than a state of spiritual *death*. That

must

---

* John xv. 22. † Rom. viii. 7. ‡ Psal. c. 3. § 1 John iii. 8.

must be *evil* indeed, that transforms the servants of God, those who are bound by *a threefold cord* to his service, into the slaves of Satan. It was the glory of Adam, that he was *the son of God**: But sin makes the subjects of it the children of the devil. It changes the heir of eternal life into a child of wrath and heir of hell. It effaces the image of God, and imprints the image of the wicked one. Justly may the Lord say: *They have corrupted themselves; their spot is not the spot of my children; they are a perverse and crooked generation. Do ye thus requite the Lord, O! foolish people and unwise? Is not he thy Father that hath* BOUGHT *thee? Hath he not* MADE *thee, and* ESTABLISHED *thee* †.

FROM what has been said on this subject, we may infer,

1. THAT those who have never seen sin to be *evil and bitter*, have no fear of God. We do not say, that all who have had this view of sin really fear him; for this depends on the nature of the discovery obtained. But we are certain, that those who have had no discovery whatsoever of the evil and bitterness of sin, have no fear of God. This is an inference native from our text; because *forsaking the Lord* by sin, and having no *fear* of him, are used as expressions of the same import. *It is an evil thing—that thou hast forsaken the Lord thy God, and that my fear is not in thee, saith the Lord God of Hosts.* This cuts off all obdurate sinners, who never had their consciences burdened by a sense of sin, whatever be their pretensions to what is called moral rectitude or virtue, from all claim to the character of *fearers of God*.

2. THE danger of entertaining trivial thoughts of sin. This is nothing else than for a man to think lightly of his own ruin, yea, his eternal ruin; and what is unspeakably more, to contemn God, against whose being and perfections it is the most daring attack. Certain it is, that all who think little of sin in this world, will, at least in the world to come, be convinced of their extreme folly. May the Lord grant you an earlier discovery

---

* Luke iii. 38. † Deut. xxxii. 5. 6.

covery of it, for then it will be too late. *For they that go down to the pit, do not show forth God's praise.* Those who are strangers to the evil of sin, are truly in a miserable situation. They are languishing under a dreadful disease, and know not their sickness. They are going on in a state of the most deplorable enmity; and know not, or care not, that they are adversaries to God, and that God is their adversary. Sinners, you cannot chuse a worse enemy than God. You would be safe with, yea, from every other enemy, were God your friend. But his arm is strong against his adversaries. His fury shall burn to the *lowest hell, towards those who go on in their trespasses.*

3. WE may see the dreadful ingratitude that is in sin. This charge God exhibits in verse 21. *Yet I had planted thee a noble vine, wholly a right seed: how then art thou turned into the degenerate plant of a strange vine unto me?* What would you think of a child, who, although under God, owing his being, nourishment, education, and every temporal comfort, to his parents, would yet rise up against them, and seek their destruction? He that striketh his father or mother, is cursed of God, and reprobated of man. But every sinner is a parricide. This is all the return that we have made to our kind and compassionate Father in heaven; we *have lifted up the heel against him.* Sin is such a miracle of ingratitude, that God appeals the justness of his complaint, even to the irrational and inanimate creatures; because these are, in their different orders, unspeakably more attentive and obedient than man, and have all fulfilled the end of their creation, but in as far as prevented by his rebellion: *Hear, O heavens! and give ear, O earth! for the Lord hath spoken. I have nourished and brought up children, and they have rebelled against me* *.

4. WE may infer the impossibility of delivering ourselves from sin. This is declared, verse 22. *For though thou wash thee with nitre, and take thee much soap, yet thine iniquity is marked before me, saith the Lord God.*

* Isai. i. 2.

The ſtain of ſin is ſo deep, that all the *nitre* and *ſoap* of our own doings or ſufferings can never waſh it out. They ſhall be as ineffectual as waſhing in the waters of Jordan would have been, for the removal of Naaman's leproſy, without the ſpecial command of God. All the ſinner's own waſhing makes him only the fouler in the eye of his judge. It is but *adding ſin to ſin**.

Finally, We may learn the neceſſity of waſhing in the blood of Chriſt. If every other method of purification will be unavailing, there is ſurely the greateſt reaſon for applying to his precious blood. This is the *fountain opened for ſin and uncleanneſs* †. The virtue of this fountain correſponds both to the evil and bitterneſs of ſin. It is *opened for ſin;* and thus takes away its *bitterneſs*, with reſpect to all the conſequences of *guilt*. It is *opened for uncleanneſs;* and ſo removes that abominable *pollution* flowing from the *evil* of its nature. *The blood of Chriſt cleanſeth us from all ſin.* It removes the *dominion* of ſin, when applied in regeneration; its *guilt* in juſtification; its *filth* in gradual ſanctification; and at length, its very *being* in the ſoul, in the perfection of holineſs, when the believer is tranſlated to glory.

---

* Iſai. xxx. 1. † Zech. xiii. 1.

SERMON II.

On the BITTERNESS of SIN.

JER. ii. 19.

——*Know therefore and see, that it is an evil thing and bitter, that thou hast forsaken the Lord thy God.*——

SIN may be fitly enough compared to that *little book* which the Angel gave to John, and commanded him to eat. *It was sweet as honey in his mouth, but it was bitter in his belly.* The sweetness of sin to the carnal nature, in the commission, often overpowers all sense of its evil in the mind or conscience of the sinner. But its bitterness will be found by him at some period or other. Although it may not operate so speedily as in the case of the Apostle in the Revelation; yet, in the end, its effects will be as sensible, and far more alarming. When his iniquity, like the *roll* given to the Prophet Ezekiel, is spread out before him, he shall then assuredly see, that it is *written within and without*, and that it contains nothing *but lamentations, and mourning, and wo*[*]. This metaphor, indeed, is expressly used in the word of God. *Though wickedness be sweet in his mouth, though he hide it under his tongue; though he spare it, and forsake it not,—yet his meat in his bowels is turned, it is the gall of asps within him.—Surely he shall not find quietness in his belly* [†]. In the preceding discourse, we have a little considered the evil of sin; we now proceed to what was proposed,

III. To speak of its *bitterness*.

1. SIN is so *bitter* in its consequences, that it hath deprived us of all *good*. It hath robbed us of the image of

---

[*] Rev. x. 9, 10.; Ezek. ii. 9, 10. [†] Job xx. 12, 13, 14. 20.

of God; which, as it was the higheſt teſtimony of his favour, was the tenure by which every other was held. *Man being in honour, continued not; but became like the beaſts that periſh.* Having caſt away the Divine likeneſs, he could no longer enjoy the communications of God's love; but muſt neceſſarily become the object of his deteſtation. His favour is not only the foundation of all good, of the enjoyment of every bleſſing, of what nature ſoever; but is itſelf the very compound and eſſence of all good. *Life lies in his favour;* yea, *his loving kindneſs is better than life.* But man, by the entrance of ſin, hath loſt the favour of God, converted his beſt friend into an enemy, and thus voluntarily bereaved himſelf of all the bleſſings that he either enjoyed or hoped for.

Sin makes the greateſt ſeparation poſſible between God and man. Therefore in the verſe before us, it is called a *forſaking* of *the Lord our God,* and it provokes the Lord to forſake us, and to *hide his face, ſo that he will not hear.* When we compare man's firſt eſtate, as the child of God, the friend and favourite of Heaven, a kind of link between heaven and earth, as partaking both of ſpirit and matter, cloſely united in one perſon, and this dignified by original righteouſneſs,—with his ſtate as a ſinner, caſt out of God's preſence, friendſhip and protection, become *as the beaſts that periſh,* and changed into the link of a dreadful union between earth and hell; juſtly may we confeſs, with the deepeſt ſenſe of the wickedneſs of our apoſtaſy, *that it is an evil thing and bitter, that we have forſaken the Lord our God.* Our moral diſtance from God, as ſinners, removes us farther from him than even our natural diſtance as creatures. For ſin incapacitates us for the ſervice and enjoyment of God; whereas our natural diſtance was, in ſome manner, diminiſhed by the participation of the Divine image in holineſs. Made like to God, although infinitely removed from him by our finite nature, we were qualified for glorifying and enjoying him.

Thus

Thus man forfeited all communion with **God**. Adam being *the son of God*, had that easy access to his Father, and intercourse with him, which were evidences and seals of his sonship. He delighted in the presence of God. Uninterrupted fellowship with him was the support of his soul, and the joy of his life. But as soon as sin entered, he not only ceased to enjoy, but ceased to desire communion with God. That voice of majesty and love, the sound of which was wont to fill his heart with the highest delight, thenceforth inspired him with shame and terror only. Instead of going forth to meet his Father and friend, instead of cheerfully answering his call, *he was afraid and hid himself.*—Sin, as it deprived man of communion with God in the present life, excluded every hope of life eternal. His expulsion from the earthly paradise, was a declaration of his exclusion from *the paradise of God*. The guard of cherubims, and of the flaming sword, that was *set upon Eden to keep the way of the tree of life*, declared the impossibility of salvation by that covenant which was already broken.—As he lost all spiritual and eternal blessings by sin, he also forfeited his right to every temporal blessing. Man, by becoming *like the beasts*, lost his dominion over them. Common mercies are vouchsafed to us as sinners, only as bread and water are to a criminal, until the time arrive, when either the sentence of the law is executed, or he partakes of the clemency of his Sovereign.

2. Sin hath subjected us to all *penal* evil. That is called *penal*, which is of the nature of punishment, which respects our guilt, and is inflicted by God as a vindictive judge. Thus it is distinguished from *moral* evil or sin, which is its procuring cause, and from that chastisement, which, although in its own nature evil, yet to the children of God bears in it nothing of punishment, and eventually works for their good. It hath subjected us to the curse of the law; for *the law saith, Cursed is every one that continueth not in all things.* The unavoidable consequence of disobedience to the law, in its *commanding* power, is a subjection to its *condemnatory*

natory sentence. It hath exposed us to the wrath of God, both in this life, and in that which shall never have an end; the effects of which we may consider afterwards. Offended justice hath nothing in reserve for sinners, but *indignation and wrath, tribulation and anguish* *. The afflictions of this life are all the fruits of sin. To those who are under its power they are really penal; they discover God's wrath, although in a limited respect, and are presages of that dreadful portion which is still in reserve. It is sin that hath subjected our nature to corruption. The body of man being gross matter, hath not in itself, indeed, a principle of immortality; but without the evil of sin, the holiness of the soul would have preserved it from decay. It would have been confirmed in this state of incorruption, as a fruit of the love and power of God, in the same manner as the bodies of the glorified saints, shall be, although without the intervention of a Mediator.—It is sin that gives to death, not only its *sting*, but its very being. For death being a punishment, there could have been nothing of this kind without sin. Therefore, as descriptive of the glory of that state which insures a complete deliverance from sin, it is declared; *There shall be no more death* †. The people of God are indeed subject to its *stroke*, because *it is appointed for all men once to die*. But they are freed from its *sting*, by their interest in the death of Christ; and thus, to allude to the words of Agag ‡, to them *the bitterness of death is past*. The tree of the cross of Christ makes the waters of death, which are naturally bitter, sweet to all believers §. Being delivered from the *power of the second death*, the first can do them no harm.—Here it may be inquired; "If believers be delivered from "the *sting* of death," through the death of Christ, why "not also from its *stroke*?" The death of Christ undoubtedly had sufficient merit to have delivered all his people, not only from the *sting*, but also from the *stroke* of death, had God so determined; because the greater includes

---

* Rom. ii. 8, 9.   † Rev. xxi. 4.   ‡ 1 Sam. xv. 32.
§ Exod. xv. 23.

includes the lefs. If it was sufficiently meritorious to deliver them from spiritual and eternal death, much more to deliver them from what is only temporal. Perhaps, the translation of Enoch and Elijah may be considered as proofs of this. But God had determined, that all his people, these two excepted, should taste of natural death. Were it his pleasure, he could easily complete their sanctification, as well as their justification, in a moment. But as this would be unsuitable to the world they live in, it is his will, that their sanctification should be gradually advanced by ordinances and providences, especially by those of a trying nature: and as he hath seen meet gradually to sanctify them by afflictions, he hath appointed the *stroke* of death to be the mean of perfecting this work.—But it may be said, " If Christ " was not to purchase deliverance for his people from " temporal death, there was no necessity for his dying " literally; it had been enough for him to have sustain- " ed the full measure of Divine wrath, which would " have removed the *sting*, without subjection to the " *stroke*." To this we reply, That Christ could not possibly sustain the full measure of Divine wrath, or the full energy of the curse of the law, without natural death. *For without the shedding of blood there is no remission.* He was to *give his soul an offering for sin.* The law expressly demands, that *the soul that sinneth* should *die.* God, in sovereign mercy, admitted of a surety instead of the principal offender. But he could not, in justice to himself, so far dispense with the law, as to alter or abridge the penalty. Besides, our Lord, by his temporary continuance in the grave, was to sanctify it as a bed of rest for all his people; and by his glorious resurrection, receive for himself, as their Surety, a legal acquittal from the sentence of the law; that they, through his righteousness, thus declared to be complete, might obtain justification, and by virtue of his resurrection, be raised to newness of life in this state, and to eternal blessedness at length.

3. Sin hath introduced *disorder* into the whole *creation* of God. It had this fatal effect in heaven itself.

There,

There, before the being of sin, the most perfect harmony reigned. Every thought, and expression, and action of all the angelic hosts, was directed to the highest end,—glory to God supreme. Then, without one discordant note, all these *morning-stars sung together, and these sons of God shouted for joy.* But how dreadful the change produced by sin! It made a temporary blank in heaven. Myriads of angels, once as holy as any around the throne, being alienated from the service of God, and having lost his image, were banished from his presence, and from the glorious society of their former companions; banished for ever, without the most distant prospect of reconciliation, and condemned to everlasting punishment. But when sin had made its entrance into heaven, it could scarcely be expected that it should long remain a stranger to earth. That presumptuous spirit who made war against God within the very limits of his throne, soon transferred it to his footstool. He who had laboured to dethrone God in heaven, could not rest without a strenuous effort to rob him of his glory on earth. What he in vain attempted against the glorious Original, he soon effected on man, his holy, but mutable image. God, for the more illustrious display of his perfections, permitted man to abuse the freedom of his will, by listening to the temptation of Satan, and transgressing the covenant. As man was thus alienated from the love and service of God, deprived of his favour, and subjected to the curse of his broken law; he was also bereaved of the society of holy angels, and secluded from their friendship. As it was his glory to be *made but a little lower than they**, having the same *glorious crown* of the Divine image, eminently consisting in holiness, conferred on him, although shining with inferior lustre; when he trampled this crown under foot, he was justly deprived of this honourable society, as being an unfit companion for the sons of God. As created in the likeness of God, he was constituted his vicegerent on earth, and *made to have dominion over the works of his hand, and*

to

---

* Psal. viii. 5.

to have all things under his feet*. But all thefe works, as revenging the quarrel of their injured Creator, rofe up in arms againſt this ungrateful rebel. Thofe very creatures that, in his ſtate of innocency, paffed before him in review, acknowledging their fubjection, and receiving names from him correfpondent to their natures, after his fall, difowned his authority, declared themfelves his enemies, and waged war againſt him. The curfe immediately aimed againſt him, reached them alfo, and introduced an unceafing enmity amongſt the different fpecies of creatures, that before lived in peace. The very ground that he trode on, being curfed for his fake, as a perpetual monitor of his fin, inſtead of the rich fruits that it formerly produced fpontaneoufly, prefented him with *thorns and thiſtles*, and feemed to grudge the fcanty fubfiſtence that nature requires, by demanding as its price, *the ſweat of his brow*.

Thus the Apoſtle, in the moſt ſtriking language, defcribes the effects of fin on the lower creation, as fubjecting *the creature to vanity*, to *the bondage of corruption*, to a ſtate of the moſt *earneſt expectation of deliverance. For we know that the whole creation groaneth and travaileth in pain together until now*, Rom. viii. 22. The inferior creatures feem to treat all the dominion that man aſſumes over them, as if it were mere ufurpation. It muſt indeed be remembered, that God, in the covenant which he eſtabliſhed with Noah, made a grant of thefe for his ufe. But there is no grant of abfolute dominion over them fpecified, as before the entrance of fin. Nay, it appears, that this new and folemn grant would never have been vouchfafed without a relation to the Covenant of Grace. Temporal mercies, indeed, flow from God as a Creator. But only through an intereſt in this Covenant, can we have a proper right to them, be delivered from the curfe, naturally attending them all, as the juſt defert of fin, and receive a fpecial bleffing with them. For whatever grant is made to mankind in general of the ufe of the creatures; they only have

* Pfal. viii. 6.

have a proper lordſhip over them, who are within the bond of the everlaſting Covenant. For it is expreſſed as the privilege of the righteous ; *Thou ſhalt be in league with the ſtones of the field, and the beaſts of the field ſhall be at peace with thee* *. In alluſion to the diſorder introduced into the intelligent creation of God, in the ſeparation of man from the love and fellowſhip of holy elect angels, Paul repreſents it as *the myſtery of* God's *will, that in the diſpenſation of the fulneſs of times, he might gather together in one,* or *gather together unto an head, all things in Chriſt ; both which are in heaven, and which are on earth* †. In reference to the diſorder introduced into the lower creation, the ſame Apoſtle declares, that *the earneſt expectation of the creature waiteth for the manifeſtation of the ſons of God* ‡.

The IV. thing propoſed is, to ſhow by what proofs ſinners may know and ſee that ſin is evil and bitter.

They may *know and ſee* this,

1. By the *commands* and *threatenings* of the *law*. The principal end that God had in view in exhibiting theſe to men as ſinners, was to declare the nature and the puniſhment of ſin ; or, in the words of our text, to make them *know and ſee that it is an evil thing and bitter, that they have forſaken the Lord*. By the commands of the law, we may ſee the holineſs of God, and, of conſequence, the evil of ſin ; by its threatenings we are aſſured of his juſtice, and, therefore, of the puniſhment of ſin. The law was never revealed to man ſince the fall for juſtification, but only for conviction and ſelf-condemnation ; *That every mouth may be ſtopped, and all the world may become guilty before God:— For by the law is the knowledge of ſin* §. Here we do not ſpeak of the illuſtrious uſe, and abſolute neceſſity of the law, as a rule of life and everlaſting obedience to *believers*, in the hand of Chriſt the Mediator, but only of its deſign and uſe with reſpect to men as *ſinners*. A diſcovery

---

* Job v. 23.   † Eph. i. 10.   ‡ Rom. viii. 19.
§ Rom. iii. 19, 20.

discovery of the holiness of the precept, and of the strictness of the penalty, makes the sinner know, that he can have no expectation of salvation, by attempting obedience to the one, or satisfaction to the other. By the operation of the Holy Spirit, it is a mean to lead him out of himself, and to reduce him to the necessity of seeking salvation in the obedience and sufferings of the glorious Surety. *For the law is a schoolmaster to bring us to Christ.* It is, indeed, a severe schoolmaster. But all its severity is necessary to banish from the heart of the sinner his foolish hope of salvation by his own doings, either in whole or in part. Now, what is the language of the law to transgressors? *The soul that sinneth, it shall die;* yea, *dying thou shalt die.* It not only threatens death, but death in all its extent; death temporal, spiritual and eternal. The law, which is the first refuge of every sinner who becomes sensible of guilt, is his worst enemy, and acts the part of an accuser. The justice of God, with which he endeavours to compound matters, appears as a vindictive and inexorable judge, who will remit nothing of the rigour of the law. Death, whom he endeavours to mollify and bribe by fair promises and forced resolutions *, appears as his executioner, and the servant of both.

2. By *terrors* of *conscience.* These are the necessary consequences of a discovery of the commands and threatenings of the law, when the sinner sees no way of hope opened up by them, and knows not of any other; if he is not left to abandon himself to greater *excess of riot*, and to dissipate his apprehensions, arising from a sense of sin, in an uncontrouled indulgence of it. Often, indeed, he seeks a remedy from giving loose reins to his disease. He looks for health and peace in the progress of his destructive malady. Terrors of conscience, as they are the fruit of sin, are to the sinner a declaration of its evil and bitterness. Cain was a striking example of the power of a diseased

---

* Isa. xxviii. 15.

eased conscience. This murderer of his brother had such a sense of his sin, at least of the demerit of it, that he feared an avenger of blood in every one of his brethren. So loud was the cry of innocent blood in his conscience, that he expresses himself in such a manner, as if he had been sensible that he deserved as many deaths as there were men in the world to inflict them: —*It shall come to pass, that every one that shall find me shall slay me* *. We have a very affecting description of the end of the wicked man, notwithstanding all his worldly comforts, Job xxvii. 20—22. *Terrors take hold on him as waters, a tempest stealeth him away in the night. The east-wind carrieth him away, and he departeth: and as a storm hurleth him out of his place. For God shall cast upon him, and not spare: he would fain flee out of his hand.* Job, although a child of God, elsewhere expresses an affecting sense of these in his own soul, chap. xxx. 15—17. *Terrors are turned upon me: they pursue my soul as the wind; and my welfare passeth away as a cloud. And now my soul is poured out upon me: the days of affliction have taken hold upon me. My bones are pierced in me in the night-season; and my sinews take no rest* †.

Men, under a sense of guilt, are sensible, that because of their iniquities they deserve nothing but eternal and ineffable wrath; and they have the first fruits of this in these awful terrors of conscience that haunt them even in this life. A fear of wrath frequently spreads a gloom over their happiest days, and evaporates the spirit of their most ravishing enjoyments. The terrors of the Lord often embitter the cups of the drunkard, dissipate the delights of the wanton amidst his darling debaucheries, or, in a moment, turn to dross all the treasure of the avaricious earthworm, so that it appears to him as of no more value than *the dust, or the mire of the street*, like which it has been *heaped up* ‡. The reason of this dissatisfaction, attending carnal enjoyments, is assigned by the Prophet Ezekiel, chap. vii. 19. *Their silver*

---

* Gen. iv. 14.   † See also Job vi. 4.   ‡ Zech. ix. 3.

silver and their gold shall not be able to deliver them in the day of the wrath of the Lord: they shall not satisfy their souls, neither fill their bowels; because it is the stumbling-block of their iniquity. They can reap no comfort from their worldly or sensual gratifications in the day of Divine indignation; because the indulgence of these is the very cause of it. These can never afford them comfort, because they are the source of their trouble. Amidst all their joy, *the sound of a shaken leaf shall chace them.* Scarcely had the impious Belshazzar profaned the holy vessels of the temple of the Lord, and observed the fingers of a man's hand writing on the wall of the palace, before *his countenance was changed, and his thoughts troubled him; so that the joints of his loins were loosed, and his knees smote one against another*. All his noble Princes, his wives and concubines, his costly dainties, and generous wines, all his pomp and glory, yea, all his gods in whom he trusted, could avail nothing to deliver him from the terrors of his conscience, when the hand of the God of heaven was upon him. No companions, no joys can avail the man whose soul is pierced with *the arrows of the Almighty.* When in company, he wishes for solitude, that, if possible, he may find peace there. When in solitude, he finds a troubled conscience such a bad companion, that he rushes back into the throng, and endeavours to silence it by the noise of mirth and folly. When it is night, he wishes for day: *When he lies down, he saith, When shall I arise and the night be gone? and is full of tossings to and fro, unto the dawning of the day* †. When it is day, he languishes for night, that he may hide his head in darkness. But he learns, that *there is no darkness nor shadow of death, where the workers of iniquity may hide themselves* ‡. He finds himself *beset behind and before, and the Lord's hand still lying upon him. If he say, Surely the darkness shall cover me, then is the night light about him.* After all his attempts, he is forced to acknowledge, although in another sense than the Psalmist;

Yea,

---

* Dan. v. 6.   † Job vii. 4.   ‡ Job xxxiv. 22.

Yea, the darkness hideth not from thee, but the night shineth as the day; the darkness and the light are both alike unto thee *.

3. From the *complaints* of God's *people*, on account of sin. Here we shall not mention the complaints of sin that arise from some experience of legal terror, but such only as flow from a constant sense of its filth and abominableness to the holy God; because *those* proceed especially from a discovery of its guilt, and do not properly belong to their exercise as Christians; whereas *these* proceed from a ruling and permanent hatred of it in their hearts. They every where, when rightly exercised, represent it as their heaviest burden; and however great their afflictions, they consider sin as greater than any other. We have a remarkable instance of this in David, after he had offended God in numbering the people; as if his strength, and the strength of Israel, had consisted in the multitude of his subjects, and not in the Lord of Hosts, who was *the chariots of Israel, and the horsemen thereof*. He said unto the Lord, *I have greatly sinned in that I have done; and now I beseech thee, O Lord, take away the iniquity of thy servant; for I have done very foolishly;* 2 Sam. xxiv. 10. The first thing that smote his heart was not a fear of the effects of his sin, but a sense of its evil and vileness. We are not to imagine, that this proceeded from ignorance of God's design to chastise him severely for it; for before he spoke these words, he had received an intimation of the Divine purpose. From the tenor of this part of the scripture-history, we evidently see, that this confession of sin was in consequence of God's declaration by the mouth of his Prophet. Before this, it would seem, he had no due sense of his sin. But the reason of his speaking in this manner is given in verse 11. *For when David was up in the morning, the word of the Lord came unto the Prophet Gad.* A sense of the dishonour he had done to God, was more affecting to him than even the prospect of that dreadful calamity

* Psal. cxxxix. 12.

with which he was threatened.—With the same temper of mind he elsewhere expresses his sense of the burdensome nature of sin. *Mine iniquities are gone over mine head; as an heavy burden, they are too heavy for me* *. How very different is the language of the sinner from that of the saint under a sense of sin! The sinner considers it only with respect to its effect, in punishment; but the saint, with respect to its evil nature, in offending God. This was the complaint of Cain; *My punishment is greater than that I can bear.* But how much more noble is the language of Joseph, *How can I do this great wickedness, and sin against God.* The Christian, however heavy his afflictions, never appears miserable to himself, but as lying under the burden of sin. The holy Apostle Paul very pathetically describes his afflictions in the work of the gospel. He approved himself *the minister of Christ, in much patience, in afflictions, in necessities, in distresses, in stripes, in imprisonments, in tumults, in labours, in watchings, in fastings* †. Such a multiplicity of evils would have made a sinner cry out, *O wretched man that I am!* But notwithstanding the variety and constancy of his trials, he found consolation in them, he found something to alleviate his distress. *We are troubled on every side, yet not distressed; we are perplexed, but not in despair; persecuted, but not forsaken; cast down, but not destroyed* ‡. He reserves his complaint of misery for sin. He could see nothing of real wretchedness in his situation, but as it arose from the pollution and prevalence of his own iniquity: *O wretched man that I am! who shall deliver me from the body of this death* §. There is not, there cannot be any real misery in the world, but what is the fruit of sin, or consists in the power of sin itself.

As sin is the greatest burden of the saints on earth, deliverance from it, and perfect conformity to Christ is the greatest joy of heaven. This is represented as a matter of much greater importance than deliverance from

---

* Psal. xxxviii. 4.   † 2 Cor. vi. 4, 5.   ‡ 2 Cor. iv. 8, 9.
§ Rom. vii. 24.

from all afflictions; yea, as the cause of the other. *The inhabitant shall not say, I am sick: for the people that dwell therein shall be forgiven their iniquity* *. Deliverance from sin has the precedence to the enjoyment of God; for however inestimable this privilege, perfection in holiness is the foundation of it, that without which there can be no enjoyment of God, or, were it possible there could, that without which there could be no happiness in this enjoyment. Therefore the enjoyment of God is given as the evidence of complete deliverance from sin, or, in other words, of complete conformity to Christ; as referving the principal place to the latter: *When he shall appear, we shall be* LIKE *him; for we shall see him as he is* †.

4. By the *punishments* inflicted on sinners in *this life*. *The Lord is righteous, he hath cut asunder the cords of the wicked* ‡. The threatenings of the word are indeed a fuller declaration of God's anger against sin, than all his providential dispensations; because all the punishment inflicted on sinners in this world, may be justly considered as an earnest only, compared to the full wages awaiting them in the world to come. But there are many dispensations of Providence recorded in Scripture, in which we may read the evil and bitterness of sin in the most legible characters; although these dispensations were meant as preludes only of that indignation which is in store.—The destruction of the old world by a deluge of waters, was an awful display of the evil of man's iniquity, and most evidently declared, that he had thereby lost all title to this earth, to life, or to any of its comforts. So great was the corruption of man, that it is metaphorically represented as extending to the very earth on which he trode. *God looked upon the earth, and behold, it was corrupt; for all flesh had corrupted his way upon the earth* §. So great is his indignation at sin, that he would not only destroy all flesh, but the earth itself, by defacing its beauty, and spoiling it of the most striking remains of that

---

* Isai. xxxiii. 24.   † 1 John iii. 2.   ‡ Psal. cxxix. 4.
§ Gen. vi. 12, 13.

that original grandeur which was impressed on it at the creation, when prepared as an habitation for innocent man. God could not *smell a savour of rest from the earth*, till it was thus washed by the flood *; nor could his Church be saved from the common destruction but by water, which is a figure of the same kind with that *baptism*, which *doth now save us* †. We are not to apprehend that this tremendous judgment was inflicted, because the world was then a great deal worse than it has ever been since. We have reason to think, that it is as bad now as it ever was since the creation. There are crimes perpetrated in our time, which, in all probability, were unknown to sinners before the flood. Indeed, corrupt human nature is ever radically the same; but since that awful æra, Satan and the wicked world have enjoyed a series of about four thousand years for acquiring greater experience, and making new discoveries in the practical science of sin. This is a science of such a kind, that no man needs to be taught the rudiments of it. For it is born with every man, and it is his first work to reduce it into an art. But there are refinements in it, the invention of which has required no small labour of that wisdom which is both *sensual and devilish*. As it is evident, that the world is at least no better now than before the flood; and as God hath nevertheless assured us, that he will not again bring an universal destruction upon it, till the general conflagration; we may be assured, that *that* judgment was intended as an awful and *perpetual* declaration of the desert of sin, and of that sacrifice which Divine justice requires every hour; and also as an illustrious display of the forbearance of God towards *the world* still *lying in wickedness*.

The destruction of Sodom and Gomorrah, and the cities of the plain, contained the same lesson of the evil of sin. In that already mentioned, it was indeed expressed by water, and in *this* by fire. But both were

---

* Gen. viii. 21. † 1 Pet. iii. 20, 21.

were types of the final judgment; and *this*, although not so universal, was yet more literal, and not merely a type of the destruction of the world by fire, but of the eternal punishment of the wicked: for *they are set forth for an example, suffering the vengeance of* eternal *fire* *. This awful visitation is expressed in the most striking language: *The Lord rained upon Sodom and upon Gomorrah brimstone and fire from the Lord out of heaven*; Gen. xix. 24. Their destruction came from that very quarter to which they should have looked for salvation. The cry of their sin was so loud, and the cry of Divine justice so importunate, that even righteous Lot, while he lingered, is represented as in danger of being consumed in the iniquity of the city. The punishment was so just, and the danger so imminent, that one retrospective glance of regret or curiosity instantly converted one of the four, saved from destruction, into a perpetual monument of disobedience and folly, ver. 15, 16. 26.

THE overthrow of all the Israelites who came out of Egypt, except two persons, was an awful declaration of God's anger against sin †. It was on this account, that all the seven nations of Canaan were devoted to destruction.—We might further mention many instances of the destruction of individuals, as of Korah, Dathan, and Abiram, Nadab and Abihu, upon whom the Lord visibly executed his judgments, to show how abominable sin is in all.—But the time would fail us to enumerate them. God, in his infinite wisdom, saw meet to exhibit these visible testimonies of his displeasure, in a more frequent, observable and tremendous manner in those ages, in which there was not so clear a discovery of his hatred of sin as is given in his written word; or when Revelation was confined to one people, and the Church, being in a state of minority, laboured under the bondage and terrors of a legal dispensation. But even since the commencement of the Christian dispensation, since the more general propagation

---

* Jude, ver. 7.   † 1 Cor. x. 5.

propagation of Christianity, God hath discovered, in a very discernible manner, his detestation of sin, by the course of his providence with nations, and especially in the destruction of the Jews. If men would but read the language of Divine providence, and compare it with the threatenings of the word, with former examples of a like nature, in what light would they view the desolations brought on cities and nations, by fire, by famine, by sword and pestilence, but as so many testimonies of the evil and bitterness of sin? *He turneth the fruitful land into barrenness, for the wickedness of them that dwell therein*; Psal. cvii. 34. So literally is this threatening verified in the course of providence, that travellers can scarcely believe the authenticity of ancient histories, and infidels presume to deny the truth of the holy Scriptures; because they find some of the countries, which are there described as so fertile and beautiful, so wonderfully changed, that they can scarcely think them the same: while all this is only a proof of the truth of God's word, in the accomplishment of his threatenings, because of the wickedness of the inhabitants in former or later ages. Nay the judgments which, in our own times, are often executed upon individuals, who have been distinguished for their iniquities, are sometimes so striking, and evidently proceeding in so immediate a manner from the hand of God, that even the most obdurate are forced to consider them as the punishment of sin, and as a declaration of its unspeakable desert. Indeed, if men can discover any plausible vent for their infidelity, by the apparent intervention of *secondary* causes, however remote, the generality of observers will attribute the most uncommon effects to these, rather than give so severe a wound to their own sin, as to acknowledge them to be the effects of the immediate interposition of the *first* Cause, and affecting displays of Divine vengeance.

5. MANY *see and know the evil and bitterness of sin*, by their own *eternal* misery. Those who, still in this life, continue strangers to these things, notwithstand-

ing all the testimonies that God gives of his displeasure, shall see and know them to their fatal experience, in that life that shall never have an end. The damned in hell see what sin is by their eternal exclusion from the presence of God, from the love of Christ, from the society of the godly; and they shall learn it more fully by their eternal sufferings both in soul and body. Although they could *give all their* former *substance for* * that love which they have despised to the end, it would not procure one renewed offer of it. They shall never enjoy the least degree of that blessed communion with God, which many of them have considered as a delusion, although they could shed as many tears for it as might extinguish the flames of hell. They shall never, for one moment, enjoy the society of the godly, although, as its price, they should be willing to suffer as many years of torment, as they have committed sins. They shall never be able to redeem their souls, although for every soul they could give a world in exchange †. Although they renounce all their infidelity; yet the more they believe, they can only tremble the more ‡. Though they should become preachers in hell, it could not procure one drop of water to cool their tongues §. All the pomp of the greatest will avail them nothing there. *Hell will only enlarge herself, and open her mouth without measure, that their glory and their multitude, and their pomp, may descend into it.* It will only be the more *moved to meet them at their coming* **. There can be no alleviation of misery there, by imparting it to others. Their only comfort, if we may speak of comfort in hell, is to get new companions in misery ††. The presence of the body, that was formerly the minister of sin, can be no consolation; for this can only give greater extent to suffering. Annihilation, consisting in the reduction of both soul and body to non-existence for ever, which is the greatest dread of

---

* Cant. viii. 7.   † Matth. xvi. 26.   ‡ James ii. 19.
§ Luke xvi. 24. 27.   ** Isa. v. 14.; xiv. 9.   †† Ezek. xxxii. 31.

of human nature, acting according to natural principles, would there be the greatest blessing. But the wicked in hell shall be eternally dying, and yet, after millions of ages, be as eternally remote from death, as when they first began to suffer.

It has now indeed become a fashionable doctrine, to deny, or at least to talk with uncertainty, of the eternity of hell. Men, under a pretence of exalting the Divine perfections, as if they knew better what were suitable to them than God himself, consider it as inconsistent with these, that he should punish sinners of mankind, or even devils with everlasting suffering. But for this doctrine there is not the least shadow of foundation in the word of God. On the contrary, the expressions that are used, evidently denote *eternity* in its strict and proper sense. The burnings of *hell* are declared to be *everlasting* *; its punishment, *eternal damnation* †, and *eternal fire* ‡. Nay, expressions, denoting eternity, are redoubled and heaped one upon another, to leave no pretence for imagining, that only a very long course of suffering is meant. Hell is represented as *a lake that burneth with fire and brimstone*, where the wicked are *tormented for ever and ever* §. If these expressions are to be understood in a limited sense, as only denoting a long continuance in suffering, which yet admits of a termination; on the same ground, the eternity of the blessedness of the saints is set aside. For there are no stronger expressions used to denote this. *They possess the kingdom, and shine as the stars for ever and ever* **. *They reign for ever and ever* ††. Yea language itself can afford none stronger, even to express the existence of God, in relation to that eternity which is to come ‡‡. Only it is to be observed, that when applied to him, they are to be understood in a sense infinitely higher than is applicable to any creature, as including his necessary existence.

This

---

* Isai. xxxiii. 14. † Mark iii. 29. ‡ Jude, ver. 7. § Rev. xx. 10.
** Dan. vii. 18.; xii. 3. †† Rev. xxii. 5. ‡‡ Exod. xv. 18.

This doctrine, instead of doing honour to the Divine perfections, offers them the greatest insult. But this is a disguise which Satan ordinarily uses when he transforms himself into an angel of light, that with the greater ease he may impose on man's weak and corrupt reason. He pretends to pay far greater regard to the truths of God than they ever have met with before, and to make a sacrifice to the Divine perfections that God utterly disclaims. For, if it be not consistent with the glory of the Divine nature, that one perfection should be glorified at the expence of another; how can we suppose that *goodness* is, in some distant period, to triumph over *justice*, nay, over *faithfulness* in the threatening? Or, if there be no way of salvation but through Christ, and if there be no redemption after death, how can *goodness* be displayed to those who have been finally impenitent, in abridging their torments, or in affecting their annihilation? Nay, the idea seems to imply in it, not only the grossest absurdity, but the greatest blasphemy. For it supposes that some of the Divine perfections can cease to be, or at least cease to operate, which is the same; that holiness, justice and faithfulness, are as it were to subside, and be lost in the nature of God, as if wearied out with punishing. If *mercy* shall be eternally displayed in the blessedness of the righteous; there is the very same reason for the eternal display of *holiness*, *justice* and *truth*, in the misery of the wicked. Besides, this presumptuous doctrine has the greatest tendency to relax the authority of the Divine word, to weaken the force of all its threatenings, and of all its promises also, and to encourage sinners in sin; because it presents a distant prospect of deliverance from wrath. Should it be said, that this prospect is so distant, that the fondest mind can have no dependence upon it; let it be considered, that there is no prospect so distant, no dawn of hope so uncertain, nothing that seems within the reach of possibility, but a mind, willing to deceive itself and

take

take indulgence in fin, will eagerly grasp at, rather than abandon its natural present and beloved enjoyments. Those who insinuate such doctrine, can be considered in no other point of view, when urging its congruity to the Divine perfections, than as *speaking unrighteously for God*. And what is the origin of such an idea in any man's mind, but the love of sin, and ignorance of its evil? For it evidently discovers a greater love to the *sinner*, than either to the glory of the *Lawgiver*, or to the righteousness of the *Redeemer* *.

6. IN the sufferings of the *Son of God*. We mention this last, not because it is last in order of nature, or the last discovery that the sinner obtains of the evil and bitterness of sin, but because it is the greatest discovery of both. All the threatenings of the law, terrors of conscience, temporal judgments, complaints of the godly, yea, all the sufferings of hell are but feeble declarations of the evil of sin, compared with those of Christ. All the sufferings of devils and wicked men through eternity, can never contain

---

* We cannot view this doctrine in any other light than as a strange attempt to revive, even among Protestants, the justly exploded doctrine of purgatory ; to revive it with accumulated absurdity. Papists have devised and adhered to *that* doctrine, for their own *interest* ; because it gives such influence to the clergy. Protestants, for the *honour* of their *feelings*, and to afford some consolation to sinners continuing in their iniquities, have devised *this* as an improvement on the former. They reject the Popish purgatory as ridiculous, and yet present the world with a new scheme much more pregnant with folly. Papists plead for a purgatory, while time endures, between death and judgment. Refining Protestants, for a purgatory after judgment. Papists make their purgatory a preservative against hell. But those wiser teachers make hell itself only a purgatory. *Those* make their purgatory a preparation for the eternal unalterable state. But *these* make the eternal state itself only a preparation for some unknown, unimaginable alteration. Seeking to be wise above, yea, against what is written, they transfer the idea of time into eternity, attribute succession and change to that state which admits of neither ; and so in reality convert eternity into time.

contain such a discovery of the holiness and justice of God, in the hatred and punishment of sin, as the sufferings of *the Lord of glory*. These indeed were but the sufferings of one person, and only continued for a time. But the peculiarity of this discovery is owing to the infinite dignity of the Person, as he is God in our nature; whence his temporary sufferings have an infinite value. Were it possible that we could look to the end of eternity, if, for a moment, we may apply to this astonishing subject, the inadequate language of time, we might have some idea of a satisfaction to justice by the sufferings of the damned: but because eternity precludes the very apprehension of an end, and because the wicked are for ever contracting new guilt; we can only have a notion of satisfaction, and of consequence, of the evil of sin, by the eternal duration of their sufferings. But in the temporary sufferings of Christ, we have a *full* display of the evil and bitterness of sin, because he at once sustained the *full* load of infinite wrath for his people. *The Lord hath laid on him the iniquity of us all**. We cannot indeed see the evil of sin in the person of Christ, for he had no sin of his own; nor had he any pollution, as arising from sin imputed. But the guilt of all the sins of his people was laid on him, and he bare the accumulated sufferings due to them all. He sustained in time as many hells of suffering, as there were sinners to redeem.

As both soul and body were by sin subjected to suffering, and to be saved from it, he suffered in both. His whole life was a life of humiliation, and therefore, to him who *was in the form*, the state *of God*, a life of suffering and satisfaction, as well as of obedience. His obedience and suffering were so interwoven, that we cannot well distinguish them. There was suffering in all his obedience, and obedience in all his suffering. He *learned obedience by the*

* Isa. liii. 6.

the things that he suffered *; and *he became obedient unto death* †. Although heaven was his throne, and earth his footstool; yet so great was his voluntary suffering, that even on his footstool he *had not a place where to lay his head*. But however great and constant his sufferings, during the course of his obedience, from weariness, faintness, hunger, thirst, temptation, poverty, reproaches, and every evil and infirmity that did not imply sin; yet his sufferings became vastly more intense from the commencement of his agony, till he said, *It is finished*.—The sufferings of his body, as proceeding from the hand of man, were great; in his being scourged and buffeted, in bearing his cross, having his head pierced with thorns, his hands and his feet with nails, and his body suspended in the agonies of crucifixion. Yet the outward sufferings of his body were little, compared with those which it endured, as the partner of his soul. Blood issued from the wounds which his cruel executioners inflicted; but it issued from every pore of his body, as the fruit of his soul-sufferings. The sufferings of his body, even as partner with his soul, were still as nothing compared with those that he felt in his soul itself. So unspeakable were these, that *his soul was exceeding sorrowful, even unto death* ‡. It was compassed with sorrows on every side. This did not proceed from any bodily sufferings, for it was the chief cause of his severest sufferings of this kind; but from a dreadful sense and feeling of the infinite wrath of God as a Judge, due for all the sins of his people, lying upon him. Under this tremendous load, he was deserted of his Father; and being deprived of the light of his countenance, he endured a dreadful conflict with the powers of darkness §, and suffered the pangs of hell **. That same *breath of the Lord's indignation, that kindleth the fire of hell* ††, kindled such a fire in his holy human soul, that his *heart*

---

* Heb. v. 8.   † Phil. ii. 8.   ‡ Mat. xxvi. 38.
§ Luke xxii. 53.   ** Psal. xviii. 5.   †† Isa. xxx. 33.

heart was melted like wax in the midst of his bowels *. All the wailings and howlings of the damned to all eternity, will fall infinitely short of expressing the evil and bitterness of sin with such emphasis as these few words; *My God, my God, why hast thou forsaken me?* It is only a discovery of sin in the sufferings of Christ that is of a saving nature. Nor can a view of his sufferings as *man*, with what feelings soever of natural affection and sympathy it be attended, be of any avail here. It is only a believing view of his sufferings as *God-man*, and a cordial acceptance of, and reliance upon them as the atonement for *our* sins, that can be profitable for salvation. *Surely*, saith the Church, *he hath born* OUR *griefs, and carried* OUR *sorrows:—He was wounded for* OUR *transgressions, he was bruised for* OUR *iniquities: the chastisement of* OUR *peace was upon him, and with his stripes* WE *are healed* †.

We shall conclude this discourse with a brief exhortation to three classes of persons.

1. To those who are secure in sin.

Your state is truly deplorable. You are pining under a dangerous and destructive malady; yet ye know it not. We would therefore offer you a few directions, relative to your present mournful situation. (1.) Be much engaged in reading and meditating on the word of God. Ponder its threatenings. Consider the judgments which it records, as inflicted on sinners. Be concerned especially to obtain a due apprehension of the spirituality and extent of the holy law, all the precepts of which reach to the heart, and concern its most secret thoughts, and the first imaginations of these thoughts. For *the word of God is quick and powerful, and sharper than any two-edged sword, piercing even to the dividing asunder of soul and spirit, and of the joints and marrow; and is a discerner of the thoughts and intents of the heart* ‡.

The

---

* Psal. xxii. 14.   † Isa. liii. 4, 5.   ‡ Heb. iv. 12.

On the Bitterness of Sin.

The law of the Lord is perfect, converting the soul: the testimony of the Lord is sure, making wise the simple *. The Apostle declares, from his own experience, that he *had not known sin but by the law* †. (2.) Diligently attend on the public dispensation of ordinances. The word preached is the ordinary mean that God blesses for conviction and conversion. It was while Peter preached, that the murderers of Christ were *pricked to the heart, and cried out, Men and brethren, what shall we do* ‡ ? It was only while the lame man waited at the pool, that he met with Jesus, and was healed by him. Christ, the personal wisdom of God, and the great Prophet of his Church, declares the blessedness of those who carefully regard his institutions, not as if all should be eternally blessed who do so, but because a dispensation of the Gospel is an inestimable privilege in itself, and a regular attendance on it, the only appointed order in which we are allowed to expect *the blessing from the God of Jacob, even life for evermore. Blessed is the man that heareth me, watching daily at my gates, waiting at the posts of my doors. For whoso findeth me, findeth life, and shall obtain favour of the Lord* §. (3.) Improve afflictions as a mean for discovering sin. This is their language from God to you, as he declares in the verse wherein our text lies: *Thine own wickedness shall correct thee, and thy backsliding shall reprove thee; know therefore and see,* &c. And how is this accomplished ? It is by means of the afflictions procured by them, in which your wickedness and backsliding may be clearly seen. *Surely it is meet to be said unto God, I have born chastisement, I will not offend any more. That which I see not, teach thou me ; if I have done iniquity, I will do no more* **. (4.) Meditate on the aggravations, consequences, and desert of sin. In this manner the Prophet Nathan dealt with David about his great transgression, 2 Sam. xii. He declares

---

* Psal. xix. 7. † Rom. vii. 7. ‡ Acts ii. 37.
§ Prov. viii. 34, 35. ** Job xxxiv. 31, 32.

declares the aggravation of his sin from a consideration of the many mercies that God had bestowed on him already, and of those also which he might have conferred afterwards, ver. 7, 8. Then he charges home his sin upon his conscience, as a transgression of the commandment of the Lord, as *doing evil in his sight*, ver. 9. Then he denounces judgments against him, and against his house for ever, as justly procured by his iniquity and ingratitude, ver. 10.—12. And last of all, he exhibits the bitter fruit of his sin, in *giving great occasion to the enemies of the Lord to blaspheme*, ver. 14. (5.) Beware of giving loose reins to sin; because it is of a very hardening nature. There is great danger of your being *hardened through the deceitfulness of sin*. Your disease may run on so far, that like a paralytic person, you may become altogether insensible. By a continued uncontrouled course of sin, your conscience may become *seared as with a hot iron*. (6.) Be frequently and fervently engaged in prayer to God for a discovery of his holiness, majesty and love. This has a direct tendency to discover the evil of sin. It had this effect on Job. Therefore he addresses himself to God in the following manner: *I have heard of thee by the hearing of the ear: but now mine eye seeth thee. Wherefore I abhor myself, and repent in dust and ashes* *. Such a discovery operated in the same way on Isaiah. When he *saw the Lord high and lifted up*, and heard the awful proclamation of his holiness, he cried out, *Wo is me; for I am undone, because I am a man of unclean lips* †. (7.) Pray that the holy Spirit may give you a living view of the evil of sin, especially in the sufferings of Christ. It is his work to convince of sin. He *takes of the things of Christ, and shews them unto us*. His work, in this respect, is the subject of promise; and therefore it should be matter of earnest prayer: *I will pour upon the house of David, and upon the inhabitants of Jerusalem, the spirit of grace, and*

---

* Job xlii. 5, 6.   † Isa. vi. 5.

Ser. 2. *On the Bitterness of Sin.* 45

of supplications; and they shall look upon me whom they have pierced, and they shall mourn *.

2. To persons who may be under convictions of sin.

(1.) Consider the advantages arising from these. Although, by no means, saving in themselves, yet, under the blessing of God, they tend to bring the sinner to Christ; for as long as men think themselves whole, they will not apply to the Physician. Convictions do not make you more welcome to the Physician; but, if not abused, they will make him more acceptable to you. (2.) Cherish your convictions. Many, as soon as they find the law working on their consciences, do all in their power to silence it. When terrified by the roaring of the lion, they endeavour, either to shut their ears, or to stop his mouth, by banishing every thing that tends to disturb their peace in sin. When Cain went out from the presence of the Lord under convictions of sin, he employed himself in building a city, in order to banish them; as would seem from the connection of his history, Gen. iv. 16, 17. Many plunge themselves into the world; and *the cares of it, and the deceitfulness of riches choke the word, and it becometh unfruitful.* Although your serious improvement of convictions cannot insure you of conversion; yet the Lord may be justly provoked to depart from you for abusing them. His Spirit *will not always strive with man,* and *wo is unto you,* Sinners, *if* God *depart from you* †. Felix endeavoured to smother his convictions by a proposed delay; and it does not appear that they ever returned ‡. (3.) Beware of lingering under convictions. Ephraim is represented as an unwise son, because he staid *long in the place of the breaking forth of children.* This is the way to lose a sense of sin: for light, if not improved, often becomes weaker, nay, is sometimes altogether turned into darkness. (4.) Rest not on convictions,

as

---

* Zech. xii. 10.   † Hos. ix. 12.   ‡ Acts xxiv. 25.

as if they were enough, as if they were a fatisfying evidence of falvation. The religion of many profeffors, we fear, goes no further than this. They have fome knowledge of fin, and they think all is well with them. (5.) Confider the danger of filencing convictions, by fleeing to a falfe refuge. This is only trying to make *Satan caſt out Satan*. This is to go out of one bad fituation into a worfe: for the cafe of perfons, who reſt on their own righteoufnefs, is more dangerous and hopelefs than even that of publicans and finners. (6.) Earneſtly pray for converting grace. This God hath promifed. *I will heal their backſlidings; I will love them freely; for mine anger is turned away from him.* Let your prayer be that of Ephraim, *Turn thou me, and I ſhall be turned, for thou art the* Lord *my God**. How neceſſary and valuable foever thofe things are, which we have already mentioned, as means for difcovering the evil and bitternefs of fin, ſtill they are means only: and they will never be of any faving benefit to you, without the efficacious operation of the Spirit of God. (7.) In a dependence on this promifed grace, endeavour the prefent exercife of faith in Chriſt: God is efpecially calling you in his word, and particularly, by the common operations of his Spirit, in convictions of fin, to embrace Chriſt as freely offered to you in the Gofpel. The compaffionate Saviour is as really propofing this queſtion to every one of you, as he did in the days of his fleſh, *Wilt thou be made whole?* The convictions of a troubled confcience, like the acute pangs of a difeafed perfon, are calling aloud for an application to the Phyfician; and *is there not balm in Gilead, is there not a Phyſician there?* Embrace the blood of Chriſt, which is that precious balm that alone can heal your difeafed fouls. Believe his record, with particular application to yourfelves, when he teſtifies to every individual, that *in him there is eternal life.* Confidently endeavour to reſt on the foundation of his gracious, particular and unconditional

* Jer. xxxi. 18.

conditional promises, to trust in his name: and *his name is called Jesus, because he saves his people from their sins.* This *name of the Lord is a strong tower; thither the righteous runneth and is safe.*

3. To those who have not only a sense of sin, but a persuasion of deliverance from it.

WE would exhort you, (1.) carefully to enquire, whether this be on a sure foundation. Many apprehend, that they are free from sin, while they are only *free from righteousness.* Try your own hearts by the word, depending on the omniscient Spirit, that you may discover, whether you have really improved the blood of Christ as the only ground of pardon. Unless you have a satisfying, solid and constant rest *here*, you ought not to speak peace to yourselves. If you rest on any other foundation, you are *speaking peace when sudden destruction is at the door.* (2.) Be afraid of losing this comfortable sense of deliverance from sin. None who are interested in the blood of Christ, can be altogether deprived of its efficacy. They can never bring guilt upon their *persons*, guilt, in relation to God as a judge.—But they may bring guilt on their consciences, by obscuring their sense of pardon. Endeavour to maintain a constant fear of sin as the greatest evil; for *it separates between us and our God*; and although it cannot separate his people from his *love*, it often separates them from the *evidences* of it, by *causing him to hide his face.* (3.) Strive to obtain further discoveries of the *evil* of sin. Apprehend not, that, in this respect, you have attained. The believer can never have a full sense of sin, till he be perfectly freed from it. We always look on sin, in this world, with a partial eye; because we cannot entirely separate the idea of sin from the personal interest we have in it; we cannot separate sin from our own minds in judging of it. As an evidence of this, we are generally disposed to be much more severe on the sins of others than our own. Even those sins that we love and indulge in ourselves, we hate and despise,

spise, when we see them in others; although they contain nothing but a portrait of our own hearts, justly delineated. The saint will then fully know the *evil* from which he has been delivered, when he fully enjoys the *good* to which he is redeemed; not merely the *bitterness* of sin, by a discovery of the *joys* of heaven; but the *evil* of sin, by the enjoyment of complete *holiness*. Here he is only *pressing forward and following after*; but then he *shall know, even as he is known,* and apprehend that for which he is also apprehended of Christ. (4.) Let the prevalence of sin be your daily burden. This, we have seen, is the greatest burden that believers have, while in this tabernacle. Let your desires be constantly directed towards that happy state, in which sin shall be no more. (5.) Make daily application to the blood of Christ for sprinkling. Although you can never contract new guilt in relation to God as a *Judge,* you are daily provoking him as a *Father;* and you need daily to apply to the fountain opened. Therefore be concerned constantly to improve it for removing the guilt contracted against your loving Father, and for washing away your daily defilement. *And the very God of peace sanctify you wholly: and may your whole spirit, and soul, and body be preserved blameless unto the coming of our Lord Jesus Christ.*

SERMON III.

On the PLAGUE of the HEART.

---

1 Kings, viii. 38.

——*Who shall know every man the plague of his own heart.*——

MAN has naturally an ardent desire of knowledge. This is a faint memorial of that perfect image of God at first impressed on his heart in creation, of which knowledge was a principal feature. It is also a striking indication of the immortality of his soul, and of that glorious perfection after which he ought eagerly to aspire. This thirst for knowledge is discovered in a thousand different ways; according to the difference of the temper and affections of the mind. But it is truly deplorable, that an inclination in itself so excellent, should be so sadly misapplied; and that men acting according to their natural impulse, should universally occupy their minds with things comparatively trivial, to the total neglect of the *one thing needful*. While many inquire into the nature of God, and into that of their own souls, as matters of mere speculation, as subjects of curious and entertaining investigation; how few are disposed to contemplate God, as he reveals himself in love and mercy to sinners through Jesus Christ, and to study themselves, as creatures that stand in the most absolute need of so gracious a revelation? While many amuse themselves, by inquiring into the faculties of the soul, and by descanting on the noble powers of which man is possessed; how few are anywise concerned to search into his unspeakable loss in the depravation of these faculties, the causes of this loss, the consequences of it, the power of indwelling corruption,

corruption, or, in a word, as Solomon expresses it, *to know every man the plague of his own heart.*

These words are a part of Solomon's prayer at the dedication of the temple. His father David had resolved to build an house for the Lord, but was prevented, being warned of God, that this work was reserved for his son. Accordingly Solomon engaged in it after the death of his father: and having finished the building in the most magnificent manner, he solemnly consecrates it by prayer and sacrifice, to the service of JEHOVAH. In his prayer he enumerates different cases, in which he entreats the Lord's gracious answer from his holy temple. The words of our text refer to some heavy judgment, which Solomon supposes might come upon Israel, because of their iniquities; *famine, or pestilence, or blasting or mildew.* He supplicates, that, in this mournful situation, the Lord would interpose for their deliverance, when he should be addressed, either by individuals, or by the whole nation; and especially, when the persons, so addressing him, should not only be affected with the outward judgment, but with their own sins; and not merely with their outward transgressions, but with the sins of their hearts, as the source of all others, and the primary cause of all judgments. By this mode of expression, Solomon does not mean to limit God, as if he should never grant a deliverance, but when his people were deeply affected with the plagues of their hearts. But he mentions this as an argument with God, urging the exercise of his sympathy and compassion towards them, and the removal of his judgments, when they should be brought to a due sense of their sins. The expression may also intimate the line of duty, the way in which God's people are to expect, that their prayers shall be heard and answered.—This is only when they are humbled before him on account of their iniquities. Thus it declares to us, as it did to his ancient people, that those who address God's throne for deliverance from judgments, and are

yet

yet hardened in their sins, have no reason to expect that they shall receive the answer of prayer.—Nor does he mean to insinuate, that it could be supposed, that the throne of God should be so approached by all his people, as that every individual should know and be deeply affected with his own sins. For this is a case that never did, and we may venture to say, never will happen in any general reformation. But as he here points out what is the duty of every one in his approach to the mercy-seat, he also supposes what might be the attainment of a great many of these afflicted supplicants. Here an universal expression is used to denote a great, although it should not be the greatest part; of which we have many other examples in scripture. We have an expression of the very same import, used on the same subject, Ezek. vii. 16. *All of them mourning, every one for his own iniquity.*

The *heart* is taken in different senses in scripture. Sometimes, in a more general sense, it denotes the soul, with all its faculties, understanding, will, conscience, affections; and with all its adjuncts, as wisdom, prudence, thoughts, desires and wishes. More strictly, it signifies the will and affections; which are the most operative powers of the soul; the peculiar seat of desire or reluctance, of choice or rejection; and the immediate springs and principles of action. Here it may be proper to observe, that when we may afterwards speak of the heart, or any particular plague of it, we shall generally understand it in the first of these senses, as denoting all the faculties of the soul; and do not mean to confine ourselves to a nice philosophical discussion of the different faculties as the subjects of different sins. Although sin has eminently its seat in the will and affections; yet we may speak of it in its influence on both the superior and inferior faculties, under the general denomination of the *heart;* by which they are so often collectively expressed in scripture. By the *plague* here mentioned, we understand *sin.* There are some indeed who apply this expression to the

the particular affliction or judgment, to which either individuals, or the nation in general, might be subjected; and in confirmation of this opinion, adduce the parallel passage in 2 Chron. vi. 29. where the words run in the following manner; *When every one shall know his own* sore, *and his own* grief.—But it must be observed, that the difference here principally depends on the translation: for the same word, there rendered *sore*, is in this place rendered *plague*. Although there is another expression added,—*and his own grief;* yet this will by no means restrict the force of the preceding one to affliction: because *sin* should be much more the subject of our grief than any affliction; as every affliction derives its essence, sting and bitterness from sin; and as the cause should naturally be considered before the effect, or at least, the cause should principally engage our attention*. Besides, affliction in general, and particularly any outward stroke, such as those mentioned in the preceding verse, cannot be denominated *the plague of the heart*, with such propriety as sin. Afflictions of this kind are more properly the plague of the *flesh*, and can only be that of the *heart* in a derivative and secondary way. The proper and original sense of the word rendered *plague*, seems also in this place to restrict it peculiarly to sin. For the word used in the original properly signifies any evil of a contagious and abominable nature. Now, although the word, when used with respect to the pestilence, or any outward calamity, may bear this sense; yet when the heart is spoken of as the seat of this plague, we must necessarily understand it of sin: for this alone, in a spiritual sense, as affecting the heart, and especially as seated *in* it, is of a contagious and abominable nature; and this

---

* The Psalmist uses the same figurative mode of expression, Psal. cxxxix. 24. *See if there be any way of pain*, or *grief in me*, as in the margin. In the text, it is with propriety rendered *any wicked way*, because the connection evidently limits the phrase to sin, the source and procuring cause of all pain or grief.

this cannot with propriety be said of any outward disease, because of its effects *on* the heart, in producing grief or affliction. The same word here rendered *plague*, as signifying a disease of an infectious nature, is often used in this proper and original sense in scripture. It often denotes the plague of leprosy, which was considered as so infectious and abominable, that not only the garment which the leper wore, but the very house in which he dwelt, was unclean. It signifies the pestilence, as in verse 37. It is also used to express diseases, which are contagious and loathsome. So in Psal. xxxviii. 11. David complains, that his *friends stood aloof from* his *sore*, or from his plague; which he had described before as a *loathsome disease that filled* his *loins with pain*. Now, these different uses of the word, according to its strict and primary sense, as denoting an abominable and infectious evil, illustrate the necessity of understanding the plague of the heart in reference to *sin*; because this, as affecting the *heart*, may, with much more propriety than any thing else, be called a *plague*.

That we are to understand this expression of sin, and not of affliction, at least of sin in a peculiar manner, and only of affliction subordinately, as the fruit of sin, seems undeniably evident from the words of Solomon recorded in verse 39. *Give to every man according to his ways, whose* HEART *thou knowest; for thou even thou only knowest the* HEARTS *of the children of men.* This solemn appeal to God, as the Searcher of hearts, must certainly determine the plague formerly mentioned, as seated in the heart, to be sin. The appeal here made refers to his infinite knowledge of this plague, and their exercise under it. For if it must be limited, or principally referred to any temporal calamity, there was no occasion for an appeal to Omniscience; because any temporal calamity of such a nature as those specified, would not only be obvious to it, but to every indifferent spectator. The connection that is also stated
between

between the *ways* and the *heart* of the person in this supposed situation, as intimating that whatever knowledge a man might have of his *heart*, if it did not influence his *ways*; or what strictness of *conduct* soever a man might attain, if it did not proceed from a true knowledge of the plague of his *heart*, would be unacceptable with God; clearly demonstrates that the plague here mentioned is meant of *sin*. Indeed the connection farther stated between the uprightness of a man's heart, as influencing his conduct, or the holiness of a man's conduct as proceeding from an upright heart, and God's gracious interposition in a time of calamity, is not to be considered as expressive of any thing meritorious, either in his practical knowledge, or holy practice, as entitling him to any blessing from God. For although the Old Testament Saints lived under a legal dispensation, still it was a dispensation of the same covenant that we are under, which proposes all its rewards as of grace, and not of debt. But this connection declares the ordinary course of God's operation, in averting afflictions, when by means of them he has brought his people to a sense of sin, and turned them to himself; as he *chastens them not for his pleasure, but for their profit*. It may also intimate, that although the Lord is often pleased, in his compassion and forbearance, for a time to remove judgments from guilty individuals or nations, in consequence of a reformation on their part, perhaps merely of an external kind, they nevertheless are only warranted to expect either a partial or total removal of judgments, when they *turn unto him with their whole heart*.

What is farther proposed in opening these words is,

I. To make some observations mostly founded on the text. And,

II. To illustrate the necessity and importance of knowing the *plague* of the *heart*.

I.

I. It is proposed to offer some observations.

It may be observed then,

1. That sin has all the evil *qualities* of a *plague*. It is of the most *abominable* nature; therefore it may justly receive this appellation. Under the law, leprosy was pronounced to be a plague; the leper was shut up by himself, by order of the priest; and if his leprosy was confirmed, he was not suffered to enter the camp, but obliged to dwell alone in a separate habitation. This certainly, in a spiritual sense, represented the abominable nature of sin. He who labours under this plague, during the continuance of its power, is excluded from the presence of God, and from all communion with him. The sinner who is finally unbelieving and impenitent, who notwithstanding all the means he enjoys, so far from being cured, despises them all, like the incurable leper, is entirely cast without the camp, for ever separated from God, and from his people. Sin is unspeakably abominable to the holy God. Therefore he pleads with sinners, in the most tender and affectionate manner, that they would not commit it. *Oh! do not that abominable thing that I hate.*—A plague is especially an *inward* distress. All its external eruptions, instead of constituting the disease itself, only declare its internal power, as infecting the whole mass of blood and humours, and rendering nature totally unfit for the performance of its proper functions. Thus sin, the plague of the heart, is especially an *inward* malady. All its loathsome appearances, in the conversation, instead of constituting the disease, are only its symptoms, as may be afterwards more fully illustrated.

Sin, like a plague, is also *infectious;* and, indeed, the contagion of this plague is universal. From one man this fatal distemper hath been communicated, without a single exception, to every individual, in every successive generation of his descendants, according to the ordinary course of nature. *Our first father hath sinned, and we have all born his iniquity.*

iniquity. This is a plague that hath infected the whole man. External plagues affect the body alone; but this hath affected both foul and body: the foul in all its powers, and the body in all its members. *The whole head is sick, and the whole heart faint. From the sole of the foot, even unto the head, there is no soundness in it; but wounds, and bruises, and putrefying sores: they have not been closed, neither bound up, neither mollified with ointment**. As it is originally infectious, in the corruption of our whole nature, it is secondarily so by example. Men are not merely, by the depravity of their nature, incident to this plague. They do every thing in their power to increase its fatal symptoms, and to extend its ravages, by greedily pursuing all iniquity. Any natural plague, as affecting the body, communicates its own virulent nature to every thing within its reach, and turns it to rottenness and corruption. So doth sin. It not only impairs the whole nature of him who is under its dominion, but communicates pollution to all his actions. Those duties, that are in themselves good, become evil as performed by the sinner. *The prayer of the wicked is abomination to the Lord.—Their solemn meetings are iniquity; their appointed feasts his soul hateth.* Even their natural and civil actions are contaminated by this plague. *The very plowing of the wicked is sin.*

It is *incurable* as to all that man can do. No earthly means can remove the plague. Notwithstanding all the attempts of Naturalists to account for this disease upon physical principles, it has generally been considered by thinking persons, as more immediately, than any other, inflicted by the hand of God, and as a disease that could be removed by no human endeavours †. This is one reason why, under the

---

* Isa. i. 5. 6.

† We are sure, from the testimony of Scripture, that this disease has been, in different instances, immediately inflicted by God's hand.

the law, the person infected with leprosy, or any other plague, was obliged to have immediate recourse to the priest*. So the plague of sin, although brought on man by himself, wherein the resemblance fails, is absolutely incurable, as to all that can be effected by the wisdom and power of creatures. Although this spiritual leper should *wash himself with nitre, and take much soap, yet* his *iniquity* would be *marked before* the Lord. Nothing but the infinitely precious blood of Christ can remove this plague.

It is also *consuming* and *deadly*. It is the nature of a plague to diffuse itself through the subject infected, and to corrupt and consume it.† Sin is the seed and principle of corruption in our nature; and if it be not removed, shall consume both soul and body. So the Psalmist confesses; *My strength faileth because of mine iniquity, and my bones are consumed* ‡. Therefore the Church also complains; *Thou hast consumed us because of our iniquities* §. Sin is the mortification of our natures. It not only subjects us to *natural* death, as part of the sentence of the broken law, and diffuses a principle of mortality through our bodies; but is also the *spiritual* mortification of our souls; for it subjects the immortal part to a spiritual mortality. This is presently discovered by the unfitness of all the powers of the soul for the service of God, which is their highest end and proper employment; by the loss of his image in original righteousness, and by

---

hand. Particularly, there were two kinds of leprosy common among the Jews, which seem to have been utterly unknown among other nations, and which they, notwithstanding all their obstinacy, always viewed as the immediate fruits of Divine judgment. These were, the leprosy in garments, and in the walls of an house; by which we are not to understand any typical defilement; nor are we to view the ordinances about them as signifying the danger of conveying the infection from a leprous *person;* for these were two kinds of leprosy, spreading and corroding, distinct from each other, and totally different from a *bodily* leprosy. *Vid.* Univ. Hist. vol. iii. p. 157.—159.; Poli Synops. Crit. in Lev. xii. 47.

* Lev. xiii. 2, 3, 5, &c. † Numb. xii. 12. ‡ Psa. xxxi. 10. § Isa. lxiv. 7.

the want of fellowship with him. It is finally discovered in that eternal death, which is especially *the wages of sin*, and in which the soul, in a spiritual sense, everlastingly endures consumption, corruption, and perdition, and yet never attains the wished-for destruction or annihilation.—The words of our text, viewed in their connection, afford a beautiful and striking contrast between the *outward* plague mentioned in ver. 37. and the *inward* one mentioned in ver. 38.; as intimating, that whatever outward plague sinners may be under, there is still a more loathsome one within; that how fatal soever the pestilence may be, *which walketh in darkness, and wasteth at noon-day*, it derives all its deadly power from the plague of the heart, which is, in its own nature, much more destructive;—and as declaring, that whatever outward calamity overwhelms the children of men, they can never make a right improvement of it, unless they turn their eyes inward to that running sore of sin, that while their flesh may be loathsome to themselves, should make their souls much more so; as it renders them unspeakably loathsome to God, and is the source of every thing else about them, which is evil or abominable.

2. Sin is with the greatest propriety denominated the plague of the *heart*. For it hath properly its seat here; and it is the heart that defiles the whole conversation. The body, indeed, is active in sinning as well as the soul; and for this reason subjected to the curse in conjunction with it. But then the body is only the tool of the soul in sinning. Therefore our members are said to be *the instruments of unrighteousness unto sin*. They are only the instruments: the soul is the principal agent, the primary director. The heart alone is the subject of will, choice, consent and approbation. The influence of the heart is therefore necessary to the being of all *outward* sin. The Apostle, indeed, declares, that *with the mind he served the law of God, while with the flesh the law of sin*[*]. But *the flesh* is not here to be understood of the body, but of the

---

[*] Rom. vii. 25.

the unrenewed part of the man. This he opposes to his new nature, which alone he accounts worthy to be called his *mind*. Could we suppose an evil action to be committed without the smallest influence or consent of the mind, it would cease to be evil, it would altogether lose the nature of sin, which, in order to its being, as an external act, must have the consent of the will in some degree or other. Man, in this supposed case, could be no more accountable than the brute, which is entirely destitute of reason. But all sin has its first rise in the heart. The sin of our nature has its residence, nay, its reign there, before it be expressed by any open immorality. All outward sins spring from this as their fountain.

HERE we do not mean to insinuate, according to the doctrine of Papists, that the consent of the will is necessary to the essence of sin. For it is undeniable, that we are chargeable with innumerable *thoughts*, which, although they may not so far ripen in the secret chambers of imagery, as to receive the consent of the will, are yet sinful, and often exceedingly so; as proceeding from the exuberant corruption of the heart, *all the imaginations of which are only evil continually* * ; as tending in themselves to open acts of wickedness; and as being of the nature of those inordinate motions of the heart, which the scripture calls *covetousness* or *lust*; and which the Apostle declares he would not have known to be sin, unless he had seen by the light of the Holy Spirit, that the law had expressly prohibited them †. To a carnal unenlightened mind the tenth commandment, delivered in these words, *Thou shalt not covet*, may appear to be unnecessary, as containing a material repetition of what is forbidden in the eighth. Paul, while the Pharisee, seems to have entertained some such unjust apprehension. But *when the commandment came*, he found even heart-sin to be *exceeding sinful* ‡ : and every man who truly knows the plague of his own heart, must admire both the grace and holiness of God, manifested in the addition of this to all the other precepts of the moral

* Gen. vi. 5.   † Rom. vii. 7.   ‡ Rom. vii. 13.

ral law; viewing it as a necessary key for opening up the spiritual meaning and extensive application of all those preceding, which, in the *manner* of expression, being confined to the principal and overt acts of each of the sins referred to, would unavoidably, as to the *matter* of them also, by every carnal mind be confined to these. Even this most spiritual precept, with respect to the manner of expression, seems only to comprehend those actings of covetousness that regard our neighbour's property; which verbal limitation appeared, in the infinite wisdom of God, most suitable to the comparative darkness of the legal dispensation. Yet it must be evident to every mind *led by the Spirit*, that it clearly pronounces even the first motions and most secret risings of *lust* in the heart to be sin, whatever be the object to which they are directed; whether they regard the first or second table of the law; and though they be nowise indulged, but suppressed by grace. For a corrupt fountain can send forth nothing but bitter streams; and all such motions are directly opposed to that universal spirituality which the law requires.

EVEN *outward* sins may be committed without a formal consent of the will; such as those of ignorance, of surprise, and also of omission, when the neglect is not voluntary. Believers likewise do what they *would not*, what they *hate*. When, therefore, we speak of the consent of the will as necessary to outward sin, *in some degree or other;* all that we mean is, to express the constant influence of the heart on the life; and to illustrate the folly of those who think that their hearts may be *pure*, while their hands are not *clean*. For even in sins of ignorance, surprise and omission, there is a tacit and virtual consent; because either a man does not improve the means of light he enjoys; or he consents to sloth and carelessness, which are the occasions of his surprise or omission. The Christian also, although his *mind*, his will, as renewed, continues to disapprove and oppose known sin, yet consents with his will as far as it is carnal.

BUT

But not only has *sin* properly its seat in the *heart*; but it is the sin of the *heart* that defiles the conversation. This is another evidence of the justness of that denomination given to it in our text. Were there no sin in the *heart*, there could be none in the practice. Our Saviour was *harmless and undefiled* in his conversation, without the least sin or defect, personal guilt or pollution of any kind; because he was *holy* in his nature. This was the foundation of the innocence and blamelessness of his life. Had he not been *the holy child Jesus*, it could never have been said with regard to his life, that *there was no guile found in his mouth*. Thus the *heart* is the fountain of all defilement. It is the plague of the heart that infects the life. Our Lord was careful to inform his disciples of this. *Do ye not perceive,* said he, *that whatsoever thing from without entereth into the man, it cannot defile him. That which cometh out of the man, that defileth the man. For from within, out of the heart of man, proceed evil thoughts,* &c. *All these things come from within and defile the man**. And again, *A good man, out of the good treasure of his heart, bringeth forth that which is good; and an evil man, out of the evil treasure of his heart, bringeth forth that which is evil; for of the abundance of the heart, his mouth speaketh* †.

3. Every man should be especially *concerned* about his *own* sin. He ought to make his *own* spiritual plague his peculiar study. There are a great many professors, who make a mighty outcry against the sins of others, against those of their neighbours, of their fellow-professors, of the nation in general, or of the age in which they live. They pretend to be deeply humbled on account of *these* sins. Yet they are entirely careless about their *own*. It is good to be duly and zealously affected with the sins of others. This is our indispensable duty; because the glory of God is concerned in it. But all professions of sorrow for the sins of others are unavailing, false and hypocritical, unless they be attended with, or flow from

---

* Mark vii. 18.—23. † Luke vi. 45.

from an affecting conviction of our own sin, and ingenuous sorrow before the Lord on this account. Such empty professions are like those of the obdurate Jews, who acknowledged themselves to be *the children of them that had killed the prophets;* and as a sort of reparation for the crimes of their fathers, *built and garnished the sepulchres* of these holy martyrs; while, after all, they were *partakers with their fathers in their evil deeds,* because of their own unbelief, which instigated them to persecute Christ and his disciples. How preposterous is it for us to acknowledge that others are sinners, and that our fathers have sinned; unless we be deeply affected with our own guilt, and thence influenced to confess, in the bitterness of our hearts, that *we have sinned with our fathers, and been too long the workers of iniquity* *. While we acknowledge the sins of preceding generations, under a heartfelt conviction of that dishonour thereby done to God, and as deprecating the judgments thus entailed on us; we ought, in a particular manner, in our confessions, to recollect and enumerate *their* sins as aggravations of *ours;* because, according to the testimony of God in his word, *their* sins, with the judgments attending them, are set before our eyes as beacons to deter us from following their wicked example. This consideration seems to have been viewed and confessed by the returning Israelites, in different periods, as a peculiar aggravation of *their* guilt †. All the professions that we make of sorrow for the sins of others, are but a solemn insult offered to the omniscient and infinitely holy God, unless we have a just apprehension of our own sin; because we profess to be humbled before him for that which we are entirely ignorant of, as to its evil and abominable nature. It is a profession of sorrow for that which never occasioned to ourselves one moment of sorrow, or one tear of anguish. Yea, our profession of sorrow for the sins of others, while we remain insensible as to our own, is a great aggravation of our guilt, and enhancement of our condemnation. For when we

---

* Psal. cvi. 6.   † Ezra ix. 7.—Jer. iii. 25.

we declare our sense of the guilt of others, and are unaffected with our own, wherein we accuse others, we condemn ourselves, proclaim our obduracy, and declare that we are inexcusable. Where shall we find a resemblance of this hypocritical conduct? Shall we compare it to that of a man who joins himself to the company of those who have discovered, and are bitterly lamenting the murder of one of their relations or friends, who weeps as bitterly, and, to appearance, as sincerely as any of them; nay, earnestly wishes that the cruel murderer were discovered; and, to his professions of grief, adds the most poignant invectives, even denounces the severest threatenings, and imprecates the heaviest curses on the guilty person; while he is himself the murderer, or an accessory to the crime?

4. EVERY man should especially *search* into the sins of his *heart*. Therefore Solomon interrupts the tenor of his address to God by this striking parenthesis; *who shall know every man the plague of his own heart*. It is not enough that we know our own plague. We must be peculiarly concerned about that of our *heart*. Knowledge of this kind is to us of the greatest importance. This appears from what we have already seen, that the heart is the proper *seat* of sin, and that it is this which *defiles* the man. He who is a stranger to his heart, can never know the multitude of evils that compass him about, and that he is ever in danger of falling into. For the heart of every man hath in it the seeds of all sin. There every iniquity, however atrocious, lies as it were in embryo; and that all men do not follow courses equally wicked with those of the worst, is not because their hearts are naturally better than others, but is principally owing, either to the restraining, or to the renewing grace of God. Every human heart is a spiritual Babylon, *a hold of every foul spirit, and a cage of every unclean and hateful bird**. Therefore the Spirit of God represents the heart of man as *desperately*

---

* Rev. xviii. 2.

sperately wicked*; not wicked in some, but in the highest degree. This expression properly signifies any disease so inveterate as to baffle all the force of medicine, a disease absolutely incurable; and when used metaphorically to denote the wickedness of man's heart, it intimates that this is so great, that all human expedients, all the exertions of natural ability, all the powers of man's reason or will are utterly insufficient to remove it, or of themselves to withstand its increasing force; that with regard to all that man can do, the wickedness of the heart is a desperate case; that it is a disease which nothing but sovereign grace and almighty power can conquer.

Man hath been sometimes called a *microcosm* or *little world*. He hath been thus denominated in a physical sense, because of the wonderful nature of his frame, in which all the principles dispersed through the rest of the universe are collected and combined: but this designation most properly belongs to him in a moral sense, and particularly to his heart. This is, indeed, a world in miniature. As all the accounts of robberies and murders, of perjuries, treasons and rebellions, of wars and devastations, are only narratives of the particular operations of inward corruption: the heart itself is a compend of the history of mankind from the fall to this very moment. It discovers, at least in the seed and principle, all those lusts that have produced so much mischief among the children of Adam. Here you may discern that Deceit, which hath so often ruined, not individuals only, but empires; that Avarice, which hath ransacked the bowels of the earth, and fathomed the abysses of the ocean for its gratifications, nay, sacrificed whole nations to its golden idol; that Ambition, which hath at times brought greater destruction on mankind than all the diseases to which our fallen nature is subject. Here you may perceive the workings of that Cruelty, which hath rendered man a greater monster, in the destruction of his own species, than any beast of prey; that Sensuality, which hath converted him into a greater

---

* Jer. xvii. 9.

greater brute than any of those whose *spirit goeth downward;* that Unbelief which made him crucify *the Lord of glory;* and that Atheism, that hath made him deny the being of his Creator. Even in the same heart, according to the variation of age, circumstances and temptations, you may discern the motions of almost all those lusts that engage the world at large, and, for near six thousand years, have kept it *lying in the wicked one.* It is deemed a peculiar excellency in an historian, if he clearly points out the secret springs of those actions which he narrates. But how accurately soever a man should describe the conduct of nations, and unravel the mysteries of their politics; if he knows not the mystery of iniquity in his own heart, he wants that key which can alone admit him to a just view of *the treasures of wickedness,* and discover to him the true origin and nature of those enormities that he describes. Could a man fairly read his own heart, by the light of the Word and Spirit, it would afford him a just and compendious history of the world. He would find the history of Cain abridged in his own Anger and Revenge; of Pharaoh in his Obduracy; of Balaam in his Covetousness; of David and Bathsheba in his *Filthiness of Spirit;* of Absalom in his Disobedience; of Rehoboam in his Self-confidence; of Nebuchadnezzar in his Vanity; of Sennacherib in his Ambition; of Rabshakeh in his Presumption; of Ahab, Jezebel and Manasseh in his Enmity against God; of Judas in his Deceitfulness; of the Heathen nations in his Ignorance and Blindness of mind; and of the Church of Israel in his Unbelief and Rebellion. It is granted, indeed, that all these corruptions do not rage with equal violence in the same heart, or break out in the conversation. But, at one time or another, a man, who is acquainted with himself, will find the workings of every one of these in a greater or less degree. And how could he find their motions, however secret or imperfect, if the principle of each of them did not reside in his heart*?

Thus,

---

* In one point of view the heart of the Christian is a more striking

Thus, without the knowledge of the heart, a man can never have a juſt apprehenſion of the evil nature of ſin. This, indeed, is mournfully diſplayed by the dreadful effects of inward depravity which appear in the enormities of the life, like ſo many empoiſoned ſtreams ruſhing from a deadly fountain. But all the enormities of the life, dreadful as they are in many inſtances, are ſtill inſufficient to declare the full malignity of the nature of ſin. This is an original found only in the heart, that no external repreſentation, however ſtriking the reſemblance, can perfectly expreſs. In the heart of man, in his natural condition, ſin ſits enthroned as a ſovereign, gives forth laws for the whole of his conduct, employs an unſpeakable variety of luſts as the executioners of its determinations, and retains all the powers of the ſoul, and all the members of the body as its abject ſlaves and devoted emiſſaries. Notwithſtanding the ſhocking outbreakings of corruption, and flagrant impieties that iſſue from the heart; we have but a mere ſample of what is within. And if theſe outbreakings are ſo ſhocking, theſe impieties ſo flagrant, if the wickedneſs of the heart diſcovers itſelf in ſo ſtriking

ſtriking miniature of the world than even that of the natural man. His corruptions, indeed, are not ſo powerful; but they all exiſt in the principle. Beſides, there is the vigorous oppoſition of grace. Here we have, on a ſmall ſcale, a repreſentation of all the politics of the great world. We diſcern the workings of that wiſdom which is *deviliſh*, which employs greater political ſubtilties than were ever brought into action among men; and of that alſo which is *from above*, endeavouring to counterplot the other, although *without hypocriſy*. Here we find corruption daringly proclaiming war againſt the ſoul, and againſt that divine principle which reſides in it; and grace proclaiming war againſt corruption; *the fleſh luſting againſt the ſpirit, and the ſpirit luſting againſt the fleſh.* You ſee them actually engaged on the field of battle; legions of luſts, aided by their auxiliaries, legions of devils, ſtruggling againſt *the hidden man of the heart,* and his various graces. For *what will you ſee in the Shulamite? as it were the company of two armies.* In a word, you may perceive ſometimes the one and ſometimes the other victorious; the new creature *lifted up and caſt down again.* The Chriſtian is the true Gad. *A troop ſhall overcome him; but he ſhall overcome at the laſt.*

striking a manner, although man is restrained by the bonds of society, by the force of human laws, by regard to his character and interest, by the terrors of conscience, by desires of happiness, by the fears of a future state, and by the common operations of the Spirit; what a dreadful discovery would the heart make of itself, were it freed from all these restraints? Were it possible that the most wicked man in the world could take a naked view of his heart, could see it stripped of all the false glosses that he puts on his crimes, of all the restraints to which they are subjected, and of all the ideal virtues and artificial refinements, which he considers as an ample indemnification for his vices; he would shudder at himself, start back from the dreadful picture with horror and amazement, and imagine that it was rather the representation of a devil, than of a man. If a Saint of God, whose nature had been renewed by the power of the Holy Spirit, whose lusts had been mortified, in whom the dominion of sin had been broken, and a principle of holiness implanted, on a discovery of his own heart, with all these advantages, could cry out; *Behold, I am vile, what shall I answer thee* *; if another, on the same discovery, although *not behind the chief of the Apostles*, was made to acknowledge that he was *the chief of sinners* †; what must the wickedness of the heart of man be, in its full force and dominion, as it appears in the eyes of the omniscient God!

We learn, from what hath now been said, the dreadful ravages that sin has made in our nature. It has degraded man, who was once the resemblance of his Maker, into the likeness of *the beasts that perish*. It has made man, the lord of the creation, more vile than the vilest of the brute creatures, which were given him as his subjects. It has changed the image of God into the image of Satan, converted the sanctuary of God into a kennel of lusts, the friend of Jehovah into his enemy, the son of God into the child

of

---

* Job xl. 4. † 1 Tim. i. 15.

of Beelzebub. From this confideration, be exhorted to take a view of the guilt and vileness of your nature, and of the unspeakable wickedness of your hearts. *If the heavens are not clean in his sight, if he hath put no trust in his holy ones, if he charged his angels with folly;* may we not justly exclaim, *How much more abominable and filthy is man, who drinketh up iniquity like water!* As children of the first Adam, you are children of wrath; and doubly so, as sinners by many actual transgressions. Thus, you are not only exposed to temporal death, which is the greatest extent of any natural plague; but while ye continue under sin, by the power of this spiritual plague, subject to, and lying under an awful sentence of spiritual death, being destitute of original righteousness, of the love of God, communion with him, and conformity to him. For as a plague wastes the natural beauty of man, the plague of sin hath *consumed your beauty like a moth.* Nay, you are also exposed to eternal death: and what this is, in its full meaning and extent, who can declare? The enlarged capacities of damned spirits, and even the superior powers of devils themselves, together with all their experience of suffering, can never be able to express the dreadful nature of that condemnation, which consists in their being *punished with everlasting destruction from the presence of the Lord, and from the glory of his power!* No man can form just conceptions of natural death, but he who has felt its stroke. But this sting of death, this eternal death, although it may be felt, yet cannot be described even by its miserable subjects. *Who knoweth the power of thine anger?* Blessed are they who know it only, by its glorious contrast, in the fruits of everlasting love! This view of the detestableness and guilt of sin should influence you to seek a discovery of the Saviour. This is your consolation, that *his name is called* Jesus, *because he saves his people from their sins.* He superabundantly restores all that man hath lost by the fall. There is value in his blood, fully commensurate to all the demerit

merit of your sin; and *he is able to save them to the uttermost, that come unto God by him.*

This subject affords a decisive test, by which you may know, whether you are still under the absolute power of the plague of sin? Have you hitherto confined your views of sin, and your sorrow for it, to the outward man? Have you never pursued this enemy into the secret recesses of the heart, where it lurks like a lion in his den? Have you been grieved for the sins of your life and conversation, but ready to overlook or excuse the secret thoughts of wickedness, which *lodge within you?* Or, if you have been grieved for these as sinful and dishonouring to God, when indulged by you; yet have you never reviewed the first motions of the heart towards sin, as really sinful in themselves; have you never considered these corrupt figments of the heart, in their abominable nature and wicked tendency? Then, you need not be in the least hesitation to conclude, that you are yet strangers to the sinfulness of sin, and to your own hearts; and that the fatal plague is consuming you within, however its external wounds may be smoothed over by a conversation generally blameless. You are in no better situation than Paul before his conversion; perhaps in a situation not so good. For *touching the* outward *righteousness of the law he was blameless;* although, like you, he was ignorant of the nature and evil of secret lust.—We do not say, that all who are convinced, that the secret motions and first risings of sin in the heart are sinful, or who make a profession of sorrow for them, are really delivered from the power of sin; for convictions may go very far. But we are certain, that none can habitually view these as sinful, because of their opposition to the infinite holiness of God, can have them as their daily burden and grief at the throne of grace, and be still striving in the strength of Christ, to resist and subdue them,—but those who are savingly acquainted with *the plague of the heart.*

SER-

SERMON IV.

On KNOWING THE PLAGUE OF THE HEART.

1 Kings viii. 38.

—Who shall know every man the plague of his own heart.—

ALL the knowledge that a man can, by any means, acquire, is utterly unprofitable, if he know not *himself*; and all his self-knowledge is equally unprofitable, if it be not practical. But alas! how many learned fools are there in the world, who know a great deal, and yet *know nothing as they ought to know;* who, in some sense, *have all knowledge,* and yet are *nothing;* because they are strangers to themselves, and of consequence strangers to God. For the saving knowledge of God, and that of ourselves, are inseparably connected, and have a mutual influence on each other. As the sun, when he appears in the natural world, by affording so striking a contrast between light and darkness, excites in the mind the most just ideas of the horror of that universal night which preceded his rising; and on the other hand, as the horror of this darkness most effectually demonstrates the inestimable value of his light: in like manner, a saving discovery of God, by means of the word, invariably tends to display to us our own hearts in their just and natural colours; and a saving discovery of our hearts will certainly recommend the infinite excellency and perfections of God.

On this subject we have already observed, that sin hath all the evil qualities of a plague; that it is with the greatest justness and propriety, denominated the plague of the heart; that a man should be in a particular

ticular manner concerned about his *own* sins; and that the sins of the *heart* especially require our attention. We now proceed to observe,

5. That every man has some sin more *prevalent* in his heart than any other. Therefore *the plague* of the heart is mentioned in the singular number, as especially referring to this predominant sin. The Apostle calls it *the sin that doth so easily beset us**. The prevalence of one sin above every other in a man's heart, may be owing to his natural constitution, to his temper, or to his situation in life, and its attendant temptations. We cannot, indeed, say with some, who, from ill-guided zeal against the Pelagian heresy, have gone to an extreme on the other side, that original sin is of the substance of the soul. Yet it must be acknowledged, that our nature is so contaminated by it, that this bitter root is as it were interwoven with our very frame. We shall not pretend to assign the natural causes of that great variety of constitutions to be found among men. But it is a fact beyond dispute, that the very temperament of the body has great influence on the qualities of the mind; and that this, according to its variations, produces a peculiar tendency to some sins more than to others. As this is one principal source of the diversity of tempers among men, so also of the different attachments to different lusts. Owing to this, some have a powerful bias to pride or passion; others to revenge and ferocity; and others again to the lust of the flesh in its various branches, to uncleanness, gluttony, drunkenness, or the like. Custom may have great influence. But as the habits of sin are not like many others, which are properly the consequences of repeated acts, but on the contrary, are their causes and springs; it must be granted, that, in most cases, where particular habits are deeply confirmed, they may be traced up to a constitutional tendency.—The temper, whether forward or timid, social or reserved, gentle or austere, calm or fiery, exposes a person to the commission

* Heb. xii. 1.

mission of sins that are nearly connected with each of these dispositions.—The situation in life hath also very great influence in this respect. Different ranks in society and employments in life have different sins, or temptations peculiar to them, or more intimately connected with them, to which those who occupy them are exceedingly exposed.

Now, this predominant sin may, with the greatest propriety, by way of distinction, be denominated the *plague of the heart*. For although every sin is entitled to this character, that of which we now speak, is so in a superlative sense; because it presides in the heart as corrupt, and principally infects and contaminates the conversation. While a man continues under the absolute power of this iniquity, it very often characterises him in life, and marks, in a striking manner, every part of his conduct. According to its peculiar nature, he is esteemed avaricious, lustful, or ambitious; vain, proud, cruel, or deceitful. This prevalent sin may be viewed, either as it is found in a natural man, or in one renewed by grace. In the natural man it appears in its proper form, without any changes or disguises whatsoever; or with those only that are enforced by secondary considerations. But in a renewed person, the prevalent sin of the heart often turns itself into a new channel; so that it is not discovered with so much ease as it was formerly. The predominant principle of pride will, after conversion, appear as legality, and in this shape harass the believer: for what is legality or self-righteousness, but just the natural pride of the heart disguised, or terminating upon God as its object rather than man? Obstinacy of temper will often discover itself in the exercise of a Christian, in the sin of unbelief. Ambition will assume the name of spiritual pride. A rash forward temper will break out in self-confidence. Doubting and despondency will often mark the exercise of those who are naturally fearful or jealous. We do not here pretend to lay down a general rule, or to assert, that universal experience declares, that the predominant

dominant sins of renewed persons undergo a change as to their objects. For although, in all believers, the reigning power of every lust is subdued, often the same lust operates in them in the same manner as before conversion, however different the degree of its operation. Nor can it be with any shadow of justice affirmed, that any sins, appearing more openly in their unregenerate state, afterwards discover themselves under the form of unbelief or legality; as if these sins had been strangers to their hearts before. For it must be evident, that these very sins formerly exercised a dominion, now destroyed. But surely it is not going too far to affirm, that lusts destroyed as to their power, often deviate into another channel; and that those which openly appeared in the conversation, afterwards operate more secretly in the heart, and eminently influence the Christian's exercise towards God.

It is evident, that Peter was naturally of a very forward temper; and after he had been effectually called, how often did he discover this disposition, by trusting to his own wisdom or strength? In general, the distinguishing features of one's temper, according to the natural constitution, most powerfully characterise the whole conduct after conversion, whether good or bad; and those affections, which are especially discovered in a natural state, appear either to advantage or disadvantage, after a gracious change. For grace does not altogether remove the natural affections of any man, or in general entirely alter their constitutional peculiarities; but subdues them in as far as they are sinful, or, when their nature is such as to admit of it, communicates a new and holy propensity. The same affection of *zeal* that hurried Paul, while in his Pharisaical state, to the greatest extremities against Christ, when rectified by the power of the Holy Spirit, distinguished him from all the other Apostles, by his unequalled diligence in the service of his Lord. The same *forward* temper, which, when left to itself, plunged Peter into the most shameful self-confidence; as sanctified by grace, and under the direction of the Spirit, made him generally precede his brethren in confessing Christ, and surpass them all in the boldness and sublimity of his confessions. The beloved disciple's natural warmth of affections eminently appears in his renewed state, by his great attainments in the grace of Christian love. Indeed, there have been, and may be instances of persons once under the absolute predominancy of a particular corrupt affection, who, after conversion, have been less under the power of it, than of any other. For the Lord works in his children in a manner entirely sovereign, uses various methods of operation, and does not confine himself to any fixed rule. But we imagine, that the case referred to is very rare, and will seldom occur where there is not an eminent degree of sanctification.

6. Every man ought to be *peculiarly acquainted* with his *predominant* sin. This seems to be especially meant in the words of our text, *who shall* KNOW *every man* THE PLAGUE *of his own heart*. This is peculiarly necessary, because it is by this sin, that we most frequently dishonour God, wound our consciences, mar our own comfort, and hinder our progress in religion; and it is this that most forcibly hurries on the sinner to every *excess of riot*. The predominant sin is Satan's strong hold in the heart. With this he is particularly acquainted. He hath too much discernment not to know what sin most *easily besets* each of us, far better than we ourselves do: and he hath paid particular attention to all the means, occasions and circumstances which lead to the commission of it. While he hath this under his direction, he is less concerned about our other iniquities. He well knows, that this is the weak side of every man, but especially of the believer; and he most frequently attacks him here. Those sins that are not so firmly rooted in the heart, as being less agreeable to the temper, constitution or situation of Christians, are less under Satan's influence. They have far less inclination to them than to this; and therefore with regard to them, temptation is not felt.

felt so powerful. Or perhaps these are mortified in a greater degree than their predominant sin, which, as being more agreeable to their natures as men, has a much stronger hold of them. Our endeavours to mortify other corruptions, if we neglect this, if we be not principally concerned about it, and watchful over it, will be as fruitless as the feeble attempts of a foolish general, who, in besieging a city, should turn his whole attention to the outposts, without giving himself any trouble about the main strength; or who, in endeavouring to obstruct the course of a river, should pay more attention to the smaller streams than to that which contains the force of the waters. We find that the exercise of the saints has been always in an eminent degree directed towards the mortification of this sin. Therefore, in the words formerly mentioned, the Apostle exhorts the Hebrews in this manner; *Laying aside every weight, and the sin that doth so easily beset us, let us run with patience the race that is set before us* *. The Christian life is here described by language borrowed from a race. He calls them to *lay aside every weight*, in imitation of the runners, who used to cast their cloaks and every part of their dress that could anywise encumber them. Our sins in general may be meant by the metaphorical expression, *every weight;* as *the sin which doth so easily beset us* denotes that particular corruption which hath such strength in the heart, as to be peculiarly its plague. It is said to *beset us*, because like any unseen obstruction that would precipitate him who runs in a race, this powerful lust is still ready to overturn the spiritual runner, or, according to the idea naturally conveyed by the word, to throw him headlong. The Psalmist was peculiarly engaged in mortifying that sin to which he was most subject. This he distinguishes by the appellation of *his* iniquity. *I was also upright before him, and I kept myself from* MINE *iniquity* †. He likewise calls it by way of eminence, the *great* transgression. *Keep back thy servant also from*

presumptuous

---

* Heb. xii. 1.   † Psal. xviii. 23.

presumptuous sins; let them not have dominion over me. Then shall I be upright, and I shall be innocent from the GREAT *transgression**.

7. THE knowledge of the heart is attended with great *difficulty*. The heart is an hidden thing. It therefore requires searching. The frequency of the calls given us in the word to this exercise, clearly intimates the difficulty of the work. As the heart is not obvious to the natural eye; as little will it be obvious to a superficial observer.—This species of knowledge is attended with great difficulty, because of the *deceitfulness* of the heart. It eludes our examination, and exhibits a false portrait of itself. Where there is nothing but *folly*, it presents us with the appearance of *wisdom*; where there is naught but *impotence*, it pleads the greatest *ability*; where *ignorance* reigns, it pretends to superior attainments in *knowledge;* where all is *deceit*, it imposes upon us a feigned *integrity*; and amidst the rage of *unsubdued lusts*, it claims an eminent degree of *holiness*.—The power of *self-love* is another source of that difficulty attending the knowledge of the heart. We survey it with a partial eye. As it presents a false shew to us, we are willing to be imposed on; we are chargeable with wilful blindness; we obstinately shut our eyes against the light, and are really afraid to admit it. Indeed, the natural man does not merely survey his own heart with a partial eye. For, strictly speaking, in a spiritual sense, we are blind, we are *as if we had no eyes*. And as a man, naturally blind, can have no idea of colours; as little can he, who is spiritually blind, discern the true and native complexion of his heart.—The difficulty attending this knowledge is greatly increased by the activity of *Satan*, who throws a mist over the eyes of the natural man, and does every thing in his power to exclude the light. For his kingdom is the kingdom of darkness; and as long as his subjects continue ignorant of their hearts, there is no danger of their being alienated from his service. As he exerts himself to

the

* Psal. xix. 13.

the utmost to hinder sinners from knowing their own hearts; he is not satisfied with preventing as far as possible this important discovery. He endeavours artfully to persuade them, that matters are all right, that they need give themselves no anxiety about eternity; nay, that they are absolutely certain of life everlasting.

8. THIS knowledge is *attainable*. Solomon plainly supposes this in these words, *who* SHALL *know*. Were not this the case, the duty of searching the heart would not be so frequently and earnestly inculcated. Therefore when it is said, *Examine yourselves, whether ye be in the faith; prove your ownselves; know ye not your ownselves* * *? Let us search and try our ways, and turn to the Lord* †; we are to consider these as so many declarations, not merely of our duty, but of the attainableness of this knowledge. This indeed is the real attainment of all believers. They receive a just and affecting discovery of their hearts, according to the characters that God hath given them. We find Solomon himself emphatically expressing his convictions on this subject, in the following question; *Who can say, I have made my heart clean, I am pure from my sin* ‡ *?*

9. THE saving knowledge of the heart flows only from the operation of the *Spirit*. Before the heart has been the subject of his saving influences, not only does it remain under the full power of its natural wickedness; but the sinner, its miserable subject, continues grosly ignorant of its deplorable situation. Convictions of sin and terrors of conscience may have a temporary effect in discovering to him his wickedness, but these are generally occasioned by outward acts. He may be, in some measure, affected with a sense of the wickedness of the sin particularly committed. But even this sense proceeds from secondary considerations only, such as the injury it does to himself, or to society. He is not at all affected with a sense of the wickedness of his heart; or

---

* 2 Cor. xiii. 5.   † Lam. iii. 40.   ‡ Prov. xx. 9.

or if he feel any thing like this, it is effaced by the first temptation. The sinner may, like the wicked Ahab, *go softly* * for a time; but he is entirely unacquainted with the exercise and resolution of good Hezekiah, which he thus expresses: *What shall I say? He hath both spoken unto me, and himself hath done it: I shall go softly all my years in the bitterness of my soul* †. Indeed it is the last conclusion that a natural man wishes to draw from the sin of his life, that his heart is wicked. He will charge his sin upon the power of temptation; or foolishly suppose some kind of fatality attending him; or even impiously presume to accuse God as the author of it, rather than impute it to his idol-heart as its source. But the holy Spirit discovers the hearts of sinners to themselves. This is his peculiar province. *He shall convince the world of sin.* And he shews them their inward wickedness; for he convinces them of the sin of unbelief; and this, you know, hath its seat in the heart: *He shall convince the world of sin,—because they believe not* ‡. So the Psalmist addresses Christ in relation to his work by the Spirit; *Thine arrows are sharp in the heart of the king's enemies; whereby the people fall under thee* §. The hearts of all are equally under his power. Even *the king's heart is in the hand of the Lord, as the rivers of water, he turneth it whithersoever he will.* This discovery he makes to sinners by means of the Word. This is the instrument which the Spirit employs in opening up to them those wounds and diseases in their own hearts, to which they were formerly strangers. *For the word of God is quick and powerful, and sharper than any two-edged sword, piercing even to the dividing asunder of soul and spirit, and of the joints and marrow, and is a discerner of the thoughts and intents of the heart* **. The law is the immediate mean of this discovery: for the Spirit brings home the law on the conscience, manifesting its purity, perfection

---

* 1 Kings, xxi. 27. † Isa. xxxviii. 15. ‡ John xvi. 8, 9.
§ Psal. xlv. 5. ** Heb. iv. 12.

perfection and extent. Thus sin appears to be *exceeding sinful;* and when *the commandment comes* in this way, the sinner dies to all his apprehensions of the goodness, innocence and purity of his heart. The word of God is the glass in which he obtains a just view of himself; and the holy Spirit shining on the word, and thence into the heart, is that light which enables him to obtain it.

But it must be remembered, that what discovery soever the sinner obtain of his sin by means of the law, it can be of no saving benefit to him, if it proceed no farther, if the love of God in Christ be not efficaciously manifested, and *shed abroad in the heart.* For all the self-knowledge that a man can attain, unless it be the fruit of the Spirit's gracious operation, is entirely unconnected with salvation. A person may, in this respect, be taught of the Spirit in a *common* manner, and yet eternally perish. He may, by the power of the Word on his conscience, and by the terrors of the law, discover, in some measure, that his heart is full of wickedness, that he is abominable to the holy God, that he is exposed to his wrath and curse; and after all be a castaway: because this knowledge, as it is not the fruit of the Spirit, working in a saving and converting manner on his heart, is entirely different in its nature and effects. There are these great distinctions between that knowledge which flows from the common operation of the Spirit, and that which is the fruit of his saving operation;—between that knowledge which is consistent with a state of condemnation, and that which certainly demonstrates a state of justification. By the former, a man especially sees the wickedness of his heart as destructive. In consequence of the latter, he chiefly views it as detestable. The first is found in a person, while his love to sin is unimpaired; but the second is always attended by an abhorrence of sin. The retaining of sin in the practice is compatible with the one; while the other invariably produces the renunciation of every iniquity, how dear
soever

soever to corrupt nature. The knowledge of sin, by the common work of the Spirit, proceeds from the fear of God as a judge and an enemy: but that knowledge, which is the fruit of his saving work, from the love of God as a father and a friend. Whenever a man becomes truly acquainted with *the plague of his heart*, he immediately endeavours to mortify and destroy it. There is the same difference between those who know their hearts in a common way, and those who know them savingly, as there was between the Israelites, who in the wilderness were stung by the fiery serpents, and consumed by their poison, because they improved not the remedy, and those who, knowing that the brazen serpent was held up to them, turned their eyes to it and were healed. Those who are enlightened by the Spirit only in a common way, though they may have some conviction of their plague, yet, by reason of unbelief, still remain under its power. But those who are savingly enlightened, are enabled by faith to look to Him who was typified by the brazen serpent; and thus they are delivered from their plague.

10. A *saving* knowledge of the plague of the heart includes a true sense of its *evil*. If our sense of sin proceed no farther than a knowledge, belief, and dread of its consequences, as it exposes us to eternal destruction; we are like a man who knows no more about the disease he is infected with, than that by means of it he is in danger of death; but is entirely ignorant of its name, nature, and distinguishing symptoms. If we know the *plague of the heart* aright, we will have a deep and affecting sense of its *evil*, as opposed to the nature, law, government, holiness, and love of God, especially as manifested in Christ; and as depriving us of his image, and making us the children of Satan. But on these things we do not particularly insist, having endeavoured to illustrate them formerly. We have no due sense of sin, unless we really see it to be a *plague*, not only

as

as confuming to our nature, but as abominable, infectious and incurable by any means in the power of the creature. He would be ignorant indeed, who had no other idea of a confirmed leprofy, than as outwardly deforming his body; without knowing that it defiled the whole mafs of blood, and affected the very fprings of animal life. And fhall we not account him grofsly ignorant of the nature of fin, who views it only as defiling his converfation, but has no juft apprehenfion of the heart as its principal feat, of his being deftitute of original righteoufnefs; and underftands not that all the leprous fpots which appear in his life, proceed from the contamination of all the powers of his foul? A juft fenfe of fin imports a conviction that *every imagination of the thoughts of the heart is only evil continually.* It is not fo much the blots of the converfation that humble the fpiritual leper, who truly knows his difeafe, as a difcovery of his inward defilement; which is fo obftinate, that all outward wafhings can as little remove it, as water externally applied, could naturally remove a confirmed leprofy.

11. The knowledge here referred to implies *hatred* of this plague, and *loathing* of *felf* on account of it. The Pfalmift appeals to God, as to his hatred of every wicked way. It is matter of promife: *Then fhall ye remember your own evil ways, and your doings that were not good, and fhall loathe yourfelves in your own fight, for your iniquities and for your abominations* *. This was the attainment of Job, when the Lord anfwered him out of the whirlwind; *I have heard of thee by the hearing of the ear; but now mine eye feeth thee. Wherefore I abhor myfelf, and repent in duft and afhes* †. Under the law, it was commanded with refpect to the leper, in whom the plague was, that *his clothes* fhould *be rent and his head bare, and that he* fhould *put a covering upon his upper lip, and cry, Unclean, unclean* ‡. We cannot imagine why the law of leprofy fhould be fo ftrict, and the whole procefs in the cafe of this plague be fo particularly appointed of God; if it was not

---

* Ezek. xxxvi. 31.   † Job xlii. 5, 6.   ‡ Lev. xiii. 45.

not that this loathsome disease is so striking a representation of the nature and effects of sin, as it is unquestionably its bitter fruit; and that God was pleased to mark it out, in so uncommon a manner, as a peculiar emblem of these. The two first circumstances here enjoined were tokens of sorrow, and intimate to us, that all who truly know the plague of sin will be deeply affected with its evil. The next circumstance of a *covering upon the lip*, seems to have typified the infectious nature of sin; as if the very breath of the leper had carried contagion in it. He was also to cry, *Unclean, unclean*. This not only signifies that filth which is in sin, the leprosy of the soul, but that all who know it savingly, have a deep and affecting sense of their defilement, and loathe themselves on this account. The same expression is used by the Prophet Isaiah, when he *saw the Lord high and lifted up*. Then he said, *Wo is me, for I am undone, for I am a man of* UNCLEAN *lips* *. The use of these words on this occasion is an infallible commentary on the type; and clearly proves, that their proper and spiritual application is only to the *plague of the heart*. The Church makes materially the same confession elsewhere: *We are all as an unclean thing* †. The leper must certainly have been loathsome to himself, when cast out of the camp, and separated from the society of others. Even his own company would be burdensome; because every thing about him, and around him, perpetually reminded him of his filthiness. In like manner, every sinner, who really knows his own plague, must appear to himself vile, loathsome and detestable.

12. This saving knowledge of the heart is matter of *promise*. The promise is to the sinful creature a rich supply of all that he wants, an inexhaustible treasure of strength for obedience to the commandment, and an unceasing ground of comfort in every duty, and under every trial. Whatever the sinner is insufficient to perform, whatever the soul indispensably requires, whatever the precept enjoins,—the promise amply

contains

* Isa. vi. 5, 6.   † Isa. lxiv. 6.

contains and freely exhibits. As it contains medicine for every difeafe, balm for every wound, healing for every plague to which the heart is liable; it alfo fecures the gracious difcovery of all thefe difeafes, wounds, or plagues, which would otherwife confume us without being known. Therefore it is faid; *Then* SHALL *they remember their own evil ways.* And again, *The heart of the rafh fhall underftand knowledge. It is written in the prophets, and they fhall be all taught of God.* Remarkable to this purpofe are the words of God by Ezekiel *. *I will eftablifh my covenant with thee, and thou* SHALT *know that I am the Lord :—*THAT *thou mayft remember, and be confounded, and never open thy mouth any more becaufe of thy fhame, when I am pacified toward thee, for all that thou haft done, faith the Lord God.* The declaration that the Lord made to the fame Prophet, when he took him in vifion to behold the wickednefs committed in the temple at Jerufalem, he fulfils to all thofe who are the fubjects of a faving work of the Spirit. He faid unto him, *Son of man, feeft thou what they do, even the great abominations that the houfe of Ifrael committeth, that I fhould go far off from my fanctuary? But turn thee yet again, and thou fhalt fee greater abominations.* Then he faid to him, *Son of man, haft thou feen what the ancients of the houfe of Ifrael do in the dark, every man in the chambers of his imagery? But turn thee yet again, and thou fhalt fee greater abominations that they do* †. Thus the Lord deals with every chofen veffel. He takes him into *the chambers of imagery* that are in his own heart, and difcovers to him the *abominations* done there in the *dark*, of which he had formerly no juft apprehenfion. Befides, this knowledge is of an increafing nature. The more that the perfon fees of his heart, the lefs good will he difcern in it, and the more evil. No believer gets a full view of his *inward part* at firft. There is a progrefs in this, as in the other parts of fanctification. Indeed, he can never get a comprehenfive view of it, becaufe there is in it fuch an inconceivable

* Ezek. xvi. 62, 63.   † Ezek. viii. 6, &c.

ceivable depth of iniquity. But accordi[ng as he pro]grefs in grace, he advances in the know[ledge of him]felf; and fees a great deal more of his [own sinful]nefs than he could ever have imagine[d before.] The Lord leads him as he did the Prop[het from one] heart-plague to another, from one *cham*[ber of imagery] into another; ftill faying to him, *I wil[l shew thee] greater abominations.* Thus we are ma[de wife, if] *we follow on to know the Lord.*

It muft appear from what has been [said, that you] fhould be much more concerned about [the plague of] the heart, than about thofe of the bod[y. Were any] of you affected in your bodies with a di[stemper] that made your company burdenfome t[o your] friends, and even loathfome to yourfel[ves; filled] you with unfpeakable pain, and expo[sed you to ex]treme danger; that made you unfit for [the duties] and enjoyments of life; and prefented [you with an] immediate and awful profpect of deat[h; would you] not tremble, and be filled with terror [and confu]fion; would you not implore every po[ssible help,] and eagerly embrace the moft uncert[ain hope of] deliverance? Sinners, your cafe is un[speakably] deplorable. You may enjoy health of b[ody, and peace] of mind. But your fouls are infected [with a plague] inexpreffibly more dreadful and malig[nant than any] bodily calamity; a plague which is the [primary] malady to which your bodies are fu[bject, which] gradually wafting your conftitutions, [will at length] make you return to the duft; a plag[ue that renders] you abominable to God, to angels, [and to all the] righteous; and that would render yo[u abominable to] yourfelves, were your eyes open to fee [it; a plague] that not only in its confequences affec[ts you,] but impairs your fouls; that diffufes [its malignity] through all your faculties, and confign[s you to] eternal fuffering; nay a plague—th[at all human] means are abfolutely ineffectual to remo[ve.] And this is the plague of *fin*. Perh[aps you see] little of it, becaufe you do not fee its im[portance.]

like those of an outward contagion. But can you shut your eyes, or harden your feelings against the innumerable diseases, pains, sicknesses, sufferings, calamities, and outward plagues, of which this is the fountain: against death itself, of which this is the cause? Can you shut your eyes against the multitude of evils, —murders, adulteries, fornications, thefts, wars and devastations, which are all the natural fruits and certain evidences of this *plague of the heart? From whence come wars and fightings among you? Come they not hence, even of your lusts, that war in your members* * *?* Perhaps, you are undismayed at the thoughts of it, because you have a world of companions in suffering; because all your brethren of mankind are infected in the same manner. But would it lessen the pain, or the danger of an outward plague, that it affected all the inhabitants of the same city or country with yourselves? Would not its horrors be equal to you? And do you imagine, that it can anywise lessen the guilt, the pollution, the misery, or the danger of your situation, that *the whole world lieth in wickedness?* Or, can it diminish the terrors of hell, that there will be millions of sufferers besides you? Ah! No. Every soul will be so absorbed in its own sufferings, that the society of others can be no alleviation. Nay, may we not rather suppose it to augment their sufferings? The consciousness that the wicked will have of their zeal and activity in enticing others to sin, in encouraging and hardening them in it, will eternally prove an unspeakable enhancement of their common misery.

Since this plague is so dreadful, the symptoms of it so evident, and its consequences so fatal; will you deign to bestow a serious thought on it? Is it not *a fearful thing to fall into the hands of the living God?* Can you read of the poor woman, who laboured under a certain bodily plague for twelve years; and who, that she might be freed from it, had patiently *suffered many things of many physicians,* and had cheerfully

* Jam. iv. 1.

fully *spent all she had; although she was nothing bettered, but rather grew worse* * ;—without thinking it worth your trouble to *suffer* some anxiety, and *spend* some little of your time in considering the nature of your spiritual plague, and endeavouring to obtain deliverance? Can you read of her eagerness, without one upbraiding thought for your own indifference; although your danger and misery exceed hers, as much as the soul is better than the body? Can you read of her patience and profuseness in spending her all, while she had only a mere probability; and can you excuse your own wantonness and obduracy, while the word of God proclaims to you the certainty of a cure? You must undoubtedly accuse her as a fool, who spent her all for her body; if you will not condescend to avert your minds for a little from the world, to spend one serious thought, one moment's reflection for your precious souls? But, sinners, do you really believe that you have souls? The question may seem strange, but it is certainly necessary. For your invariable conduct, in preferring your bodies to your souls, would naturally suggest the idea, that you did not sincerely believe the existence of the latter. At any rate, if the soul be as much better than the body, as eternity exceeds time; and if, notwithstanding, you pay much more attention to your bodies than to your souls; unquestionably you practically deny their immaterial nature and eternal existence. Can you really believe that you have souls formed for immortality, and also that they are infected with a destructive and abominable plague; and after all give yourselves no concern about them? Neither God nor angels, men nor devils, will esteem you serious in your pretended persuasion of these truths, till you evidence it by a very different conduct. If you would be thought to believe these awful matters, apply yourselves diligently to discover your spiritual plagues; and especially that sin which may by distinction be called the *plague* of your heart,

that

* Mark v. 25.—34.

that fin which doth fo eafily befet you, that iniquity which you roll as a fweet morfel under your tongue; elfe it will prove your eternal ruin. This muft be dealt with as Agag, whom Samuel *hewed in pieces before the Lord in Gilgal.*

Seek a difcovery of your plagues by the Holy Spirit. Efpecially be concerned to put the work of fearching your hearts into the Lord's hand, faying, *Examine me, and prove me, try my heart and my reins, O God; and fee if there be any wicked way in me at all, and lead me in thy way everlafting.* He alone can truly difcover them to you. Improve the promife by pleading it in the exercife of faith. Try to truft your fouls on it as the ground of your hope; while, at the fame time, you are engaged in endeavouring duty. Like that woman formerly mentioned, ftrive to prefs through the crowd that you may get near to Chrift. You muft *prefs into the kingdom of heaven;* prefs through the crowd of lufts that oppofe you within, of the cares and allurements of this world, of wicked men and devils that oppofe you without; prefs through all this crowd, that you may get to Jefus. *For the kingdom of heaven fuffereth violence, and the violent take it by force.* Under the law, as foon as any one difcovered the plague of leprofy, he was to appear before the prieft. Show yourfelf, poor, guilty, defiled finner to this great Highprieft; and if you *touch but the hem of his garment, you fhall be healed.* One *touch,* by faith, of the GARMENT *of falvation, the robe of righteoufnefs,* that *vefture dipped in blood,* will *dry up your plague,* will remove both the guilt and pollution of your fin. Stedfaftly credit his promife. *I have feen his ways, and will heal him;—I will heal their backfliding, and love them freely, for mine anger is turned away from him*: and this kind Phyfician, this compaffionate Highprieft will make you *feel within yourfelf, that you are healed of your plague;* and as certainly fay to *you,* as to that poor woman, *Thy faith hath made thee whole, go in peace, and be whole of thy plague.*

SERMON V.

On the NECESSITY of KNOWING the PLAGUE of the HEART.

---

1 Kings, viii. 38.

———Who shall know every man the plague of his own heart.———

SELF-KNOWLEDGE was considered, even by unenlightened heathens, as so indispensably necessary, that it was a motto engraved on one of their temples, *Know thyself.* Thus they made *the stone cry out of the wall* to every one who entered, that without this important acquisition, he was a vain worshipper. How many professed Christians are there, who may well blush at this relation, as they have never reckoned the knowledge of themselves a matter deserving their attention! Nay, are there not multitudes who industriously avoid the investigation of their own hearts? The greatest part of professors are as averse to look into themselves, as if the sight of their spiritual plagues would increase their malignity. They are as much afraid of being jealous of themselves, as if it were the greatest sin they could be chargeable with; as if a persuasion of the goodness of their own hearts were the only faith that the Gospel required. We see many as reluctant to fulfil the counsel of the Prophet to good Hezekiah, by setting their houses in order, and settling their worldly affairs, as if it would hasten the stroke of *the king of terrors.* But thousands are overcome by a far more destructive folly. They are as much afraid of inquiring into the state of their hearts, and endeavouring to have them *set in order,* according to the Word, as if a doubt of their salvation,

salvation, even while continuing in fin, would certainly expofe them to eternal deftruction. Is it a very bad fign of traders, when they are afraid to look into the ftate of their worldly circumftances? Surely then, if perfons conftantly avoid the exercife of felf-examination, it is a decifive evidence that they are in a ftate of bankruptcy for eternity. A man's wounds muft be noifome indeed, if he cannot bear the fight of them, if he be afraid of his own company; and he muft be deeply confirmed in the moft deplorable ftate, who will rather turn his eyes any way, than to *the plague of his own heart*. But all fuch pretended Chriftians have the fame infcription on their hearts that Paul obferved on the Athenian altar; *To the unknown God:* and they will ever continue to *worfhip him ignorantly*, till they become better acquainted with themfelves.

THE II. head of the method is to illuftrate the neceffity of fuch a knowledge of *the plague of the heart*, as we have endeavoured to defcribe.

1. THIS knowledge of the heart is neceffary, becaufe without it there can be no due knowledge of God*. The perfections of the Divine nature being infinite,

---

* WHEN we fpeak of the faving knowledge of the heart as of fuch importance, that without it there can be no faving knowledge of God, &c. &c. it is by no means intended, that the former can precede the latter. For whatever apprehenfions a man may entertain of the evil of his own heart; they are only of a *legal* nature, they belong to the old Covenant, and are connected with its curfe, unlefs they proceed from a faving difcovery of God in a regenerating work of the Holy Spirit. In regeneration, according to the order of nature, a true difcovery of fin, as *the plague of the heart*, is antecedent to the exercife of faith in Chrift as the Healer; becaufe the illumination of the *underftanding* precedes the gracious inclination of the *will*. But as this work is inftantaneous, and as the parts of it know no difference in order of time, faith may juftly be viewed as going before this knowledge, in as far as it is evident to us, and properly exercifed by us; becaufe this is the firft grace of the Spirit that is exercifed in the renewed heart; as it is only in confequence of a faving apprehenfion of God in Chrift that fin appears in its natural wickednefs

and

infinite, are therefore entirely above our comprehension as *creatures*. But they are doubly incomprehensible to us as *sinners*. There is naturally a twofold vail between us and them. There is the vail of creature-weakness, which renders it impossible for us to form adequate apprehensions of the nature of God. But there is also the vail of moral depravity, and actual pollution, which so darkens the mind, that it cannot form even those apprehensions of his glorious attributes, which were competent to it in the state of innocence. Sin throws a mist over all the Divine perfections, that conceals their beauty, and robs them of their lustre; not in reality, but only in the mind of the sinner himself. Now, it is only in consequence of the total removal of sin, that we can entertain just apprehensions of God. But as none, while in this world, are entirely delivered from sin, there is another way in which the defect, arising from our imperfection, is, in some measure, supplied, and by which man attains such discoveries

and deformity, and so as immediately to produce the exercise of *evangelical* mourning. Then only can we *remember our own evil ways*, when he has accomplished his promise of *giving the new heart and right spirit*, (Ezek. xxxvi. 26.—31.) Therefore, when we assert the necessity of this knowledge, in relation to a saving acquaintance with God and eternal interests, we only speak of these things, as pointing out the indispensable connection of the one with the other, and to illustrate the folly and blindness of those who flatter themselves that they are savingly acquainted with God, while ignorant of themselves.

Nor is it meant, that the knowledge of the heart is in any sense our *title* to believe, or the foundation of our boldness in any duty we perform. The gracious offers and promises of the Gospel, the endearing relation which Christ bears to mankind-sinners as a Kinsman redeemer, and the intrinsic merit of his blood, are alone the warrant of faith; and his righteousness is the only foundation of our approach to God in every duty, whether in the first act of faith, or in any subsequent act in the Christian life.

Nor, still farther, do we mean to put the knowledge of the heart in the place of *faith* as embracing the righteousness of Jesus Christ. But we consider this knowledge as inseparably connected with all genuine faith in the performance of every religious duty. As *without faith it is impossible to please God*, that faith is nowise pleasing to him, that carries not along with it this saving knowledge.

discoveries of God as are connected with salvation, and are the happy prelude of a perfect knowledge of him in glory, according to his limited capacity. This end is effected, when he is blessed with a real and affecting discovery of *the plague of his heart.* While this remains in full power, the sinner views every thing, even the nature and perfections of God himself, through a false medium,—the supreme love that he hath to sin. But when the power of sin is broken, instead of viewing objects through this medium, he uses it rather as a contrast. Instead of judging of them according to their conformity to sin, and subserviency to the indulgence of it, he estimates their dignity and worth by their contrariety and disconformity to this *plague of the heart.* Sin is the heart-idol, the god of every natural man, by which he frames his ideas of right and wrong, of agreeable and hateful: and till this idol be cast down, he will assuredly form a false judgment of every thing moral in its nature. Yea, so blind is he, that he virtually esteems God to be *altogether such an one as himself,* and fondly imagines that he will *approve his sin.* But when his eyes are opened to the evils of his heart, he judges in a manner entirely different.

This knowledge is especially necessary in order to a right apprehension of the perfections of holiness, justice and mercy in God. While we continue ignorant of ourselves, we think very unjustly of Divine *holiness.* Although this is that perfection, according to which God essentially hates sin, as directly contrary to his nature; yet the ignorant sinner cannot suffer himself to think that sin can be really hateful to God, because he loves it so much himself. Or, if he allow that God hates it, he cannot believe that he hates it so much as the Scripture represents. But when the Holy Spirit discovers to him his own heart, he sees sin to be so extremely hateful in itself, and so unlike to God, that he is fully persuaded it must be the object of his infinite abhorrence. Without the knowledge of the heart, one can have no suitable

idea of the *juſtice* of God. According to this perfection, he eſſentially puniſhes ſin, as contrary to his nature, and as a rebellion againſt his authority. But the ſinner, as long as he ſees only the fair ſide of ſin, as agreeable to his ſenſes, without perceiving its filthineſs, cannot imagine that God will puniſh men for that which is ſo natural to them, and which appears to him ſo innocent. He would eſteem this to be cruelty rather than juſtice. The many threatenings contained in the Word againſt ſin, he views rather as beacons ſet up to deter men from it, than as declarations of what God is really determined to do. Nay, rather than believe all theſe threatenings, he would indulge himſelf in an idea much more grateful to his corrupt heart, that perhaps the Scripture is only a *fable cunningly deviſed*, for the peace and order of civil ſociety. But when he ſees his own heart, and learns the malignant nature of ſin, his conſcience affixes its ſeal to every curſe written in the book of God. He perceives that he, who in Scripture claims the character of God, would be unworthy of it, were it not eſſential to his nature, not only to hate, but to puniſh ſin. For were it eſſential to him to hate ſin, and not to puniſh it; he would of neceſſity be an inactive being, who willed what he was not able to perform; and was therefore unfit for being the Moral Governor of the world; whoſe will muſt be a law to his creatures, and whoſe acts muſt confirm his law, and proclaim his authority. While ignorant of his heart, a man can have no juſt ideas of Divine *mercy*. He reckons it poſſible for God to pardon ſin without a ſatisfaction; and imagines, that if he depend on the mere general mercy of his nature, he is ſafe for eternity. But when he obtains a view of the myſtery of iniquity and abomination in his heart, he is fully convinced, that God cannot, conſiſtently with himſelf, pardon ſin, which is ſo atrocious an offence againſt his nature, without a full atonement. While a ſtranger to himſelf, he was totally ignorant of the
connection

connection and confiftency of the Divine attributes, or of that relation which they bear, one to another. But now he fees that there would be a variance amongft them, that is a variance in God himfelf, could one be glorified to the injury of another. While ignorant of his heart; he had a low eftimation of the Divine mercy in the method of falvation through Jefus Chrift; he faw no furprifing love, nor unparalleled grace in this difplay; he viewed it all with an unaffected indifference. But when he has once feen his vile felf, his filthy and impure heart, he is aftonifhed at the fovereign love of God, in ever entertaining thoughts of compaffion to fuch defpicable worms, and efpecially in giving fuch an incomprehenfible evidence of it, as to fend his own Son to die for them. Then, in aftonifhment at his former darknefs, he cries out; *O the depth of the riches, both of the wifdom and knowledge of God: how unfearchable are his judgments, and his ways paft finding out! I will fing of the mercies of the Lord for ever.*

2. This knowledge is neceffary in order to a due improvement of the *remedy* provided in the gofpel for the *plague of the heart*. This is the Lord Jefus Chrift. Indeed he is both the *remedy* and the *Phyfician* who applies it. This is a remedy of fovereign efficacy. There never was a fingle inftance of its failure. *Is there not balm in Gilead, is there not a phyfician there?* The balm that this Phyfician applies, is his own blood. *For the blood of Chrift cleanfeth us from all fin.* The only plague of the foul is fin; and what form foever it affume, the blood of Chrift will infallibly remove it. But we cannot improve this gofpel remedy aright, without a knowledge of the difeafe. It would be vain for a diftreffed perfon to apply to an earthly phyfician for the removal of an inward difeafe, were he entirely unacquainted with its feat. However great the attention of the phyfician, however confummate his fkill, they would be both ufelefs to his patient, if he could give him no information of the nature and fymptoms of his complaint. In like manner, we can make

make no suitable improvement of the heavenly Physician, or of the remedy provided for us, while we remain entire strangers to our spiritual plagues. Indeed, the resemblance fails here: for although an earthly physician, however accomplished, often can only guess at the nature of an inward disease, but cannot declare it with absolute certainty; our Physician, whose name is *Jehovah the Healer*, can not only remove the disease when made known, but can discover it without the smallest difficulty. For he knows the heart; and whenever he enables a sinner to improve himself as the remedy, he, at the same time, favours him with a clear discovery of the plague. Often indeed, a man's plague is in some measure made known to him, while he is left under its power. But always where the cure is wrought, there is a discovery of the plague. And it is necessary that it should be so; for otherwise the patient would have no just apprehensions of his obligations to the Healer. A conviction of the dreadful nature of his malady, when attended with deliverance from it, will be a prevailing motive to the exercise of gratitude to his sovereign benefactor.

Without a due knowledge of the *plague of the heart*, we will never make a personal application to the Physician, nor a particular appropriation of the remedy to ourselves. Why is it that the greatest part of the hearers of the gospel rest satisfied with a general notional faith in Christ, as a common Saviour; but are nowise concerned to embrace him as their own? The reason is; they have no real discernment of the fatal plagues of *the inward part*, and are thus entirely ignorant of their need of him. They please themselves with a general knowledge of their sins, and therefore rest satisfied without a particular interest in the Saviour. They say; *We are rich, and increased with goods, and have need of nothing; and know not that they are wretched, and miserable, and poor, and blind, and naked.* Therefore they despise his counsel, and will not *buy of him gold tried in the fire, that they*

they may be rich, nor white raiment that they may be clothed, and that the shame of their nakedness do not appear; nor anoint their eyes with eye-salve, that they may see *. For they that be whole, in their own apprehension, *need not the physician,* i. e. they do not see their need of him, *but they that are sick* †.—This knowledge is absolutely necessary to give us a just idea of the importance of salvation. Why is it that multitudes account it such an easy matter to be saved; apprehend, that they can at any time believe in Christ, and repent of their sins; that in their dying moments they can implore mercy; and that their salvation will be so easily accomplished, as to be the certain fruit of a languishing prayer, of a feeble wish, or even of one serious thought, when life is fluttering on the lip, and when the soul is already on the very confines of eternity? These false and ruinous imaginations are the native consequence of their ignorance of themselves, of the evil nature of sin, and of the plague of the heart. This is the great reason why thousands of thousands, who enjoy a gospel-dispensation, esteem it such a trifling privilege, and from Sabbath to Sabbath, from year to year, wilfully continue to despise the gracious offers of healing and deliverance; to *trample under foot the Son of God, to count the blood of the covenant, wherewith he was sanctified, an unholy thing, to do despite unto the Spirit of grace;* and so inevitably and obstinately perish.

This knowledge is not only necessary to the sinner, but constantly so to the believer, that he may thence learn to make a daily improvement of the remedy. Although the dominion of sin is subdued, yet he sins every day. The plagues of his heart are always appearing, one after another; and they can only be prevented from prevailing against him, by a constant unremitted application to Jesus the Physician. Although the power of every plague is broken, yet the remains of every one are to be found in his heart; for he will never be entirely delivered from them in this world.

* Rev. iii. 17, 18.   † Matth. ix. 12.

world. It is the falutary air of that heavenly land, *where the inhabitant fays not, I am fick; the leaves of that tree,* which *are for the healing of the nations,* and the water of that *river of life that proceedeth from under the throne of God, and of the Lamb;* that can alone remove all the fymptoms and confequences of this fatal plague.

3. This knowledge is neceffary to all genuine *repentance.* Whatever forrow we have for fin, unlefs it proceeds from a right knowledge of our own hearts, is only *the forrow of the world,* and is unconnected with falvation. Befides, it is generally a forrow for the fins of the life, rather than for thofe of the heart. But whenever a perfon obtains a difcovery of *the plague of his own heart,* he is made to *forrow after a goaly fort.*—He can have no juft view of the *caufe* of forrow, till he get a juft view of the fin of his heart; becaufe fin hath its feat, its empire there. We cannot fee it aright, but as it appears there in its natural light, without any difguife. Without this, all the forrow that a man hath for fin, is only *wafhing the outfide of the cup,* or *of the platter, while the infide is full of naftinefs.* After all the tears and fighs fpent in this kind of repentance, he is no better than a *whited fepulchre, fair without, but within full of rottennefs and corruption.*—Our forrow for fin will otherwife be very *fhortlived.* If it proceed not from a knowledge of the heart, it will be as tranfitory as the joy of thofe hearers, reprefented under the metaphor of the *ftony ground.* Like grain without a proper root, it will foon fade away. For all genuine repentance has its root in the heart. It penetrates as far as fin itfelf. *Legal* repentance goes no farther than the *confcience; Gofpel* repentance reaches to the heart, ftrictly viewed, as influencing the will and affections; becaufe legal repentance takes place without the knowledge of the heart, but evangelical repentance always carries this along with it.—The knowledge of *the plague of the heart* opens a *new fcene* for the exercife of repentance. One, who hath never before mourned over any evils

but

but those of the life, upon a view of the heart, sees innumerable evils and iniquities there, greater than he hath ever been left to commit in his outward conversation. Such a saving discovery is so affecting, as to give a keener edge to repentance, than it ever had before. Knowledge that is so humiliating, will make our sorrow more lively.—The necessity of this knowledge to the exercise of all true repentance is evident from this, that it is the repentance of the heart which is *required. Therefore also now saith the Lord, turn ye even to me, with* ALL YOUR HEART,—*and rend your* HEARTS, *and not your garments* *. But how is it possible to *rend the heart*, or to *turn to the Lord with the heart*, if the heart itself be unknown?

4. This knowledge is necessary to all acceptable *worship*. One branch of Divine worship is particularly specified in the passage before us; this is *prayer*. *What prayer or supplication shall be made by any man who shall know the plague of his own heart.* Without this knowledge, there can be no right praying. Until a person be acquainted with *the plague of his heart*, he is at a loss what to pray for; his mouth is often shut before God; he has no proper sense of his own spiritual necessities. But as soon as the state of his soul is unfolded by the Spirit, he sees an extensive field opened to him, and always finds enough within himself as matter of prayer, although there were nothing else that required his attention. Here he sees the most ample ground for confession, petition and thanksgiving. He has much to confess; for the plagues of his heart are just so many enemies against God within him, which he would wish ever to mourn over. His heart affords abundant reason for petition; for he finds it necessary daily to implore the destruction of all these lusts that are enemies to God, and seeking his destruction, and to entreat rich supplies of grace for enabling him faithfully to maintain the struggle against them. He has also sufficient ground of thanksgiving; because the Lord hath not left him to

* Joel ii. 12, 13.

to commit all those sins that his own wicked heart would have led him to, or suffered him to proceed to *the same excess of riot* with others, whose hearts were naturally just as good as his. When he sees the senses of the drunkard, as well as his substance, worn out by intemperance; when he contemplates the misery of the unclean person, whose conscience and life are equally wretched by a sense of his guilt, and the consequences of it; or when he turns his eye to those, who, for theft, or robbery, or murder, are brought to an untimely end; and at the same time, finds such a desperate wickedness in his own heart; what reason has he to bless the Lord, that he hath not suffered him to proceed to the same degree of open iniquity! The Christian's own evil heart discovers such a depth of sin, such a multitude of iniquities, that with the word as his rule, and the Holy Spirit as his interpreter, he needs no other prayer-book. There he sees more matter, than would employ him all the days of his life. *If I should count them,* saith he, *they are more than the hairs upon my head:* nay he perceives continued reason for thanksgiving that he is out of hell. *It is of the Lord's mercies that we are not consumed.* Indeed, without this knowledge of the heart, all the prayers that one presents to God, are, in his esteem, *vain oblations,* they never *enter into the ears of the God of Sabaoth.* Paul, before his conversion, was a strict Pharisee, *touching the righteousness of the law blameless;* and undoubtedly, in this state, he had offered up many prayers to God. But he was then ignorant of his own heart. He was then *alive,* in his own apprehension, *without the law,* without a knowledge of its spirituality and extent, and of his own disconformity to it; and during all this time, he never once prayed in God's account, because he never knew his inward wickedness, and was proceeding on a false foundation. But no sooner does he get a view of this by the Spirit, no sooner does *the commandment come,* and sin appear sin, and become *exceeding sinful,* than God takes as particular notice of his prayer, as if

he

he had never tried the exercise before. *Behold he prayeth*[*].

We shall only mention another ordinance as confirming the observation; this is the Lord's supper. It is expresssly enjoined, *Let a man examine himself, and so let him eat of that bread, and drink of that cup* [†].—Now, it is not simply the performance of the duty of self-examination that is required. The command implies the necessity of a saving knowledge of the heart, of the evil of sin, of Christ as the only remedy, and the necessity of a personal interest in this remedy. Therefore is that awful caution added; *For he that eateth and drinketh unworthily, eateth and drinketh damnation to himself, not discerning the Lord's body;* and every one *eateth and drinketh unworthily*, who partakes of this ordinance ignorantly, without a saving discernment of the plague of his own heart; for without this, there can be no discernment of that healing efficacy which is in *the Lord's body*. No kind of religious worship can be acceptable to God without the knowledge of the heart. For it is indispensably required, in all the worship we give him, that we *worship him in spirit and in truth*. Now we cannot *worship God in spirit*, when we do not know our own spirits. That service can never be spiritual, which proceeds from a heart ignorant of itself. Nor can we thus *worship him in truth*. Our confessions and supplications are only the language of the lip, or at most the effusions of a frightened conscience, till we know ourselves. Till then we are never really serious in any act of adoration.

5. It is necessary for the *keeping* of the heart. To this duty we are earnestly exhorted in the word of God; and it is certainly a duty of the greatest importance. *Keep thy heart with all diligence* [‡]. The words may be read, *Keep thy heart* ABOVE *all* KEEPING, as signifying, that the utmost vigilance is required. And a very forcible reason is subjoined; *for out of it are the issues of life.* All our actions, which are *the issues*

---

[*] Acts ix. 11.   [†] 1 Cor. xi. 28, 29.   [‡] Prov iv. 23.

sues of life, whether natural, civil, or religious, spring from the heart. This is the fountain of them all, whether they are good or evil, whether they lead to life or death: because the heart, strictly understood, as denoting the will and affections, is the operative power of the soul. Of the same import is the declaration of our Lord; *These things which proceed out of the mouth, come forth from the heart, and* THEY *defile the man.* We have already seen that sin, the spiritual plague of man, properly has its seat in the heart, and that thence it infects and defiles the conversation. It will therefore follow, that it is of the last consequence that the heart be *kept* with peculiar care. We do not mean from this to insinuate, that man is capable of himself to keep his heart. The contrary is declared in the Holy Scriptures. *The way of man is not in himself. Cursed be man that trusteth in man,* that is, that trusteth in *himself;* Jer. xvii. 5. and the reason is given in ver. 9. *For the heart is deceitful above all things, and desperately wicked.* Being so deceitful, he cannot keep it. But the *keeping* of the heart is a duty incumbent on us, which, although we cannot perform in our own strength, we must endeavour in the strength of the Lord. For while he requires of us, that we trust in him, *do good,* and *delight* ourselves *in the Lord,* he, at the same time, enjoins us to *commit our way to him,* and promises that *he will bring it to pass**. As the *keeping* of the heart is of such importance, it is a duty, to the performance of which, the knowledge of the evils of the heart is indispensably requisite.—We cannot attain to the *keeping* of the heart, unless we attain to *humility.* Now, the knowledge of the evils of the heart is necessary to the exercise of humility. Therefore these two are joined together in scripture. We learn their connection from the exercise of the Prophet Jeremiah, who speaks in this manner: *Remembering mine affliction and my misery, the wormwood and the gall: my soul had them still in remembrance, and is humbled in me* †.—Tranquillity of soul in the service of God

---

* Psal. xxxvii. 3, 4, 5. † Lam. iii. 19, 20.

God is one important branch of the *keeping* of the heart; and this cannot be attained without the trial and knowledge of the heart. Let us here attend to the exhortation of the Pfalmift: *Commune with your own heart, and be ſtill**. The *ſtillneſs* that is here meant, is a bleſſed ſettlement of heart upon God; a reſt and reliance of ſoul on him, as our ſtrength and ſupport, according to the uſe of the ſame word; Pſal. xxxvii. 7. *Reſt in the Lord.*——

But to ſpeak more comprehenſively of the *keeping* of the heart, it conſiſts in the conſtant *mortification* of *ſin;* and in the lively *exerciſe* of all *grace*. Now, the knowledge of the heart is undoubtedly neceſſary in the higheſt degree, for the *mortification* of ſin. For how can its plagues be ſubdued, unleſs they be diſcovered. Vain are all a perſon's pretences to mortification, if he remain unacquainted with his heart. One might as well pretend to ſubdue an enemy, before he ſaw him, either in the field, or in the camp; nay, even before he knew who his enemy was! Our Lord evidently ſuppoſes the knowledge of ſecret corruptions, as lying at the very root of mortification; and not merely a general knowledge of them, but a particular acquaintance with that luſt, or *plague of the heart*, which eſpecially requires it. Therefore, he ſays, *If thy hand or thy foot offend thee, cut them off, and caſt them from thee: if thine eye offend thee, pluck it out, and caſt it from thee* †. This implies, that as luſts may be as dear to us as the moſt uſeful members of our body, we ought to be as particularly acquainted with them, that we may, through the Spirit, ſubdue them, as with our eyes, our hands, and our feet; and that thoſe who have not this diſtinct and particular knowledge of their heart-plagues, are as ignorant in a ſpiritual, as thoſe in a natural ſenſe, who *cannot diſcern between their right hand and their left*. Would it appear the extreme of folly in a perſon infected with a malignant diſeaſe, plague, or mortification in his body, from which the metaphors, both in the

---

* Pſal. iv. 4.   † Mat. xviii. 8, 9.

the words of our text, and in thofe now mentioned, are evidently taken,—to perfuade himfelf that he was entirely free of all danger, before he were rightly acquainted with the nature of his difeafe; or, in order to remove it, to lop off a limb at a venture, without knowing which of his members was particularly affected? And is it not alfo the extreme of folly, in a fpiritual fenfe, for a perfon to pretend he has made progrefs in mortification, who remains hitherto a ftranger to the *plague of his heart?* Therefore, the Pfalmift propofes this queftion: *Wherewith fhall a young man cleanfe his way?* And gives fuch an anfwer as denotes, that the way to fubdue fin is firft to fearch it out; *by taking heed thereto, according to thy word**. And, in another place, he makes this declaration: *If I regard iniquity in my heart, the Lord will not hear me.*

Nor can the believer make progrefs in holinefs, or attain to the vigorous exercife of grace in any other way. Is it incumbent upon a fovereign to be well acquainted with the moft defencelefs places of his kingdom, where there is the greateft danger of invafion? Ought a general particularly to know the weakeft places of the wall, where his enemy is moft likely to make an attack, or effect a breach, that the moft powerful fupplies may be directed to thefe quarters? And ought not the Chriftian to be efpecially acquainted with his own heart, that he may know where his lufts are ftrongeft; where the plague of fin rages with greateft violence; and that he may apply to the Lord for renewed fupplies of grace, fuited to his prefent neceffities. As fin and grace are two contraries in his foul, thofe graces, in a peculiar manner, require confirmation, that in their nature are directly oppofed to the moft prevalent corruptions. When his *unbelief* is very powerful, this prayer fhould be conftantly in his mouth: *Lord increafe my faith.* When *enmity* is raging, he requires a renewed communication of *love.* He needs *patience* ftrengthened, when he is ready to be overcome by *fretfulnefs.*

* Pfal. cxix. 9.

fretfulness. For, as the Lord at first subdues sin in the heart, by implanting a principle of grace; it is in the same way that he carries on the good work, and subdues sin more and more. He gives the believer renewed communications of those graces that are directly opposed in their nature to his most powerful corruptions; *grace to help him in time of need.* Now, the knowledge of the heart is necessary for this purpose: Therefore we are called to *ask, seek, and knock,* with the promise of receiving, finding, and having admittance. But how shall we not only ask, but be importunate, if unacquainted with our necessities?

6. NECESSARY for the due *regulation* of the *life.* Even as renewed by grace, we can no more accomplish this of ourselves than we can keep our hearts. For *it is God that worketh in us, both to* will *and to* do. He constantly makes use of means to bring us to holiness of life; and one mean for this purpose is, the discovery of the evils of the heart. All the pretences that men make to holiness of conversation, before they know their own hearts, are vain and hypocritical, false and fruitless. They may have some reformation of life for a time, from the convictions of their natural consciences; but it deserves not the name, as it partakes not of the nature of holiness. Outward and open sins are relinquished, only that those which are secret may be more greedily committed. The character of Ephraim, although strictly viewed, it has another meaning, will, in the way of accommodation, apply to all unrenewed men. *Ephraim is a silly dove without heart* *. Those who are ignorant of their *heart,* destitute of spiritual understanding, are, in God's reckoning, as if they were without heart altogether. Their actions are not esteemed holy by him, because they are performed without the *heart*; they want the very soul of holy actions: So it is said by Solomon, *Fools die for want of wisdom,* literally, *for want of heart;* Prov. x. 21. They also follow the conduct of Ephraim, of whom it is said, *They go to Egypt, and seek unto Assyria.*
They

---

* Hof. vii. 11.

They betake themselves to false grounds of trust, instead of confiding in divine strength. They put their trust in those actions that they falsely term holy: and although they may continue in a course of outward reformation for a time, yet often they afterwards become worse than ever. *It happenes unto them, according to the true proverb, The dog is turned to his own vomit again, and the sow that was washed, to her wallowing in the mire.* Our Lord compares their situation to *an house* that has been *empty, swept, and garnished.* But *their last end proves worse than the first**.

We have already mentioned the observation of the wise man, concerning the heart, that *from it are the issues of life.* Now, if *the issues of life* are from the heart, it is exceedingly necessary that itself should be well known; that thus, by the work of the holy Spirit in us, we may be made to *cleanse ourselves from all filthiness of the flesh and spirit, and to perfect holiness in the fear of the Lord.* Whenever the light of the Spirit shines into the heart that was formerly in darkness, it breaks out in the life by a godly conversation; and the light of the believer so *shines before men, that others seeing* his *good works glorify* his *Father in heaven.* Therefore, it is said, that *the wise in heart shall receive commandments*, whereas *the prating fool shall fall* †. Those only who have received spiritual wisdom to discern their own hearts, can either receive or obey God's commandments: and whatever professions of subjection or obedience are made by sinners, they will certainly fail in fulfilling them. It is only that *wisdom which is from above,* that is *full of good fruits.* Let us listen to the testimony of the Psalmist, with regard to the importance of knowing the heart, to the exercise of true obedience in the life: *I thought on my ways.* This implies a search into and knowledge of his heart, as well as of his life. Observe the consequence: *And I turned my feet unto thy testimonies. I made haste, and delayed not to keep thy commandments* ‡.

FROM

---

* Mat. xii. 43.   † Prov. x. 8.   ‡ Psal. cxix. 59, 60.

FROM what has now been offered on this subject, we would call and entreat you all to come to the all-powerful Physician, and to put your various plagues in his hand. *He healeth every manner of sickness and disease among the people.* There is *a fountain opened for the house of David, and the inhabitants of Jerusalem, for sin and for uncleanness.* His precious blood is the fountain: and this fountain was opened for sinners from all eternity, in the *purpose* of God. It was opened in the promises, in typical sacrifices, and other ordinances, ever since the entrance of sin: For Christ is *the Lamb slain from the foundation of the world.* Ever since it was first opened, it has been flowing for the healing of diseased souls. This fountain was *actually* opened in the death of Christ, when his side was pierced on mount Calvary, whence *came blood and water.* It is still as efficacious as ever; for it is an inexhaustible fountain,—a fountain that ever flows,—and there is the freest access to it. For it is *opened to the house of David, and the inhabitants of Jerusalem*; to rich and poor, old and young, bond and free, great and mean; to persons of every character, without any distinction. All who hear the call of the gospel, have a right to come and wash therein. And this fountain is for removing all *sin and uncleanness;* the *power* of sin, the *guilt* of sin, its *pollution,* its *prevalence,* and its very *inbeing* at length. Come then to this omnipotent Physician; for it is ground of comfort to you, that not only is this fountain opened, but Christ acts the part of a physician, by washing sinners in it, as they cannot wash themselves. He is *the angel who* both *troubles the waters,* and puts the diseased into them, that they may receive a cure. Whatever is your plague, he can easily remove it. He needs only to *speak the word, and* you *shall be healed.* You who have never had your maladies in any degree removed, should be concerned now to make a diligent improvement of his call. Have others formerly experienced the virtue of his blood ? Then make a renewed application to it. While you are called to come by faith to this fountain, as you cannot come of yourselves, although it is your duty constantly to endeavour it; remember, for your encouragement, that he is engaged to take the work of cleansing you into his own hand; and that this is his promise: *Then will I sprinkle clean water upon you, and ye shall be clean: from all your filthiness, and from all your idols will I cleanse you.*

SERMON

On the NECESSITY of KNOWING the PLAGUE of the HEART.

1 KINGS, viii. 38.

—*Who shall know every man the plague of his own heart.*—

THE enemies of Samson were exceedingly anxious to know *wherein his great* STRENGTH *lay*, that they might accomplish his ruin. It is of no less importance for the Christian to know wherein his great *weakness* lies, that he may, through the power of God, accomplish the ruin of his spiritual enemies. He is at no loss as to the seat and repository of his strength. He finds that it is only laid up in Christ his vital *Head*. But he cannot make a right improvement of the life, grace and strength treasured up in Him, till truly acquainted with his own weakness: and this he can only learn, when the Spirit discovers to him *the plague of his heart*.

On the II. head we have already endeavoured to illustrate the necessity of a saving knowledge of the heart from its connection with the due knowledge of God, improvement of the remedy, genuine repentance, acceptable worship, keeping of the heart, and regulation of the life.

7. THE necessity of this knowledge farther appears from its inseparable connection with the *purification* and *peace* of *conscience*. The *heart* and *conscience* are terms often used promiscuously in Scripture, as denoting the same thing. But if we understand the

heart

heart in its strict and proper sense, as signifying the *will* and *affections*, the *conscience* is to be viewed as a different faculty of the soul. It is that power implanted in man, by which he forms a judgment of the actions of his life, and of the very thoughts of his heart, as being either right or wrong, conformable or contrary to the law of God. Thus *the conscience beareth witness, and the thoughts the mean while either accuse, or else excuse one another* *. It is a deputy for God in the breast of man, which ought constantly to remind him of his subjection and accountableness to the Supreme Judge. But there are two evils that especially affect the conscience of every natural man, in a greater or less degree. It is *defiled* and it is *disturbed*. Sin deprives it both of *purity* and of *peace*. His conscience is *defiled*. *Unto the pure all things are pure, but unto them that are defiled and unbelieving is nothing pure, but even their mind and conscience is defiled* †. Sin is the cause of this pollution. For there can be no moral uncleanness but what springs from this fountain. The defilement of conscience appears by its incapacity to judge of the actions of the person; by its blindness in mistaking right for wrong, and wrong for right; by wilful self-perversion; by giving a judgment against its own conviction; by affording an unfair representation to the person, holding up sin in the place of duty, and calling evil good. This defilement sometimes so remarkably increases by the indulgence of sin, that conscience becomes *seared as with a hot iron* ‡. When this is the case, it seldom or never reproves; it is in a manner *past feeling*; it is nowise moved by the most atrocious offences of its subject against the Divine law. In general, a defiled conscience reproves for the grosser sins of the life only; but passes over in silence the multiplied abominations of the heart. Sin bribes it with the prospect of pleasure and peace, to give it as little trouble as possible about *outward* transgressions, and none at all about its *inward* workings: and like

---

* Rom. ii. 15.   † Tit. i. 15.   ‡ 1 Tim. iv. 2.

like an unjuft judge, who wifhes to fhare in the profits of the crime, confcience takes no more notice of it than is barely neceffary to maintain a name, and fave appearances with the world. In this ftate is the confcience of the natural man, and thus it will continue till he obtain a faving difcovery of *the plague of his heart.* Then that fupernatural light, diffufed by the Holy Spirit through the heart, reflects on confcience, and difcovers its blindnefs, unfaithfulnefs, treachery, and all the abominations lurking in it. Then confcience, inftead of being a fire that fhould have confumed fin, appears to have been only as a feeble fpark hid among afhes, and almoft entirely extinguifhed. Then it difcovers the ghofts, as it were, of ten thoufand former iniquities, the cry of whofe guilt and pollution has been ftifled by its own hand, while acting as an unfaithful watchman. Thofe actions that the finner was taught by his confcience to confider, either as very little fins, or as entirely harmlefs, he fees rifing up as from the dead, in all their number, magnitude, and aggravated circumftances. His iniquities which were quite forgotten, or very flightly remembered, like the *dry bones in the valley of vifion,* in confequence of the difcovery of his heart, by the *breathing* of the Holy Ghoft on it, firft make *a noife,* then *a fhaking,* and at length *ftand up an exceeding great army.* Then *confcience* alfo accufes the *heart,* and produces a regifter of heart-fins and fecret iniquities, of which the perfon had no apprehenfion.

But the confcience is not merely *difcovered* by means of this knowledge. It is alfo *purified.* Therefore it is faid,—*How much more fhall the blood of Chrift, purge your confcience from dead works to ferve the living God* * ? The blood of Chrift applied to this power of the foul, *purges it from* DEAD *works,* from thofe works that have been performed in a ftate of fpiritual death ; that are dead as being unacceptable to God, becaufe they proceed not from a renewed nature
and

* Heb. ix. 14.

and sanctified heart; and dead, as being deadly in their nature, and subjecting him more and more to eternal death. Conscience is thus *purged* from the pollution of these works, and from their guilt as binding over the sinner to punishment. In consequence of this, he is enabled *to serve the living God*, in the exercise of faith on him, as reconciled through the blood of Christ. Because of the necessary connection of the knowledge of the heart with the *purification* of conscience, the Spirit joins *a true heart and a pure conscience together**. *Let us draw near with a* TRUE *heart;—having our heart sprinkled from an* EVIL *conscience.* Now, our heart can never be *true*, till, by the light of the Spirit, we perceive its natural situation. Till then it is a *false* heart, and attended by an *evil* conscience. But as soon as this gracious discovery is made, and *integrity of heart* bestowed, the conscience is delivered from its habitual pollution. Farther, in the natural man, this power is not only *defiled*, but also *disturbed*. It hath no proper peace. Not only is it overwhelmed with guilt and pollution, but often distressed with a *sense* of guilt, and *fear* of deserved wrath. Indeed the conscience, in an unrenewed state, is most generally too much at peace. But the peace which it enjoys is false. It springs not from reconciliation to God, and pardon, but only from the concealment and indulgence of iniquity. It is not the fruit of a deliverance from sin, but a peace in the commission of it, arising from the smothering of its own convictions, and from the resistance of the ordinary motions of the Spirit. Now, without the knowledge of our own hearts, we can have no true peace of conscience; for otherwise our sins are either hid from us, or falsely glossed over, so that their pollution and punishment are kept out of sight. Therefore a *pure* heart and a *good* conscience are mentioned in connection: *The end of the commandment is charity out of a* PURE *heart and a* GOOD *conscience* †. That conscience is called *good*, in which the

---

* Heb. x. 22.   † 1 Tim. i. 5.

the peace of God dwells; and this is infeparable from *a pure heart,* a heart that hath both feen and been delivered from its abominations. No fooner are men favingly inftructed by the Spirit, with regard to their own hearts, than they have a real and bleffed peace of confcience. *All thy children fhall be taught of the Lord, and great fhall be the peace of thy children. In righteoufnefs fhalt thou be eftablifhed; thou fhalt be far from oppreffion, for thou fhalt not* FEAR, *and from* TROUBLE, *for it fhall not come near thee* *. *Behold I will bring it health and cure, and I will cure them, and reveal unto them the abundance of* PEACE *and* TRUTH †. It is the work of Chrift, and the way in which he carries on his work, *to give* LIGHT *to them that fit in darknefs, and in the fhadow of death, and to guide their feet into the way of peace.*

8. THIS knowledge is neceffary to enable us to form a right and impartial judgment of our *ftate* before God. *Know ye not your ownfelves, how that Jefus Chrift is in you, except ye be reprobates?*—that is, ftill at a diftance from God. He, who is not favingly acquainted with his heart, may know by the moft unqueftionable evidences, that he is a wicked man, or an hypocrite; but he can have no juft apprehenfions of the wretchednefs of his fituation. For a man to judge of his ftate merely by his actions, without looking into his heart, would argue as great ftupidity, as if one fhould pretend to judge of the real and internal fituation of a prifon or madhoufe, by looking at the ftructure of the edifice. Undoubtedly, the life is an evidence of the ftate of the heart, as the fruit is of the nature of the tree; and it is only by the external conduct that others can form their judgment, becaufe they can go no farther. But although this is the only method of judging left to others, a man himfelf muft not ftop here. Others might conclude, that their friend was perfectly well, from the healthinefs of his look, and apparent vigour of his conftitution; but it would be great folly for him to form the fame conclufion

* Ifa. liv. 13, 14.   † Jer. xxxiii. 6.

clusion from these *outward* appearances, if, from many inward symptoms, he had reason to apprehend, that there was some fatal disease preying on his vitals. It is the duty of every man to look into his own heart, to try it by the unerring rule of the word, and to implore the direction of the Holy Spirit; that he may be enabled to judge with integrity of his real state, as he appears before the holy and just God. A man can never attain this knowledge, but by the Spirit as his guide; for it is his work to *convince the world of sin*. But even by the exertion of his natural abilities, every natural man might know a great deal more of his heart than he does. However men, in general, either give themselves no trouble about this important inquiry, or wilfully blind their minds, and refuse to believe what they see. It is therefore only by the knowledge of the heart that we can apprehend our state. If from the situation of our heart we have good reason to conclude that our state is bad, we may be assured that it appears so before God. Therefore, saith the Apostle John, *If our heart condemn us, God is greater than our heart, and knoweth all things. Beloved, if our heart condemn us not, then have we confidence towards God**. When a person is in darkness about the state of his soul, or has reason to think that he is in a state of alienation from God; this affects his mind with much distrust and confusion in all spiritual exercises. But if, on the contrary, from an impartial examination of our hearts, we have reason to conclude that they are *right with* him and *found in his statutes*, and that we are indulging no known sin; holy freedom and boldness in coming to him, as our reconciled God and Father, is the native consequence.

9. The knowledge of our hearts tends to inspire us with *charity* towards our brethren of mankind. Some men are naturally less severe and censorious in their disposition than others. But genuine charity is not natural to man, and can proceed from the work

---

* 1 John iii. 20. 21.

work of the Spirit only. He makes use of means in working a conformity to himself; and a discovery of the heart is one mean eminently subservient to this end. It is a very bad evidence of any one, if he has it as his principal employment to find out and propagate the faults and blemishes of others. This is directly contrary to the rule of Christian charity, which teacheth us to *bear one another's burdens*, conceal the infirmities of each other, and *so to fulfil the law of Christ*. On this head, how cutting is that question proposed by Him, who was the greatest pattern of love that the world ever saw, *Why beholdest thou the* MOTE *that is in thy* BROTHER's *eye: but considerest not the* BEAM *that is in thine* OWN *eye?* How severe his reproof?—*Thou hypocrite, first cast out the* BEAM *that is in thine* OWN *eye, and then shalt thou see clearly to cast out the* MOTE *out of thy* BROTHER's *eye* *.— This temper also demonstrates, that he who is under its influence, is a great stranger to the exercise of *self-denial*. For, when showing an eagerness to propal the faults of others, he intends the discovery as a foil to his own excellencies; and tacitly extols himself for the supposed want of such blemishes. This is a very common, although to persons of any discernment, a very evident way of soliciting self-praise; instead of which it ought always to meet with contempt and detestation. As many follow this course to gain the approbation of man; the self-righteous Pharisee, described by Christ, endeavoured, in this way, to commend himself to God; *praying thus with himself, God, I thank thee, that I am not as other men are, —nor even as this publican* †. Such, instead of being grieved at the faults or failings of others, seem rather to rejoice in them; as they give them an opportunity of talking, and of publishing their own merits. But charity *rejoiceth not in iniquity, but rejoiceth in the truth* ‡.

The

---

* Matth. vii. 3. 5.   † Luke xviii. 11. 13, 14.

‡ The *truth* here meant, is that which is practical. For from the contrast, it is clear, that the word is used in this place in the same sense in which it is used by John; *I have no greater joy than to hear that my children walk in the truth*; Epist. iii. ver. 4.

The conduct of the poor publican was very different from this. He had seen his *own* heart; and his prayer is not the language of self-exaltation or detraction, but of confusion and contrition. *He stood afar off, and would not lift up so much as his eyes to heaven, but smote upon his breast, saying, God be merciful to me a* SINNER. And it is declared, that *this man went down to his house justified, rather than the other;* that is justified, while the other was condemned. For that this is the sense of the expression, is evident from Christ's application of the parable to his hearers: *Every one that exalteth himself shall be abased, and he that humbleth himself shall be exalted.*

HE who hath seen *his own heart* by the light of the Spirit, perceives so much evil in *it*, that he finds little time to contemplate the defects of others. When he *sees transgressors he is grieved, because men keep not God's law.* When their actions are *doubtful*, he endeavours to put the best construction on them they can bear; knowing that *charity believeth all things, hopeth all things, and thinketh no evil,* where it can find any room to think good of the person or action.— When the evil nature of the action is *evident*, he endeavours to view all the alleviating circumstances attending it; and from the knowledge of his own heart, reflects, that had his temptation been as strong, he might have done as ill, perhaps much worse. He always finds so much wickedness in his inward part, that he is ashamed to be harsh or uncharitable to others. He knows, that were God to leave him but for a moment, he would instantly follow their example. Therefore, *if a brother be overtaken in a fault,* he tries to *restore him in the spirit of meekness, considering* HIMSELF, *lest he also be tempted.* Our Lord, by his answer to the Scribes and Pharisees, when they brought him a woman taken in adultery, taught them the necessity of knowing their own hearts, that they might learn mercy and compassion to others. *He said unto them; He that is* WITHOUT SIN *among you, let him first cast a stone at her.* This reproof was so penetrating, that it had a prefent effect on them all, by making them afhamed. *For they who heard it, being convicted by their own confcience, went out one by one, beginning at the eldeft even unto the laft **.

10. NECESSARY as an excellent guard againft Satan's *temptations.* As he is the great adverfary of our falvation, it is a leading branch of the Chriftian warfare to refift his attacks; and the complete defeat of this foe will conftitute an eminent part of the faint's victory. To the attainment of this victory the knowledge of our own hearts is abfolutely neceffary. As Satan is well acquainted with them, and knows all our corruptions; to them he applies himfelf in a fpecial manner, that, if poffible, he may accomplifh our ruin. The lufts of the heart are his great inftruments. He ftill endeavours to blow up the fire of corruption within us into a flame. The predominant fin in every man, is the weapon that he principally wields againft him for his deftruction. This pretender to God's empire in our hearts, hath always a difaffected party within us; and, for gaining his end, at leaft in fo far, he hath nothing more to do than to ftir this up to actual rebellion againft God. Our corruptions are juft the devil's forces, which, notwithftanding the many defeats he meets with by the power of Divine grace, he ftill rallies again, and brings on the field with renewed impetuofity. Were it not for thefe lufts that dwell in our hearts, Satan could have no power over us. He was entirely baffled and routed in all the attacks that he made on our great Head, whether in the defert, or in the garden, immediately after his baptifm, or during his dreadful agony; becaufe he had no fin, no inward principle to work upon. Therefore Chrift declared his defeat, even before he made the affault: *The prince of this world cometh, and hath nothing in me* †. If Satan had nothing in us, nothing of his own, nothing in oppofition to God; he would depart from us, as unfuccefsful as he did from Chrift. But he hath a powerful hoft within us ready for his reception.

* John viii. 7. 9.   † John xiv. 30.

reception. *What will ye fee in the Shulamite, but as it were the company of two armies?* It is therefore neceſſary that we be well acquainted with our hearts, that we may, in the ſtrength of grace, reſiſt Satan when he makes his attacks. We are exhorted to *watch and pray, that* we *enter not into temptation* *. Our watching is eſpecially to be directed to our hearts, to the luſts that war there; becauſe it is among theſe *enemies of our own houſehold* that Satan will raiſe his head: and we can only improve the knowledge of our hearts aright, by intreating the Lord's protection and guardianſhip. *For except the Lord keep the city, the watchman watcheth in vain* †.

11. Necessary for the *revival* of the Lord's people in a time of ſpiritual bondage. Chriſtians are ſubject to ſad declenſions from the exerciſe of godlineſs. They are ſometimes *dried and withered like the graſs; as bones ſcattered at the grave's mouth;* they have as little activity, and ſeem to have as little life as dead men's bones; or, *as when one cutteth and cleaveth wood upon the earth* ‡. They appear to be as ſapleſs and uſeleſs as the ſplinters of wood that fly from the ax; or, as the words may be rendered, *as when one cutteth and cleaveth the earth.* They ſeem to meet with as little regard or compaſſion from God, as the earth does from the huſbandman, when it is plowed up by him. Now, the knowledge of their own hearts neceſſary to their *revival;* for it is generally becauſe of the indulgence of ſome ſecret luſt, that they are deprived of the ſenſe of God's love, and of the comforts of communion with him. It is only by obtaining farther acquaintance with their hearts, that they can find out that luſt, that hidden enemy which offends God and deprives them of his preſence. Therefore, Aſaph, when he was in ſo mournful a ſituation, by the hiding of God's countenance, that *his ſore ran in the night and ceaſed not; that his ſoul refuſed to be comforted; that he remembered God, and was troubled; that he complained, and his ſpirit,* inſtead of being

* Matth. xxvi. 41. † Pſal. cxxvii. 1. ‡ Pſal. cxli. 7.

being revived, *was overwhelmed within him; that his eyes were held waking, and he was so troubled that he could not speak;*—had recourse to his own heart, most probably to discover the procuring cause of the Lord's contending. These are his words: *I commune with mine own heart, and my spirit made diligent search**: Thus did he endeavour to find out that heart-plague which deprived him of all comfort, and made him even question *the loving-kindness of the Lord.* And he was successful in his inquiry. He found that unbelief was the plague. *And I said, This is mine infirmity.* As it is the duty of Christians, under desertion, to review their hearts with the greatest care, to subject them to the most rigid scrutiny, to endeavour to search out all the lusts that rage there, and especially that particular lust which hinders their peace, and earnestly to supplicate the direction and counsel of the Spirit, who knoweth and searcheth the heart; it is generally in this way that the Lord recovers them from backsliding. He, by the motions of his Spirit, stirs them up to self-examination, and anew opens up their hearts to them in their vileness and wickedness, discovers their particular plagues, and so brings them back to himself. Then he hears this pleasant declaration from his backsliding children, when overcome by a sense of his love, and of their own unworthiness, as from repenting Ephraim: *After I was instructed, I smote upon my thigh.* Then he speaks in this comfortable manner of them: *Is Ephraim my dear son? is he a pleasant child? for since I spake against him, I do earnestly remember him still; therefore my bowels are troubled for him: I will surely have mercy upon him, saith the Lord*†. This was the exercise of David, after he got an affecting view of his great transgression; *Against thee, thee only have I sinned;* and therefore he prays; *Create in me a clean heart, O God, and renew a right spirit within me* ‡. The Lord declares that in this manner he would deal with his ancient people, after eminent defection from himself; *Therefore, behold, I will allure her, and bring her into the wilderness, and speak comfortably*

* Psal. lxxvii. 6.   † Jer. xxxi. 19.   ‡ Psal. li. 4. 10.

comfortably unto her; or, *speak to her heart,* by a discovery both of her sin, and of her deliverance from it. *I will give her the valley of Achor for a door of hope.* *Achor,* signifying *bitterness,* is here figuratively used to denote true *sorrow* for sin. It follows, as the fruit of this; *She shall sing there as in the days of her youth, and as in the day when she came up out of the land of Egypt**. The Lord brings back his people to himself, by exciting them to renewed acts of faith and evangelical repentance, proceeding from a renewed discovery of the heart; and he gives them a new influx of joy, like that which they felt in the *day of espousals,* when first delivered from the worse than *Egyptian* darkness and bondage of sin. Indeed, the knowledge of the heart is essential to the very being of a saint, and to all right exercise.

12. NECESSARY for convincing us of the wisdom, justice, and love displayed in all Divine *dispensations.* As long as a man continues ignorant of his own heart, he remains a stranger to the operations of God's hand towards him. When afflicted, either he views not the rod as sent because of his iniquities, or he complains of it as heavier than these deserve. He is ready to say with Cain; *My punishment is greater than I can bear.* He presumes, at least in heart, to accuse God of folly, injustice and cruelty in his dispensations. The reason of this arrogance is, that he has no just idea of the desert of his sins; far less of their evil and abominable nature. Therefore this is the improvement of afflictions which God requires of sinners, that thence they learn the *evil* and *bitterness* of sin; that they apprehend the wickedness and malignity of their iniquities, by the severity of their punishment. *Thine own wickedness shall correct thee, and thy backslidings shall reprove thee: know therefore and see, that it is an evil thing and bitter, that thou hast forsaken the Lord thy God, and that my fear is not in thee, saith the Lord God of hosts* †. Indeed the influence of Divine dispensations, and of the knowledge of the heart is mutual. By the dispensations

* Hof. ii. 14, 15. † Jer. ii. 19.

fations of Providence concurring with the Word efficaciously applied, we see the evils of the heart: and by the knowledge of these evils we perceive the justness of those dispensations. That the dispensations of Providence are instrumental in discovering the evils of the heart, is evident from these words already mentioned; *Thine own wickedness shall correct thee, and thy backslidings shall reprove thee:*—and that the knowledge of the evils of the heart, on the other hand, is subservient to the discovery of the justness of these dispensations, appears from the words of Moses to the children of Israel; *Thou shalt remember all the way which the Lord thy God hath led thee, these forty years in the wilderness, to humble thee, and to prove thee, to know what was in thine heart* *. They were to make use of that sense which they had of their sins, that humbling and affecting sense which was the fruit of the Lord's dealing with them, as a mean of convincing them of the wisdom, justice and love of God, in continuing them so long, and afflicting them with so many severe dispensations in the wilderness, for the purpose of accomplishing this heart-humiliation.

The children of God perceive a display of *wisdom* in these trying dispensations; because when ordinances have been ineffectual, he makes these successful. They see *justice* in them, because they deserve infinitely more on account of their sins. They also discover the greatest *love* in them, because God hath their salvation in view, and because their trials are attended by the power of the Holy Spirit for this end. Therefore, though at first under these dispensations they are *as a bullock unaccustomed to the yoke,* spurning and fretting under them, viewing them rather as destructive than as healing; yet when the blessing attends them, they are made to speak and think in a very different strain, saying unto God; *Turn thou me, and I shall be turned, for thou art the Lord my God.* Then they know that *it is surely meet to be said unto God,*

---

* Deut. viii. 2.

God, I have born chastisement; I will not offend any more: that which I see not, teach thou me; if I have done iniquity, I will do no more. The afflictions of wicked Manasseh were blessed as the means of humbling him, and discovering to him his own heart; and the fruit of this humiliation was a persuasion of the equity and mercy of the Divine procedure. For *when he was in affliction, he besought the Lord his God, and humbled himself greatly before the God of his fathers, and prayed unto him: and he was intreated of him, and heard his supplication;—then Manasseh knew that he was God**.

13. The saving knowledge of the heart is farther necessary, as a mean of obtaining deliverance from *personal afflictions*. We are not to imagine that it is in any degree the meritorious cause. This knowledge can have no merit before God. For if it be of a saving kind, it proceeds from him alone; it is his own free gift. But it may safely be considered as a mean employed by the Spirit, preparatory to the removal of trying dispensations. This is evidently implied in the passage before us:—*What prayer or supplication soever be made by* ANY MAN, *who shall know the plague of his own heart,—then hear thou in heaven thy dwelling place, and forgive, and do, and give to every man according to his ways, whose heart thou knowest;* or, as the words may be, and are translated by some, *Then thou* WILT *hear, thou* WILT *forgive, &c.* for they may not only be understood as a *prayer*, but as a *prophecy*. Afflictions are often sent to the unconverted, and in subserviency to the word, sanctified for turning them to God; according to his promise, *I will cause you to pass under the rod, and I will bring you into the bond of the covenant.* As it is often the Lord's design in sending affliction to bless it, for bringing them into union with himself; when this end is served, he, in mercy, removes the affliction. To this purpose is the testimony of the Church,—*Such as sit in darkness, and in the shadow of death, being bound in affliction*

---

* 2 Chron. xxxiii. 12, 13.

affliction and irons; because they rebelled against the words of God, and contemned the counsel of the Most High:—they cried unto the Lord in their trouble, and he saved them out of their distresses *. The Lord severely afflicted Manasseh because of his sin, and as a subordinate mean of the conversion of this *vessel of mercy*. He deprived him of his kingdom, and loaded him with bonds and fetters in Babylon. This affliction he blessed, for shewing him his own evil heart, and the wickedness of his ways; and when he was brought truly to know and confess his iniquities, the Lord delivered him from adversity. For it is declared, that when *he was in affliction, and humbled himself greatly before the God of his fathers; he brought him again to Jerusalem, into his kingdom* †.

This is especially the case with the children of God. When displeased with them, he applies the rod to excite them to search their hearts, and try their ways, for discovering the causes of his controversy. When they are made to know their iniquities, and to bewail them in an evangelical manner, he often removes the stroke of his hand. *He withdraweth not his eyes from the righteous;—if they be bound in fetters, and be holden in cords of affliction: then he sheweth them their work, and their transgressions, that they have exceeded. He openeth also their ear to discipline, and commandeth that they return from iniquity. If they obey and serve him, they shall spend their days in prosperity, and their years in pleasures* ‡. Christians, these afflictive visitations are all in love; and you ought to be more concerned about the sanctification than about the removal of them. But it is lawful for you, in submission to the Lord's will, to pray for deliverance from adversity, when, by means of it, your compassionate Father hath accomplished his gracious purposes. *If thou return unto the Almighty, thou shalt be built up; thou shalt put away iniquity far from thy tabernacles. Thou shalt make thy prayer to him, and he*

shall

---

* Psal. cvii. 10, 11. 13. 17.—20. † 2 Chron. xxxiii. 12.
‡ Job xxxvi. 7.—11.

shall hear thee.—When men are cast down, then thou shalt say, There is lifting up ; and he shall save the humble person *. Job was a striking instance of the truth of this. For when he was humbled before the Lord, and made to know more of his heart, to acknowledge that he had *uttered* what *he understood not, things too wonderful for* him, *which* he *knew not*,—and *to abhor himself, and repent in dust and ashes;*—the Lord turned again his captivity; chap. xlii. 3. 6. 10. Of the same import is the declaration of God by the Prophet Hosea; *I will go* and *return to my place, till they acknowledge their offence, and seek my face : in their affliction they will seek me early* †. Nay, sometimes the Lord, in dealing with his people, employs a conviction of their sinful courses as a comfortable preventative of that affliction, to which he would otherwise subject them. When they have dishonoured him by sin, and, from a due sense of it, are humbled before him, in mercy he averts the chastisement they have deserved ; because the end which he hath always in view with respect to them, is already gained by the operation of the Spirit, in bringing them to repentance. God never inflicts the rod on his children, but when it is necessary. He *chastens, not for his pleasure, but for their profit.* When truly humbled for their iniquity, he not only often withholds the rod, but returns to them with great loving-kindness. Thus he addresses his backsliding people, to show how unwilling he is to afflict them ; *Return thou backsliding Israel, saith the Lord, and I will not cause mine anger to fall upon you ; for I am merciful, saith the Lord, and I will not keep anger for ever. Only acknowledge thine iniquity, that thou hast transgressed against the Lord thy God :— Turn, O backsliding children, saith the Lord, for I am married unto you* ‡.—Christians are often excited to concern about sin, and to an ardent desire of pardon, more immediately from an apprehension of the deserved chastisement, than from a sense of its evil. They are more, in such a situation, under the influence of fea than

---

* Job xxii. 23. 27. 29.   † Hos. v. 15.   ‡ Jer. iii. 12, 13.

than love. But the Lord, in infinite fovereignty and condefcenfion, ufes even this more unworthy motive in them for awakening them from that fecurity and obduracy which naturally follow fin, and by fuggefting motives of a filial and evangelical kind, gradually brings them to genuine repentance.

You who are yet ftrangers to your hearts, may, from what hath been faid, learn the neceffity of *purity* and *peace* of confcience. Your confciences are *defiled* by fin. But apply to the blood of Jefus Chrift, that they may be fprinkled, that thus they may be *without offence, both towards God and man.* Seek *peace* of confcience. Is not this power often difturbed and diftreffed with a fenfe of your guilt, and fear of eternal indignation? You can only enjoy peace by an application to the blood of the Lamb: *for he hath made peace by the blood of his crofs.* Perhaps, you find no trouble from your confciences. It may be, they are *feared* and *hardened through the deceitfulnefs of fin.* You have got them fo quieted, that they feldom or never reprove you. But, O finners! confider that it is a *delufive* peace. It is all a dream. It cannot be lafting. You will have an awakening fooner or later. And if mercy do not interpofe, your temporary, fhort-lived peace will iffue in an eternal war with confcience. This is that *worm that dieth not*, that fhall for ever gnaw the hearts of finners in hell. All whofe confciences are not favingly awakened under the found of the gofpel, fhall experience a tremendous awakening by the found of the *laft trump*, when it fhall be faid, *Awake, thou that fleepeft, and come to judgment.* Confider that this is a *deftructive* peace. It is working for your everlafting ruin, like the repofe that a man takes on the brink of a precipice, before he is dafhed in pieces. *At the laft it biteth as a ferpent, and ftingeth like an adder.—Yea, thou fhalt be as he that lieth down in the midft of the fea, or as he that lieth upon the top of a maft* *. This peace is like the fleep of a mariner upon a topmaft,

---

* Prov. xxiii. 32. 34.

in the midst of a dreadful storm. The next billow sweeps him into eternity. This is only *saying peace to yourselves, while there is no peace.* For *there is no peace, saith my God, to the wicked.* It is *saying peace and safety to yourselves, while sudden destruction cometh upon you, as travail upon a woman with child, so that ye shall not escape.* That you may attain this delightful peace of conscience, this true, abiding and saving peace; be exhorted to apply to God for a discovery of the evil of your hearts, and an interest in the *blood of sprinkling*: for otherwise you can only bring a scurf over the sore, whilst the plague remains in all its virulence and malignity.—Consider that there is a dreadful filth in sin, which is one reason why it is called a *plague.* Seek to have the pollution of your persons purged away by the Spirit of Christ, applying his blood for cleansing you; and to be delivered from that shame which flows from a *sense* of guilt, and which is the inseparable concomitant of pollution, that you may *have boldness before God.*

Those who are truly acquainted with their hearts, should labour for a revival in the time of spiritual bondage. Be not satisfied, while the Lord hides his countenance. Search out the plagues of your hearts, that you may come to Christ with the finger on the *sore;* like Esther, when she *touched the golden sceptre,* saying, *The adversary and enemy, is this wicked Haman.* Be frequent and fervent in prayer for a farther discovery of your hearts; that you may see more reason to bless the Lord even for your trials, to acknowledge that *in truth and righteousness he hath afflicted you;* and to say, *Blessed is the man whom thou chastenest, O Lord, and teachest out of thy law.*

SERMON VII.

On HEART-KNOWLEDGE as connected with NATIONAL REFORMATION and DELIVERANCE.

---

1 Kings, viii. 38.

―――*Who shall know every man the plague of his own heart.*―――

THERE is nothing that a man will not more readily believe than any thing bad about himself. How quick-sighted soever he be to the faults of others, and even to those of his nearest friends, he is, in a great measure, blind to his own. The reason is; man naturally worships self, and puts it in the place of God. He is especially unwilling to believe any thing to the prejudice of his heart. He will far more readily allow faults in his practice. For as self is an idol that receives universal homage, the heart is its temple, and it seems highly sacrilegious to charge it with defilement. Such an imputation is a stroke at its dominion. Thence when men cannot deny or even palliate the vices of their lives, they lull themselves with the pleasing idea of the goodness of their hearts: and the character of *a good heart*, when bestowed on any one, is reckoned a powerful apology for a very wicked practice. But it is one great design of God, in the revelation of his will to sinners, to cast down this cursed idol. Therefore our Lord represents self-denial as the first lesson of Christianity. *If any man will be my disciple, let him deny himself.*

In the preceding discourse we have illustrated the necessity of knowing the plague of the heart, from its infeparable connection with the purification and peace of confcience;—for enabling us to form a right and impartial judgment of our ftate before God;—as a powerful incitement to charity towards others;—as an excellent guard againft the temptations of Satan;—for the revival of the children of God in a time of fpiritual bondage and declenfion;—for convincing them of the wifdom, juftice and love difplayed in all Divine difpenfations;—and alfo as a mean of obtaining deliverance from perfonal afflictions.

14. THIS knowledge of the heart is neceffary to all true *national reformation.* The generality of men think in a very trivial manner on this fubject. If a day of general fafting and humiliation be obferved by the nation, it is confidered as all that is neceffary; nay, by many, as a kind of atonement for all national fins. But as the one is not only a very fuperficial, but a very unjuft view of the matter; the other is impious. There are many effential ingredients in true national reformation; among which we may reckon the following.

1. IT is neceffary that the members of a nation fhould as *individuals* know, and be duly affected with their *own* particular fins, and efpecially with the fins of their hearts. This Solomon fuppofes to be indifpenfably requifite to all genuine public repentance: *What prayer or fupplication foever be made, by all thy people, who fhall know every man the plague of his own heart.*—Many are apt to look upon national fins as fomething that they have little connection with, fomething that they are not immediately concerned in; as if a nation itfelf were fome kind of exiftence different from the individuals that compofe it. But what is a nation? Is it not a fociety of individuals, united by a common form of government, and by the fame laws? Is not every perfon in this fociety a conftituent member of it? Can we therefore think of national fins, without viewing them as committed by the perfons that compofe this nation? They become national, when committed or acceded to by the

the generality, or, at leaft, by the leading part of the nation. When this is the cafe, every individual, except in as far as he does his utmoft againft them, is concerned in the guilt, and expofed to the punifhment. Single perfons being then the conftituent members of a nation, it follows that national fins derive their very being from individuals, and only become national, as they are committed or approved by the bulk of fingle perfons who conftitute the nation. But as *public* fins originate from private perfons, it is therefore neceffary that every man fhould know his own fins; and as the fins of every individual take their rife from his heart, it is not fufficient to a thorough national reformation, that every man fhould have fome general acquaintance with his own fins. It is neceffary that *every man know the plague of his own heart*. All fins, whether public or private, fpring from this bitter and polluted fource. National corruption may be compared to a corrupt tree. The branches reprefent the different individuals in the nation, every one of which hath his fhare in the general corruption; and the root, with which all the branches are connected, may reprefent the heart, from which the corruption of all thefe individuals fprings. Thus national reformation can only be faid to begin at the root, when it begins at the heart. Therefore, when the Lord would defcribe a thorough reformation in the cafe of Ifrael under public calamities, he declares that they fhould *be on the mountains, like doves of the vallies, all of them mourning, every one for his iniquity* *.

2. EVERY one fhould know, and be deeply grieved for the particular *fhare* that he has had in the *general* trefpafs. It is not enough that individuals know the plague of their own hearts, or view their iniquities, as accumulating the general guilt. They ought to confider the active hand they have had with others in national trefpaffes. Every man fhould be acquainted with his own guilt, whether it hath been difcovered by

finful

---

* Ezek. vii. 16.

sinful silence, or by personal instrumentality; by unfaithfulness in not reproving, or endeavouring, according to his station, to prevent or punish the sins of others; by following others in their courses of defection; or perhaps, by taking a lead in the general transgression. Can we really view the rejection of the precious gospel as a national iniquity, without considering our partnership in guilt, by the abuse of our distinguishing privileges, by our obduracy under the dispensations of grace? Can we consistently look on the breach of solemn covenant-engagements as an eminent part of national guilt, without judging with regard to ourselves, how far we have dealt unfaithfully in God's covenant? Can we be truly convinced that security under judgments is one of our public sins, without acknowledging that our own hearts afford the most affecting evidence of the general infatuation? Shall we pretend to confess that carnal confidence is another bitter ingredient, filling up the cup of our iniquity, and calling for a *cup of trembling* from the hand of the Lord; if we do not, at the same time, confess that we have often been ready to distrust our God, and to look for deliverance from an arm of flesh? Can we sincerely lament the mournful prevalence of every species of iniquity; without remembering how little we have endeavoured to stem the torrent by our fervent prayers, faithful warnings, and holy example? The Lord complains of all professions of public repentance as deceitful and unacceptable to him, if they are not attended with this particular inquiry. *I hearkened and heard, but they spake not aright; no man repented him of his wickedness, saying, What have I done* *? General confessions, even of general iniquity, are in God's sight nothing but evasions. Although a man should confess public sins with the greatest particularity possible, yet unless he confess them as his *own*, according to the hand he has had in them, it is nothing but a superficial and deceitful acknowledgment.

3. THERE

* Jer. viii. 6.

SER. 7.   *National Reformation and Deliverance.*   129

3. There muſt be a *joint, public* and *particular confeſſion* of national ſins. Solomon takes this alſo for granted in his prayer, ver. 47. *If they ſhall bethink themſelves in the land whither they were carried captives, and repent, and make ſupplication unto thee,—ſaying, We have ſinned, and have done perverſely, we have committed wickedneſs,—then hear thou.*—If ſins become national, as being committed by the leading, the repreſentative part of a nation, by the bulk of its members in a ſocial capacity, or as overſpreading the generality of a nation ; they muſt be confeſſed in as public and ſocial a capacity as that in which they were committed. When the Lord raiſed up Ezra, and afterwards Nehemiah to be inſtrumental in the reformation of his people, *there aſſembled out of Iſrael, a very great congregation,* and jointly confeſſed their ſins, and *all the people wept* *. Therefore when God would bring his backſliding children to repentance, he commands that all orders of perſons ſhould meet in a ſolemn aſſembly, for confeſſing their ſins, and imploring his mercy. *Gather the people, ſanctify the congregation, aſſemble the elders, gather the children, and thoſe that ſuck the breaſts. Let the prieſts, the miniſters of the Lord, weep between the porch and the altar, and let them ſay ; Spare thy people, O Lord, and give not thine heritage to reproach* †.—Nor is it enough that this confeſſion be ſocial and public ; it muſt alſo be *particular.* Nations, in their pretended reformations, moſt frequently ſatisfy themſelves with a general acknowledgment of ſin, and profeſſion of ſorrow for it. But there ought to be a diſtinct and explicit enumeration of the cauſes of provocation. In this manner was the High-prieſt, by the expreſs command of God, to make confeſſion on the head of the live goat, on the great day of atonement. *He ſhall confeſs over him* ALL *the iniquities of the children of Iſrael, and* ALL *their tranſgreſſions in* ALL *their ſins* ‡. In all the examples of the moſt general and apparently ſincere reformations among God's ancient people, we

VOL. I.   R   may

* Ezr. x. 1. ; Neh. viii. 9.   † Joel ii. 16, 17.   ‡ Lev. xvi. 21.

may obferve great particularity in mentioning thofe fins that were moft offenfive to their God. When he was wroth, becaufe they had rejected him from being king; they entreated Samuel to *pray for them, that they might not die; for,* fay they, *We have added to all our other fins this evil, to afk us a king* *. In the faft proclaimed by Ezra, the people made a particular confeffion of the newly difcovered guilt of mingling with the heathen †. Nehemiah particularly confeffed the guilt of perfons of different ranks in Ifrael. *Neither have our kings, our princes, our priefts, nor our fathers kept thy law, nor hearkened unto thy commandments, and thy teftimonies, wherewith thou didft teftify againft them. For they have not ferved thee in their kingdom, and in thy great goodnefs that thou gaveft them, and in the large and fat land which thou gaveft before them, neither turned they from their wicked works* ‡.

4. This muft be attended with a confeffion of *former* iniquities, of the iniquities of our fathers. Many will be ready to fay; " What have we to do with thefe? " They muft anfwer for themfelves, and not we for " *them.*" But the fins of our anceftors are like a debt lying on any fubject. You know that, in law, he who intromits on a fubject becomes liable for all the debt. So, we ferve ourfelves heirs to the guilt of our forefathers by our own iniquities, by continuing in the practice of the fame fins, or of others that refemble them. In this cafe, we fin WITH *our fathers;* or, LIKE *them, we prove a ftiff-necked and rebellious race.* But either way, we materially approve of all that they have done againft God. National fin is metaphorically reprefented as a fwelling tide, which rifes higher and higher, by the inftrumentality of the children in adding to the iniquity of their fathers: *Our iniquities are* INCREASED OVER *our heads.* It is compared to the growth of a tree, which becomes taller and ftronger every year, till at length it hides its top in
the

* 1 Sam. xii. 19. † Ezr. ix. 10. 14. ‡ Neh. ix. 34, 35.

the clouds.—*Our trespass is* GROWN UP *unto the heavens* *. When the children walk in the steps of their fathers, the guilt is accumulated, and the cry of it waxes louder and louder. This increase of guilt is compared to the growth of man from infancy to maturity, or described, at least, as something growing up with him. In this manner, national sin gathers strength by the activity of one generation after another. *We have sinned against the Lord our God*, saith the Prophet Jeremiah, *we and our fathers, from our* YOUTH *even unto this day* †.

Now, it is just with God to punish the children for the iniquity of their fathers, when they claim it as their own by walking in their ways. Not only does the Scripture uniformly declare, that our *God visits the iniquities of the fathers upon the children*, even unto many *generations of them that hate him;* but reason itself assents to the equity of this procedure. For a nation must still be viewed as one great *whole*, without regard to difference of time, or change of the individuals that constitute it: as it is still esteemed the same river, that comes from one source, and retains one channel and course, although every moment there is the succession of a new body of waters. There is even a considerable difference between the relation that a child bears to his immediate parent, and that which succeeding generations bear to the preceding in a nation. Although the child shall bear his father's iniquity, if he follow his example, yet the guilt is more immediate in the case of a nation. For when the individual parent is dead, the *person* is gone, and quite a different one succeeds. But the *nation* must still be viewed as the same, without regard to the change of persons. It could never, at any period of time, be said, as in the case of individuals, that the nation is properly altered; because, although there be a succession of generations, it is gradual and indiscernible. Thus the Lord often addresses the same people, as if they were still the same persons

---

* Ezr. ix. 6. † Jer. iii. 25.

persons with the generation before them. *Even from the days of your fathers, ye are gone away from mine ordinances* *. To the same purpose, the whole time of God's forbearance, and of the continuance of a dispensation of grace with a wicked nation, is represented as *one day;* because the nation itself is viewed as *one whole*, without regard to succession :—*All day long have I stretched out my hands unto a disobedient and gainsaying people.* The guilt of children is highly aggravated above that of their fathers, if they continue in the same ungodly courses; because the iniquity of their fathers is held up to them as a beacon to deter them from following their wicked example. Therefore, it is only in the exercise of cordial confession, lamentation and repentance that we may warrantably look for deliverance from the guilt of the iniquity of our fathers: for, *saith the Lord, Behold it is written before me; I will not keep silence, but will recompence, even recompence into their bosom, your iniquities, and the iniquities of your fathers together.* And why *recompence the iniquity of the fathers* into the bosom of their children? Because they continued in the same sins :—*your fathers, who have burnt incense upon the mountains, and blasphemed me upon the hills;* THEREFORE *will I measure their* FORMER *work into their bosom* †. So Christ informs the Pharisees, that by killing the Prophets whom he would send, they would *fill up the measure of their fathers*, and bring upon themselves *all the righteous blood shed upon the earth, from the blood of righteous Abel to the blood of Zacharias* ‡. Accordingly we find, that in all the national confessions of Israel, they connected the iniquity of their fathers with their own §.

5. It is necessary that there be a joint and cordial *application* to the *blood* of Christ for *remission*. Why does Solomon so frequently mention in his prayer that temple which he had built? Why does he so particularly

---

* Mal. iii. 7.   † Isa. lxv. 6, 7.   ‡ Mat. xxiii. 32.—35.
§ 2 Chron. xxix. 6.   Ezr. ix. 7.   Psal. cvi. 6, 7.   Neh. ix. 16.—29.

particularly intreat, that God's *eyes may be open towards that house night and day; even towards the place of which he had said; My Name shall be there; that he may hearken to the prayer which his servants should make towards that place*, verse 29.? Why does he speak of it, in the verse immediately under consideration, as not only necessary that *every man should know the plague of his own heart*, but what would seem rather to weaken the climax, as being, in a comparative point of view, a matter of far less moment, that he should *spread forth his hands towards* that *house?* Why does he limit the answer of the prayer of those who might be in a state of captivity, by requiring that they should *pray towards their land, and towards the house built for God's name?* In a word, why does he assume this as an indispensable requisite in every one of the cases supposed? Could there be any charm in looking to the temple, or towards the land where it stood? Could prayer be in itself more acceptable from one quarter of the heavens, than from another? No, surely. All places are in themselves alike to that God, whose *is the earth and the fulness thereof*, who *fills heaven and earth*. But this limitation typically declared the absolute necessity, in every age, of having the eye of faith directed to Him, *the vail* of whose *flesh* was prefigured by the literal temple; to Him, who *in very deed hath dwelt with man upon earth*, although *heaven, yea the heaven of heavens cannot contain* him, the necessity of approaching God in every duty through *the Word made flesh*. Their eyes were to look to that place of which Jehovah had said, *My Name shall be there*, only in relation to that great Prophet, who was to *destroy the temple of his body and raise it up again*, with respect to whom he had long before given them this warning. *Beware of him and obey his voice, for my Name is in him**.

It is to be lamented, that in our public professions of repentance, there should be so great a prevalence of a self-righteous spirit; that our confessions, and prayers,

---

* Exod. xxiii. 21.

prayers, and fupplications fhould be confidered as the meritorious caufe of the removal of God's anger,—or as means to recommend ourfelves to his mercy; while the eye is but faintly directed to the only propitiation. Repentance of fo legal a nature, inftead of enfuring the fuppofed ends, of expiating our fins and averting the Divine indignation, unfpeakably increafes our guilt, and fubjects us to that awful curfe pronounced by the mouth of the Prophet Ifaiah; *Wo to the rebellious children,* faith the Lord, *that take counfel, but not of me; and that cover with a covering, but not of my Spirit; that they may add fin to fin* *. This legal conduct is a confirming evidence of our rebellion againft God. It is an obftinate rejection of his counfel; a weak attempt to fcreen ourfelves from the tremendous effects of his anger, by a covering as feeble as a fpider's web. Nay, it is only an *adding of fin to fin,* of renewed guilt to that formerly contracted, of the fin of our own defiled righteoufnefs to the fin of our unrighteoufnefs. This fin is doubly hateful and difhonouring to God, becaufe it is committed under the pretence of atoning for former guilt, and appeafing incenfed juftice. How extremely different is this conduct, from that commanded by him whofe name is Counfellor, in his addrefs to the lukewarm Church of Laodicea; *I counfel thee to buy of me white raiment that thou mayeft be clothed, and that the fhame of thy nakednefs do not appear* †! He counfels us to accept of his own perfect righteoufnefs as our covering from the piercing eye of Divine Juftice. But we prefer the counfel of our own hearts, and of Satan; and cover ourfelves *with a covering,* although *not of his Spirit.* But our repentance can never be of a right kind, unlefs it entirely renounce itfelf, as the ground of acceptance with God; and be attended with a believing appropriation of the blood of Chrift as the only atonement for fin, as the only meritorious caufe of Divine mercies. Never will public repentance be agreeable to the commandment of God, till there be a united

---

* Ifa. xxx. 1.   † Rev. iii. 18.

united and cordial application to this blood of sprinkling, every man knowing *the plague of his own heart,* and his particular hand in the national guilt; being affected with abounding sins, and the sins of former generations; and thus, under a conviction of the necessity of this precious blood to wash away sin, improving it for his own iniquities, and pleading its efficacy for those of his people. This is intimated to us by the typical ordinance of the *scape-goat* among the Israelites. On the great day of atonement, the High-priest was to lay both his hands upon the head of this goat, and confess over him *all the iniquities of the children of Israel, and all their transgressions in all their sins, putting them upon the head of the goat, and to send him away into the wilderness* *. Thus a whole people ought not only to confess their sins; but, in the exercise of faith, to transfer them over to Christ, who was typified by the scape-goat; that they may be no more remembered.

6. NATIONAL reformation implies solemn public *vowing* to God. When he at first espoused the Israelites to himself, he brought them into a covenant of duty. This they often renewed, after being chargeable with great apostasy. Indeed, we have scarcely an instance of any remarkable reformation among them, or effusion of the Holy Spirit on the Church of Israel, without the performance of this duty. In the history of that great reformation, accomplished by means of Hezekiah, it is not expressly said, that they entered into covenant; but we find the king himself declaring, *It is in mine heart to make a covenant with the Lord God of Israel, that his fierce wrath may turn away from us* †. We do not say that the express form of an oath is absolutely necessary; but sure we are, there can be no true public reformation without the substance of the duty. And this much we find in that reformation: For *in Judah the hand of God was to give them one heart, to do the commandment of the king, and of the princes, by the word of the Lord.*

---

* Lev. xvi. 21. † 2 Chron. xxix. 10.

Lord*. But, in general, the very form was strictly observed. Joshua, before his death, made a covenant with the people, in which he took them engaged to adhere faithfully to God †. That worthy priest, Jehoiada, who was the instrument of reclaiming Israel from the worship of Baal, *made a covenant between the Lord, and the people, and the king, that they should be the Lord's people* ‡. It hath been often objected, that " the example of Israel is not binding on us, " because covenanting was peculiar to them on " account of the theocratical nature of their go- " vernment; and was simply their oath of allegiance " to God as their king, even in a political capacity." It is indeed granted, that this was the nature of their government, and that it is therefore without a parallel. But it does not necessarily follow, that the duty of which we speak was inseparably connected with the theocracy. For God declared the theocracy to be dissolved on the part of the people, when they asked a king like the rest of the nations. Thus he said to Samuel, who judged Israel, when he was displeased at their proposal: *They have not rejected thee, but they have rejected me, that I should not reign over them* §. And although it would seem that the Lord did not entirely dissolve it on his part, yet, if the duty of swearing to him had been indispensably connected with that kind of government, no covenant could have been owned by him, which, like that of Jehoiada, and several others, admitted of an earthly king as a party. Had this solemn oath only or principally respected God as king of the Jewish state, the very admission of another into such an oath, would have made the whole void; for he must have accounted this oath of allegiance to him an insult, when, at the very time, an earthly political head was acknowledged. But whatever general reference this duty had to the judicial, undoubtedly it especially respected the moral law. The only thing particularly mentioned by Joshua, in the covenant that he made,

is

---

* 2 Chron. xxx. 12. † Josh. xxiv. 25. ‡ 2 Chron. xxiii. 16.
§ Sam. viii. 7.

is the worship of the true God in opposition to that of idols *. It is undeniable from the consequence, that this was the thing especially in view in Jehoiada's. For they immediately broke down the images of Baal. Those made by Asa and Josiah were of the same nature †. We are far from saying, that these covenants excluded the ceremonial institutions. In the circumstances of that people, no covenant could have been acceptable with God that did so. They were as much bound to refer to these as we are to our more spiritual ordinances. Nor is it denied, that, in some instances ‡, such solemn engagements expresly contained a judicial penalty, arising from the nature of their dispensation. But the temporal penalty could no more affect the essence of the covenant itself than a penalty affixed to any contract among men can alter its nature. The penalty was merely an addition, suited to their peculiar situation, and entirely distinct from the obligation itself. For the very idea that a penalty suggests is, that something else is the matter of the engagement (*a*).

Vol. I.   S   This

---

* Josh. xxiv. 15.   † 2 Chr. xv. 12.; xxiii. 3.—14.   ‡ 2 Chr. xv. 13.

(*a*) There is reason to apprehend that some are enemies to this duty, because they cannot in their minds separate the idea of public vowing from that of persecution. But if this duty was ever meant, under the New Testament, as an instrument of violence, it was grosly perverted; and in as far as it hath been thus employed, it hath been dreadfully abused. The Israelites were bound to punish errors in doctrine by *civil pains*, because, according to the peculiar nature of their government, heresy was treason against their King. But the *kingdom of heaven* is, in its whole form and administration, at an unspeakably greater distance from the kingdoms of this world, than the legal dispensation was. So far is the King of Zion from giving any encouragement to violence, that it is his unalterable decree, that *all they that take the sword, shall perish with the sword* *. It is by no means the character of the Christian Church, but of Antichrist, and it is his condemnation also, that *he that leadeth into captivity, shall go into captivity, and he that killeth with the sword, must be killed with the sword* †. If the religious opinions of any man do not necessarily endanger the state, that rule certainly applies; *To his own master he standeth or falleth.* And if any one think otherwise, let him answer that question; *Who art thou that judgest another man's servant* ‡? There is but
one

* Mat. xxvi. 52.   † Rev. xiii. 10.   ‡ Rom. xiv. 4.

This duty was also eminently blessed of God at the Reformation from Popery. There is scarcely a Protestant Church that hath not engaged in it. Often in this land hath it been a mean of reviving, or of establishment. Our fathers, when leaving the bosom of the Roman Church, in this manner devoted themselves to God. And in later times, when the Church was groaning under the yoke of Prelacy, after a few had been led to this duty, in a short time the greatest part of the nation, with those of our neighbouring kingdoms, willingly offered themselves to the Lord. It hath, indeed, become fashionable, not only with the enemies of religion or liberty, but with many who are the declared friends of both, to run down the enthusiasm of that period, and indiscriminately to hold up the characters and conduct of the principal actors to derision. But such persons consider not, that it is to those very men, whose characters they so wantonly abuse, whose conduct they, while *at ease*, so rashly condemn, that under providence they are indebted for that religious and civil liberty which they enjoy; that their treasure and blood were the price of those invaluable rights, which they daily boast of, and which other nations envy. We wish not either to deny, or to palliate the excesses of some, who were once engaged in this cause, and afterwards manifested that their hearts were not right with God, or the infirmities of those worthies whom God raised up for such arduous work; although much might be pleaded from the necessity of the times, and from the intimate connection of the natural and spiritual rights of man. But unquestionably there was then a more eminent effusion of the Spirit on the Church of Christ in this land, than either former or later ages have known, and many dated their conversion from that period, who afterwards appeared as eminent witnesses for Jesus, and testified their sincerity by *resisting unto blood*.

That so little is said on this head in the New Testament,

one Lord of conscience. *There is but one Lawgiver, who is able to save, and to destroy:* and the natural inference from this is, *Who art thou that judgest another?* Jam. iv. 12.

tament, need not seem surprising, when it is so clear as a moral duty from the Old, and the subject of many promises that undeniably respect the Gentiles in gospel-times. Some learned writers, indeed, who appear not to have had this duty expressly in their eye, have proved that the word *, sometimes rendered *profession* †, and sometimes *confession* ‡, almost invariably signifies a *covenant*, and that these words, *Let us hold fast the profession*, should be translated, *Let us hold fast the covenant of our faith* §. It seems also difficult to understand the following words in another sense: *This they did, not as we hoped, for first they gave their ownselves to the Lord* **. We cannot imagine that this is meant of the ordinance of the supper, because it was so frequently dispensed in the Apostolic age, that it could never be matter of surprise to an Apostle to find a Christian Church engaged in it. Nor can it with any shadow of reason be supposed to have been a covenant entered into at the formation of these Churches, as particular congregations. Not only does Paul, in the beginning of the chapter, design them *the churches of Macedonia*; but it undeniably appears, from the Acts of the Apostles, that they were regularly constituted long before; nay, that they were planted and established, even before there was a Church among the Corinthians themselves, to whom Paul thus relates their conduct. Were these words to be understood of a covenant confined to the first framing of a Christian Church, they would imply a very gross absurdity,—that Paul expected they should have made a liberal contribution to the Christians at Jerusalem, before they were properly Christians themselves, and that he was agreeably surprised it was otherwise.

SUFFICE it to say, that there are other things retained among the generality of Christians, without dispute, which might bear fully as much as the obligation of this duty. It is evidently, *a reasonable service*, agreeable to the ordinary practice of Christians,

---

* ὁμολογία. † 1 Tim. vi. 12.; 2 Cor. ix. 13.; Heb. iii. 1.; x. 23. ‡ 1 Tim. i. 12. § Vid. Wolfii Cur. Philolog. in 2 Cor. ix. 13.; Heb. iii. 1.; x. 23. ** 2 Cor. viii. 5.

stians, in their secret exercise; nay, to the established method of procedure among men, as to moral obligations. When a Christian hath departed from God, in the indulgence of sin, he renews his engagements to him in the strength of promised grace, and vows that *henceforth he will not go back.* If Job did right in making a covenant with his *eyes,* because they had been instruments in sinning, and snares to his imagination, by administering fewel to corruption; it must be the duty of all those who have enticed one another to sin, or encouraged one another in it, *mutually* and *jointly* to engage, in the most solemn manner, that they will *do no more wickedly.*

When subjects have broken their oath of allegiance to a Prince, he, on their return to him, requires new engagements, and devises stronger bonds, if possible, than those that they have formerly broken. Is the King of Zion the only Sovereign who hath no right to require the strongest obligations from his subjects; to bind them to his service by every moral tie which is of force with the human mind? It is strange, indeed, that men, who in the most common transactions of life, cheerfully submit to solemn oaths, and to a frequent repetition of them; who so often invoke God as a witness and judge, should be so reluctant to deal with him as a party; that those, who without hesitation will swear to man as oft as he pleases, should revolt at the idea of *swearing* so much as once, *to the Lord of Hosts!*

7. This reformation must be *practical.* When Solomon prays for a merciful deliverance to his people, if led captive into the land of the enemy; he not only supposes that they should *repent, and make supplication,* and confess, saying, *We have sinned, and have done perversely;* but that they should renounce the practice of those sins, which had procured Divine vengeance. This is evident from the following words in verses 48. and 49.; *If they shall*—return *unto thee with all their heart, and with all their soul*—*then hear thou.* This is more fully expressed in
the

the parallel paſſage, 2 Chron. vi. 27.—*Hear thou from heaven, and forgive the ſin of thy ſervants, and of thy people Iſrael, when thou haſt taught them the* GOOD WAY *wherein they ſhould walk.* A change of courſe, as well as a change of heart, is included in all true repentance. Our pretended repentance is but a ſolemn mockery of God, unleſs it include practical reformation. Therefore, when the Lord exhorts the Church of Epheſus to repent, he exhorts her alſo to forſake her ſins: *Remember therefore from whence thou art fallen, and repent, and* DO *. All repentance, deſtitute of this, is in God's account only *holding faſt deceit,* and *refuſing to return* †. He complains of this as a demonſtration of the deceitfulneſs of Iſrael, in their profeſſions of repentance, that they turned not from their wicked courſes ‡. *When he ſlew them, then they ſought him; and they returned, and enquired early after God. Nevertheleſs they did flatter him with their mouth, and they lied unto him with their tongues. They turned back and tempted God:—they tempted and provoked the Moſt High God, and kept not his teſtimonies.* In all the examples of real reformation among that people, we find that their profeſſions of repentance were attended by a turning from their wickedneſs. In the time of Ezra, they not only confeſſed their ſins, but ſeparated themſelves from the people of the land, and put away their ſtrange wives §. In the reformation accompliſhed by means of Nehemiah, they ſeparated from Iſrael all the mixed multitude; they ſanctified the houſe of the Lord, which had been profaned; the portion of the Levites, which had been withheld, was given them; they alſo turned from profaning the Sabbath; and the ſtrange wives were again put away **.—Thus it appears, that unleſs *national* repentance hath all the qualities of genuine *perſonal* repentance, it is not of a right kind: and it is reaſonable to think ſo, becauſe the circumſtance of its being national cannot alter the

* Rev. ii. 5. † Jer. viii. 5. ‡ Pſal. lxxviii. 34. 36. 41. 56.
§ Ezr. x. 11.—19. ** Neh. xiii. 3. 8. 9. 12. 19. 28.

the *nature* of the duty itself, but only gives a greater extent to its exercise.

In the *last* place we observe, That this is the surest way of obtaining *deliverance* from *outward plagues* and *public judgments*. This course is pointed out by Solomon, in the prayer before us, verse 37. *If there be in the land famine, if there be pestilence,* &c.—*then hear thou;*—or as it may justly be said, *then thou wilt hear*. For this is not to be viewed as a prayer only, but also as a promise and prophecy of that conduct which the Lord would observe towards his people. The same is declared by Jehosaphat, when he had proclaimed a fast, and assembled all Judah before JEHOVAH, to implore his protection from their enemies *. *If when evil come upon us, as the sword, judgment, or pestilence, or famine, we stand before this house and in thy presence (for thy Name is in this house) and cry unto thee in our affliction, then thou wilt hear and help.* Afterwards we find him addressing the people in this manner; *Hear me, O Judah, and ye inhabitants of Jerusalem, Believe in the Lord your God, so shall you be established* †. And the Lord fought for them, and turned their enemies one against another; and *when they looked unto the multitude; behold they were dead bodies fallen to the earth, and none escaped.* But this declaration of Solomon had the highest attestation possible; for it was confirmed by an immediate revelation from God himself ‡; *and the Lord appeared unto Solomon that night, and said unto him, I have heard thy prayer.*

THROUGH the whole Scriptures, God recommends this repentance of the heart as the most proper course for eviting national calamities. So he speaks by Moses to Israel: *But if thou shalt seek the Lord thy God, thou shalt find him, if thou seek him with all thy heart, and with all thy soul. When thou art in tribulation, and all these things are come upon thee, if thou turn to the Lord thy God, and shalt be obedient to his voice, (for the Lord thy God is a merciful God), he*
will

---

* 2 Chron. xx. 9.   † 2 Chron. xx. 20.   ‡ 2 Chron. vii. 12.

will not forsake thee, neither destroy thee, nor forget the covenant of thy fathers, which he sware unto them *. This course Samuel recommends unto Israel, as that in which they were to expect deliverance from their enemies: *If you do return unto the Lord with all your heart; then put away the strange gods from among you, and prepare your hearts unto the Lord, and seek him only; and he will deliver you out of the hand of the Philistines* †. So the Lord speaks by Jeremiah: *If so be they will hearken, and turn* EVERY MAN *from his evil way, that I may repent me of the evil which I proposed to do unto them, because of the evil of their doings* ‡. Indeed, the Lord is so compassionate, and so unwilling to destroy, that he hath often averted impending judgments from a guilty people, when their reformation was only of an external kind. This he did with regard to the Israelites, even when their repentance was feigned and hypocritical. *When he slew them, then they sought him. Nevertheless, they did flatter him with their mouth, and they lied unto him with their tongues: For their heart was not right with him, neither were they stedfast in his covenant. But he, being full of compassion, forgave their iniquity, and destroyed them not;* Psal. lxxviii. 34, 36, 38. Although the reformation of the Ninevites was only external and temporary, yet the Lord spared them. *God saw their works, that they turned from their evil way; and God repented him of the evil, that he had said he would do unto them, and he did it not* §. But this kind of reformation is not attended by a removal of the Lord's anger. He may suspend the stroke; but he does not avert it altogether. *For all this his anger is not turned away; but his hand is stretched out still.* The punishment is not remitted. It is only suspended for a time: And, we may add, the longer that judgments are delayed, the more heavy are they when inflicted. Thus, it is declared, Lev. xxvi. 23. *If ye will not be reformed by these things, but will walk contrary unto me:*

---

* Deut. iv. 29, 31. See also ch. xxx. 1, 10.   † 1 Sam. vii. 3.
‡ Jer. xxvi. 3. See also ch. xviii. 7, 6. ch. xxxvi. 3.
§ Jonah iii. 10.

me: *then will I also walk contrary unto you, and will punish you yet seven times for your sins.* Although a person or people *break off* their *sins by an outward righteousness,* and their *iniquity by shewing mercy to the poor;* yet it is only *a lengthening of* their *tranquillity* *. This was the case with Nineveh. For, although the Lord spared it at that time, when they outwardly repented at the preaching of Jonah, yet he destroyed it not long after; as was particularly foretold by Nahum in his prophecy. When Elijah had denounced the judgments of God against Ahab, that wicked king *rent his clothes, and put sackcloth upon his flesh, and fasted, and lay in sackcloth, and went softly.* And because he humbled himself, although only in a legal and external way, God brought not the evil in his days. But the judgment was only delayed. For the Lord said, *In his son's days will I bring the evil upon his house* †.

WE see, then, that it is only such a public reformation as is described in the words of our text, when *every man knows the plague of his own heart,* that is succeeded by a real deliverance from threatened, impending, or inflicted judgments; and that the calamity can only be deferred for a little, when the reformation is merely external. We may consider the doctrine as applicable to us, in the present melancholy situation of affairs. It must naturally have occurred to every thinking person in this nation, that God hath, this season, been threatening us with his three great judgments, the Sword, the Pestilence, and the Famine ‡. The Sword has not only been threatened; but it has actually desolated our borders. During the progress of a long and fatal war, many thousands of our countrymen, and many thousands of our brethren on the other side of the Atlantic, have fallen victims to its cruel devastations. Our once victorious fleets have turned their backs to their enemies: and *the desired haven* hath been the tomb of many of our

---

* Dan. iv. 27. † 1 Kings xxi. 27, 29.
‡ This Sermon was preached in November 1782.

our mariners. There has been a general apprehenſion of an invaſion from ſome foreign foes: and if we judge of the juſtneſs of our fears by the greatneſs of our demerit, we muſt conclude that we have too much reaſon for theſe apprehenſions. If we compare them with God's awful threatenings, denounced in like circumſtances, we may well tremble. For this is his declaration: *I will bring a ſword upon you, that ſhall avenge the quarrel of my covenant* *. This ſeaſon we have alſo been threatened with the Peſtilence. A contagious diſorder hath prevailed, which, if it hath not ſwept off many, has yet infected the greateſt part. Can we here paſs over in ſilence the mercy which the Lord mixes with his judgments? This ſtroke has been very gentle, as if it were a premonition of a far more ſevere viſitation, if we continue in our ſins; and, at the ſame time, a loud call to avoid farther calamity, by turning to the Lord our God. Whatever phyſical theories may be formed about this diſeaſe, we muſt ultimately reſolve our difficulties by one of a religious kind,—the anger of the Lord againſt a guilty people. And if we go on in our national treſpaſſes, unqueſtionably we have the greateſt reaſon to dread more tremendous diſplays of his indignation in this manner. For, in the ſame paſſage in which he threatens the Sword *to avenge the quarrel of his covenant,* the Peſtilence alſo is denounced: *If you will not be informed by me by theſe things,—when you are gathered together within your cities, I will ſend the peſtilence among you, and you ſhall be delivered into the hand of the enemy.* Can the moſt ignorant or hardened among us be blind to the Lord's controverſy with regard to the harveſt? He hath been evidently frowning through the whole ſeaſon. Do we not already feel the effects of his judgment in this reſpect? And do not the preſent gloomy appearances forbode that we ſhall feel them with greater ſeverity? At any rate, although the Lord ſhould be pleaſed to prevent our fears in the iſſue, the preſent diſpenſations of his Pro-

* Lev. xxvi. 25.

vidence wear a very threatening aspect, and loudly declare, that if we be not visited with Famine, it is only because he *is slow to anger*, and doth *not stir up all his wrath*. In this respect, the Providence of God concurs with his Word. For in the passage already referred to, not only are the Sword and Pestilence threatened, but Famine also. *And when I have broken the staff of your bread, ten women shall bake your bread in one oven; and they shall deliver you your bread again by weight; and ye shall eat it, and not be satisfied.* Are we then threatened with judgments so awful? Do we already feel them in some measure? And shall we not consider these things as a call to turn to the Lord by national repentance? You see the only way in which this repentance can be real, in which you may expect a merciful deliverance from judgments. It is by turning to him with the heart, by knowing *every man the plague of his own heart.* For *if there be in the land famine, if there be pestilence, blasting, mildew, locust, or if there be caterpillar: if their enemy besiege them in the land of their cities; whatever plague, whatsoever sickness there be: what prayer and supplication soever be made by any man, or by all thy people Israel, who shall know every man the plague of his own heart, and spread forth his hands towards this house: then thou wilt hear in heaven thy dwelling-place, and forgive, and do, and give to every man according to his ways, whose heart thou knowest.* The Lord promises, that when he is intreated in this manner, he will *forgive their sin and heal their land**. Every one of you should be active, according to your different stations, in promoting reformation among others. If the nation should still continue obstinate in wickedness; yet, as individuals, and as a congregation professing to witness against the defections, both of former, and of present times, it is *your* duty to return to the Lord, by searching out *every man the plague of his own heart*, and saying, in deep contrition, *What have I done?* Thus, you will at least deliver your own souls; and perhaps the Lord may

---

* 2 Chron. vii. 14.

Ser. 7. *National Reformation and Deliverance.* 147

may spare you in the day of public calamity. You should also be earnest in prayer, that he may bring others to repentance, that he may turn the nation in general to himself, and thus *turn from the fierceness of his anger against us.* Seek, that the Lord may give you the same spirit and exercise with the Prophet Jeremiah, and that his language may be really yours : *O! that my head were waters, and mine eyes a fountain of tears, that I might weep day and night for the sins of the daughter of my people.*

We shall conclude the discourse with some more particular improvement of the subject.

We infer, 1. The necessity of searching the heart. We have endeavoured to illustrate the necessity and usefulness of the knowledge of it. Now, the evidences of the necessity of this knowledge are just so many arguments for self-examination. For we can only expect acquaintance with our hearts in the path of commanded duty. And we are expressly enjoined to examine them carefully by the word, depending on the promised direction of the Spirit. The Lord often, in a sovereign manner, discovers to a sinner his heart, when he is in a state of security and indifference. But it is incumbent on us to be in the use of instituted means; and God hath appointed this, of self-examination, as a special mean for attaining the knowledge of the heart.

2. That it is by the heart that God judgeth of a man's profession of religion. He does not estimate the worth of religious duties by their multitude, by the apparent fervency of the worshipper, or by the time spent in the performance of them. But he tries whether they proceed from the heart. Often a poor weak prayer is accepted of him, as flowing from the heart; when another, delivered with the greatest fluency of diction and warmth of natural affection, is rejected, because it proceeds not from this source. These services only are acceptable to him, in which the spirit is engaged. Therefore, he here requires the knowledge of the heart as necessary to every kind of prayer

prayer or fupplication. God judgeth in a very different manner from man. For *the Lord feeth not as man feeth: for man looketh on the outward appearance; but the Lord looketh on the heart.* We judge of a man's heart by his profeffion, taken in conjunction with his deportment; but God judgeth both of a man's profeffion, and of his deportment, by his heart.

3. That the Lord employs different means in bringing men to the knowledge of their hearts. The ordinary ftated mean, under the influence of the Spirit, is the Word. But if perfons continue to reject this, when God is about to turn them to himfelf, he often vifits them with the rod. Perfonal or public afflictions are fometimes fanctified for this purpofe. The Lord can make famine, or fword, or peftilence efficacious, where the Word has long been rejected. This is fuppofed in the words of our text, viewed in their connection. But even when finners are brought to know themfelves by means of the rod, it is attended by, and ufed in fubferviency to the Word, which is the great ordinance of God for falvation.

From this fubject, you, who have obtained a faving acquaintance with your hearts, may be exhorted.

1. To cultivate this acquaintance. You, who are God's children, have indeed feen them; but you have not feen all their wickednefs, nor can you fee it all in this world. You muft attain perfection in knowledge, before you can juftly know the former evils of your own hearts. In that happy place, where you fhall be completely delivered from their plagues, you will fee with the cleareft light the unfpeakable evil of them. There you will look back on them with fafety, when you are *brought through fire, and through water.* Did the Chriftian in this world fee all the wickednefs of his own heart, it would be in danger of driving him to defpair. But although you cannot now fully difcover this myftery of iniquity, it is indifpenfably incumbent on you to be ftill preffing after farther knowledge of it; and, for this end, to be much engaged in felf-examination. This
is

is not merely neceffary when you are about to make folemn approaches to God. It fhould be your daily exercife. Corruption is ftill working in your hearts. You fhould, therefore, ftill keep a ftrict eye on it, and diligently inveftigate its workings. Sometimes it changes its manner of operation, and takes a new channel. It appears to the believer in an unexpected form. When it thus changes its appearance, he is in danger of being overcome, before he obferve its machinations. The frequent exercife of self-examination will greatly affift you in prayer. Thus you will know what you need to afk of God, what bleffings are moft fuitable to your prefent neceffities, what iniquities you need efpecially to have fubdued. It will tend greatly to keep the confcience pure, and without offence. It will alfo be an excellent help to the exercife of mortification; and to this exercife we would alfo

2. EXHORT you. It is not enough that you feek farther acquaintance with your hearts. You muft more and more ftrive for the deftruction of their iniquities. Beware of thinking that fin is fufficiently fubdued. If you indulge this idea, you will certainly fall before your lufts. If you imagine that *your mountain ftands ftrong*, and that you *fhall never be moved*, you will provoke the Lord to *hide his face*. The Ifraelites were commanded to carry on war with Amalek *from generation to generation.* Sin is a fpiritual Amalek in your hearts, with which you muft not even make a truce. There muft be no ceffation of arms in the Chriftian warfare. In this fenfe we may apply the word of the Lord by the Prophet Jeremiah; *Curfed be he that doth the work of the Lord deceitfully; and curfed be he that keepeth back his fword from blood*[*]. Self-examination may be confidered as an hand-maid to mortification. Therefore, when you have difcovered the plagues of the heart, you fhould bring them anew to the crofs of Chrift, that you may be *crucified with* him, and fo *live.* For, *if ye do mor-*

tify

---

[*] Jer. xlviii. 10.

tify the deeds of the body, ye shall live. Mortify therefore your members which are on the earth, and be concerned wholly to *put off the old man with his deeds.* But beware of attempting this duty in your own strength, either natural or spiritual. It is only *through the Spirit* that you can *mortify the deeds of the body.* On every renewed discovery of sin, make a renewed application to the blood of the Saviour. Thus you will receive a daily pardon of the guilt contracted against God as your Father, and daily intimations of that irrevocable pardon, which hath formerly been intimated to your consciences, the sense of which you are apt to lose by your transgressions. Always, when you see or feel your plagues, as being stung by the fiery serpents of sin, turn the eye of faith to *the Son of man,* who was and is *lifted up.*

But here, perhaps, some doubting person may inquire, " How shall I know if I have obtained a saving " acquaintance with the plague of my heart?" In answer to this, you may attend to the following things. As it is our duty to endeavour to *strengthen the weak hands, and confirm the feeble knees,* and also ministerially to separate *between the clean and the unclean;* so, dear brethren, it is your duty to try yourselves, while we mention some scriptural evidences for this purpose. If you are savingly acquainted with *the plague of your own heart,* you have seen it to be hateful, as being contrary to the holy God, to his nature, and to his law; as being the very reverse of infinite purity. You hate sin, because it is that *abominable thing* which God *hateth.* You have seen yourselves to be miserable on account of it. You have been convinced that you were exposed by sin to the wrath and curse of God, both in this life and in that which is to come. But, notwithstanding the destructive nature of sin, you desire to hate it, more because it is abominable to God, than because it is ruining to yourselves. It is not so much a discovery of its danger, as of its evil, that makes you abhor it. You loathe yourselves on account of this plague. You cannot

Ser. 7. *National Reformation and Deliverance.* 151

not look on yourselves, as sinners, with any satisfaction. Like Job, you abhor yourselves, and *repent in dust and in ashes*. You are fully convinced that you cannot recover yourselves from it; that, as soon might *the Ethiopian change his skin, or the leopard his spots*; that all your washings could never make you clean; that they could only defile you the more. You have seen Christ as the only remedy. You are persuaded that there is nothing, either in heaven or on earth, that can wash away the guilt and the filth of your sin, but the blood of Jesus; that *there is not another name under heaven, given among men, by which you can be saved*. You are willing to embrace him as your remedy. You adore the wisdom and the love of God, in providing one so infinitely precious; and it is the unfeigned and earnest desire of your hearts, to receive him, who is *come in the name of God to save you*. You could not think of parting with Christ, of renouncing all lot and portion in him, for ten thousand worlds. You desire to claim him, in the seraphic language of the Psalmist; *Whom have I in heaven but thee, and there is none in all the earth that I desire besides thee*. You wish to apply to the fountain of his blood, that you may be washed from all sin, and from all uncleanness. The plague of the heart is your daily burden. It is the greatest grief that ever you had in the world, that you so greatly dishonour God. While *in this tabernacle, you groan, being burdened*: you experimentally know the propriety, the peculiar emphasis of the Apostle's language, *O! wretched man that I am; and who shall deliver me from the body of this death?* In a word, it is your constant aim to get sin mortified and subdued. You daily endeavour to come to the cross, that your corruptions may be *nailed* to it. There is no lust whatsoever in your heart, that you wish to spare. Those that are most pleasant to the old man, you especially want to have destroyed. The sin, that to the unrenewed part is precious as a *right eye*, you endeavour to *pluck out;* that which is useful as a *right hand,*

hand, you strive to *cut off, and cast from you.* Your dependence is on the promise, *He will subdue our iniquities.* This you make your plea at the throne. Is this the state of thy heart, desponding disciple? Then thou mayest safely conclude, that thou art indeed truly acquainted with its plague. *Sin shall not have dominion over you, for you are not under the law, but under grace.*

Those who are still unacquainted with their own hearts may be exhorted to try the duty of self-examination. While engaged in this duty, in obedience to the command of God, he may be pleased to give you a saving discovery of them. Whether this should be the result or not, it is, at any rate, your indispensable duty; for you know that God requires it: *Examine yourselves, prove your ownselves, know ye not your ownselves, how that Christ is in you, except ye be reprobates?* The importance of the duty, and the difficulties attending the due performance of it, instead of discouraging you, should be improved as motives not only exciting you to try it, but to use the greatest diligence and earnestness. Both the importance of the duty, and its concomitant difficulties are implied in this threefold exhortation. The very expressions used denote the necessary diligence. The word rendered *prove* is a metaphor taken from the trial of metals by the touchstone or otherwise. Therefore, it intimates the accuracy and impartiality which are requisite in this investigation. As the Israelites were obliged to search their houses, before eating the passover, lest any fragment of leaven should be any where concealed; so you must assiduously search your hearts for the discovery of every sin. Take the word of God for your *rule.* This is the standard by which you must judge of your hearts. *To the law, and to the testimony: if they speak not according to this word, it is because there is no light in them.* This word is *a discerner of the thoughts and intents of the heart.*— Earnestly pray for the Holy Spirit as your *guide.* Say unto God, *O! send forth thy light and thy truth,*
the

the light of the Spirit to attend the truth of the word. It is his promise, *I will put my Spirit in you,—then shall ye remember your own evil ways. I will remember my covenant with thee,—that thou mayest remember and be confounded, and never open thy mouth any more, because of thy shame; when I am pacified toward thee, for all that thou hast done, faith the Lord God* *. Engage in this duty with due deliberation. It must not be done carelesly. Consider that your eternal all is at stake. You should chuse a proper time and place, without incurring the danger of interruption or distraction. Try yourselves as in the presence of God, and endeavour to get your spirits impressed with an awful sense of his omniscience. Remember that he addresses you in this manner; *Be still, and know that I am God.*—When you have done all you can in the way of duty, acknowledge the unprofitableness of your service; and be concerned to roll the work on God himself, pleading that he would accomplish it for you. Let this be your prayer; *Search me, O God, and know my heart; try me, and know my thoughts.*—Whatever discoveries you obtain of your hearts, come to God in earnest prayer for the destruction of their plagues; and endeavour a cordial application to the blood of Christ, both for justification and sanctification; that *the body of sin may be destroyed, that henceforth you may not serve sin.*

* Ezek. xxxvi. 27,—31. Ch. xvi. 62, 63.

SERMON VIII.

On the ATHEISM of the HEART.

Psalm xiv. 1.

The fool hath said in his heart, There is no God.

*H*E *that cometh unto God*, faith the Holy Spirit, *must believe that he is.* Without a firm perfuafion of his being and perfections, there can be no acceptable worfhip. That fervice which proceeds not from faith in God, according to the revelation that he hath given of himfelf in the Word, is no better than idolatry: for although we profefs to worfhip the true God, if we do not really believe in him as fuch, it is the fame as if we worfhipped a falfe god. Now, idolatry in God's account is nothing better than atheifm; becaufe if we do not worfhip the true God, ftrictly fpeaking we worfhip no God at all; for *an idol is nothing in the world.* Therefore the Spirit of God reprefents the idolatrous Heathens as Atheifts. They are faid to be *without God in the world*, or, as the expreffion is, according to the original, *Atheifts in the world.* Thus it appears that the worfhip offered to God that flows not from faith in him, according to his own revelation, is the creature of our own fancy. Nay, it is a folemn mockery of the Majefty of heaven, and a profanation of his bleffed name under the pretence of honouring it. If we apply this rule to the fervices of the greateft part of gofpel-hearers, it is to be feared they will be *found wanting.* For the heart is naturally a fink of atheifm. Therefore the Holy Spirit gives this affecting defcription of the natural man; *The fool hath faid in his heart, there is no God.*

THE

THE perſon ſpoken of is ſaid to be a *fool*. This phraſe, as here uſed, is not to be confined, according to its full meaning, to one who is really deprived of the exerciſe of reaſon. We muſt underſtand it of the ſinner;—not merely of him who is addicted to the habits of vice, and to a life of groſs impiety; but of every one who is under the power of the natural wickedneſs of his heart, under the dominion of ſin, or in an unrenewed ſtate; although his life ſhould be externally ſober and blameleſs. And in this ſenſe it is moſt frequently and almoſt univerſally uſed in Scripture. So it is ſaid, Pſal. xlix. 10. *The fool, and the brutiſh perſon periſh;*—and, Eccleſ. ii. 14. *The fool walketh in darkneſs*. In both theſe places the expreſſion evidently denotes that folly which is of a ſpiritual kind. Do men in general reckon him a fool, who, in the concerns of this life, gives himſelf up to indolence, indifference and prodigality; while they confer the character of a wiſe man on him who, by honeſt diligence, endeavours to provide a ſufficient ſuſtenance for himſelf and family? With far more reaſon is the man whoſe mind is ſo engroſſed by the trifles of time that he neglects eternity, in a ſpiritual ſenſe pronounced to be a fool; as oppoſed to him, whoſe labour and anxiety are eſpecially engaged about that portion, which is large as the unlimited deſires, and laſting as the endleſs duration of his ſoul. It is declared of this ſpiritual fool, that he hath ſaid in his heart, *There is no God*. Theſe words do not expreſs the perſuaſion of the ſinner, but his affection and deſire. He is not convinced that there is no God, but he wiſhes that there were none. Thus, the expreſſion may be ſtrictly and literally read as a wiſh or deſire; *The fool hath ſaid in his heart, No God*. For the words, *there is*, are a ſupplement. He ſays it *in his heart*. For few will dare to avow it to the world. Aſk the unregenerate man, if he believes the exiſtence of a God? He will be enraged at the queſtion, as offering him the higheſt inſult. 'Yet God, who cannot err,

directly

directly charges him with atheism. It is observable here that he is not introduced as saying, *There is no* JEHOVAH, this being that name which peculiarly denotes the existence of God. But the language ascribed to him is, *There is no Elohim.* This word in the original denotes God as the Governor of the world; and the use of it here expresses the wish of the sinner that there were no Providence, that God did not observe his conduct, and that he would not call him to an account.

The words thus viewed afford the following doctrinal proposition; That every unrenewed man is under the power of atheism.

The plan we propose in discoursing from them is,

I. To make some general observations on the subject;

II. To endeavour to show that every natural man is under the power of atheism; and,

III. To illustrate the consequences of this inward depravity.

The first thing proposed is to make some general observations on the subject.

1. It may be observed, that there cannot be a *speculative* atheist in the world. By a speculative atheist we mean one who is firmly convinced in his mind that there is no God. Many, under the temporary influence of Satan's temptations and power of their own corruption, have called in question the existence of a God. But we cannot believe that there ever was any person in his senses who, for any length of time, disbelieved this great and fundamental truth. Some men, from the wickedness of their hearts, have tried to make others believe that this was their creed; but we are persuaded, that even then, amidst all their pretensions, they have found it impossible to shake their minds loose of their convictions of the being of God. There are so many invincible demonstrations

of this truth, that the human mind, in its worſt ſtate, cannot entirely reſiſt their force.—The works of Creation contain ſo powerful a demonſtration of the exiſtence of the Supreme Being, that a man muſt wilfully ſhut his eyes, ere he can preſume to deny it. The whole of his works are ſo wonderful, and ſo exactly correſpondent to the end deſigned in their creation, that we muſt neceſſarily acknowledge that they could never be produced by any creature, and that they could only be the effect of infinite power concurring with infinite wiſdom. It is not conſiſtent with reaſon to ſuppoſe, that this creation, ſo regularly and beautifully diſpoſed, could have been caſt into its preſent form by a fortuitous concourſe of atoms, as ſome have pretended. Blind chance could never be the cauſe of effects ſo univerſally well-ordered. They could proceed from an intelligent Being only: and this Being can be no other than God.—The works of Providence are alſo a demonſtration of the exiſtence of God. Who, but an infinite Being, could ſupport the world in the utmoſt regularity for ſuch a long courſe of ages, although conſtantly expoſed to deſtruction by the force of devouring elements, which carry on a perpetual war againſt each other, and ſeem to threaten the univerſe in general? God's dealings with man in his moral government declare his being and preſence. Wickedneſs does not in this life paſs unpuniſhed; for men would thence conclude that there was no Providence. Nor are all evil actions puniſhed; leſt men ſhould infer that there was no ſtate of retribution. But there is ſuch a mixture of mercy and juſtice diſcernible in the management of the world, that there is evidently much reſerved for a future ſtate, both in the way of reward and puniſhment: and, at the ſame time, there are ſuch inſtances of righteouſneſs being rewarded, and of wickedneſs being puniſhed, even in this life, as clearly to manifeſt that there is a God who *judgeth in the earth.*

THIS

This truth is further demonstrated by the tendency of all earthly things to destruction. For, when we see our fellow-creatures in general daily perishing around us; the greatest kingdoms and empires, after gradually arriving at the summit of their glory, falling to ruin; immeasurable oceans washing themselves away by their perpetual action; and the earth on which we tread mouldering down to destruction, or consuming itself by its own fires;—we are laid under the necessity of concluding, that there must be some one great cause and last end, who, as he hath at first given being to this universe, is gradually unhinging its frame and bringing it forward to dissolution. Job seems to have had this view of matters. He speaks as one fully satisfied that the constant changes of this lower world were a convincing proof of the being and agency of a supreme cause. *The waters fail from the sea, and the flood decayeth and drieth up.—And surely the mountain falling cometh to nought: and the rock is removed out of his place.—The waters wear the stones:* THOU *washest away the things which grow out of the dust of the earth, and* THOU *destroyest the hope of man* *.—To find a proof of the existence of a Deity, man needs not go farther than himself. He cannot attentively view the structure of his body, which is formed with such singular wisdom, and discovers so much beauty and regularity; or consider the powers of his soul, which place him so far above the brute creation, and capacitate him for enjoyments so ineffably superior to any thing this world can afford; nor can he contemplate the admirable union of two principles so exceedingly different as gross matter and pure spirit; without exclaiming with heart-felt astonishment; *I am fearfully and wonderfully made.* Nor acting as a rational creature, can he withhold this inference; *He that built all things is God.*

The dictates of conscience also afford the same testimony. There is a witness in man's breast, proclaiming this great truth, which all the subtilty, labour

---

* Job. xiv. 11, 18, 19.

bour, and ingenuity of man, will never be able to silence. Whence proceed those terrors of conscience, which the most wicked men, even such as have gloried in atheism, have felt at times, but from an inward conviction, and Divine impression on their minds, of the existence of God? This is a witness, which, however it may be silenced for a time, will speak out to the confusion of the sinner, sooner or later. This is so convincing an argument, that heathens themselves cannot resist its influence. For the Apostle declares, that *the Gentiles, who have not the law, are a law unto themselves; which shows the work of the law written in their hearts, their conscience also bearing witness, and their thoughts the mean while accusing, or else excusing one another* *.—This is a truth that receives the consent of all nations. However different from each other, or false in themselves their notions on this subject, no nation has ever been found that did not believe the being of a God. Some, indeed, proceed so far in absurdity and impiety, as to worship the Devil. But even this horrible extreme demonstrates their secret conviction of the existence of some invisible Power, totally distinct from chance or secondary causes, to whose agency the prosperous or calamitous events of life must be ascribed.

2. There have been, and there are many *heart-atheists*. By this designation we mean those, who, although they do not in their judgments disbelieve this fundamental doctrine, yet ardently wish in their hearts that they had no ground to believe it. A sense of sin, and a conviction of its desert, have, by reason of their unbelief, produced this impious wish. When men consider themselves as atrocious transgressors of God's law, as rebels against the Sovereign of heaven and earth, they feel a desire that there were no God to observe their conduct, and to punish them for it. The sinner, from his violent attachment to a course of iniquity, is apt to imagine that it would be a happy thing for him, were this the case; for then he

---

* Rom. ii. 14, 15.

he would have full scope in sin; he would act the brute without any restraint, and without any sting from conscience; he would cautiously endeavour to escape punishment from men, and he would be delivered from the appalling apprehension of any other. He would be content to die the death of a beast, whose *spirit goeth downward*, that he might enjoy, without any interruption, the envied life of a beast. The existence of a God is so ungrateful an idea to a wicked man, that he wishes by all means to get rid of it. Hence it is, that when his conscience accuses him, and threatens him with destruction, instead of attempting a reformation of his life, or inquiring into the real state of his heart, he plunges anew into the mire of iniquity, and wallows there till he has choked all his convictions. This awful truth, which haunts him as his own shadow, he wishes buried in eternal oblivion. Say, guilty sinner, hast thou not sometimes felt such a wish in thy heart? When alarmed by a sense of God's justice, pursuing thee as a wretch obnoxious to everlasting destruction, hast thou not perceived a secret desire in thy soul, discovering itself in such language as this: "O! what a happy "thing would it be for me, if there were *no God?*"

3. There are many *practical* atheists in the world, even among those who make a profession of Christianity. Such men, although they believe the being of God, do notwithstanding live as if there were none; and thus *by works deny him.* Their life is a practical denial of his being, because it is a life of impiety. In this sense the Psalmist understood it. *The transgression of the wicked saith within my heart, that there is no fear of God before his eyes**. It said so within his heart. Their sinful conduct led him to form this judgment concerning them. The wicked are no more impressed by a sense of the presence of the great God, than if he were not the witness and judge of their actions. What shall we think of drunkards, gluttons, profane swearers, Sabbath-breakers, unclean persons, and the like? We must certainly

account

---

* Psal. xxxvi. 1.

account them practical Atheists. They live as if they were never to die. They spend their time, as if there were no eternity to follow. They take up their rest in sensual enjoyments, like that fool, who having filled his granaries, said to his soul; *Take thine ease;* not reflecting that in a moment their souls may be required of them. It is the language of their conduct, *Who is the Lord, that we should obey him? We know not the Lord, neither will* we *let our lusts and idols go. Depart from us, for we desire not the knowledge of thy ways.* Practical Atheists are more inconsistent than mortal Deists, who make the nearest approach to speculative atheism, by denying the mortality of the soul, and a future state. For if men can once persuade themselves that their souls shall perish with their bodies, and that there shall be no awful hereafter, when they must give an account of the deeds done in the body; it is not surprising that they should say to themselves, *Let us eat and drink, for to-morrow we shall die.* But while others profess to believe that God will assuredly reckon with them, and that their souls will endure for ever, either in a state of consummate blessedness, or of inconceivable misery; how astonishing is it, that these affecting and important truths should have no influence on their hearts or lives! They are self-murderers; for they wilfully and resolutely devote their never-dying souls to *everlasting destruction from the presence of the Lord, and from the glory of his power.*

4. Every man is *naturally* an Atheist in heart. The justness of this observation, however degrading to the powers of human nature, which are in general so highly extolled, will evidently appear, if we consider that every man is naturally under the absolute dominion of sin. Now, where sin is, there are all its seeds and branches; and atheism, however shocking, will be found among the rest. This may be traced to the natural depravity of the heart, as its root. By the transgression of God's covenant, our nature became entirely corrupt. It was transformed into a copious

fountain of all iniquity. And atheism stands at the head of that black list of sins, which defile the heart of man, and render him *guilty before God.* This was the first sin that made its appearance in the world. It introduced every other in its train. It assumed the dominion in his heart, before he outwardly transgressed the law. Whence was it that our first parents presumed to eat of that tree, the use of which God had denied them, but from the entrance of atheism into their hearts. They listened to the suggestions of the Devil, and obeyed him rather than God. Their beneficent Creator had given them all earthly blessings, and restricted them only as to one tree in paradise. Satan stepped in with his temptations? *Yea,* saith he, *hath God said, Ye shall not eat of every tree of the garden?* and, at the instigation of Satan, they disbelieved God; and so they fell. Atheism first stole into their hearts; then it broke forth in their practice; and produced the most baleful consequences to themselves and all their posterity. And as atheism introduced every other sin into the world, there is atheism in every sin that a man commits. As it was the origin of the evil of sin, so the greatest malignity that is in sin consists in this, that it is a stroke at the very being of God. Every sin is an attempt to deprive him of Deity; for it is a rebellion against his sovereign authority and moral government. Sin is a denial of subjection to the law of God, and of consequence a virtual denial of his essence: for unless he be God Supreme, and entitled to universal homage and obedience, he cannot be God.

5. The natural atheism of the heart is greatly *confirmed* and *increased* by continuance in *sin.* This holds as to every particular corruption. As the seeds of all sin are in every heart, whence is it that in some many of them do not spring up as in others? Either they are sanctified from the womb, and the living principle of sin is thus destroyed as to its reign, ere it acquire strength from habit; or they are laid under greater

greater reftraint by common grace; or fin takes a different channel in them from that in which it appears in others. But while any remain under the dominion of fin, notwithftanding all common reftraints, it is always confirmed and increafed by practice. If a man be not delivered from the natural power of atheifm, it takes a firmer hold of his heart, and fpreads its bitter roots more extenfively. He who, perhaps, in confequence of a religious education, had in his early years a fear of many fins, a fenfe of the neceffity of prayer and other duties, by gradually yielding to fin, at length proceeds fo far as to *laugh at the fhaking of the fpear.* Hence it is that fome, who at firft have only *faid in their hearts,* at length prefume to fay even with their lips, *there is no God.* From the hiftory of the fall of our firft parent, we have a ftriking proof of the rapid progrefs of atheifm in the heart. As it entered, in confequence of temptation, by means of a doubt, after outwardly tranfgreffing the law, he fhows that he is loft to a fenfe of the Divine perfections; for he tries to hide himfelf, as if the fhadow of a few leaves could conceal him from that eye before which *hell is naked, and deftruction hath no covering.* Nay, to fuch a pitch does atheifm rife in his heart, that he lies in the very face of God. He fays, *I was afraid, becaufe I was naked;* when it was not his bodily nakednefs, but the caufe of it, that filled him with terror. He even proceeds fo far, as virtually to accufe God as the author of fin: *The woman, whom thou gaveft to be with me, fhe gave me of the tree, and I did eat.* Since atheifm went thus far in its very birth, we need not wonder that in thefe laft times, men who have gone as far on this head, in a fpeculative way, as the human mind can well go, have dared to exhibit the fame charge againft their Maker. When, therefore, we fpeak of *natural,* or of *heart-atheifm,* we do not intend that principle merely as it at firft fubfifts in the heart, but as confirmed by continuance in a natural ftate.

6. There

6. THERE is atheism in the heart of every *Believer*. This, indeed, as well as every other lust, is subdued, when the power of sin is broken in regeneration; so that he is not, like the unregenerate, under its dominion. But it still hath, and will continue to have a being in the heart, till the old man be fully destroyed. Nay, at times it greatly prevails. Hence it is that he feels so much distraction, deadness and indifference in the performance of religious duties. Hence he so often offends his God, and even falls into sins which are atrocious in their nature, and attended by very aggravating circumstances; although, for former offences of the same, or of a similar kind, he has been sharply reproved by his own conscience, by the convincing influences of the Spirit, and by fatherly chastisements. For were the impression of the being of God sufficiently powerful, it would prevent him from offending his loving and compassionate Father by the transgression of his law. Thus, we discern atheism breaking out in the exercise of eminent saints, whose lives are recorded in Scripture. From this corruption Asaph seems to have had various assaults. When he saw the afflictions of the righteous, and the prosperity of the wicked, he was in danger of denying the reality of all religion, and for a moment spoke the language of atheism. *Verily, I have cleansed my heart in vain, and washed my hands in innocence;* Psal. lxxiii. 13. But this was only a temporary atheism, unlike to that of the unregenerate, which continues with them as long as they are estranged from God. For this was his exercise, only till he went into the sanctuary of God. Then he *understood their end*. He also discovered the same atheistical propensity with regard to his own experience, when he said; *Hath the Lord forgotten to be gracious;* Psal. lxxvii. 7. But he soon learned that this was his *infirmity*. David gives an account of the working of the same corruption. *I said in my haste, All men are liars;* Psal. cxvi. 11. But when freed from it, so great is his sense of the mercy and importance

importance of the deliverance, that he is at a loss to know what he should *render to the Lord for his benefits;* because he had *delivered his soul from death,* his *eyes from tears, and* his *feet from falling.*

The observations already offered on this subject suggest to us the following inference; That the power of sin in the heart of man, must be truly dreadful, and its nature unspeakably abominable, as it practically denies the being of God. This is the greatest affront that can possibly be offered to him. It is the greatest presumption that the creature is capable of, to deny the existence of his Creator, or to wish and desire in his heart that there were no God.

From this subject, melancholy as it is, a ray of comfort breaks forth to the children of God amidst all their adversities. For this strange language, *There is no God,* is that of fools only. The wicked heart would rejoice if this assertion were true. But this, Believer, would be thy greatest grief. It would rob thee of all the sweetness of life, of all thy riches for time and eternity. For this is their foundation, that there is a God; and herein they consist, that this God is thy God. He is thy portion; and were it possible thou couldest be deprived of him, nothing in the universe could supply his place to thee. He is thy God in covenant, engaged to be thine for ever. For he hath said, *I will make an everlasting covenant with them, that I will not turn away from them to do them good, but I will put my fear in their hearts, that they shall not depart from me.* It is thy greatest consolation, that thou canst claim him as thine, and say with assured confidence, *This God is my God, and he will be my guide* over *death.* All the perfections of God are on thy side. His wisdom is engaged for thy direction, his power for thy protection, his holiness for thy sanctification; his justice ascertains thy pardon; his love secures the communications of his Holy Spirit to thee; and his faithfulness

is

is pledged for thy preservation in a state of grace, and for thy admission into glory at length.

You, whose hearts habitually discover their enmity against God by such impious wishes, may learn from this subject the necessity of entreating a discovery of your natural folly. For this is the source of all these atheistical thoughts and desires. *Ask wisdom of God.* By receiving this you will have *the fear of the Lord.* For this is *the beginning of wisdom.* If you had this fear of God, you would be actuated by a true and firm faith in his being. Plead that he may deliver you from folly, open your eyes to your danger while at a distance from him, reveal himself to you in his dear Son, and make you wise to eternal salvation.

SERMON IX.

On the EVIDENCES of HEART-ATHEISM.

Psalms, xiv. 1.

The fool hath said in his heart, There is no God.

THE world we live in is a world of fools. The far greater part of mankind act a part entirely irrational. So great is their infatuation, that they prefer time to eternity, momentary enjoyments to
those

those that shall never have an end, and listen to the testimony of Satan in preference to that of God. Of all folly that is the greatest, which relates to eternal objects; because it is the most fatal, and when persisted in through life, entirely remediless. A mistake in the management of temporal concerns may be afterwards rectified. At any rate it is comparatively of little importance. But an error in spiritual and eternal matters, as it is in itself of the greatest moment, if carried through life, can never be remedied; because after death there is no redemption. The greatest folly that any creature is capable of, is that of denying or entertaining unjust apprehensions of the being and perfections of the great Creator. Therefore, in a way of eminence, the appellation of *fool* is given, by the Spirit of God, to him who is chargeable with this guilt: *The fool hath said in his heart, There is no God.*

The II. thing proposed, in the illustration of our text, is to show that every natural man is under the power of heart-atheism.

1. This appears from his *neglect* of *religious duties*. An open contempt of the external practice of Religion is not universal. Great as the wickedness of the world is, we have reason to thank God that there are still some who call upon his name. Yet aversion to the duties of Religion is natural to all. There cannot be a more certain evidence of this, than the extreme difficulty which religious parents find in prevailing on their children to attend Divine worship. From their early years, they give ample demonstration that this is a work burdensome and unnatural to them; and they gladly embrace every opportunity of withdrawing their necks from the yoke. Any employment whatsoever is exceedingly more agreeable to them than the service of God their Maker. This must, indeed, be partly attributed to their reluctance to restraint of any kind. But while it is undeniable, that this very reluctance is a proof that they are naturally *children of disobedience,* it must be evident that they

give

give more abundant proofs of it with respect to religious duties than any thing else. However short the service, their every look and motion cries out, *What a weariness is it?* And as aversion to the duties of Religion is natural to all, a great part of men practically discover it by a contempt of the ordinances of Divine appointment, whether secret, private, or public. Thus, it is declared: *The wicked, through the pride of his countenance, will not seek after God: God is not in all his thoughts;* Psal. x. 4. So great is the pride of the wicked, or unregenerate person, that he wishes to have no superior, to acknowledge no being higher than himself. He wants to be lord of his own conduct. Therefore he scorns to give homage to God. Nay, so great is his impiety, that he would think it too much condescension to pass one thought concerning him: *God is not in all his thoughts;* or if he deigns at any time to think of God, all his thoughts are pointed directly against him: as the words may be read, *Every thought in his heart is, There is no God.* This is virtually the language of every thought. And wherefore is it that the wicked man neither serves God, nor so much as properly thinks of him? The reason is, he has no just apprehension of his Being and Providence. He has, indeed, some trivial, abstract, and unaffecting notions about the existence of God. But he does not firmly believe this great truth, that God will call him to an account. This reason is added in the 13th verse of the Psalm formerly cited. There the question is asked, *Wherefore doth the wicked contemn God?* Attend to the reason assigned: *He hath said in his heart, Thou wilt not require it.* He flatters himself that God will not reckon with him for his neglect of ordinances and unholy life. We can scarcely imagine that even the greatest part of ungodly men absolutely disbelieve the Providence of God, and a future judgment. For men must have their consciences dreadfully seared ere they can lose all impressions of these great truths. But it is most probable, that whenever these ideas come across their minds, they

they treat them as if they were *old wives fables*. If they cannot really difbelieve a future reckoning, they at leaft wifh to perfuade themfelves that there is none. In the Pfalm in which our text lies, the infpired Penman gives it as an evidence of the atheifm of the wicked, that *they call not upon the Lord* *. They do not acknowledge and adore him in the duties of his own inftitution. When we fee men as backward to bow a knee to God, and filled with as much contempt at the idea, as if they were independent creatures; or, as carefully avoiding a place of worfhip as if it were a place of infection; we are forced to conclude, that their impious conduct proceeds from the atheifm of their hearts, and that they have no juft and abiding perfuafion of the Divine being and attributes. For if there be a God, unqueftionably he muft be entitled to adoration ; it muft be the duty of all his intelligent creatures to draw near to him with holy homage. And, as he ought to be worfhipped, it muft belong to himfelf to fpecify that kind of worfhip which is moft fuitable to his nature and agreeable to his will. And, as it muft belong to him to require it, it muft be our indifpenfable duty to obey his commandments and obferve his inftitutions ; and if we refufe this homage and obedience, it neceffarily follows that we have no right impreffions of the being of God ; as thefe, wherever they are, will produce religious adoration. Thofe, then, who deny God that worfhip which he requires, practically deny his being, becaufe thus only can they acknowledge their faith in him : and they undeniably proclaim it as their fecret wifh, that there were no God.

2. The power of heart-atheifm appears by *hypocrify*. As many demonftrate their atheifm by neglecting Religion altogether, others difcover it by the manner in which they perform religious duties. They profefs to be remarkably ferious in their prayers, and praifes, and other fervices. They may perhaps be reckoned great faints by others. But it is all mere

* Verfe 4.

mere show. Their hearts were never seriously engaged in any duty. They may, like the Pharisees, even *disfigure their faces, that* to others *they may appear* exceedingly devout. But still it is all a solemn farce. There is no truth in their appearances. Whence proceeds this conduct, but from the natural atheism of their hearts? The Apostle gives an account of some *who have a form of godliness, but deny the power thereof* *. All, who have nothing more than a form of godliness, do actually deny its power. As they practically deny, they show that they do not really believe with their hearts the reality of religion; because theirs consists in a mere form. And by denying the reality of religion, they materially deny the existence of God. For if a mere form be sufficient, then it cannot be God who is worshipped; for *God is a spirit, and they that worship him must worship him in spirit and in truth.* Those who imagine that mere bodily service will be acceptable to him, deny him to be a spiritual being, and so deny him to be God. When he denounces a woe against his ancient people for their hypocrisy, he traces it up to their atheism. *Wherefore the Lord said, Forasmuch as this people draw near me with their mouth, and with their lips do honour me, but have removed their heart far from me, and their fear towards me is taught by the precept of men: therefore, behold, I will proceed to do a marvellous work,* &c. Then it follows,—*Wo unto them that seek deep to hide their counsel from the Lord, and their works are in the dark, and they say, Who seeth us? and who knoweth us* †*?* He considers this as the very language of atheism, *Who seeth us? and who knoweth us?* and surely with the greatest justice. For men would never presume to offer such an affront to God if they really considered him as their present witness, and as their future judge. The strict observation that God takes of the whole of our conduct, the certainty of a future judgment, and the awful discovery that will then be made of the secrets of the heart,

* 2 Tim. iii. 5.   † Isaiah xxix. 13, 14, 15.

heart, are the arguments ufed by Chrift in diffuading his difciples from imitating the wicked example of the Pharifees in their hypocritical conduct. *Beware ye of the leaven of the Pharifees, which is hypocrify. For there is nothing covered, that fhall not be revealed; neither hid, that fhall not be known. Therefore, whatfoever ye have fpoken in darknefs, fhall be heard in the light* *. Our Lord reckoned this exhortation of fuch importance to his difciples, both for time and eternity, that as the introduction of a moft memorable difcourfe, and at a very remarkable time, when *there was an innumerable multitude of people gathered together, infomuch that they trode one upon another,* the greateft part of whom he doubtlefs knew to be actuated by unworthy motives, he particularly addreffed thefe words to the twelve: *He began to fay to his difciples, firft of all, beware ye of the leaven of the Pharifees.* As this corrupt leaven is mournfully diffufed through the hearts of believers themfelves, it calls for their peculiar attention to that natural atheifm, which ftill dwells in them, and which is the fource of the other. It is for want of a due impreffion of the being of God on their minds, that with refpect to formality and hypocrify in religious duties, they have fo much reafon to complain that their *hearts are like a bow that fhooteth deceitfully.* But in this refpect there is a great difference between real Chriftians and hypocrites. All the fervices of the latter are performed under the influence of an hypocritical fpirit: but with Chriftians this principle prevails only in part; and in as far as it prevails, it is their habitual burden.

3. THIS corruption of the heart breaks out in the *profanity* and *fenfuality* of the life. The whole labour of many is merely to gratify their fenfual appetites. Carnal pleafure is their higheft aim. They travail with iniquity of every kind, they wallow in every fpecies of debauchery; paying no more regard to their immortal fouls than if they were as vile as their perifhing bodies; nay, far more vile than them. For they treat the foul as if it had been given them

* Luke xii. 1—3.

for no other end than to be a drudge to the flesh, in *making provision* for it, as if it were designed as merely a principle of animation to the body, supplying it with the capacity of brutal gratification. What shall we think of these men, but that they are under the power of heart-atheism? For had they any just notions of the being of God, they would tremble at the idea of living like beasts. There are others, again, who, in their common conversation, profane the holy name of God. They use such freedom with his name, as they would suffer no man to use with their own. They invoke him for blessing, preservation, pity, and mercy in the most irreverent manner. They call upon him to witness the merest trifles. They swear in a rash and unhallowed way by his attributes, by his faithfulness, goodness, and grace. Nay, they take God's prerogative out of his hand, by denouncing his curses against those who offend them. They will even go the length of calling on the devil, as if he, who is the greatest adversary of God, deserved that homage, which belongs to him only.

Many, instead of keeping the first day of the week holy to the Lord, as he hath commanded, make it a day of idleness, and wander up and down like persons who know not what to do with themselves; or presume to do those works that are lawful only on other days. What can we think of such profaners of God's holy name and day, but that they are under the power of atheism? For were they duly affected with a sense of his being, they would shudder at the thought of taking his name in their mouth in an irreverent manner; and they would *call the Sabbath a delight, the holy of the Lord, and honourable.* Can we reckon those sensual persons, who constantly riot in wickedness, any better than Atheists*? *There is no fear of God before their eyes.* The Psalmist points out atheism as the spring of the sensuality and wickedness of the life; or in other words, the wickedness of the life as the fruit and evidence of the atheism

of

* Isaiah lviii. 13.

of the heart *. Men are here represented as *having all gone aside,* because they have universally in their natural state lost a proper sense of the being of God. Their departure from the way of holiness is the inevitable consequence of that impious doctrine of their foolish hearts; *There is no God.*

4. By *perjury.*—This is a sin that awfully prevails among us, and the commission of it is a mournful proof of the power of atheism. An oath is a very sacred thing. It is appointed by God to be *an end of all strife.* He who takes it, in the most solemn manner calls on God to witness the truth of his testimony, and to inflict all his curses upon him, if he swear falsely. He invokes God both as his witness, and as his judge; and avows his willingness to answer to him for the truth of his declaration. Every oath judicially made is in some sort an anticipation of the final judgment. A man thus cites himself immediately to the bar of God, and practically asserts that he would be nowise afraid to answer him for his conduct in the present instance the next moment. Now, if he swear falsely, it is a striking demonstration of the power of atheism in his heart; for he denies the perfections of the Divine nature. He denies omniscience; for by his perjury, he virtually refuses that God knows his heart. He denies Divine faithfulness; because he calls upon the true God to bear witness to a lie. He denies his holiness; for his conduct declares it to be his persuasion that God can *dwell with iniquity.* Yea, he puts his power and justice to defiance, by thus *rushing against the thick bosses of his bucklers.* By denying the perfections of God, he denies his very being; for he, who swears falsely by the true God, materially affirms that *there is no God.* Therefore, an oath is called a swearing by the life of God, or by his being †; as intimating that he who swears falsely, denies the being of God. When he forbids the awful crime of perjury amongst his ancient people, the argument by

which

* Verse 2, 3. † Jer. v. 2.

which he enforces the prohibition is his very being, as JEHOVAH. *Ye shall not swear by my name falsely, neither shalt thou profane the name of thy God: I am* JEHOVAH *. The use of this argument, a powerful one indeed, derived from his own incomprehensible essence, denotes that he who swears falsely by his name, denies him to be JEHOVAH, to be the self-existent, independent, and eternal Being.

5. SINNERS discover the atheism of their hearts, by the *false apprehensions* they entertain of the *justice* and *mercy* of God. Alas! we cannot mention the sad prevalence of these delusive notions, without the deepest regret. The mournful experience of almost every day, presents us with affecting instances of their fatal effects. How often do we see men stepping into eternity, big with hopes of salvation; while they rest on a very false foundation? Are there not many, within the circle of our own observation, who are lost in ignorance of the principles of revealed religion; devoted to wickedness, habitual swearers or drunkards, who, notwithstanding, do not entertain the smallest doubt of obtaining eternal happiness? How mournful is it to hear a man on a sick-bed or death-bed, when interrogated as to his hope for eternity, reply, without the least hesitation, "God is merciful, and this "is all my confidence;" and when further asked, "How " his justice is to be satisfied, as he is just as well as mer- " ciful;" to find him entirely at a loss for an answer? The frequency of this case, makes it the more deplorable. Have we not found many, on the very brink of eternity, seemingly confident of a happy meeting with God, merely because of the mercy of his nature; while as ignorant of the blood of the Lamb, the only channel in which this mercy can find a vent in the salvation of sinners, as Heathens who never heard of a Saviour. But such wretches do not consider, that a " God all mercy is a God unjust;" that it is inconsistent with his nature to glorify one perfection at the expence of another; that if mercy

be

* Levit. xix. 12.

be manifested towards sinners, it can only be through a perfect atonement to Divine justice. Now, whence is it that they have such gross notions about the perfections of God? Whence do they err in matters of such great importance? They are under the reigning power of atheism in their hearts. They cannot find such a God in the Word as would answer their corrupt desires: therefore they create such a God in their own imaginations; a God whose mind is in a state of tumult and uproar, whose perfections are at war with each other! But to frame such an idea of God, is to undeify him, to deny him existence. For he who is God, is possessed of all perfection, which could not be the case, were there any discord among his attributes. Sinners, you cannot make yourselves such as God requires you to be; therefore you presume to make God such a one as yourselves, and imagine that he will approve your sins *. You trifle with his mercy, as if it were a patent for iniquity; and sport with his justice, as if it were a mere bugbear, fit only to frighten children. But were you not heart-atheists, you would tremble at the view of that flaming sword, that shall pierce through the heart of every sinner, who does not embrace the mercy of God, through the propitiatory sacrifice of his dear Son.

6. MEN farther discover the power of this principle by not being influenced in their conduct by an impression of the Divine *omnipresence* and *omniscience*. That God is every where present, is a truth very evident from scripture. The Psalmist expresses his sense of this in a very striking manner. *Whither shall I go from thy Spirit; or whither shall I flee from thy presence? If I ascend up into heaven, thou art there: if I make my bed in hell, behold, thou art there. If I take the wings of the morning, and dwell in the uttermost parts of the sea: even there shall thy hand lead me, and thy right hand shall hold me. If I say, Surely the darkness shall cover me, even the night shall be light about me. Yea the darkness hideth not from thee;*

but

---

* Psal. l. 21.

but the night shineth as the day: the darkness and the light are both alike to thee*: It is also a Divine truth, that as he is every where present, he sees all things that take place, and knows, not only the actions of men, but the very *thoughts and intents* of their hearts. *Neither is there any creature that is not manifest in his sight; but all things are naked and opened to the eyes of him with whom we have to do* †. Now men are naturally destitute of any proper sense of these attributes; and so demonstrate that they are under the power of atheism. They are evidently without a due sense of his omnipresence and omniscience; for it is their great aim, when committing iniquity, to hide it from the eyes of men; and if they are successful in this, they seem entirely devoid of any other concern. They are nowise affected by a sense of that great truth that impressed the mind of Abraham's Egyptian bondwoman, when she thus addressed God who spake to her; *Thou God, seest me*: else they would be as much afraid in secret as before the world; considering the sons of men as worms and grasshoppers in the presence of that God, with whom *all the nations are less than nothing, and vanity.* There are no gates or bars, no concealments of any kind, that can seclude us from the presence of God, or remove from us his all-seeing eye. *Am I a God at hand, saith* JEHOVAH, *and not a God afar off? Can any hide himself in secret places, that I shall not see him? saith* JEHOVAH: *Do not I fill heaven and earth? saith* JEHOVAH ‡. There is a threefold repetition of his awful, essential name, to declare that omnipresence is essential to his nature, and to convince us of the necessity of a constant sense of it. Our foolish attempts to conceal our actions from men, while we are regardless about their being seen by God, is a certain evidence that we are without a due sense of his being. Therefore is the exhortation given, *Be still, and know that I am God;* as intimating that those who go on in a course of iniquity, who are *like the troubled sea, when it cannot rest, whose waters cast*

---

* Psal. cxxxix. 7.—12.   † Heb. iv. 13.   ‡ Jer. xxiii. 23, 24.

cast forth mire and dirt, do not know, acknowledge and believe in God, as God; as he reveals himself in the Word, and as he is in his own perfect essence. For were men duly affected by this truth, that he is God, or truly acquainted with it, they would *be still.* The impression of it would restrain them from the practice of iniquity.

7. By their disregard of the *threatenings* of God's *law.* These are directed against sinners; and so dreadful are they, that at first view one would be apt to imagine, they would make *the ears of every one that heareth* them *to tingle.* He threatens to rain *snares, fire and brimstone, and an horrible tempest,* or, *the spirit of storms,* the very essence of them, *upon the head of the wicked.*—He declares that *the wicked shall be turned into hell.* Mens own consciences, if not greatly seared, must tell them that this is a character applicable to themselves, and that therefore they deserve the punishment threatened. But when *the lion roars,* they are *not afraid.* They harden themselves against the *curses written in the book of God.* They hear them with as little concern as if they had no reason to apply them to themselves. It is such an obdurate and wicked person as this that Moses describes, as one *whose heart turneth away from the Lord,—a root that beareth gall and wormwood; who, when he heareth the words of the curse, shall bless himself in his heart, saying, I shall have peace, though I walk in the imaginations of my heart, to add drunkenness to thirst.* Attend to the dreadful sentence pronounced against this sinner; *The Lord will not spare him, but then the anger of the Lord, and his jealousy shall smoke against that man, and all the curses that are written in this book shall lie upon him, and the Lord shall blot out his name from under heaven* *. God farther declares his indignation against those who make light of his threatenings: *Wo unto them that draw iniquity with cords of vanity;—who say, Let him make speed, and hasten his work, that we*

may

---

* Deut. xxix. 18.—20.

may see it; and let the counsel of the holy One of Israel draw nigh and come, that we may know it *. Now, such persons evidently discover the power of atheism in their hearts; for as they know themselves to be sinners, they would tremble at the threatenings of the word, were they not lost to a just sense of the being of that God who denounces them.

8. By their *rejection* of the *Gospel*. To all unregenerate men the Gospel of Christ is *a stumbling-block and foolishness*. They, in their carnal wisdom, account the infinite wisdom, displayed in the plan of redemption, folly. They scorn the idea of being indebted to the cross of Christ for salvation. They would rather be saved any way, nay, they would rather run the hazard of damnation, than be saved by the obedience and sufferings of a *crucified* Redeemer. Now, wherefore does the natural man reject the Gospel and Christ offered in it? Because he is under the reigning power of atheism. He does not credit the testimony that God gives in his word, that *the Gospel is the power of God, and the wisdom of God;* and that in Christ there is eternal life. Thus he calls *God a liar*. He impeaches his faithfulness; and by denying him the honour of this attribute, denies his very being. For *he* is not God, who is not the God of *truth*.—It is evident that the atheism of the heart prompts men to reject the Gospel. For if they once lose a proper sense of that great truth, the being of God, they also lose a due impression of the certainty of a future state: and if their minds be not deeply impressed with the truth of a coming judgment and state of retribution, they will never find motives so powerful as to incline them to embrace the Gospel, even in a rational manner, and to endeavour obedience to God's commandments. For in the case supposed, they will conclude that it must be the wisest conduct for them, to make themselves as happy as possible in this life, by the indulgence of every sin. Therefore *they say unto God, Depart from us.*

* Isa. v. 18, 19.

us *. Paul certainly acted *as a wife master-builder,* when, in his addrefs to a Heathen, he laid the foundation of *the faith in Chrift,* by proving the certainty of a *judgment to come* †. As he had the greateſt reaſon to apprehend the unbelief of Felix in this matter, not only from the uncertainty of the Heathen doctrine, but from the wickedneſs and practical atheiſm of this Heathen's life; he undoubtedly diſcovered *that wiſdom given to* him, in eſtabliſhing *the principles of the doctrine of Chrift,*—by declaring *the reſurrection of the dead, and eternal judgment* ‡; knowing that while Felix continued in unbelief or uncertainty about theſe, he would deſpiſe all warnings *to flee from the wrath to come.* And this will invariably be the caſe with ſinners under a Gofpel-diſpenſation. While they continue Heathens in principle, they can be Chriſtians in name only. While they doubt of a God to puniſh, they will not embrace a Saviour to redeem.

9. By their *contempt* of the *godly.* There are many who not only neglect the duties of religion themſelves, but ridicule thoſe who act otherwiſe. Religious exerciſes are the ſubject of their profane mirth; thoſe who fear God are their laughing-ſtock; and they watch every opportunity of turning the force of their weak and malicious wit againſt them. But whence proceeds this contemptuous conduct? From their atheiſm, ſurely. For if they believed the being of God in a right manner, ſo far from deſpiſing his people, they would reckon them *the excellent ones of the earth,* and place *all their delight* in them. But they conſider them as deſpicable, hateful perſons; becauſe they forget that *there is a God who ruleth in the earth, in whoſe eyes vile men are deſpiſed,* but who *giveth grace to the humble.* This of ſcorning is, in the Pſalm before us, given as one of the characters of the Heart-atheiſt, and as a fruit and evidence of his atheiſm, *The fool hath ſaid in his heart, There is no God. You have ſhamed the counſel of the poor, be-*
cauſe

* Job xxi. 14.   † Acts xxiv. 24, 25.   ‡ Heb. vi. 1, 2.

cause the Lord is his refuge*. " You have reprefented " the conduct of the man who is poor in fpirit as a " foolifh and fhameful thing, as mean and unmanly; " merely becaufe he trufts in God."

This fubject then informs us what *fcorners* are in God's account. They are *fools*. They reckon themfelves very wife; and as if their own defpicable prejudices were the ftandard of truth, they take a liberty in laughing at thofe who worfhip the Moft High, and make Religion the conftant fubject of their infignificant raillery. But God reckons them fools, nay, practical atheifts. Think with yourfelves then, you who make a mock of the righteous, who laugh at prayer, at the worfhip of God in families, and other exercifes of devotion, who call fuch things mere cant and enthufiafm, duly confider it, whether you will indulge your mirth at the expence of falvation; whether you will ceafe to reckon the godly fools, or fubmit to be reckoned fools by God; whether you make a wife choice in purchafing a little mirth in *time*, at the expence of *weeping, and wailing, and gnafhing of teeth* through *eternity?* Count the coft. Are you fatisfied that your prefent profits will fufficiently indemnify you for all future lofs. For be affured, that if ye indulge your laugh at his people, God will in his turn laugh at you. *He that fitteth in the heavens fhall laugh, the Lord fhall have you in derifion.* And you had better bear the fcoffs of all the atheifts and ungodly on earth, nay, of all the devils and damned fpirits in hell, and their curfes too, than the fcorn of God. That is an awful word; *Becaufe I have called and ye refufed, I have ftretched out my hand, and no man regarded; I alfo will laugh at your calamity, and mock when your fear cometh: when your fear cometh as defolation, and your deftruction cometh as a whirlwind: when diftrefs and anguifh come upon you.*

We may alfo learn the neceffity of having *the heart purified by faith.* For a fcriptural faith in the being of God, and this alone, is inftrumental
in

* Verfe 6.

in subduing the natural power of atheism. As long as a person remains an unbeliever, his heart continues a sink of impurity; and, as a proof of this, he remains under the power of atheism. But when *he cometh unto God,* in the exercise of true faith, he is made to believe, in a right manner, *that He is.*

IN a word, from this subject, we may learn the great importance of having right apprehensions of the nature of God. An error, as to this fundamental article of Religion, is the origin of almost every other that hath crept into it. From ignorance of the Divine nature, arise unjust apprehensions of sin. He who conceives falsely of God, esteems sin to be a small matter. God himself assigns this as the reason: *Thou thoughtest that I was altogether such a one as thyself.* False notions of punishment must be traced to the same origin. He who reckons sin a light thing, cannot believe that God will punish it in all the extent threatened. From the same source proceed unjust apprehensions of pardon. To him who thinks sin trivial in its nature, it seems easy for God to overlook it. This also produces unjust notions of duty. He who disregards the spiritual nature of God, will deem it enough to offer him carnal services. Thus, errors, with respect to sin, punishment, pardon, or duty, all originate from ignorance of the Divine nature. The sinner thinks falsely of sin, because he hath never seen the glory of that Holiness, in the proclamation of which seraphs cover their faces with their wings. He deceives himself with respect to punishment, because he knows not that God *who will by no means clear the guilty.* He entertains unjust apprehensions of pardon, from his ignorance of Divine Mercy. And he errs in his notions of duty, because he is a stranger to *God* the *Spirit.*

SERMON X.

ON THE CONSEQUENCES OF THE NATURAL ATHEISM OF THE HEART.

PSALM xiv. 1.

The fool hath said in his heart, There is no God.

HAVING made some general introductory observations on this subject, and considered the *evidences* of heart-atheism; we now proceed,

III. To illustrate the *consequences* of it.

THE things we are about to mention are not to be considered as so inseparably connected with this corrupt principle, as always to attend it without any variation. For those who have their hearts delivered from the natural power of atheism, are also delivered from its natural consequences, in their full power: and there are even many who still remain under the dominion of heart-atheism, and yet do not experience all its effects. But we would wish it to be remembered, that the things we have in eye are the natural consequences of atheism; that in itself it has this tendency; and that it would operate in all its dismal consequences on every unrenewed man, were he not restrained by grace. God, as the Creator, Preserver, and Benefactor of mankind, bridles this corruption with respect to its effects, even as to the *vessels of wrath*, from good will to his creatures. For
bad

bad as the world is, were atheism suffered to take its full sway in the hearts of men, it would be inexpressibly worse; nay, perhaps we may add, that the wickedness of men would be altogether insufferable. When we speak of the *natural* atheism of the heart, we do not at all mean a *confirmed* principle of atheism, in the absolute denial of a God: for then it would be preposterous to speak of its consequences in the manner intended; but only the original principle of corrupt nature, as strengthened by continuance in sin, prompting to this, pregnant with atheistical wishes, and producing an atheistial practice.

The natural atheism of the heart tends,

1. To *apostasy* from the true *faith*. The ground of faith in the doctrines of the holy Scripture, in opposition to those of error, must be the authority and faithfulness of God speaking in his word. A Christian believes these doctrines, which he finds in the Bible, to be true, and the contrary to be false; because God, *who cannot lie*, hath revealed them. This is the only solid ground of faith; and if a man puts any other in its room, he offers injury to the Most High. If he sets up his own corrupt reason as the standard of truths revealed in the Word, he ceases to believe as a Christian, and gives a faith to Scripture nothing superior to that which he gives to any human testimony or composition. Now, when a professor gives up with this ground, of the Divine authority, on which he formerly *seemed* both to himself and others, to stand, he naturally inclines to renounce these very doctrines so established, because of their mysterious nature. He proceeds to bring them to the crooked rule of his depraved reason, to see whether they will tally with it, or rather, whether they will be measured by it. And because he finds them above the comprehension of his reason, he concludes they are contrary to it; and, of course, relinquishes them as unworthy of faith; and in their stead substitutes the doctrines of error. He begins to enquire *how* and *why* these things are so and so; and because he cannot give the reason, arrogantly concludes,

cludes, that to suppose them to be, as the language of Scripture declares, is to conclude without reason: although, all the while, he has the most decisive proofs which reason can demand, that they are the matter of a Divine Revelation.

Now, whence do men so easily renounce the true ground of faith, and embrace the false foundation of reason; but from their want of a Scriptural and Divine faith in that God who thus interposes his authority in attesting his own word? Did they firmly and sincerely believe God to be such as he declares himself to be; they would find no difficulty in believing his word, barely on his own authority; they would not startle at founding their faith upon a *Thus saith the Lord;* they would not dare to reject Divine truths because mysterious, and above the line of reason; or to embrace vile and pernicious errors in their room. But if a person has no just and scriptural impressions of the being, majesty, and perfections of God on his mind, it affects him little, whether the doctrines he believes be true or false, if they please his own fancy. Thus he is entirely destitute of a proper antidote against delusion.

From these considerations, it appears that the atheism of the heart directly tends to apostasy: and we see how easy it is for one who has not a right faith in the true Religion to embrace a false one. We may suppose the case of a person apostatising from Protestantism to Popery, and turning back to the polluted embraces of *the mother of harlots.* This must flow from the atheism of his heart. For if he had a due sense of the being, perfections, and authority of God speaking in his word, he would never leave a pure Divine Religion for an idolatrous one; he would never prefer the merit of works called good, of fastings, and penances, and prayers of saints, to the righteousness of Christ, for salvation; and he would be at no loss to apply these characters to the Romish Church, which are given in Scripture to *the mother of abominations.* Again, suppose a person, educated in the
pure

pure doctrines commonly called Calvinistic, to embrace Arminian principles. This apostasy must also originate from the atheism of his heart; for had he a right apprehension of the nature and attributes of God, when he finds the doctrine of *particular* election clearly declared in God's word, he would never dare to start such an objection as that; " How can it be " just with God to choose some and reject others?" and thence to conclude, that he *must* force another meaning on the language of the Holy Ghost; because this scriptural faith would remind him that the God whom he worships is absolutely sovereign in all his dispensations, and unaccountable to any creature. He would never maintain the doctrine of man's *free-will* to good in his fallen state: for the belief of this doctrine shows the want of faith in God's free grace. He would not deny the *perseverance* of the Saints; because this would display ignorance and unbelief of the love and faithfulness of God, which are essential perfections of the Divine nature. He would not presume to assert that Christ died for *all* men; because this would be an impeachment both of the wisdom and justice of God; for then all men should be saved. Nor would he imagine that the Spirit could be *resisted* in his efficacious operations;. for this is a denial of omnipotence. As little could he apprehend that man's own *doings* could be the ground of his salvation; for this would discover ignorance of the holiness of God, which demands complete satisfaction to his justice, as well as perfect obedience to his law.

2. To produce an apprehension that there is no truth in Divine Revelation, and, consequently, that all Religion is a *human device*, a plan wisely designed and politically framed for laying restraints upon vice, and for promoting order, peace and government in civil society. Whence have so many fallen into the dreadful gulph of deism, which consists in denying the reality and necessity of any revealed Religion, and asserting that the light of Nature is sufficient to lead men to eternal happiness; whence is

Vol. I.   A a   it,

it but from the natural atheism of the heart, acting under less restraint than in most cases? The denial of all Divine Revelation is the natural consequence of this principle of atheism. For if men once lose sight of the true foundation, the whole superstructure of course falls to the ground. Now, the fundamental doctrine of all religion is, that there is a God: but if men lose all just and proper apprehensions of the nature and perfections of this Being, the transition to infidelity is very easy. Indeed, atheism and deism have a reciprocal effect on each other in man's heart. For as natural atheism, if not restrained, hath a direct tendency to produce infidelity: on the other hand, if men are left of God to fall into deism, to deny the truth and divinity of that religion which is revealed by God; it tends greatly to increase the natural atheism of the heart, and to drive them to the horrid extreme of denying *all* religion whatsoever, whether natural or revealed. The Epicurean Philosophers, of whom we read, Acts xvii. 18. proceeded this length. For they not only rejected revealed religion, of which they gave evidence in esteeming the great Apostle of the Gentiles, when preaching Jesus and the resurrection, a *babbler*; but they denied all natural religion, and taught that men ought to give full indulgence to their passions, and live according to the dictates of their own minds. For doctrine so strange, they assigned these reasons; that although there was a God, he never troubled himself with the affairs of men, and that he would not call them to an account for their conduct. The natural atheism of the heart, aided by temptation, had this effect upon David, although it was only temporary: *I said in my haste, all men are liars* *. Here the Psalmist seems to have reflected even on the holy Prophets of God, as if they had only deceived him by their predictions; and thus he tacitly charged God himself with unfaithfulness, by denying the truth of his word.

But

* Psal. cxvi. 11.

But if this was its effect on a child of God, what must it be on the unregenerate, when suffered to exercise its full sway!

3. To give *loose reins* to all manner of *iniquity*. Indeed, the unrestrained indulgence of sin, may be viewed either as the cause, or as the consequence of atheism. It cannot be the cause of the *natural* atheism of the heart; for this must be traced up to the universal corruption of our nature by sin. But it may be justly considered as the cause of great progress in it. Actual sin is a sweet balsam to the original atheism of the heart, which, far from healing, only cherishes and spreads the sore. As the heart naturally wishes that there were no God; as atheism lies at the root of all sin; when sin is greatly indulged, it hardens the conscience, and removes farther and farther from it a sense of the being and perfections of God. The sinner, in the war he carries on against God, may be compared to a soldier, who, in his first action, or perhaps at the commencement of any action, feels a panic seize his heart at the near prospect of death; but this wears off by degrees, till at length he faces danger, without any dread of the consequences. In general, the advances towards speculative atheism, in the denial of Providence, or of a future state, or in uncertainty about both, are made and used by the corrupt heart as a salvo for the indulgence of sin. When a sinner finds that it is greatly his interest that there were no God, he endeavours also to make it his faith, if we may use the expression, about that which unhinges the foundations of all faith, whether in a Divine or human testimony. But as the indulgence of sin greatly increases the natural atheism of the heart, and assists it in making rapid progress towards that which is speculative; heart-atheism, on the other hand, looses the reins to sin, and takes off the remaining restraints lying on conscience. What is it, but this, that makes a man tamper with eternal destruction? The abominable iniquities of the Gentiles are described as the consequences of the indulgence

gence of their natural atheism : *Becauſe that when they knew God, they glorified him not as God, neither were thankful, but became* vain *in their imaginations, and their* fooliſh *heart was* darkned ;—*Wherefore God alſo gave them up to uncleanneſs.*—*For this cauſe God gave them up to vile affections :*—*And even as they did not like to retain God in their knowledge,* or rather in acknowledgment, *God gave them over to a reprobate mind, to do thoſe things which are not convenient ; being filled with all unrighteouſneſs, &c.* *. The words immediately following our text, may alſo be viewed as a declaration, both of the proofs, and of the conſequences of heart-atheiſm. *The fool hath ſaid in his heart, there is no God.* Obſerve the effect this language, or wiſh of the heart, hath on his practice. It is the parent of *abominable works* †, of univerſal pollution ‡, of groſs ignorance, of perſecution of the ſaints, of contempt of Divine worſhip §, and of profane ſcorning **.

4. To produce unreaſonable and ill-grounded *fears*. One would apprehend, that he, who has in a great meaſure ſhaken off the fear of God, would be regardleſs of every *other* being. But God, in his righteous judgment, often orders it otherwiſe, and *turns the counſel* of thoſe *into fooliſhneſs,* who deſpiſe the only proper object of fear ; by making them afraid of what cannot poſſibly injure them, at leaſt without his permiſſion. He diſcovers their great weakneſs, by making them, who have caſt off the fear of the Creator, tremble at the creature, and frequently at the creature of their own imaginations only. Thus he threatens thoſe that *will not hearken unto* him, *but walk contrary unto him :*—*I will ſend a faintneſs into their hearts, in the lands of their enemies :* '*and the ſound of a ſhaken leaf ſhall chaſe them ; and they ſhall flee, as fleeing from the ſword, and they ſhall fall when none purſueth* ††. And again, *A dreadful ſound is in his ears : in proſperity the deſtroyer ſhall come upon him* ‡‡. *The wicked flee, when no man purſueth* §§. God hath often accompliſhed

---

* Rom. i. 21. 24. 26. 28. † Verſe 1. ‡ Verſe 3. § Verſe 4.
** Verſe 6. †† Lev. xxvi. 21. 36. See alſo Deut. xxviii. 65, 67.
‡‡ Job xv. 21. §§ Prov. xxviii. 1.

accomplished his threatenings on those who have confirmed their natural atheism by atrocious sins. How often have murderers found a punishment in their own breasts, arising from their constant terrors, far more severe than any punishment that man could inflict? Cain made great progress in atheism, and actually *went out from the presence of the Lord;* whence many conclude, that he renounced the service of the *living God*, and was the father of Polytheism, by inventing the worship of many false deities. But he *went out* with a trembling heart: for he was afraid of an enemy in every human creature: *It shall come to pass*, saith he, *that every one that findeth me shall slay me**. This was the case with the atheistical fools, described in the portion of scripture under consideration. For as this Psalm is elsewhere repeated, we find this important enlargement, *There were they in great fear, where no fear was* †.

5. To drive to *despair*. It is the atheism of the heart, taken in one point of view, that makes the sinner imagine there is no mercy for him. It proceeds from the want of a just apprehension of the nature and perfections of God, that the guilty wretch views him as only encompassed by terrors; for he reveals himself in the Word, as a God *pardoning iniquity, transgression, and sin;* all kinds, and every degree of sin, but that which is in its own nature unpardonable, as being a malicious, despiteful, and obstinate rejection of the very remedy. He exhibits pardon for the most abominable sinner out of hell, through the obedience and sufferings of his own Son Jesus Christ. But when a sinner apprehends there is no mercy for him in God, it manifests that he has no due faith in that revelation which God gives of himself. It gives him the lie, when he says, *I, even I, am He that blotteth out thine iniquities, for my name's sake.* Thence we find, that many of those who have been eminently given up to the atheism of their hearts, have died in despair. Some professed atheists, indeed, through the dreadful force of their corruptions,

* Gen. iv. 14. 16.   † Ps. liii. 5.

tions, and the powerful aid of the great adversary of souls, have braved it out to the last. But others have been made monuments of Divine justice, even in this life; and those who have tried to disbelieve the being of God, or would have persuaded others they actually did so, or have thought and spoken of God, as if he had been like themselves, and laughed at the idea of hell; have often been left to the most awful terrors of conscience before death, have experienced a hell in their own consciences, and have thus been made *terrors to themselves and all around them.*

There are many instances which confirm the truth of this observation, on record with the Church, in the writings of those *men of God,* who have diligently attended to the dispensations of his Providence. Many such things have taken place in our own time: But the false tenderness of relations, and the diabolical assiduity of friends in infidelity and companions in wickedness, conceal them from the world; because the former have a greater regard to the glory of the creature, than of the Creator; and the latter are unwilling to let any thing transpire, that may expose themselves to the contempt they deserve, or tend to awaken others to consideration, whom they, like their master, are still *seeking to devour.* Perhaps, instead of glorifying God, by confessing to the world such striking evidences of his Being and Providence, they deem it a meritorious sacrifice to the memory of their deceased friends, and service to their surviving brethren, to belie the convictions of their own consciences, by trying to persuade the world that they died with a jest in their mouths, with the greatest fortitude, and with the firmest belief in their damnable principles; while the recollection of the horrors *themselves* have witnessed, is ready to *work wrath* in their breasts, at the very moment they disavow them. Besides, infidelity has come to such a pitch, and so awfully pervades all ranks of men in the age in which we live, that these things are little attended to, even when discovered. The pretence of a brain-fever, or
of

of the intoxicating power of some medicines, *generously* administered to banish the sensations of pain, and the thoughts of eternity, is both offered and received, as a satisfactory solution for such disagreeable appearances as are denominated in Scripture *the terrors of the Lord*. When men have so incorporated atheism with their notions of Revealed Religion, as to deny the sovereignty of his distinguishing *mercy*, when he *plucks brands out of the fire;* while many others, no worse than they, are left in it: need we be surprised that a righteous God should suffer them to be so far hardened, as also to deny the sovereignty of his *justice*, when he as it were casts some *into* the fire, even in this world, and sets them up as monuments of his indignation; while others, of the same kidney, go down quietly to hell, *with a lie in* their *right hand?*

6. To hurry men into eternal *perdition. The wicked shall be turned into hell, and all the nations that forget God.* If mercy prevent not, eternal ruin must be the lot of all who are chargeable with this impiety, who forget him in their lives, or wish to forget him in their hearts. It is but just with God, that those, who have obstinately refused to entertain such apprehensions of him as are correspondent to the revelation given in his own precious word, should learn to think more justly by the force of punishment; that those, who, while on earth, have either tried actually to disbelieve his Being, or have fostered such thoughts of him as amount to a denial of it, should be made to *believe and tremble* in hell: that such as have refused to listen to the thunders of the Law, and also to *the still small voice* of the Gospel, and to accept of the mercy of God streaming through the blood of Jesus, to learn his nature and will from the book of the law, and to read the demerit of sin in the sufferings of the Redeemer;—should read it by the direful glow of an awakened conscience, and by the light of that *fire that shall never be quenched.*

THIS subject affords ground of exhortation to those who are delivered from the natural power of atheism, and

and to such as still remain under it, and perhaps are entirely ignorant of their situation.

We would exhort you who are freed from the dominion of this corruption, to pray earnestly for deliverance from its remaining power. There is still an atheistical principle in your hearts. Christians, the grace of the Spirit subdues every corruption. But it will totally eradicate none, till it be consummated in glory. As long as you remain in this vale of tears, you must struggle with the plagues of your own hearts. Maintain a constant war with this plague: for it mingles itself with every other, and appears in the heart on every motion of sin. Daily endeavour the mortification of it. There is grace in Christ for this end. Therefore earnestly desire the communication of it. He hath promised, *I will give them an heart to know me, that I am* Jehovah*.

2. Strive to resist atheistical thoughts. These sometimes arise from the corruption of your own hearts; sometimes they are darted in by Satan; and often they are excited by his operations on your corruption. But from what quarter soever they proceed, guard against them. Give them not so much as a hearing. The very listening to the suggestions of Satan, or motions of the corrupt heart, is an inward defection, a partial declension to atheism. Therefore, whenever you find any such thoughts arising in your hearts, try to dispel them by the Divine word; *Get thee behind me Satan.* Immediately hold up *the shield of faith.* It is this alone that can *quench the fiery darts of the wicked one*; and it will quench them *all.* We may add, that the first boss of this buckler is that great truth, "There is a God." Immediately betake yourselves to prayer. The best and surest way to obtain deliverance from temptations to atheism or any other sin, to quench any of Satan's darts, is, by entertaining a deep sense of your own weakness, immediately to fly to God as your refuge, for a supply of strength from him. It was thus the Apostle Paul resisted

* Jer. xxiv. 7.

resisted the *messenger of Satan*. He *besought the Lord*. Although the temptation continue after prayer, you must not be discouraged; you must not give up with the duty; but persist in it, till you obtain the answer. You see that Paul did not merely pray, but he *besought the Lord thrice*: and then he was favoured with a gracious return; *My grace is sufficient for thee, my strength is made perfect in thy weakness*.

3. BEWARE of indulging *secret* sins. For these are eminent temptations to atheism. Many commit sins by themselves that they would be ashamed to commit before any one in the whole world, however mean and insignificant the person might appear. Now, secrecy is the temptation to the sin; and the regard paid to this temptation is not only an effect of atheism, but an inlet to its further ravages. A person indulging any known sin in secret, which he could not commit before others, is, for the time, an atheist. He does not *endure, as seeing him who is invisible*. The present language of his heart and conduct is; *No eye seeth me*: and by the continued indulgence of secret sins, he is in great danger of habitually forgetting that *God seeth*, and that *the most High taketh knowledge*. A sense of the danger of these sins prompts the holy Psalmist to present this prayer; *Cleanse thou me from secret faults*. Ever remember that the Lord *sets your secret sins in the light of his countenance*.

4. IMPLORE a continued sense of the *presence* of God on your mind. Remember at all times, in all companies, and in all employments, that the eye of God is fixed on you. Remember this, when you are most in company, or most alone. By a sense of this, and by the due improvement of it, you will have reason to say with that Ancient; "When I am most alone, "then I am least alone." For thus you will maintain constant communion with that God who is ever present with you; from whom *the darkness hideth not, but the night shineth as the day*, as *the darkness and the light are both alike unto him*. Remember that he not only

sees your most secret actions, but your inmost thoughts; that they are all *naked and opened unto the eyes of that God with whom* you *have to do*. Endeavour, therefore, through his grace, to retain a constant impression of his command on your spirits; *Be still, and know that I am God; I will be exalted*.

We shall conclude, by addressing you who are still under the dominion of heart-atheism.

Perhaps you may all deny the character. It never belonged to you. For you always believed the being of God. You would reckon him a monster who did not. But if your conduct shall be found on examination to be such as demonstrates that you have no real persuasion of this fundamental truth, then surely, it will be vain for you to deny the justness of the charge.

Do you live without secret or family prayer? For we do not reckon upon that, in which you join out of compliment to the religion of your country. And will you dare to say, you truly believe the being of a God? If you do so, give the same proof that blinded heathens afford. For they call on their gods. If an inspired Apostle denominates them *atheists in the world* *, because they do not worship the true God; with how much more propriety may this character be given to those who worship no god at all, who are, in every sense of the expression, *without God in the world?* All faith, if sincere, according to its kind, whether its object be true or false, will produce worship as its necessary fruit. But you do not adore that God in whom you profess to believe. Therefore, you do not really believe in him. If you still assert that you do, you only give another evidence of the truth of what we say; for God, the Searcher of hearts, adduces it as a proof of atheism, that men *seek not after*, and *call not upon God;* and expressly declares of the man who *will not seek after God*, that *God is not in all his thoughts*. And by still maintaining that you believe in God, although you do not

call

---

* Eph. ii. 12.

call upon him, you *make* that very God, in whom you profels to believe, *a liar*. Such is your faith in him. Perhaps fome of you worfhip him, but you do it hyprocritically; your hearts habitually denying the language of your lips. But if you believed him to be a God of incomprehenfible majefty, you would not dare to offer him fo grofs an infult.

Do you live in fin, and yet pretend to believe in God? If there be a God, his name muft be *holy and reverend*, never to be ufed rafhly or profanely. But do you cuftomarily take his *name in vain*? If fo, you cannot ferioufly believe that it is worthy of reverence. And if not, as little do you believe that he is himfelf worthy of reverence. For, even among men, the refpect we have for any perfon is generally teftified by that which we pay to his name. But if you do not believe that God himfelf is worthy of reverence, you believe not that he is God. Do you live in fin of any kind? Do you delight in it? Is it the fource, the effence, the confummation of your blifs? Is it your fupreme pleafure? Then furely, you do not truly believe in God. This is a proof that he himfelf gives of the truth of the doctrine of our text: *They are altogether become filthy*. No man who is *altogether filthy* can love infinite Holinefs. If a man believe in God, he muft believe him to be infinitely good; and, therefore, to be the chief good to his foul. But he who makes fin, the direct contrary of God, his chief good, his *exceeding joy*, by denying God to be fo, virtually denies his being. For he fays, that he is unworthy of fo much love; thus denies him to be infinitely good; and of confequence, to be God.

Do you difbelieve vindictive Juftice? You of courfe deny infinite Holinefs. For juftice, in the punifhment of fin, is merely the difplay of holinefs in the hatred of it. Now, if you refufe in heart that there is a Being who will punifh fin, not merely of the groffeft kind, but all fin, where no fufficient atonement is produced, you *fay in heart*, *There is no God*.

For

For if there be a God, he muſt be *of purer eyes than to behold iniquity*. If you live without an habitual ſenſe of Divine omnipreſence and omniſcience, you virtually deny theſe perfections. Did you really believe that your earthly ſovereign were hearing you, ſurely you would not venture to utter treaſon againſt him. But when you daily utter and practiſe treaſon againſt the Sovereign of heaven and earth, no other reaſon can be aſſigned for your conduct, than that you do not believe his preſence. But he, who is not believed to be every where preſent, is not believed to be God.

Are you not alarmed, though continuing in ſin, at the threatenings of God's law? Then it muſt unavoidably follow, that you do not believe them. This is a concluſion that you would form in any other caſe, in which you were not yourſelves parties. Were it aſſerted that an army was at the very gates of a city, waſting with fire and ſword, and ſparing none of any age or ſex; you would undoubtedly conclude, with reſpect to any man who ſhould pay no regard to this intelligence, nor uſe any means for his ſafety, either that he was deprived of his reaſon, or that he did not believe the report. You will not ſubmit to the former concluſion as to yourſelves; and it is impoſſible that you can evade the latter.

Did you ſee one committing robbery or murder; did you warn him, that if he continued in his wicked courſe, the ſentence of the law of his country would certainly be executed upon him at length; if he ſtill perſiſted in the commiſſion of his crime, would you not conclude, either that he did not believe that the law would lay hold on him, or that he did not fear death? Apply this to yourſelves. If notwithſtanding all the threatenings you read and hear, you ſtill go on in ſin; are we not under a neceſſity of concluding either that you do not believe that theſe threatenings will be accompliſhed, or that you care not although they ſhould? If the former be the caſe, you diſbelieve the

the being of God; for you deny his juſtice and faithfulneſs: if the latter, matters are juſt as bad; for you pretend to believe in a God whom you do not fear. But theſe things are irreconcileable. For God himſelf faith: *If I am a father, where is mine honour? and if I am a maſter, where is my fear?*

Do you reject the blood of Chriſt as offered to you in the Goſpel? The firſt conſequence is, that you diſbelieve the Bible. For it aſſures you that you muſt be miſerable, if you do. But this is not all. You alſo in your hearts join in the creed of fools, recorded in our text. For even your own conſciences at times condemn you for ſin. When, therefore, you deſpiſe to ſpend one thought about a remedy offered to you as of infinite value and efficacy, you ſay in fact that there is no God to puniſh ſin, that is, as we have already ſeen, that there is no God.

In a word, do you laugh at thoſe who fear God? Did you believe that pſalm, in which our text lies, to be of Divine inſpiration, you would acknowledge this to be an evidence of atheiſm. But by continuing to *ſit in the chair of the ſcorner*, you ſhow that you diſbelieve Divine Revelation, you really laugh at all religion; becauſe you ridicule thoſe who obſerve that worſhip which is inſtituted in the Word. And as you not only pour contempt on this, but on every thing that looks like the fear of God; as you propoſe no ſubſtitute for this inſtituted worſhip; as while deſpiſing this, you obſerve no other; you in fact laugh at God himſelf, and ſay that it is not worth your while to ſeek him, or call upon him in any way.

Are theſe things ſo? Then, God will never reckon you ſerious in believing his being. Nor will any of his creatures, capable of impartial judgment, do ſo; whether Angel, Saint or Devil. Having thus, we hope, proved the juſtneſs of the charge, or ſhown to whom the deſcription contained in our text belongs; we earneſtly call you,

1. To

1. To confider that there is a God, and that he takes notice of all your actions. To illuftrate the folly of the finner's apprehenfion, That there is no Providence, that God nowife interefts himfelf in the affairs of men, the Spirit here declares, that *the Lord looked down from heaven upon the children of men, to fee if there were any that did underftand, and feek God.* This is a form of fpeaking after the manner of men; for the eye of Omnifcience does not, like that of man, need to travel over objects diftinctly and feparately, in order to have a juft notion of them. God fees all things by one intuitive glance. For this reafon it is faid, that *all things are naked and opened unto his eyes.* The moft fecret things are fo obvious to him, that they are as it were fpread out before him. *The Lord looketh from heaven, he beholds all the fons of men; from the place of his habitation he looketh upon all the inhabitants of the earth.* Unbelieving, atheiftical Sinner, if thou continueft in this ftate, it were well for thee that thy wifh were realized, that there were *no God.* But know, poor worm, that thy rebellious defires can never deprive the eternal and omnipotent God of being; nor fhall they deprive thee of the hated immortality of thy own exiftence, when the thread of natural life is cut in funder. Thy wifhes for annihilation fhall never reduce thee to nothing. But if thou remaineft under the power of atheifm, thou fhalt be fet up as a monument of the juftice of God to all eternity. Although thou fhouldeft never be delivered from the power of atheifm on earth, the torments of hell fhall deliver thee from this. There fhall not be one Atheift there. The tremendous nature of the fufferings, and the aftonifhing power of God in fupporting a finite being under them, fhall fully convince thee of his exiftence, and that he is a God who *will by no means clear the guilty.* Confider, unawakened finner, that there is a coming judgment, and that the inconceivable terrors of that day fhall difplay the madnefs of

of thy atheism. Then shall that God, of whom thou hast no fear now, if mercy prevent not, appear to thee clothed in terrors, the very appearance of which shall be ready to dissolve thy existence. Then shall guilty sinners *cry to the rocks and mountains, Fall on us and cover us from the wrath of him that sitteth on the throne, and from the wrath of the Lamb.*—Then *the sinners in Zion shall be afraid*, and cry out, *Who among us shall dwell with the devouring fire? Who among us shall dwell with everlasting burnings?* Know that, in that awful day, God shall open *the book of his remembrance,* and all thy sinful thoughts, and words, and deeds, shall be disclosed before assembled worlds. Then those impious thoughts and actions, by which thou hast, either in heart or conduct, virtually denied the being of a God, shall fill thee with horror and confusion.

2. ENDEAVOUR to attain a firm and proper persuasion of this great truth, That there is a God. Seek to have it engraved on your hearts, as *with an iron pen and lead in the rock for ever.* Contemplate God in his works, and especially in his word. *Search the Scriptures, for in them you have eternal life,* whether you *think* so or not. There are more striking evidences of the being of God to be found in his word, when accompanied by the Spirit, than in all his works. The holy Scripture contains innumerable internal proofs, that it is a book infinitely superior to any human or created understanding. Pray for the power of the Spirit to attend the reading and hearing of his word. Diligently attend on the means of grace, and pay the strictest regard to the holy Sabbath. Sabbath-breaking is generally an introduction to every heinous sin, and greatly increases the atheism of the heart. For when men lose a sense of the holiness of God's day, they soon lose a sense of God himself. Avoid the company of those who are mockers of Religion. It is dangerous to associate with such. If they make no farther impression,

sion, they may at least make you ashamed of the slight profession of religion you still retain. Say of them as Jacob of his cruel sons ; *O my soul, come not thou into their secret: unto their assembly, mine honour, be not thou united.*

3. APPLY to God for the destruction of all sin, and particularly of the sin of atheism. Come to him that he may remove all that power of unbelief, which is in your heart. Try the language of him in the Gospel ; *Lord, I believe, help thou mine unbelief.*

4. IN the strength of promised grace embrace him as your God and Father in Christ. He is, in the Word, offering himself to you in this amiable character. *The sons of the stranger that join themselves to the Lord—them will I bring to my holy mountain. I am found of them that sought me not.—I am your God.* Now, it is only a believing apprehension of him in this character that can deliver you from the power of atheism. But if brought, by the influences of the Spirit, to receive him as a God of love, as your Father ; you will not only believe aright that there is a God, but find to your comfortable experience that he is *the rewarder of all them that diligently seek him.*

SERMON XI.

On the DECEITFULNESS of the HEART.

JEREMIAH xvii. 9.

The heart is deceitful above all things.——

ALL Gospel-preaching, with regard to any certain effect on those who hear it, is, to the servants of Christ, like drawing *a bow at a venture*. It is the Holy Spirit alone, who can so direct the Word as to smite the sinner *between the joints of the harness* *, and make it *a discerner of the thoughts and intents of the heart*. But there are some subjects that have a more native tendency, as means to accomplish this desirable end, than others which have equally the sanction of inspiration. Among those, we consider a view of the evils of the depraved heart as demanding a principal place. There is, indeed, a method of treating of the heart, which is now, alas! too generally adopted, that can be as little conducive to the recovery of diseased souls, as the assistance of a physician would be to one in imminent danger, who should lay it down as his first principle, by which all his future conduct was to be regulated, that his patient was in perfect health. To discourse to a sinner of the noble dispositions of soul that he once possessed, and of the perfection of heart that originally belonged to him, as if he still retained them in their primitive state; is only to ridicule his misery and make him despise the remedy. Such sermons might have done well enough for man in a state of innocence. To him they would have been lessons of gratitude, and also of duty. But to address fallen man in this manner, is only to pursue a laborious method of increasing the depravity of his nature, and of leading him farther astray from God. Christ, the great Prophet of the Church, and the great Pat-

* 1 Kings, xxii. 34.

tern of all Gospel-ministers, as he hath set us an example of preaching to the heart, hath also pointed out the manner of treating this subject. Instead of flattering his hearers with delusive descriptions of their own excellencies; their inward wickedness was a topic on which he greatly insisted. One evil that he often illustrated to his hearers was the deceitfulness of their hearts. This was the substance of all the accusations which he exhibited against the Pharisees. Therefore does he so frequently upbraid them as hypocrites. If some are offended at this way of preaching, they declare themselves to be of the same Spirit with that perverse generation, which rejected *the great Apostle of our profession*. All the Prophets who appeared before him preached in the same style. Thus did Jeremiah address the professed people of God in his time; *The heart is deceitful above all things*.

In the preceding part of this chapter, we have a declaration of the iniquity of the children of Judah, and of those judgments that the Lord was about to inflict as the punishment thereof. In verse 5. he denounces a curse against *the man that trusteth in man*; that trusteth in him either for temporal or spiritual salvation; that trusteth either in another, or in himself, in any respect. The 6th verse expresses both the essence, and the evidence of the curse. For, as a demonstration of the vanity of his confidence, *he shall be like the heath in the desert, and shall not know when good cometh*. He shall be desolate and unfruitful, like the bleak and barren heath in the wilderness, that knows no distinction of seasons, that is as unprolific in summer as in winter. This allusion will appear to be remarkably beautiful and expressive, if it be remembered that the heath, as it never bears fruit, does not even begin to blossom till about harvest, when almost every other plant is on the decline. The genial influence of the sun, the cooling breezes and refreshing dews of summer, are all lost on it. Like this barren production of the desert, is the self-righteous sinner. He is on every hand surrounded by fruitful trees. In common with them, he receives the waterings of a Gospel-ministry. The beams of the Sun of Righteousness shine around him. In the convincing and comforting influences of the Spirit, the north and south winds awake and blow upon fellow professors, and even the first of these on his own conscience. In a word, the dews of heaven fall on every side: but like Gideon's, his fleece is altogether dry; his heart remains obdurate, and his life is unfruitful; because *his root is rottenness*, he *trusteth in himself*, he *maketh flesh his arm*, and thus *his heart departeth from the Lord.* As a counterpart to the curse denounced against carnal confidence, there is, in verse 7. a blessing pronounced on *the man that trusteth in the Lord.* And the evidence of his blessedness is declared in the following verse. *For he shall be as a tree planted by the water, and that spreadeth out her roots by the river, and shall not see when heat cometh; but her leaf shall be green, and shall not be careful in the year of drought: neither shall cease from yielding fruit.* The Lord proceeds to demonstrate, in the words of our text, the danger of trusting in man, and the justness of the curse denounced against this false confidence, and of the awful judgment incurred; by declaring, in the most striking terms, the deceitfulness of the human heart. This may be also introduced, as the source of that strong propensity which is in man, to carnal confidence of every kind. Since both Scripture and experience verify the folly of this conduct; what can be the origin of that irresistible inclination which every man discovers to trust in himself, or in an arm equally feeble? It undoubtedly proceeds from the natural deceitfulness of his heart.

The word here rendered *deceitful*, in its simple and original sense, signifies any thing that is *crooked;* as, a crooked way. In this sense, it is opposed to one that is straight, Isa. xl. 4. *The crooked places shall be made straight.* Hence it is metaphorically applied to the heart of man, to denote its perverseness, wickedness and

and deceitfulness. Being derived from a word which signifies to *supplant*, it is with the greatest propriety transferred to the heart; because, by its deceit, it does every thing in its power to supplant God of his glory, and even itself of eternal happiness. The idea of *supplanting* may in some sense be applied to a *crooked* way, because it misleads the traveller by its windings and defiles, and supplants him of the design of his journey: but far more strictly does it correspond to the heart, because it has so many windings and wanderings of deceit; is, in a spiritual sense, *crooked*, as on every side declining from the straight path of righteousness, from the unerring standard of the Divine law; and has no truth in it. Others think that the idea is taken from a road, that has many footsteps in it, when covered with slime and mud: as if the heart were said to be full of pits and depths, to express the greatness and variety of its deceitfulness.

ALTHOUGH it were possible for us, to say all on this important subject that man can say, there would still be reason to confess, that *the one half* had *not been told*. For the deceitfulness of the heart is unfathomable. The concluding words of the verse put the understanding of every creature to defiance: *Who can know it?* But, however insufficient at any rate, for investigating this subject; we apprehend that it would be highly injurious both to it, and to you, to pass it over altogether in a cursory manner.

IT is proposed, first, to adduce some general evidences of the deceitfulness of the heart: Then to consider it more particularly, with respect to *sin*; its methods of stifling *convictions*, and of abusing them, in subserviency to *false* grounds of *confidence*; with respect to the *duties* of *religion*; the *conduct* of *life*; and *Providential dispensations*: Then to inquire why the heart is declared to be *deceitful above* all *things*: And, finally, to take notice of some things, which, although themselves deceitful, the heart of man surpasses in deceit.

BUT all that we propose from this text, at present, is to mention some general evidences of the working of this corruption.

1. MAN discovers this corrupt principle, by adopting or maintaining a *profession* of religion *hypocritically*. Many, it may be feared, in the Church of Christ, embrace a profession, when they are themselves convinced, that their hearts are *not right with God, nor found in his statutes*. It is impossible that there can be, on earth, any society of considerable extent, without bad men in it. The Church, although a society instituted by God himself, regulated by the most perfect laws, and guarded by the most tremendous penalties, is nevertheless not exempted from the intrusion of the wicked. Into the heavenly Jerusalem alone can *no unclean thing enter*. In the Church visible there still have been, and there ever will be *tares among the wheat*. The Lord of the harvest suffers it to be so, for the display of his adorable perfections, especially of his love, wisdom, and power, in gathering in his elect, even by unlikely means; and of his justice, in the final condemnation of hypocrites, who shall thus appear inexcusable. Nor, from his infinite compassion to the weakest disciple, will he suffer his servants to claim a right of judging with certainty of the state of professors, and of acting accordingly; lest, in attempting to *gather up the tares*, they *root up also the wheat with them*. This mingled state of the Church he likewise permits, for the sake of his people, that they may retain a godly jealousy over their own deceitful hearts; that they may see the danger of trusting, in any degree, to religious duties; and earnestly seek the assurance of a more solid ground of consolation. God in sovereignty also suffers this, as a stumbling-block to the wicked, who, upon a discovery of hypocrites in the Church, harshly extend this character to all its members, and boldly pronounce every religious profession to be false: because they are resolved not to believe his word, and the reality of religion, on his own testimony.

Those who are conscious of hypocrisy, may adopt and maintain a religious profession, merely in some degree to pacify conscience. When this is alarmed by a sense of sin, they are fain
to

to lull it, if possible, by the semblance of holiness. However preposterous the attempt may seem, the conscience, while in a state of defilement, easily complies with deceit, being itself under the power of deceitfulness. Others may assume a cloak of religion, that in this way they may display their natural abilities, and gain the affection or admiration of the religious. Or they may design the advancement of their temporal interests. When the Church enjoys external prosperity, hypocrites abound most; as then the appearance of godliness may be subservient to gain. Jeremiah gives a short, but striking character of such professors, when complaining of them to God; *Thou art near in their mouth, and far from their reins* *. They use religion just as it serves their own purposes. Yet they will have the presumption to pretend, nay, to boast, that they are *doing God service*, and seeking his glory; while only accomplishing their own impious designs, and perhaps transgressing the very letter of his law. Concerning them, Isaiah speaks to the righteous in his time, whom they persecuted; *Hear the word of the Lord, ye that tremble at his word; Your brethren that hated you, that cast you out for my name's sake, said, Let the Lord be glorified* †. Of this character was Jehu. He could say to Jonadab, *Come and see my zeal for Jehovah*, while he meant only to accomplish the purposes of his own ambition. But the Lord used him as his instrument in punishing the wicked house of Ahab, and the accursed priests of Baal. After all his pretences, it is declared, That *he took no heed to walk in the law of the Lord God of Israel with all his heart; for he departed not from the sins of Jeroboam, who made Israel to sin* ‡. Hypocrisy was a prevailing iniquity among God's ancient people. Of this he often complains; and, would to God! that his language were not too applicable to us: *Yet, they seek me daily, and delight to know my ways, as a nation that did righteousness, and forsook not the ordinance of their God: they ask of me the ordinances of justice; they take delight in approaching unto*

---

* Jer. xii. 2.   † Isa. lxvi. 5.   ‡ 2 Kings x. 16. 31.

unto God *. How oppofite is this bafe character to that of the children of God, who, according to the meafure of grace given them, are like the men of Zabulon, who were *not of double heart* †. Some throw afide the cloak of a profeffion, as being too cumberfome, as foon as their purpofes are ferved by it; or perhaps, when they find themfelves difappointed in their expectations. Others continue to wear it to the end, and will never be difcovered, till *the Son of man fhall fend his angels to feparate the precious from the vile.*

2. THE deceitfulnefs of the heart appears, when men difcover greater *zeal* about matters of *indifference*, or, at leaft, of comparatively *lefs* importance, than about thofe of the *greateft* moment. This is exhibited by our Lord as an evidence of the hypocrify of the Pharifees: *Wo unto you, Scribes and Pharifees, hypocrites, for ye pay tithe of mint, and anife, and cummin; and have omitted the weightier matters of the law, judgment, mercy, and faith. Thefe ought ye to have done, and not leave the other undone. Ye blind guides, who ftrain at a gnat, and fwallow a camel* ‡. They preferred the obfervation of the ceremonial law to that of the moral; and indeed, were more anxious about obedience to the leaft precept of the one, than to the greateft of the other. Thofe things that are of greater moment, and thefe which are of lefs, are both to be obferved as duties; but ftill in their own place. Thefe of lefs importance are not to be preferred to thofe of the greateft; nor is the obfervation of the one to be confidered as an apology to God for the wilful neglect of the other. Chrift calls the Pharifees *blind guides*, becaufe they *ftrained at a gnat*, &c. This alludes to the cuftom obferved by the Jews of ftraining their liquors before they drank; left they fhould fwallow any thing, however fmall, that was unclean, or that might prove prejudicial. He accufes them of *fwallowing a camel*, while they *ftrained at a gnat*. They made great ado about the leaft obfervances in religion, and even about fuch as were not of Divine inftitution, but had only the fanction of their

be-

---

* Ifa. lviii. 2.   † 1 Chron. xii. 33.   ‡ Matt. xxiii. 23, 24.

beloved traditions; while they could eafily put up with the omiffion of the cleareft and moft important duties, fuch as immediately concerned the glory of God, or the good of their neighbour. They *omitted judgment.* They were negligent of the execution of juftice between man and man. They omitted *mercy.* Inftead of relieving the diftreffed, they *devoured the houfes of widows.* They omitted *faith.* All their religion was deftitute of the leading principle of faith in God; or, as the word may be underftood, they had no fenfe of faithfulnefs or honefty in civil tranfactions. It is greatly to be lamented, that this Pharifaical fpirit prevails with many profeffors of the Chriftian religion; and much to be feared that it prevails with many who make a greater profeffion than others. Many in our time feem exceedingly zealous about the external duties of religion, who are deftitute of any regard for the internal and more fubftantial parts of it. They are perhaps regular in the obfervation of fecret, private, and public ordinances, but in a great meafure negligent of relative duties. They are undutiful hufbands or wives, parents or children, mafters or fervants. You can have little dependance on their word, or confidence in their uprightnefs in civil dealings. Perhaps they carry on a practice of deceit, extortion, and oppreffion in fo fecret a manner, that although fufpected by all around, no one can prove it. They are indeed commendable in their attention to inftituted duties. But is this to be put in the room of every thing elfe? Perfons of this defcription feem to view the firft table as comprehending the whole law, and the bare outward obfervation of it as including the whole of religion.

There are others who go ftill farther. They place the greateft part of their religion in *fcrupulofity* about matters of mere indifference. Thofe things, for which they have no authority from the word of God, they wifh to impofe on others, as of indifpenfable obligation. The fmalleft deviation from a common form, which has no other fanction than that of cuftom, and it may be,
not

not even that of common sense, will be esteemed a grievous defection. The most innocent and necessary recreations will be reckoned unlawful freedoms. The very shape of a garment, or the dress of another, although consistent with the station in life, and with the rules of decency, will enter into their consciences; as if there were a certain sanctity in a custom, because it is a hundred years old; or, as if there never had been a change in these trifles, before the present age. We are far from defending that despicable and sinful vanity, which is so very prevalent in our times, of eagerly hunting after every new fashion, and of spending a great deal of time and money on gaudy attire. This conduct discovers an empty mind. It is to glory in what originates from our shame. But may not the pride of the heart as really appear, in an unseasonable zeal for the indifferent customs of the former age, as in an excessive conformity to those of the present? May not the affectation of an extreme peculiarity be as real a sacrifice to vanity as its contrary? Yes. For the Pharisees made broad their phylacteries, and enlarged *the borders of their garments ;* and this they did *to be seen of men.* It is no new thing for men to *wear a rough garment to deceive.*—To some the mere pronunciation of a word, however intelligible, or tone of the voice, will prove a weighty stumbling-block; as if a man should be accounted *an offender*, not only *for a word*, but for the very sound of it.

NOTWITHSTANDING all this warmth of zeal, you may perhaps find some of this character, if carefully watched, almost strangers to a principle of common integrity. They will make conscience a plea for all their impositions on others. But they more generally arise from the deceitfulness of the heart, than from any tenderness of conscience. Some of the children of God may, indeed, be very weak; and it would be sin to offend them. But, at the same time, it is the duty of ministers to show them what is religion, and what is mere whim or superstition. And it is their own duty to endeavour to get their consciences regulated according to God's Word; lest they be found chargeable with the guilt of will-worship, and of offending God by offering him *vain oblations*. Where such aptness to take offence is found, even with those who seem to be real Christians, if carefully investigated, it will appear to arise more from want of knowledge, than from tenderness of conscience: and, perhaps, the wilful indulgence of this ignorance, contrary to the clear light of the Word, which, in the most evident manner, distinguishes between sin and duty, may be a greater sin in them, than any supposed offence in matters of indifference, that can be given them by others. This temper is far more prejudicial to the interests of religion than is generally imagined. For, when professors give a false importance to matters of indifference, especially if they be more strict about these, or about things comparatively of less weight, than about the most essential; when men seem to make religion consist in absolute trifles, or are far more zealous about *mint, and anise, and cummin*, than about *the weightier matters of the law;* it induces others, who are unacquainted with its power, to apprehend that there is no reality in it at all. It is also extremely hurtful to the interests of religion in the persons themselves who indulge this spirit. For it insensibly confirms them in a Pharisaical temper; inspires them with a capricious and censorious disposition toward others; and, although real Christians, leads them to pay more attention to the externals of religion, than to a life of communion with God. This propensity is a great evidence of the deceitfulness of the heart. For in this manner, many, as it were, compound with their consciences; and enter into an engagement with them, that if they will not reprove them for the omission of *the weightier matters of the law*, they will be very rigid in the observation of things of less importance, and even lay a considerable weight upon matters of indifference. This, to those who have not the reality of religion, appears

pears an eafy way of purchafing a religious character; and the confciences of fuch, having never been purified by the Spirit, are very eafily fatisfied, and will give them peace at a fmall expence. But if any appear habitually more concerned about the outfide of religion, than about the very foul and effence of it; they give the greateft reafon for fufpecting them of hypocrify. For hypocrites are always partial in their religion. The ftudy of univerfal obedience to God's commandments is too fevere a tafk. They are therefore pleafed with a part: and they choofe that part which is leaft effential, becaufe it anfwers two of their deceitful ends; it gives themfelves lefs trouble, and it makes a greater blaze in the eye of the world.

WE would not here be thought to teach indifference with refpect to thofe things in religion, that are comparatively of lefs importance. Very far from it. All the Lord's people, according to their light and grace, will be concerned to *obferve all things, whatfoever he hath commanded them;* to *buy the truth,* however expenfive the purchafe, and to *fell it* at no price: becaufe every Divine truth, every Divine inftitution, is of infinite importance; is a part of that teftimony which *the faithful and true Witnefs* hath fealed with his ineftimable blood; and neceffarily belongs to that teftament which the great Teftator hath died to confirm, and hath *rifen again and revived* to execute. But we would expofe the folly of thofe who difcover great zeal and fervour about the lefs important matters of the law, and are fhamefully negligent of thofe of the greateft moment. We would alfo illuftrate the danger of ingrafting thofe things into religion, which are entirely indifferent; becaufe this has a tendency to lead away from the true foundation, and favours of an attempt to *add to the things which are written in the book* of God. Did not the innumerable abfurdities of the Roman Church fpring from this very fource? Carnal or fuperftitious men, difpleafed with the fpirituality of God's law, tried to

atone

atone for their neglect of *the weightier matters* of it by substituting in their room an endless variety of trivial observances, that were entirely destitute of the impress of Divine authority. These gradually swelled into a system, far more burdensome than that law of ceremonies which the Son of God abolished in his death, and as ridiculous as the human mind, in its most debased state, can be supposed capable of devising. An unscriptural scrupulosity often arises, even in real Christians, from a decline of that zeal, which hath once animated them in regard to practical religion. They feel the want of their former zeal, and must supply it some way or other. But instead of really awakening it in their hearts, and giving it a proper direction to its former objects; they deceive themselves with a mere phantom, which indeed assumes the appearance of zeal, and the place once occupied by zeal of a genuine kind. But it is merely the counterfeit of the other; it has not the same gracious origin; and it entirely differs from it in the mode of operation, being principally employed about matters of indifference. This spirit may also spring from peevishness of temper, from envy, or from ambition. A bad natural temper, in order to cover its own moroseness or virulence, may assume the mask of unwarrantable rigidity or censoriousness in religion. An envious person, who is sensible of the superiority of fellow-professors, may wish to bring them more on a level; and, at least in secret, to triumph over them, by subjecting them to his caprice. One, whose ambition is checked by meanness of station, may attempt to purchase distinction by the appearance of uncommon zeal.

But what will it avail you, professor, although you have every matter of indifference submitted to your pleasure, although you had every form of religion regulated to your mind, nay, every precious truth preserved entire: what will it avail you, though you be strict in a professed adherence to these, and unblameable in all the externals of religion? If this be all, you are but *a sounding brass, and a tinkling cymbal*.

cymbal. You may, indeed, continue in *the valley of vision,* and form the complete skeleton of a Christian. But like those ancient professors, you want sinews, and flesh, and skin; and what is worst of all, you want breath*. You are yet a dead man. You want the life, the soul of religion. Notwithstanding all your form, and your zeal about it, you *deny the power of godliness.*

3. The *short* continuance of *religious impressions,* whether on saints or sinners, is another evidence of this deceitfulness. Unrenewed men, when they have heard an awakening sermon, when they have been visited with some severe affliction, or when any arrow of conviction hath been fixed in their hearts by the power of the Spirit, are ready to apprehend that they shall be entirely different persons ever after. They set about external reformation, and, it may be, endeavour to cleanse their hearts and mortify their lusts by prayer and fasting: but, the first temptation that assails them effaces all these serious impressions, and plunges them into those sins that they pretended to forsake. Now, as the leading reason of this is, that they have not undergone a saving change in regeneration; it argues the great deceitfulness of their hearts, that all their zeal for God and religion, for the purification of their hearts and reformation of their lives, is dissipated by the first blast of temptation. Even Simon Magus had a kind of faith. It is said, that he *believed and wondered;* and perhaps he thought himself as good a Christian as any around him. But when he encountered a temptation to his ambition and covetousness, he instantly discovered that he was yet *in the gall of bitterness, and in the bond of iniquity.* 'In a short time he became one of the greatest enemies of the Christian Religion; and as is generally believed, was the founder of the impious sect of the Gnostics, who, pretending to believe Christianity, shockingly corrupted it, and intermixed it with heathen abominations. The deceitfulness that also prevails in the hearts of the Lord's people, appears by the short duration of their religious

---

* Ezek. xxxvii.

religious impressions. Often, after enjoying the most comfortable communion with God, and resolving to walk always with him, they find that the duty in which they have been engaged is scarcely ended, ere their warmth of affections and holy resolutions are vanished. Christians have frequent occasion to observe that their hearts are never more ready to be trivial, or to be carried away by vanity, than immediately after they have made the most solemn approaches to God. This may, in some measure, proceed from the temperament of our minds in this embodied state. They cannot bear to be always on the stretch. Therefore, when the faculties have been most excited for any length of time, they are in a manner exhausted, and require relaxation. But it especially proceeds from the deceitfulness of the heart, which always endeavours to escape from under the yoke of religious exercises. Even while the understanding disclaims the idea of any reliance on the work performed, as if it were in any degree meritorious, the legality of the heart may, in a secret and almost imperceptible manner, discover its power by blunting the pleasant edge that was on the spirits, as if it were now less necessary than before the performance of the duty. This shows the great necessity of that exhortation given by Christ to his disciples, immediately after the first celebration of the Sacrament of the Supper: *Watch and pray, that ye enter not into temptation.* To express the danger of slightly parting with gracious impressions, and the great prevalence of this evil with his own people, the Lord condescends to speak after the manner of men, as if his omniscience were put to a stand by it, as if *the only wise God* were himself at a loss for a remedy: *O! Ephraim, what shall I do unto thee? O! Judah, what shall I do unto thee? For your goodness is as the morning cloud, and as the early dew it goeth away**. No metaphor in nature can more justly express the transient nature of religious impressions, even on the hearts of the saints. How soon is *the morning cloud* dispelled, and *the early dew* drunk up by

---

* Hos. vi. 4.

by the scorching rays of the sun in a warm country, which generally enjoys an unclouded sky! As soon do the scorching flames of lust in the heart, especially when *set on fire of hell*, or fanned by the world's temptations, drink up, or, if we may so express it, evaporate our most serious impressions, unless we be *watered every moment* by that dew of the Holy Ghost, that *waiteth not for man, nor tarrieth for the sons of men.*

4. THIS deceitfulness appears by the many *delusions* of the *imagination*, in forming great hopes of earthly riches, honour or pleasure. Any person, who is but in a small degree, and in a natural way, acquainted with the workings of his own heart, must know how often it is hurried away, amused, and deluded by the most vain and foolish imaginations. How often does the *poor* man build himself up, and regale his fancy with the empty prospect of great riches. Even while awake, he pleasantly indulges the golden dream. He imagines to himself, how his eyes shall be dazzled with the lustre of his heaps of gold and silver. Does he try to satisfy the present cravings of nature, by feigning to himself the most luxurious feasts? It is *even as when a hungry man dreameth, and behold he eateth; but he awaketh, and his soul is empty: or, as when a thirsty man dreameth, and behold he drinketh; but he awaketh, and behold he is faint, and his soul hath appetite* *. Perhaps, he forms plans of his future operations, projects what he shall then do, what he shall say, how he shall demean himself to his former companions, and in what manner he shall spend his future wealth. How often does the *mean* man amuse his imagination with the delusive hope, we can scarcely call it hope, for it hath not probability sufficient to constitute hope; with the idea, with the supposition of honour and dignity, to which it is possible he may yet be advanced. He runs over, in his mind, the swelling titles and honourable names by which he may yet be known; fondly indulges his fancy in dwelling on them, even while his judgment declares his folly; and perhaps, enjoys more pleasure in his delusion,

* Isa. xxix. 8.

lusion, than he could enjoy in the reality. A man, in indulging his vain imaginations, often imposes upon himself so far as to try to persuade himself of the probability of that in his own case, which has no more probability with regard to him than to a million of others around him. If one of his acquaintance has been unexpectedly exalted in his situation in life, he will consider this as a strong argument for the probability of his own advancement. And is not this vanity of imagination, which all must feel in some degree, because of the natural folly of all, a decisive proof of the deceitfulness of the heart? Such it is esteemed by God: *Ephraim feedeth on wind, and followeth after the east wind.* How is the truth of this illustrated? *Ephraim said; Yet I am become rich, I have found me out substance* *. From partiality to ourselves, we may apologise for such reveries of fancy, as if they were altogether harmless, however ill-founded. But, as they demonstrate *the vanity of the mind* †; the Searcher of hearts not only declares them to be vain, but wicked: *O! Jerusalem, wash thine heart from wickedness, that thou mayest be saved; how long shall thy vain thoughts lodge within thee* ‡.

5. The extreme *reluctance* of the heart to *believe its own deceitfulness,* is a great evidence of its power. Notwithstanding the many express declarations of this contained in the word of God, and the various proofs that every man gives of it; the heart naturally refuses the charge, gives the lie to God, and flatly denies the evidence of demonstration. Now, as we conclude that he is certainly blind, who asserts that he is in darkness, and can discern no object, even while the sun shines on him at mid-day; when a man denies the deceitfulness of his heart, in opposition to the most convincing proofs from scripture, and from his own experience of its fruits; we with equal propriety conclude, that this very denial is a corroborating proof of the justness of the charge. The truth is; as a man born blind cannot see the light, or discern objects around him, unless his eyes be opened: as little can the

---

* Hos. xii. 1. 8.   † Eph. iv. 17.   ‡ Jer. iv. 14.

the heart be perfuaded of its own deceitfulnefs, till *the eyes of the underflanding be opened, by the Spirit of wifdom and revelation.* This blindnefs of mind is like the jaundiced eye, which makes a man apprehend that every thing he views is difcoloured, while the whole error lies in his own difeafed organ. Although a perfon deprived of the exercife of reafon, may fometimes imagine that all around him are mad, and that he alone is in his fenfes; we would not fuftain this as any evidence of the foundnefs of his judgment, but on the contrary, as an evidence of his infanity; efpecially when this is confirmed by the reft of his conduct. Our Lord, addreffing the Pharifees, confiders their denial of the charge of fpiritual blindnefs as a certain document of its reality: *If ye were blind, ye fhould have no fin,* i. e. " if ye were deftitute of revelation, *if I had " not come and fpoken unto you,* your fin would be un-" fpeakably lefs; or, if ye were fenfible of your own " blindnefs, it would be an evidence of your delive-" rance from its dominion:" *but now ye fay, we fee; therefore your fin remaineth;* " you are filled with ap-" prehenfions of the greatnefs of your wifdom, and of " the perfection of your righteoufnefs; and this in-" fallibly demonftrates that you are yet under the " abfolute power of fin*." Solomon feems to adopt the fame proof: *The wifdom of the prudent is to underftand his way; but the folly of fools is deceit* †. Elfewhere he fpeaks more clearly on this head. *The way of the wicked is as darknefs: they know not at what they ftumble* ‡. They cannot refufe that they do ftumble; but like a man walking in fuch grofs darknefs, that he cannot difcern objects around him, they know not the true caufe, and deny it when declared to them. So great is this reluctance, that finners, inftead of crediting what they hear from the law and teftimony, are apt to take offence at the fervants of Chrift, when they infift on the evils of the heart; as if they had a pleafure in magnifying the wickednefs of man, and in reprefenting human nature

* John ix. 41. † Prov. xiv. 8. ‡ Prov. iv. 19.

as vaſtly worſe than it really is. At any rate, they deny the applicableneſs of the doctrine to themſelves, and proudly ſay, with the vain-glorious Phariſees, *Are we blind alſo** ?

From the foregoing obſervations we may learn,

1. The origin of hypocriſy in a religious profeſſion. Of this the natural deceitfulneſs of the heart is the parent. This is the cauſe of the dreadful preſumption of ſinners in reſting on *a name to live*. Hypocriſy, indeed, whatever form it aſſumes, is juſt the acting of this corrupt principle which lies hid in the heart.

2. The only cure of hypocriſy. This is the deſtruction of the principle of deceit. One may with conſiderable ardour aim at ſincerity in a profeſſion; but he is ſtill, in God's account, an hypocrite, as long as his inward deceitfulneſs remains in full power. It is only by the removal of the cauſe, that the effect can ceaſe.

3. The danger of this courſe. You, who are ſenſible that you are falſe and hypocritical in your profeſſion, that you only ſeek your own intereſt, or the praiſe of men, ſhould conſider the awful judgments, which God denounces againſt you. *The congregation of hypocrites ſhall be deſolate. The hypocrites in heart heap up wrath; they cry not when God bindeth them. They die in youth, and their life is among the unclean. The Lord ſhall have no joy in their young men; neither ſhall have mercy on their fatherleſs and widows: for every one is an hypocrite and an evil-doer.* God ſummons all with the greateſt ſolemnity, to attend to his judgments on hypocrites: *Hear ye that are far off, and ye that are near, acknowledge my might. The ſinners in Zion are afraid, fearfulneſs hath ſurpriſed the hypocrites.* He ſummons all to attend to their language under his judgments; *who among us ſhall dwell with devouring fire? who amongſt us ſhall dwell with everlaſting burnings?* It is only by being delivered

from

* John ix. 40.

from the hypocrisy of your hearts, that you can be saved from its tremendous consequences.

Finally, we may learn the necessity of consistency in religion. It is your duty, to be zealous in all the matters of God, in all those things which are the subject of Divine Revelation. There may be a call in Providence, from a concurrence of circumstances, for displaying more zeal about one part of truth than about another; particularly when it is in danger of perishing, or generally *despised and rejected*. But beware of being so zealous about any truth of comparatively less importance, as to let those slip which are of the utmost consequence to God's glory and your salvation. All truths are pearls; but there are some of more value than others, as being more nearly connected with *the pearl of great price*. Endeavour to attain that spiritual discernment, which will enable you to distinguish between things that really belong to religion, and such as are merely indifferent. Although you ought not to part with *one jot of the law;* you must be equally concerned not to add any thing to it: for this tends to lead your minds astray from your principal concerns, and to restrain the Christian liberty of your brethren, often in things which are trivial, and sometimes in those that are ridiculous. Nay, hereby you offer *vain oblations* unto God, and are in danger of *making his commandments of none effect by your traditions.*

SERMON XII.

On the DECEITFULNESS of the HEART, with Regard to the COMMISSION of SIN.

Psalm xxxvi. 2.

He flattereth himself in his own eyes, until his iniquity be found to be hateful.

OF such unspeakable consequence is it to us, in all the duties of religion, to be delivered from our own deceitfulness, that our Lord *first of all began to say unto his disciples; Beware of the leaven of the Pharisees, which is hypocrisy.* So powerful and prevalent is it, that, like leaven, it hath diffused itself through the whole man. All the powers of the soul are tainted with it. All our thoughts, words and actions bear the marks of its pollution. The very members of our body are affected by its contaminating influence. Our eyes, and lips, and hands are taught to speak and practice deceit. So that this corrupt mixture hath *leavened the whole lump* of our nature. As our deceitfulness is compared to leaven; the Spirit of God metaphorically describes the sincerity of the saints under the notion of their being *unleavened;* therefore we are required to *purge out the old leaven,* and to *keep the feast with the unleavened bread of sincerity and truth.*

In this Psalm we have a description of sin, especially as it appears in those who have openly broken God's bands. The introduction is very striking; *The transgression of the wicked saith within my heart, that there*

there is no fear of God before his eyes. How could the *transgression of the wicked* speak within the *heart* of him, who in the inscription of the Psalm declares himself to be *the servant of* JEHOVAH? These words are generally understood as signifying that the outward conduct of the sinner, as often as he thought of it, naturally suggested this conclusion to his mind, that he was destitute of all fear of God. But they may perhaps admit of another meaning, equally agreeable to the literal reading; *wickedness saith of the wicked, within my heart, &c.* According to this view, the Psalmist meant that notwithstanding the external pretences of the wicked, and all their attempts to cover their iniquity, he was certain that they had no real sense of the presence of God, that they secretly renounced his authority. How was he assured of this? By a comparison of their conduct with the dictates of the heart. He could not indeed look into their hearts, but he could look into his own; and *there* he found corruption so strong, that were it not for the fear of God that was implanted within him, he would be as bad as they. The difference between him and them lay in this only, that he was *the servant of the Lord,* by whom his *bands* had been *loosed,* by whom he had been delivered from the dominion of his natural depravity. But when he saw such wickedness in their lives, and compared it with the tendency of the heart, as attested by his own experience, he might safely conclude that they had cast off the fear of God. For this he found was the only thing that restrained him. And this indeed was a very fair method of trial. He knew that as the hearts of all were *formed alike,* there was a secret sympathy of operation, correspondent to this similarity of frame. For *as in water face answereth to face, so the heart of man to man.* He, as well as they, was *shapen in iniquity, and conceived in sin.*

HE afterwards introduces some evidences derived from the outward conduct of the sinner, which led
him

him to form this conclusion as to his heart: *The words of his mouth are iniquity and deceit, he hath left off to be wise, and to do good.*—*He setteth himself in a way that is not good; he abhorreth not evil.* But judging from his continuance in iniquity, he previously gives an account of its progress in his heart, and of its hardening nature: *He flattereth himself in his own eyes.* The matter which this self-flattery especially concerns is sin, as appears from the following clause. He deceives himself as to its nature and consequences, its evil and aggravations; and he continues to do so, *until his iniquity be found to be hateful,* till it be fully discovered, and appear in its magnitude and atrocious circumstances both to himself and others, by some awful Divine judgment, such as that mentioned in the last verse of the Psalm. *There are the workers of iniquity fallen; they are cast down, and shall not be able to rise.* He adduces this self-deceit and continuance in it, as illustrating the truth of that judgment he had formed of the state of such a person: *There is no fear of God before his eyes. For he flattereth himself in his own eyes.* And surely the proof is incontrovertible. For a man under the bondage of sin would never *flatter himself in his own eyes,* were it not that *God is not before* them. The reason why he thinks so well of himself is, that *God is not in all his thoughts.* He hath cast off all fear about himself, because he hath no fear of God.

From these words it is proposed to mention some evidences of inward deceitfulness, with regard to the *commission* of *sin.*

Here it may be necessary previously to observe,

1. That all the proofs of the deceitfulness of the heart, which we mean to offer with regard to sin, may not be found in every person, especially in those who are under its power. As to those who work sin, whose constant employment it is to commit sin; as they do it *with greediness;* as there is no fixed
principle

principle within them oppoſing it, whatever occaſional oppoſition may be made by the natural conſcience or temporary convictions; as they require fewer excitements to the commiſſion of it: the heart does not need to unfold many of its ſtratagems, becauſe they ſin with all their heart. Some of thoſe inſtances of deceit, which we have in our eye, will be more generally found with true believers, who, as their *mind*, their renewed part is conſtantly oppoſed to ſin, however often overpowered by it, are not only hurried away by the force of corruption, but enſnared by its ſubtilty. They do not habitually, like the unrenewed, fall into the pit the moment that it is digged; nor do they voluntarily entice themſelves to the commiſſion of ſin; but they ſtruggle againſt it, till they are enticed and overcome by their own deceitfulneſs.

2. MANY of thoſe things, which are evidences of the deceitfulneſs of the heart, may be uſed as temptations by Satan. For his ſnares are generally formed upon the deceits of the heart. The wind of Satan's temptation commonly blows along with the tide of corruption within, whether by deceit, or by violence. Were not this the caſe, *Satan would be divided againſt himſelf*, and oppoſing the intereſts of his own kingdom. When he *entered into Judas*, it was only to ſtir up his natural covetouſneſs. If we may ſuppoſe him at any time oppoſing the current of any particular luſt, it is with a view to open the ſluices to one comparatively more abominable, or becauſe, from his helliſh policy, he perceives that the indulgence of one corruption would not anſwer his preſent deſigns, ſo well as the indulgence of another. The general coincidence between the deceits of the heart and the temptations of Satan, makes it extremely difficult to diſtinguiſh the one from the other: for thoſe temptations that may at one time ariſe from the corruption of the heart, may at another proceed from the activity of this adverſary. Moſt probably, there is no temptation that Satan can manage againſt a

perſon,

person, which may not, at some time, or in some measure, proceed from his own deceitfulness.

We may now observe that the deceitfulness of the heart appears,

1. In raising *doubts* in the mind, with respect to what one is inclined to, whether it *really* be *sin*. It is a very common stratagem of the heart, to make the person question the reality of sin in any particular action, when lust excites him to the commission of it; although it be directly against the clearest precepts of the law, the light of the understanding, and the dictates of conscience. Such doubts will more readily arise concerning an action, with regard to which there is nothing expressly revealed; although by clear scriptural consequence, there may be sufficient reason to conclude that it is a transgression of the law. As they appear in the mind, which, strictly viewed, is the seat of thought and reflection; they owe their origin to the heart, which is the seat of will and choice. This indeed is the leading cause of the commission of sin. The affections, which are the inferior part of the soul, and the instruments by which the will expresses its inclinations, gain the ascendant over the understanding, which is the superior. If this faculty be under the power of sin, the affections habitually take the lead. If it be partly enlightened in a gracious manner, the affections, notwithstanding, when a fit opportunity is presented, often blind it by their allurements, and subject it by their influence. Therefore, those who are in a state of nature, are said to *walk in the vanity of their mind, having the understanding darkned, being alienated from the life of God through the ignorance that is in them, because of the blindness*, or, as it may rather be read, *the hardness of their heart* *. The obduracy of the heart, its proneness to sin, is here assigned as one great reason of ignorance; because it increases the darkness of the understanding. What sin soever the heart desires to perpetrate, it wishes, if possible, to view as no sin;

* Eph. iv. 17. 18.

sin; that it may be done with less reluctance from conscience, and according to the person's deluded imagination, with less danger of punishment; as if wilful ignorance could excuse us before God. Sin was first introduced into the lower creation by a doubt. Eve first doubted the evil of eating of the forbidden tree, and the certainty of the penalty, before she disbelieved and ate.

The heart, when it prevails so far, as to inspire the mind with doubt as to the sinfulness of an action, will then urge that at the worst it can only be a sin of ignorance, and that God will either not punish it at all, or pass it over very slightly. The Spirit of God, speaking by the wise man, takes notice of this apology, and illustrates its deceitfulness from a consideration of that contempt that the Searcher of hearts will pour upon it. *If thou forbear to deliver them that are drawn unto death, and those that are ready to be slain: If thou sayest, Behold, we knew it not: doth not he that pondereth the heart, consider it? And he that keepeth thy soul, doth not he know it? And shall not he render to every man according to his works**.

2. In trying to persuade him that it is a *little* sin. If the understanding will not be betrayed into a belief that the matter proposed is no sin at all, the heart will strenuously plead that it scarcely deserves the name. Its reasonings on this head are exceedingly deceitful. It will remind the person, that *there is no man who liveth and sinneth not*; that every man has some evil about him; that it is vain for him to expect to be altogether free of sin, for thus he would claim greater perfection than any saint on earth, nay, greater than God himself hath allotted to any man in this imperfect state; and that if no man can be altogether delivered from sin, he may surely indulge himself in that which he knows is comparatively little; that it is better to commit this, than a greater one, which might probably be the case, as he cannot wholly subdue his corruptions; that it is wisdom to chuse the least of two evils, and, perhaps,

* Prov. xxiv. 11, 12.

prevent a greater sin by a less; and, in a word, that God cannot be much offended at the commission of so trivial an offence, when one abstains from many that are far more dishonouring to him. The heart, in this case, presents the same plea with Lot for Zoar; *Spare this, for it is a little one.* Ephraim is introduced as expressing its genuine language in palliating guilt; *In all my labours, they shall find none iniquity in me, that were sin* *.—" Although I am " not altogether blameless," saith the deceitful heart, " yet nothing can be found in me of so great im- " portance as really to deserve the odious appellation " of sin."

3. By representing the *mortification* of sin, as affording far less pleasure than the gratification of it. Sinners know well enough that it is necessary for them to mortify sin; because it is expresly declared, that *if we live after the flesh, we shall die*. They know that whosoever is *in the flesh cannot please God;* and that *no unclean thing shall enter within the new Jerusalem*. But their corrupt and deceitful hearts tell them, in reply to all their convictions, that the task of mortification is not only extremely difficult, but extremely unpleasant; and that it is much more for their ease and satisfaction to indulge sin, than to endeavour its destruction. The heart discloses all the pain, labour, anxiety, and struggling, that a person must undergo in crucifying one lust; and thence argues the great improbability of getting all those of the old man crucified. It heightens the colouring, and increases the dimensions of the picture, to make it the more disgustful to the eye of sense and carnal reason. Nay, it will presume to urge, not only the difficulty, but the unreasonableness, the cruelty of attempting totally to subdue sin. " Are passions," may it say, " implanted in man by his Creator, and " can we ever suppose that he requires him to eradi- " cate them? Hath he communicated desires; and " can it be unlawful to gratify them? Hath he fa- " voured us with enjoyments; and must we deny " ourselves.

* Hos. xii. 8.

"ourselves the use of them? Would it not be unjust to suppose so compassionate a Being to punish men, for what is natural to them; or to require that they should entirely devote themselves to a melancholy life, and voluntarily renounce every blessing and comfort of society?" It gives as false a representation, as if God, when calling us to subdue sin, required that we should be denied to all our natural feelings and enjoyments, while he only directs us to the moderate and innocent use of them; as if he enjoined us to deny ourselves every comfort, while he only points out the way to the real enjoyment of temporal comforts, and to the possession of those which are spiritual, endless, and unfading in their nature. The very slaves of sin, if they would suffer themselves to reflect but for a moment, must be persuaded of the falsity of this reasoning. For there is really more trouble and vexation occasioned to the sinner, in his unremitted endeavours to satisfy his corruptions, than all that is felt by the believer, in mortifying his. Lust is absolutely insatiable. Like the grave, like the barren womb, it ever cries; *Give, give, for it is not enough.* Gratify it in one instance, and this is only opening the door to its importunate cravings in another. Do every thing in your power to *make provision for the flesh*; fatigue your body, wound your conscience, waste your substance, and rack your invention in discovering renewed gratifications: and, after all, it is more unsatisfied than before. It still rises in its demands. Newly invented gratifications, as they enlarge the capacity of enjoyment, enlarge the desire. It seeks to plunge you deeper and deeper in guilt. It may delude you, by saying; "Give me this one gratification farther, and I will ask no more." But how often have you found its deceitfulness? For it hath another, and generally, a more wicked demand to present immediately after. Every corruption, how modest soever it may seem in its solicitations, on its first appearance, still seeks to drive its subject to the very utmost of iniquity that can be perpetrated

trated in its service. Add to this; that, as lust, after all its gratifications, is still unsatisfied, the soul is far more so. Thereby not only does a man purchase to himself everlasting misery, but a great portion of present anguish; so that a few moments of the horror of conscience, which has been at times felt by the most guilty sinner, inexpressibly overbalance all the transitory pleasure in the enjoyment of sin. Now, if we compare this with the exercise of the renewed soul, in the mortification of sin, we will find that the difference is exceedingly great. Every child of God, who *through the Spirit* has learned to *mortify the deeds of the body*, will be ready to declare, that he has experienced joy unspeakably more solid and satisfying in the mortification of sin, than he ever did in its gratification; and that the toil of *fulfilling the desires of the flesh, and of the mind*, far exceeds that of resisting them in the strength of grace. The one is a pleasure, succeeded and often accompanied by anguish and horror, which consume its very essence; the other, a pleasure unattended by a pang, save that which the unrenewed nature feels. The one is labour, without any reward, but that of death; the other is *a labour of love*, accomplished in obedience to an affectionate Father; a labour, which constitutes an eminent part of the present delightful enjoyment of the life of God, and which shall be finally crowned with a rich *recompence of reward*, in that state in which sin shall be no more.

4. Sin is exhibited as far more *pleasant* than it is really found in the commission. The corrupt heart and carnal affections, which are attached to sin, delineate it a attended by the greatest pleasure or advantage. The prospect of that delight, which one expects to find in the indulgence of sin, is but a gay illusion, presented by the deceitful heart. The sinner, in general, lives only by hope. He is disappointed in the gratification. The enjoyments of sin are like the apples of Sodom, which, how fair soever they appear to the eye, when grasped by the hand
are

are said to fall to ashes. *He that soweth iniquity, shall reap vanity* *. Solomon, *the beloved of the Lord*, when left to fall into a course of sin, was by the event fully convinced of the deceitfulness of his heart. From his elevated situation, he had an opportunity of making a fuller and more extensive trial than the most of men. Pushed on by the ardour of hope, he pursued pleasure through all its supposed retreats; and the result of all his gratifications and researches, is contained in that striking declaration; *Vanity of vanities, vanity of vanities; all is vanity and vexation of spirit.* The heart often seduces to indulgence in some carnal joy, some sinful pleasure; but it is found, that *even in joy the heart is sorrowful, and that the end of that mirth is heaviness.* Therefore, saith the Spirit of God; *What fruit had ye in those things whereof ye are now ashamed? for the end of those things is death* †. He does not merely refer the vanity and unsatisfactoriness of carnal enjoyments to the test of that sorrow and *shame*, which men feel, after being brought to genuine repentance. He is willing to risk the issue on the trial of those very feelings that they had in their unconverted state. *What fruit had ye in those things?* " What did all the honours, pleasures " and profits you promised yourselves in sin amount " to? Was not the sum-total not only *vanity*, but " *vexation of spirit?* Did they not, in the end, *bite* " *like a serpent, and sting like an adder?* As their " natural and direct *end*, their proper *wages* and " fruit, is death; had you not many earnests of this " in the bodily pangs, and especially in the agonies " of spirit and remorse of conscience, which closely " followed them?"

5. It represents a *renewed opportunity* of sin, as promising far *greater* satisfaction than was ever found *before*. As the person must necessarily remember that sin deluded him in the enjoyment; to set aside this objection to the renewed practice of it, the heart pledges itself, that on another trial sin will bring with it a great accession of pleasure. Sin often assumes a

new

---

* Prov. xxii. 8.   † Rom. vi. 21.

new difguife, to conceal that vanity which has been formerly found in it. Indeed, the heart fubmits to a great deal of trouble, that it may give fin a keener edge, and increafe its pleafantnefs. The finner would feem, at times, to be fatiated with the famenefs, and wearied out by the emptinefs of frequent gratification. But the heart endeavours to ftimulate him, by preparing new allurements. In enticing itfelf and the other powers to fin, it acts the fame part with the adulterefs, fo ftrikingly defcribed by the wife man; *I have decked my bed with coverings of tapeftry, with carved works, with fine linen of Egypt. I have perfumed my bed with myrrh, aloes and cinnamon* *. What a fool is the finner in thinking God a hard mafter! He is infinitely better than the deceitful heart; for it promifes and never performs: but he gives both ftrength for his fervice, and a glorious reward. The heart, as unrenewed, is a worfe mafter than Satan himfelf: for he fometimes ceafes to tempt; but the heart is never at reft: and often when Satan gives over a temptation, it takes it up again, and pufhes it with greater violence than before. The *worldly-minded* man, how much foever he has been formerly difappointed in his expectations, or in the comfort which he apprehended would arife from his fuccefs, is by his heart perfuaded to devote himfelf to the world anew, and with more keennefs than ever, under the flattering profpect of greater fuccefs, and of greater fatisfaction. The *fenfualift*, who is perhaps fick of fin, becaufe of the fatal confequences of his debauchery, is encouraged to begin again, from the falfe hope that his next fcene of diffipation will afford him pleafure, fuperior to any that he has found before. Thus the fallacious heart goes on, adding promife to promife, and hope to hope, till, in the end, either mercy or judgment difcover them to be equally vain and unfatisfactory.

6. It pleads that one may *indulge* fin *a little*, without altogether yielding to the fin particularly in view. The heart does not difcover all its depths of wickednefs

* Prov. vii. 16, 17.

ness at first, especially if there be a principle of grace to oppose it; finding it the surest course to proceed by degrees. In its temptations, as temptation is indeed ascribed to it, (James i. 14.) it goes on like Satan. The great point he aimed at, in his assault upon our spotless Head, was to prevail with him, if possible, to deny his Deity by devil-worship. But he appears at first to be very moderate in his demands. While he insinuates a doubt of the truth of his Divinity, he pretends a care for his natural life, as he was then *an hungred*; and will have him to display his power, by converting stones into bread. In his next attack, he wishes him to tempt Providence, by unnecessarily exposing himself to danger. Not till the last, does he produce his most arrogant demand of express worship from the Son of God. In like manner, the corrupt heart, in tempting to sin, seeks but a little at first, and pretends that it will be satisfied with a little. The natural conscience, at least, would recoil at the immediate proposal of the greatest wickedness. Even the wicked Hazael, when the Prophet foretold what he would do to the people of God, seems to shudder at the idea ; *Is thy servant a dog*, saith he, *that he should do this great thing* *. Elisha made no other reply than this ; *The Lord hath shewed me, that thou shalt be king over Syria*. By insinuating to him what he was, perhaps, even *then* resolved to do to his master, he proved the certainty of what he would do to Israel. As if he had said ; " The man who can " do the one, will find little difficulty with the other." The deceitful heart has enough of that *wisdom that is devilish*, to know, that if a man be enticed to tamper with sin, or to sin a little, he is in a fair way to proceed to all that excess in sin to which it wishes to hurry him. It intreats that sin should at least obtain a hearing. It insinuates that it is very weak in a man to be so jealous of his own strength, as to suppose that he can be in any danger from merely listening to what sin hath to offer for itself. Or it argues, that one may indulge sin a little, and easily retreat, when there is any

---

* 2 Kings viii. 13.

any danger of going too far; that sin is a very delicious morsel, and may be *rolled under the tongue*, without being swallowed. Thus was the heart first poisoned, by listening to the deceitfulness of Satan, and disbelieving God. Eve first looked on the tree; then she saw that it was *pleasant to the eyes;* then she proceeded to touch it; then to eat; and, last of all, to act the part of a tempter to her husband.

7. It throws a veil of *forgetfulness* over the whole soul, with respect to all the painful *consequences* of sin, formerly felt. Upon a renewed allurement to the commission of sin, even the natural conscience is ready to suggest its former bitter fruits. The heart itself, perhaps, still retains the impression of its stings. But it discovers a peculiar power of deceit in concealing these, as if they had never been; in deadening any remaining sensations of this kind; and in persuading itself that all was mere apprehension. That loathsomeness of sin, hatred of self on account of it, or fear of wrath, which the person experienced after a former indulgence, are entirely vanished; and he now appears to himself as one who *feared where no fear was*. Whence does this arise, but from the deceitfulness of the heart, that uses all its influence to suppress convictions, and to bury in oblivion a sense of the past bitterness of sin? When the Spirit works, either in a common or gracious way, by inward motions, in opposition to sin; representing it as contrary to the holy law, as dishonouring to God, as ruining to the soul; when it recals to view the former unpleasant consequences of it; or directs to the heart and conscience *a word in season;* the heart, as unrenewed, discovers its deceitfulness, by treating all these as dreams. It endeavours to ridicule a man out of any regard to them, as being childish or enthusiastic fears, and unnecessary restraints. It attempts to quench this holy fire of the Spirit's kindling, by the filthy torrent of its own corruption; to extinguish this *candle of the Lord*, by the storm of lust which it awakes. Thus all *the affliction and the misery, the wormwood and the gall*, which, in consequence of sin,

have

have formerly embittered the foul, are forgotten in a moment: as God complains to his ancient people, when reproving them for renewed tranfgreffions; *In all thine abominations and thy whoredoms, thou haft not remembered the days of thy youth, when thou waft naked and bare, and polluted in thy blood* *.

8. It entices the *imagination* into its fervice. This is not only Satan's workhoufe in the foul; but it may be viewed as a purveyor, which the heart engages in making provifion for its lufts. When finful motions arife in the heart, by it they are immediately tranfmitted to the imagination, that it may minifter fewel to corruption. This power cheerfully obeys the fummons. Being nearly connected with the fenfes, being the channel in which the ideas of external objects are communicated to the mind; it awakes within itfelf the agreeable impreffions formerly made by the indulgence of fin; calls in the affiftance of memory; invents the means of *fulfilling the defires of the flefh, and of the mind;* and thus ripens the motions of fin communicated by the heart, and remits them to it, in a more perfect form, to receive the confent of the will, by which the act is inwardly completed. Mournful is the defcription given us of this inventive faculty, in confequence of its depravation by fin: *God faw, that every imagination of the thoughts of* man's *heart was only evil continually* †. And this is ftill the cafe in the eye of Omnifcience; for God makes the fame declaration immediately after the flood, before he took another trial of man; becaufe he knew that this wickednefs was not peculiar to any age, or to any race, but inherent in human nature, in confequence of original apoftafy: and that it was not fo by reafon of example; *for the imagination of man's heart is evil from his youth* ‡. Not only is this power inftrumental in preparing the intoxicating potion of iniquity for the heart, and in hurrying on to the perfection of the outward act of fin; but it multiplies iniquities, increafes the filth, and greatly adds to the guilt of the perfon, by acting fin over and over again within itfelf,

* Ezek. xvi. 22. † Gen. vi. 5. ‡ Gen. viii. 21.

self, long after it has been actually committed, and when, perhaps, there is no opportunity of a renewed commission. It ruminates on sin; it recals the impressions it has made with pleasure, at least, without becoming abhorrence; whence a wish often arises in the heart, for as good an occasion as formerly has been either embraced or rejected. This is one article in the accusation brought by God against Aholibah, the type of the Jewish Church, expressive of her grateful recollection of ancient idolatry: *Yet she multiplied her whoredoms, in calling to remembrance the days of her youth, wherein she played the harlot in the land of Egypt* *.

9. It engages the *senses* on its side. These are volunteers to the corrupt heart, which it arms in its service, and by which it accomplishes its wicked purposes, when enticing to outward acts of sin. It is not enough to the deceitful heart to raise a confusion and combustion in all the powers of the soul. It excites a perturbation in the whole man, and tries to actuate and employ the members of the body as *the instruments of unrighteousness unto sin:* like a thief who sets the whole house on fire, that he may have an opportunity, by the confusion occasioned, of carrying off the goods that it contains. When it would allure to avarice or uncleanness, it directs the eye to gilded treasures, or to an object fit to excite sinful desires. Hence avarice is called *the lust of the eye;* and unclean persons are said to have *eyes full of adultery, and that cannot cease from sin.* Observe the progress of sin in the heart of Achan. He *saw,* and *coveted,* and *took,* and *hid in* his *tent* †. When the heart would excite to vanity or ambition; the ear shall be regaled with flattery, or the delusive sound of applause. Would it tempt to gluttony or drunkenness? It grasps at things which are pleasant to the taste. Thus, by stirring up a flame in the sensitive part of the man, he becomes a more easy prey to its deceits. For the voice of the senses will always overpower that of the understanding; if they be not *brought into subjection,* or presently restrained by grace.

* Ezek. xxiii. 19. † Jos. vii. 21. 10. In

10. In reprefenting fin as properly *one's own*, as fomething belonging to *one's felf*. As it endeavours to caft a veil over the hatefulnefs of fin, fo alfo over the horror of it, as in any degree arifing from Satan; that the perfon may more readily comply with its inftigations. When a man is enticed to fin, however pleafant it be to his unrenewed part, or to the whole man as unrenewed, how gratifying foever to his fenfes; he would yet in fome meafure recoil at the thought, were he fully convinced that Satan were *ftanding at his right hand*, feeking his utter deftruction. Now, as Satan and the deceitful heart go hand in hand in temptation, it is one of its devices, and alfo, one of his wiles, if poffible, to perfuade a man that he has no fhare in the prefent temptation. Sin, although in itfelf it would be nowife difagreeable, would yet appear fhocking, were it viewed as the immediate fpawn of the devil. But when a man confiders it merely as the offspring of his own heart, he looks upon it with far lefs reluctance; whatever may be urged againft it by a natural confcience, or by the principle of grace.

SERMON XIII.

On the DECEITFULNESS of the HEART, with regard to the COMMISSION of SIN.

Psalm xxxvi. 2.

He flattereth himfelf in his own eyes, until his iniquity be found to be hateful.

IN the preceding difcourfe, we have, in feveral inftances, illuftrated the deceitfulnefs of the heart, with regard to the Commiffion of Sin, we proceed to obferve that it farther appears,

11. By

11. By insinuating that committing such a sin *once more* cannot greatly *increase* our *guilt*. Perhaps the heart is engaged in alluring to a sin frequently committed before. In this case it urges, that it is not like the commission of a new sin, that it is only to make a very inconsiderable addition to the old score. To serve its present purposes, it may grant that if it were a new sin, a farther progress in the same kind of sinning, or a repetition of any sin with aggravated circumstances, then it would be dangerous and to be avoided. But it pleads an indulgence for an old, beloved iniquity, just as a man does for a friend, with whom he has long been on a footing of intimacy. Thus, it deludes the person by its wicked suggestions, making him believe that there is less guilt in the commission of a sin, which has been often committed before; while no reasoning can be more false: for the longer that any sin is indulged, it becomes the more provoking to God, and the more dangerous to the soul. Instead of being alleviated by the frequency, the guilt of every renewed transgression is greatly aggravated; because it is committed against the more frequent warnings of conscience, testimonies of the Lord's displeasure by Word and Providence, and instances of his unspeakable long-suffering. Therefore, a continuance in the practice of any sin, or return to it, after it has been in some measure renounced, is mentioned as a great aggravation of the guilt of any person or people: *They turned back and tempted God**. It procures an awful increase of wrath: *They have returned to provoke me to anger,—therefore will I also deal in fury; mine eye shall not spare, neither will I have pity: and though they cry in mine ears with a loud voice, yet will I not hear them* †. *They sin more and more—therefore they shall be—as the chaff that is driven with the whirlwind out of the floor, and as the smoke out of the chimney* ‡.

12. The heart will urge the *vanity* of attempting to resist the temptation. It will plead for yielding to

---

* Psal. lxxviii. 41.   † Ezek. viii. 17, 18.   ‡ Hos. xiii. 2, 3.

to the present assault, from former instances of insufficiency in opposing one of the same nature. "What?" may it say, "art thou now become "stronger than at such a time, when thou usedst "every effort to withstand a solicitation to this very "sin; but all in vain? Hast thou received any hid- "den strength formerly unknown? Notwithstanding "thy late defeat, are thy locks so well grown that "thou canst think of being victorious over thine "enemies?" It may urge present felt weakness. "Art thou so foolish," may it say, "as to think of "resistance at this time with any prospect of success; "when thy affections are already engaged, when "conscience is become more calm in its remon- "strances against the sin, when the means are at "hand, and nothing hinders the indulgence, but the "feeble reluctance of the will to a formal consent?" It may reason, according to the nature of the temptation, from the example of others who were eminent saints. "Art thou more temperate than Noah, "more righteous than Lot, more upright than Abra- "ham, who lied twice that he might save his life? "Art thou more meek than Moses, more patient than "Job, more holy than David, or more faithful than "Peter? If such cedars were forced to bow before "the blast of temptation, shall so bruised a reed, as "thou art, resist its force?" In a word, the heart may argue for any particular sin, from the propriety of saving a great deal of time, that must be otherwise lost to no purpose, and of trouble, that must otherwise be unavoidably incurred in fruitless endeavours to stem the torrent. It will insist, that it is better to yield to the temptation at once, because this at length will be the event; and that, till the temptation be gone, the mind will be unfit for every thing else.

13. It may sometimes endeavour to persuade a man, that the present commission of sin will be an *antidote* for the *future*, because he will see more of its hatefulness. So deceitful is the heart, that it will

not only reason from the pleasantness and profitableness of sin; but, if these arguments be repelled, it will change its strain so far as to reason from the very contrary. The Christian hath found, that after falling into sin, he hath felt a greater hatred of it, and keener resentment against himself for some time, than he felt before; and that he hath seen more of its abominable nature. He knows that the Lord often suffers his people to fall, that by a deeper sense of their iniquity, they may be more deeply humbled before him; when for a while, they have been languid in the exercise of religion, and little affected with a sense of the evil of spiritual apostasy. Even this signal display of infinite sovereignty, in not only permitting believers to fall into sin, but in over-ruling their falls for affecting their minds more deeply with a sense of their guilt and impurity, when grace regains the superiority, will, by the wickedness of the heart, be used as an argument for the indulgence of sin. Thus, like Satan, it *transforms* itself *into an angel of light* for accomplishing the works of darkness. It will in effect say to the Christian; " Thou art at present very dead
" in Religion, and very little affected with a sense of
" the guilt, power and filth of thy sins; thou per-
" formest no duty in a comfortable manner; and
" thou hast sometimes found, when formerly in such
" a situation, that even the commission of Sin has
" been an occasion of quickening, and of greater vi-
" gour in religious exercises; and that, for a consi-
" derable time, thou hast retained a more affecting
" sense of Sin on thy spirit. Mayest thou not, there-
" fore, at present indulge Sin a little, when it will be
" subservient to so excellent a purpose, as to enliven
" thee in the service of God." The heart, as unrenewed, reasons in this wicked manner, not because it really wishes the person to increase in humility, or that God should sovereignly over-rule his fall as an occasion of his more comfortable rising; but merely to accomplish its own ungodly designs. For such a sense of sin as it seems to plead for, as the fruit of

renewed

renewed transgression, is what, in itself, it would least of all desire.

14. The heart sometimes urges the commission of *sin*, as immediately clearing the way to the *performance* of some necessary *duty*. It uses that abominable reasoning falsely charged on the first ministers of Jesus, *Let us do evil, that good may come* *: not merely when, as we have already seen, it pretends to seek an antidote against sin, but when there may be a call to some important service to God. Then, perhaps, it pleads that this cannot be otherwise accomplished. Abraham seems to have thought, that he might venture on a lie, in saying that Sarah was his sister, when it might be the mean of preserving his life, which would otherwise, as he pretended, be in danger †. Doubtless, Jacob flattered himself that he might be excused for his lie, when he was only seeking the blessing, and saw no other way of receiving it from his Father ‡. Saul ventured to offer sacrifices, because *the people were scattered* from him, Samuel *came not within the days appointed, and the Philistines gathered themselves together against* him ‖. When he afterwards went out to war against Amalek, he *spared the best of the sheep, and of the oxen*, under the pretence of *sacrificing them to the Lord*, although he had expressly commanded him to slay them all. Even professors in our time will excuse the guilt of lying, if it be a mean of saving their character or natural life, or their property only. How often have men dared to think, nay, to avow to the world, that they *did God service*, by what are called *pious frauds*, because, as they pretend, the glory that redounds to God from the *end* justifies the *means*. But all who use such impious methods, discover that they are as ignorant of God as Saul was, according to the declaration of the faithful Prophet: *Behold, to obey is better than sacrifice, and to hearken than the fat of rams* **.

15. By

* Rom. iii. 8.   † Gen. xx. 11.   ‡ Gen. xxvii. 19.
‖ 1 Sam. xiii. 11.   ** 1 Sam. xv. 22.

15. By persuading a person to lay the commission of sin to the charge of the *flesh*, and solacing him with the idea, that although he fall into it, he does *not* really *love* it. He knows that in every believer there is a principle of corruption as well as of grace, that there is *a law in the members rebelling against the law of the mind, and* often *leading him into captivity to the law of sin*. The deceitfulness of his heart improves this by pleading, that when he sins it only proceeds from a fatal necessity, arising from this corrupt law, and that he is in some degree excusable, because it is only his flesh, and not his mind, that yields to sin. Thus it tries to persuade him, that he may grant some little indulgence to a beloved corruption; as if it flowed from an absolute necessity, and that he may, nevertheless, retain a sufficient hatred of it in his heart. We see how soon after the entrance of sin the heart sought an excuse for itself. *The man said, The woman whom thou gavest to be with me, she gave me of the tree, and I did eat.—The woman said, The serpent beguiled me, and I did eat* *.

16. It *dissuades* him from *prayer*. When in the time of temptation, the natural conscience, or the Holy Spirit, either by his common or gracious operations, directs a person to apply to the throne for deliverance, and to bring his lusts to the cross of Christ that they may be mortified; his heart, as unrenewed, dissuades him from this course. Perhaps, it reminds him that he has often tried this exercise before, in like circumstances, when he found an inclination to sin, or was assaulted by a temptation; and that it was attended with no success. Or, it may reason in so wicked a manner as this; that if God hath determined to permit his fall at this time, prayer will not prevent it; as if this were an argument against the use of means appointed by God himself for obtaining deliverance from sin; or as if the means were not, in the Divine purpose, inseparably connected with the end. Perhaps, it will suffer him to try this duty; but

* Gen. iii. 12. 13.

but still make such efforts as to baffle the professed design. He is rendered totally unfit for performing it. He prays indeed; but it is in hypocrisy. What he asks, he does not really wish to be granted. It would be a disappointment to him, were the Lord to hear him and subdue the power of his lusts. Or, if it allows him in peace to address God in prayer, it immediately renews its assault, and urges him to use his prayer as a sort of salvo with God and conscience, for the commission of the sin; insinuating to him, that it is not properly his blame that he has fallen, because he prayed for deliverance, and was not heard. It is, indeed, a sad display of the wickedness and deceitfulness of the heart, that persons sometimes as it were, prepare themselves for the more unrestrained commission of sin by their duties. This is emphatically described by Solomon, as the case with the insidious adulteress: *I have peace-offerings with me; this day have I paid my vows. Therefore came I forth to meet thee, diligently to seek thy face* *.

17. It strives to banish a sense of the *Presence* and *Omniscience* of God. Well does the corrupt heart know, that an affecting persuasion of the All-seeing Eye being on the person, as long as he retains it, will be a preservative from sin. Therefore, it does every thing in its power to efface this persuasion. It will even dare to insinuate, that perhaps God does not pay so much attention to human affairs, as we are apt to imagine; that it would be unworthy of so exalted a Being to interest himself about every trivial offence of his creatures, or, if it cannot entirely overpower this sense of the Divine Presence, it will endeavour to efface the impression of it in the mean time, and to throw such a mist over a man's eyes, that he shall lose the present effect of this persuasion, and believe the presence of God in as unaffecting a manner, as if he did not believe it at all. When he loses either this persuasion itself, or the present impression of it, he can have no guard against the present commission

* Prov. vii. 14. 15.

of sin. For, often the *fear* of God as Omniscient, awes the mind, when a sense of his *love* and of the *evil* of sin have no influence. God gives this as a reason, why men indulge sin in the secret *chambers of imagery.* Thus he said to Ezekiel; *Son of man, hast thou seen what the ancients of the house of Israel do in the dark, every man in the chambers of his imagery; for they say, The Lord seeth us not, the Lord hath forsaken the earth* *.

18. THE deceitfulness of the heart about sin, eminently appears in its *self-hardening* influence. Sin is the instrument which it uses in this work. Therefore it is said; *Exhort one another daily, while it is called to-day, lest any of you be hardened through the deceitfulness of sin* †. No man is *hardened through the deceitfulness of sin,* any other way than by reason of the deceitfulness of his own sinful heart; or, in other words, by the activity of his heart in deceiving itself. This self-hardening power of the heart by means of sin, appears, when there are different branches of any one sin, or parts necessary to the completion of it. When the heart enters on the way of iniquity, how rapid is its progress! Achan first looked on the accursed thing; he no sooner looked than he coveted; he no sooner coveted than he took; and then he hid it in his tent, thus defying the All-seeing Eye. The ease with which the heart proceeds from one sin to another, is a further demonstration of its great power in hardening itself. But a few hours seem to have elapsed between Ahab's coveting the vineyard of Naboth, and his taking possession of it; after he had, by the instrumentality of Jesabel, murdered the rightful owner, by an unparalleled prostitution of justice and religion ‡. This was also fully exemplified in the conduct of David. First he was gazing idly from the top of his house; then he fixed the eye of sinful desire on another man's wife; then he sent for her, and committed adultery; he next proceeded to horrid injustice and ingratitude, in attempting to deceive his faithful

---

* Ezek. viii. 12. † Heb. iii. 13. ‡ 1 Kings, xxi. 1.—16.

faithful servant Uriah; and, last of all, he became his murderer. Nay, so much was his heart hardened by the deceitfulness of sin, that he does not seem to have had any just sense of his aggravated iniquity, for many months after. So great was his obduracy, that he condemned himself before Nathan, without ever thinking that the parable was applicable to him. Thus the indulgence of sin has so hardening an effect, that for a time a sense of its evil seems to be entirely gone. The heart affords another evidence of its activity in self-hardening, by its extreme alacrity in framing apologies for sin. From the dreadful situation of fallen Adam, from his consciousness of the deplorable transition he had made from spotless innocence to aggravated guilt, from unspeakable happiness to inconceivable misery, one might have expected that his *mouth* would have been *stopped*, and that he would have *become guilty before God.* But instead of this, we find him impudently saying; *The woman whom thou gavest to be with me, she gave unto me of the tree, and I did eat.**. He divides the blame chiefly between the woman and her Maker; and brings in his own sin, as if it scarcely deserved to be mentioned; as if it had been an unavoidable consequence of God's gracious gift. Soon also does the heart, when engaged in the practice of sin, disregard the threatenings of temporal judgments. *They have made their hearts as an adamant stone, lest they should hear the law, and the words which the Lord of hosts hath sent in his Spirit by the former Prophets* †. Even the immediate infliction of temporal judgments cannot deter from sin. Pharoah's heart seems to grow still the harder, the more he is visited by plagues, till at length he involves himself in total destruction. The more the Israelites were punished, the more they saw God's wonders, either of mercy or of judgment, *they sinned still the more.* They proceeded from murmuring against Moses, to direct rebellion against God. Nay, so hardening is sin, that the heart gradually loses all fear

of

* Gen. iii. 12. † Zech. vii. 12.

of eternal wrath. The sinner concludes, that God is *altogether such a one as* himself. He *saith in his heart, The Lord will not require it.*

The *old man* is said to be *corrupt according to the deceitful lusts**. The *old man* denotes the unrenewed nature. It is said to be *corrupt*, or rather *corrupted*, because the longer it subsists in its power, it attains the greater strength. It becomes more and more wicked. And the great agency in effecting this progress in corruption, is ascribed to its own lusts. These are ever at work, and by their constant action, support and invigorate the habit of sin. They are here called *deceitful lusts*, or *lusts of deceit*, because it is by the vain hopes of pleasure, honour or profit, which they inspire, that men are hurried on to sin, and that the old man is gradually strengthened. Their success in corrupting the soul is in proportion to the deceitfulness of their operation. Thus, the deceitfulness of the heart is represented as the principal agent in the increase of the body of sin, the great mean of the growth of the old man, nay, as the very standard of his stature; for this exactly corresponds to the degree, and to the operation of deceit. This is given as the most distinguishing character of all the lusts of the *old man;* because it is principally owing to their wonderful power of deceiving, that they are so frequently indulged. The strength of every lust is commensurate with the power of deceit.

19. The heart will even urge God's *readiness* to *pardon* as an excitement to the commission of sin. Is it declared, that God *will abundantly pardon,* that he *will multiply to pardon?* Even this will corruption use as an argument for multiplying iniquities. This is indeed a dreadful abuse of pardoning mercy. It discovers the most shocking ingratitude to God, and the greatest wickedness in making his mercy *the minister of sin*. But the depraved heart often prophesies in the same manner with the false prophets, whom the Lord reproves. *They say still unto them that despise me; The Lord hath said, ye shall have peace: and they say unto every*

---

* Eph. iv. 22.

every one that walketh after the imaginations of his own heart, no evil shall come upon you *. Although, in a moment of temptation, the children of God may be so far left, as to abuse his mercy; yet, where this course is habitual, where sin is constantly recommended by this hope; it is a certain evidence that men deceive themselves, and that the pardon they seek is not such as God promises. To such sinners he speaks in this awful manner: *Those men have set up their idols in their heart, and put the stumbling block of their iniquity before their face, should I be enquired of at all by them? Therefore speak unto them, and say unto them; Thus saith the Lord God, Every man of the house of Israel, that setteth up his idols in his heart, and putteth the stumbling-block of his iniquity before his face; and cometh to the Prophet: I the Lord will answer him that cometh, according to the multitude of his idols; I the Lord will answer him by myself†. Unto the wicked God saith, What hast thou to do to take my covenant in thy mouth? seeing thou hatest instruction, and castest my words behind thee ‡.*

LASTLY; by endeavouring to drive one to *despair,* after the commission of sin, as being beyond the reach of mercy. The deceitful heart first flatters into sin by the hope of forgiveness; and when sin is committed, sometimes tries to frighten from applying for mercy, by representing that the opportunity is lost. It is the great aim of the evil heart, as well as of Satan, to keep a man away from God the only refuge. Therefore, upon the commission of sin, especially if it be of an atrocious nature, it would persuade him that it is vain to supplicate mercy, or to expect it. And it takes this plan, in order to harden the person in sinful courses, and to plunge him deeper into sin than before. This God declares to be the language of the heart: *They said; There is no hope, but we will walk after our own devices, and we will every one do the imagination of his evil heart* §.

WE shall conclude this discourse by calling your attention to the following things, as means for obtaining

* Jer. xxiii. 17.   † Ezek. xiv. 3, 4, 7.   ‡ Psal. l. 16, 17.
§ Jer. xviii. 12.

taining victory over the deceits of the heart with respect to sin.

1. In a dependence on the Spirit, *resist* the *first motions* of sin within you. It is necessary, that you should have a constant sense of the sinfulness of these. Because they are secret, because they are not so gross as outward acts of sin, men are fain to persuade themselves, that there may be no sin in them. But their sinfulness evidently appears from these considerations. They are repugnant to the spirituality and extent of the holy law, and to that perfection which it requires. For it reaches to the whole heart. *Thou shalt love the Lord thy God with* ALL *thy heart.* They oppose the renewed nature in believers; they carry on a war against the principle of grace in them. Therefore, they are called the *lustings of the flesh*, or unrenewed nature against the Spirit, which denotes that part of the Christian that is renewed, or, as it is materially the same, the Holy Spirit himself dwelling in them as the efficient cause of a new nature, of a new life, and of all its actings. *The flesh lusteth against the Spirit, and the Spirit lusteth against the flesh.*—Thus they also counteract and resist the motions of the Spirit. This pure Agent works in and by the new nature already implanted: and these first motions of sin constantly oppose his sacred suggestions.—They are the corrupt seed, from which all actual transgression springs up in the conversation. *For from within, out of the heart of man, proceed evil thoughts, murders, adulteries,* &c. If the fruit be evil, the root on which it grows must be correspondent. These are the instruments which Satan employs in his work. When he means to excite persons to actual sin, he blows up the corrupt spark within. By these secret motions he stirs them up to outward immoralities.—In a word, they must be evil, because they are the very imaginations of our own hearts. But *every imagination of the thoughts of man's heart is only evil,*—every figment, the first formation of thought, that is, every motion of the natural heart,

is

is *only evil continually.*—These motions being evidently sinful, it is therefore of the greatest consequence that they be resisted. For *when lust hath conceived, it bringeth forth sin; and sin, when it is finished, bringeth forth death.* These are the conception of sin in the heart, and the conception always tends to the birth. True, sin can only be said to be brought to the birth, when it is actually committed: but it hath as real an existence before, when only conceived. Against these motions you must *watch and pray.* Especially improve the Holy Spirit for subduing them. *If ye, through the Spirit, do mortify the deeds of the body, ye shall live.* All attempts to resist or subdue them, without the Spirit, will be ineffectual. This is one great end of his dwelling in believers, that acting by and on the principle of grace in them, he may *lust against the flesh. If ye walk in the Spirit, ye shall not fulfil the lusts of the flesh.* If you be thus enabled to resist the first motions of sin, it will at once defeat all the delusive arguings of your hearts.

2. BEWARE of entertaining *doubts* with regard to what Scripture and conscience declare to be *sin*. To doubt the reality of sin, is to meet the temptation half way. To doubt is to begin to fall, for it implies unbelief of God's testimony. At any rate, if you hesitate with respect to any thing, whether it be innocent or sinful, and do it with this hesitation, to you it is sin. Even in so trivial a matter as eating, *he that doubteth is damned, if he eat.* He is condemned by his conscience as guilty of sin; because he does something that he cannot do as *to the Lord*, being uncertain whether it be not a transgression of his law. In all we do, we ought either immediately or ultimately to propose the glory of God as our highest end. Now, it is impossible singly to propose this as our end in an action, about the nature of which we are uncertain.

3. CAREFULLY avoid *light notions* of any *sin*. To think lightly of sin is to think lightly of God.
For

For although some sins be comparatively less aggravated than others, yet every sin is infinitely evil, as committed against an infinitely Holy God. It is impossible that you can, at the same time, entertain light notions of sin and important notions of duty, or of God; of whose nature sin is the very reverse, who hates it with a perfect hatred, who punished it in the person of his only-begotten Son.

4. GUARD against the *solicitations* of your *hearts*. If these promise you honour, profit, or pleasure in the service of sin, believe them not. These promises are only like the tears of the crocodile, which is said to weep that it may destroy. Ask your hearts in reply, " If there be any *honour* in that which is the " shame of man, who was formed after the image of " God; any honour in being more like the Devil, " than you are already? If there be any *profit* in de- " voting your precious souls to destruction, in despi- " sing eternal life, or in preferring a filthy lust to God " himself as your portion?" Ask them, " If there can " be any *pleasure* in the ways of death, in that path " that leads down to hell, in defying the justice of an " angry God, or in procuring the anger of a loving " Father; If there can be any *pleasure* in crucifying " the Son of God afresh, in grieving and doing despite " unto the Spirit of Grace?" *Stand in awe, and sin not: Commune with your own heart—and be still.*

5. BEWARE of *tampering* or *dallying* with *sin*. This is like sporting with the point of a sword, or at the verge of a pit. Temptation is, to the corrupt heart, *sharper than a two-edged sword*, and if the point once enter, you may be *pierced through with many sorrows*. There is always a snare in sin, and if you begin to trifle with it, you may fall into it ere you are aware. Endeavour resolutely to tear yourselves away from the first solicitations to iniquity. Imitate the conduct of Joseph, who gave this repulse to the first proposals of guilt, *How can I do this great wickedness and sin against God?* If temptation become

more

more urgent, imitate his flight. For when his adulterous miſtreſs renewed her entreaties at another time, when the abſence of the family made the temptation more dangerous; *he left his garment in her hand, and fled, and got him out.* A flight from ſin is truly honourable. For it is an unfair warfare, *a man's worſt enemies* being *thoſe of his own houſe*; and it is his glory to be ſenſible of his inequality for the conteſt. It is better to ſuffer a little in your ſubſtance, or in your honour, according to the world's eſtimation, than to comply with the temptation. It is better to leave your garment behind you, like Joſeph, than afterwards to depart with a wounded conſcience. It is perilous even to reaſon with ſin, becauſe it will prejudice the carnal affections in its favour. Nay, it is ſinful to reaſon with ſin. Is it treaſonable to hear treaſon againſt an earthly Sovereign, and not divulge it? And is it not treaſon againſt the God of heaven, is it not leaſe-majeſty, but for one moment to liſten to his rival in your hearts, even although you do not actually rebel?

6. TRY to get all your *ſenſes armed* againſt ſin, or rather *barred* againſt it; for this is the beſt mode of defence. The ſenſes are the gates of the affections. It is moſt ordinarily by them that temptation to outward and groſſer ſins enters into the heart, and co-operates with the corrupt motions there. Like Job, make *a covenant with* your *eyes.* Endeavour to ſtop your ears againſt it. For he is ſaid to *walk uprightly, who ſtoppeth his ears from hearing of blood, and ſhutteth his eyes from ſeeing evil.* Strive for the *maſtery* over your taſte. *Put a knife to thy throat,* leſt thou *be given to appetite. Look not thou upon the wine when it is red, when it giveth his colour in the cup, when it moveth itſelf aright. At the laſt it biteth like a ſerpent, and ſtingeth like an adder. Thine eyes ſhall behold ſtrange women, and thine heart ſhall utter perverſe things. Yea, thou ſhalt be as he that lieth down in the midſt of the ſea, or as he that lieth upon the top of a maſt.*

7. SEEK a conſtant *ſenſe* of the *Majeſty* and *Omniſcience*

nifcience of God. When at any time enticed to fin by the deceitfulnefs of the heart, or by Satan, confider that awful injunction: *Be ſtill, and know that I am God.*

8. *Pray without ceaſing* againſt the deceitfulnefs of the heart. When by it you are folicited to fin, if in company, if you have no opportunity of retiring by yourſelf, look up to the Lord, in ejaculatory prayer, like Nehemiah, when he preſented his petition to the Perſian king. Be frequently engaged in fecret prayer for the mortification of your corruptions. Put them in the Lord's hand, in the exerciſe of faith and godly ſorrow, faying, *I am oppreſſed; undertake for me.* I *know not what to do, but* mine *eyes are towards thee.*

Above all, improve the *ſtrength* of Chriſt, and the *grace* of his Spirit for the mortification of ſin. Theſe things, already recommended, are as means abſolutely neceſſary in their own place. But if we uſe or attempt them in our ſtrength, they will be unavailing. *Except the Lord keep the city, the watchman waketh but in vain**. It is not faid, *The watchman waketh in vain*, becauſe *the Lord keepeth the city;* nor ſimply, *The Lord keepeth the city, and the watchman waketh in vain;* for either of theſe would have been a difcouragement to the uſe of means. But the declaration is ſo laid, that while it ſhows the vanity of means in themſelves, it points out their neceſſity, as having the impreſs of Divine inſtitution. For God will have us to be both diligent in duty, and denied to our diligence. So, all the means employed for mortification will be uſeleſs, unleſs we obſerve the new covenant-way. When the commandment is given, *Mortify your members,* we are to underſtand it only as elſewhere explained; *If ye through the Spirit do mortify the deeds of the body, ye ſhall live.* We muſt *work out our ſalvation with fear and trembling,* knowing and believing that *God worketh* in us. We muſt *lay aſide every weight, and run our race;* but it is only as *looking unto Jeſus, the author and finiſher of our faith.*

* Pſal. cxxvii. 1.

SERMON XIV.

ON THE DECEITFULNESS OF THE HEART, IN STIFLING CONVICTIONS.

JEREMIAH, viii. 5.

They hold faſt deceit, they refuſe to return.

FROM the connection of that paſſage formerly illuſtrated, in which the heart is declared to be *deceitful above all things* *, it is evident that the Spirit of God eſpecially refers to its deceitfulneſs in relation to the falſe grounds of confidence, on which ſinners build for eternity. In the prophetical writings, the Spirit of inſpiration often infolds ſpiritual bleſſings in promiſes, which ſeem to regard thoſe of a temporal nature only; and makes a tranſition, almoſt indiſcernible, from the one to the other: becauſe the Prophets principally *miniſtred to us the things which are reported in the Goſpel.* In like manner, ſecret ſins, affecting the ſtate of the ſoul, are frequently reproved in more general language, under the aſpect of thoſe open ſins, that were chargeable againſt Iſrael in a public or political capacity. When the Lord would only ſeem to reprove his people for truſting in an arm of fleſh for *temporal* deliverance; he means to deſcribe the far more dangerous folly of falſe confidence with reſpect to eternal ſalvation. And there is generally ſome particular expreſſion in the deſcription or reproof, which ſhows its ultimate deſign, as reſpecting

* Jer. xvii. 9.

ing the heart. In the passage referred to, God evidently rebukes his people, for their carnal confidence, during their outward calamities; and denounces a curse on those who thus rejected Him. But he gradually speaks more closely, as illustrating the extent both of the curse and of the blessing. It is said of *the man that trusteth in the Lord*, that he *shall not cease from yielding fruit*, to declare, that he continues to bring forth the real fruits of holiness. But to insinuate that the worst and most fatal species of carnal confidence, is especially meant, that which regards the state of the heart, which is hid from every created eye, which none but God can discover, either in the certainty or greatness of it; and to illustrate the unspeakable risk that men run of continuing in this delusion, he subjoins; *The heart is deceitful above all things.*

The same observation will in some measure apply to the words immediately before us. In the preceding part of this chapter, God threatens to inflict such judgments on his rebellious people, that by the residue of them, death should be chosen rather than life. Then in verse 4. he commands his servant to propose this question to them in his Master's name; *Shall they fall, and not arise? Shall he turn away, and not return?* This seems to be a declaration of what God knew to be the certain event. Yet he speaks in this manner, to leave them the more inexcusable, in consequence of his expostulation. He continues his address to them, demanding the reason of their obstinate perseverance in defection from him: *Why is this people slidden back with a perpetual backsliding?* Thus he insinuates that they could give none, that their conduct was in the highest degree irrational. Then he asserts what was evidently the case with them. *They hold fast deceit, they refuse to return.* These words, as immediately referring to the people of Judah, might denote their preposterous confidence in the assistance of neighbouring nations, or in the testimony of their false prophets, who assured them of peace and prosperity, notwithstanding all God's declarations

declarations to the contrary; and their refusal to return to him in that way which he had enjoined, by faith in his pardoning mercy through the blood of the covenant, and genuine repentance. In general, they express the conduct of sinners under the power of deceit, who reject all the calls, invitations, entreaties and expostulations of God, turn a deaf ear to all the warnings of conscience, and resist all the common operations of the Spirit.

In opening them further, we propose to consider some of the proofs that the heart affords of its deceitfulness, in the methods which it takes for stifling convictions of sin.

1. MANY *drown* their convictions in the mire of their *lusts*. When by the Word, read or heard, they are reminded of the shortness of life, and certainty of death, how do they improve these affecting doctrines? *Let us eat and drink, for to-morrow we shall die*:—reasoning worthy of a beast, could we suppose a beast, but for a moment, capable of reasoning; because it perisheth, its *spirit goeth downward*. When conscience is, in some measure, awakened because of former sins, they endeavour to overpower it, by making its load the heavier, that, if possible, it may sink under it altogether, and trouble them no more. They return as *the dog to his vomit*, and as *the sow that was washed, to her wallowing in the mire* *. *As a dog returneth to his vomit, so a fool returneth to his folly* †. No comparison can more justly represent the conduct of a sinner, who is resolved on his wicked courses. As the dog, after easing his loaded stomach, and freeing himself from sickness, devours his own vomit; so the filthy sinner, has scarcely felt the sickness of sin, in some temporary qualms of conscience, which produce a momentary resolution of renouncing it, ere he returns to *work all uncleanness with greediness*. For *the mouth of the wicked devoureth iniquity* ‡. Does such filthiness make our nature shudder, even when we see it in a brute creature! How much more abominable must

---

* 2 Pet. ii. 22.   † Prov. xxvi. 11.   ‡ Prov. xix. 28.

must the sinner, returning to his lusts, appear before Him who is *of purer eyes than that he should behold iniquity?* We are apt to wonder, when we see men going on in the greatest wickedness, in the commission of the most shocking enormities, and to apprehend that their hearts must certainly be far worse than those of others; and to be astonished that they seem to have no trouble from their consciences: but the truth is; this is just a picture of the heart of man, when *hardened through the deceitfulness of sin.* This discovers what any of us would be, did God *give us up to our own heart's lust.* The reason of their becoming so bold in sin, is not that they have no conscience at all; but that they have in a great measure silenced it. Perhaps, they met with many reproofs from conscience at first, but they immediately hurried back to the very cause of these reproofs, and *sinned still;* till conscience hath become insensible.

2. MANY extinguish convictions by flying to the *world.* Multitudes are in this manner ruined for eternity. The heart of the sinner has been affected under the word. Serious impressions have been made for a time. But *the cares of the world, and the deceitfulness of riches* render them unfruitful: *That which fell among thorns are they, who, when they have heard, go forth and are choked with cares, and riches, and pleasures of this life, and bring no fruit to perfection**. Even the innocent enjoyments of life prove the destruction of myriads. Perhaps it may be said, that among those who make a profession, more fall a sacrifice to innocent enjoyments, than to those that are in themselves sinful. They devote their hearts to them. They love them immoderately. And this as *certainly* ruins them as if they proceeded to the greatest excess; although their guilt may be comparatively less. With regard to the loss of the soul, the question is not so much, what is the enjoyment, as what is the *degree* of our *affection?* In the parable of the marriage-feast, when the servants of the king went

* Luke viii. 14.

went to inform those who were bidden, that *all things were ready; they made light of it, and went their ways, one to his farm,* and *another to his merchandise.* It was only *the remnant,* that *entreated his servants spitefully**. As related by Luke†, one excused himself, because he had made a purchase of land; another because he had bought some oxen for labour; and a third could not attend the marriage of the King's son because he was himself newly married. One had bought an estate, another was replenishing his farm, and the third was taking care of his wife. There was nothing sinful in their employments. The sin lay in preferring either the business or comforts of life to the invitation of the King, to the concerns of salvation. They preferred *broken cisterns* to *the fountain of living waters.* O! sinners, you may flatter yourselves that there is nothing evil here. But God finds two evils in this conduct: *My people have committed two evils; they have forsaken me the fountain of living waters, and hewed them out cisterns, broken cisterns that can hold no water* ‡. *Forsaking the fountain* is the first evil, which leads to the second, that of *hewing out broken cisterns,* and preferring these to the Fountain. Creature-comforts are, in their best state, only cisterns. Indeed they are of God's hewing. But they have no source of consolation from within. They must have their supplies from above; and they can contain no more than God is pleased to pour into them. But all the cisterns of sublunary enjoyments have received a fatal rent by the entrance of sin, so that they are *broken cisterns that can hold no water.* If *the poor, and the needy seek water* from them, *there is none,* even although *their tongue faileth for thirst.* For *the creature is made subject to vanity.* How great then is your folly in forsaking the Fountain, from whom all true consolation springs; in forsaking him, who is a *Fountain of living waters,* who will make all alive, and will afford eternal supplies to all, who come to him? For the water, that he gives, not only heals, refreshes and preserves from perishing by thirst, all those

---

* Matt. xxii. 4,—6.   † Luke xiv. 18,—20.   ‡ Jer. ii. 13.

those who drink it, but will be in them *a well of living water springing up to life everlasting.*—Perhaps, relations or friends may perceive them becoming serious. They call them morose and melancholy. They advise them to banish their anxious thoughts by lively company, by the vanities of life, by amusements. A drunken frolic, or a gay assembly, or a theatrical entertainment is prescribed as a sovereign remedy for a troubled conscience: and it is inconceivable, what a powerful charm such things are for lulling conscience asleep. Not only *whoredom*, but wine, and new wine take away *the heart.* The heart itself loves the prescription of such false friends, it is willing to be *taken away.* We see what a mournful effect prosperity and pleasure had upon Israel. *Jeshurun waxed fat and kicked.—Then he forsook God who made him, and lightly esteemed the Rock of his salvation* *.

3. THE hearers of the Gospel often quench their convictions, by *doubting* the truth of the *doctrine*. In this way did sin make its entrance into the world; and all along, it has proved a great support of it. The unbelief of the heart comes in to the assistance of the love of sin. " Surely," saith the sinner, " God doth " not hate sin so much as the Scripture declares. We " are not to take the threatenings of the Word in their " full extent." Perhaps, corruption and Satan may drive them the length of thinking that the whole Scripture is a *cunningly devised fable*; because it goes so much against the grain with them. When conscience, as God's deputy, threatens the sinner with destruction, as the fruit of sin, with the sword of Divine Justice; the deceitful heart acts the same part with the hearers of Jeremiah, when he denounced judgments; *They have belied the Lord, and said, It is not he; neither shall evil come upon us, neither shall we see sword nor famine* †. How many are there, who, notwithstanding all the threatenings of the Word, and warnings of the Lord's servants from it, say to themselves;

---

* Deut. xxxii. 15.   † Jer. v. 12.

selves; *Peace and safety, while sudden destruction cometh upon them, as travail upon a woman with child?* When Lot went out, and said to his sons-in-law, *Up, get ye out of this place, for the Lord will destroy this city; he seemed unto them as one that mocked* *.

4. MANY stifle their convictions, by turning them into *ridicule. Fools make a mock at sin. The scorner heareth not rebuke.* They treat the reproofs of conscience, as the men of Ephraim and Manasseh did the posts whom Hezekiah sent, warning them *to turn to the Lord, that the fierceness of his anger might turn away from them. They laughed them to scorn, and mocked them* †. They *mock* these *messengers of God, and despise his words* ‡. They make themselves *sick with bottles of wine, and stretch out their hands with scorners* §. Such *scornful men* try to persuade themselves, that they have made *a covenant with death, and an agreement with hell, and that the overflowing scourge shall not come unto them.* " What?" may they say, " have we any more reason to fear than others?
" Multitudes are as bad as we, and yet give them-
" selves no trouble about sin. These silly apprehen-
" sions are merely the consequence of a superstitious
" education, and of false ideas implanted in the ten-
" der credulous mind in youth,—old wives fables;
" which it would be as despicable in us to regard, as
" to become children over again, and tremble in the
" dark." Thus they try to laugh themselves out of convictions, just as a coward endeavours to get rid of his fear, by inward ridicule: not that they really disbelieve the things that give them trouble, but they wish to do so. And by habituating themselves to *laugh at the shaking of the spear,* like the coward at heart, they may acquire a fictitious courage, and really get the mastery over them.

5. MEN overpower their convictions, by *extenuating sin,* or apprehending that they are not guilty in the eye of the law, because free of *grosser* immoralities.

---

* Gen. xix. 14. † 2 Chron. xxx. 10.
‡ 2 Chron. xxxvi. 16. § Hos. vii. 5.

ties. This is an error very common among the hearers of the Gospel, arising from the deceitfulness and unbelief of the heart, and from their ignorance of the nature of God, and of the evil of sin. They think nothing deserves the name of sin, but such transgressions of the law as are of the grossest kind, and carry in them the *immediate* ruin of the sinner himself, or directly tend to the destruction of society. If a man be an adulterer, or dishonest, or a murderer, they will allow that he is a sinner; but if he be externally sober, they cannot think that he merits so harsh an appellation. Nay, you may be at no loss to find *some*, who are unwilling to bestow it even upon profane swearers, Sabbath-breakers, drunkards, or whoremongers. In a word, a man may do what he will against God, and against himself; if his crimes do not immediately affect his neighbours, they deserve not the name of *sin*. If a person be outwardly moral, although destitute of the very form of religion, by many he is viewed as a very good man, as an almost perfect character; because unbelief and enmity against God, declared by a contempt of external worship, are esteemed such small matters as to be unworthy of notice. It is a long time since the deceitful heart invented this false distinction. The Pharisees, overlooking their own pride, legality, unbelief, and malice, not only reckoned themselves righteous, but all who followed them: while they applied the appellation of *sinners* to Publicans and Harlots, because of the oppressions of the one, and notorious wickedness of the other. To distinguish in this manner, is going farther than Popery itself. For although Papists dream of some sins, which they call *venial*, as being of little consequence, and easily pardoned, in opposition to others, which they call *mortal*, because in their account damning in their nature; they still account the first to be sins. But those we speak of, are ready to ridicule the person who will venture to give them this name. It is, indeed, acknowledged, that there are some sins, which are comparatively greater than others,

thers, as being more atrocious in their nature, or aggravated in their circumstances. But every sin is in itself *exceeding sinful*, because the least is a rebellion against an infinite Being, and therefore damning in its nature; and such as without the justifying and purifying efficacy of the blood of Christ, will expose the person to eternal wrath. For, *by one sin*, and that against a positive precept, which many in our time deem so incredible a matter, that they reduce the whole to an allegory, *judgment came upon all men to condemnation*. Every thing that is, in any degree, contrary to the nature and law of God, is *sin;* and every man, while in this world, is a sinner: For *there is no man that liveth, and sinneth not*.

This unjust apprehension, that grosser immoralities only deserve the name of sin, is one great reason that so many gospel-hearers continue to despise the blood of Christ for cleansing. Having *escaped the pollutions of the world*, they conclude that they are innocent before God, and do not see the necessity of an application to this blood. They say, *Because I am innocent, surely his anger shall turn from me.* The prayer of such persons, like that of the Pharisee, is all in the strain of self-commendation: *God, I thank thee that I am not as other men are, extortioners, unjust, adulterers, or even as this publican* [*]. This is the reason assigned by our Lord, for his being rejected by the Pharisees: *They that be whole need not a Physician, but they that are sick. For I am not come to call the* RIGHTEOUS, *but* SINNERS *to repentance*. Therefore, he also assures them that *Publicans and Harlots* should *enter into the kingdom* before them. But this is as great folly in a spiritual sense, as it would be for a thief or robber to imagine that he was in no danger of the sentence of the law of his country, because he had not yet committed murder; or, for a man indulging himself in strong drink, to apprehend that he run no risk of intoxication, because he could still hold the cup to his head. O! what unspeakable
deceitfulness

[*] Luke xviii. 11.

deceitfulneſs does this demonſtrate in the hearts of men! They will call that innocence which God calls guilt, and that only guilt which expoſes them to puniſhment from men. Many ſuch innocents as you have dreamed themſelves down to the pit of perdition, and there learned the nature of ſin, where they could never hear of redemption. In vain, do thoſe in that ſtate of remedileſs miſery, who while here have continued to deſpiſe the *fountain opened*, ſolicit one drop of water to *cool their tongue*. Sin can no more loſe its nature, as diſhonouring to God, and ruining to your own ſouls, becauſe it does not include the ruin of thoſe around you, than fire can be ſuppoſed deſtitute of its deſtructive quality, becauſe at preſent it only burns on the hearth, and does not conſume your habitation.—Such perſons may eſteem themſelves wiſe for eternity, and examples to others, becauſe they are not ſinners of the deepeſt dye, while they obſtinately contemn ſalvation through the croſs of Chriſt, and *tread under foot the Son of God*. To ſuch the Apoſtle ſpeaks; *Let no man deceive himſelf; if any man among you ſeemeth to be wiſe in this world, let him become a fool, that he may be wiſe**. All outward ſobriety, if there be nothing more, will be utterly unavailing, and all confidence in it will in the end be found ſelf-deceit. He, who ſeems to be *not far from the kingdom of heaven*, muſt *deny himſelf*, and *become a fool* in the world's eſtimation, by being indebted to the Son of God for his righteouſneſs. There were nominal Chriſtians in the days of the Apoſtle John, who thought themſelves free of ſin. This apprehenſion he conſiders as an evidence not of ſelf-deceit only, but of their total eſtrangement from the truth: *If we ſay that we have no ſin, we deceive ourſelves, and the truth is not in us.* Nay, it is not only lying to ourſelves, but giving the lie to God. *If we ſay that we have not ſinned, we make him a liar, and his word is not in us* †. To imagine this, is only to flatter ourſelves

---

* 1 Cor. iii. 18.   † 1 John i. 8. 10.

felves in our own naughtinefs, nay, in our own iniquity. It is to fuppofe ourfelves of fome importance in the eye of God, while he utterly difclaims us. Therefore, it is a felf-deceit of the moft dangerous nature. *For if a man think himfelf to be fomething, when he is nothing, he deceiveth himfelf.* It is felfdeceit, aggravated by a vain attempt to mock God, to fet afide the force of his law, and to oppofe the very exiftence of his perfections. But *be not deceived; God is not mocked: for whatfoever a man foweth, that fhall he alfo reap. For he that foweth to his flefh, fhall of the flefh reap corruption: but he that foweth to the Spirit, fhall of the Spirit reap life everlafting* *. You would reckon him a fool, who fhould fow one grain in the fpring, and expect from it grain of a different kind in the harveft. And will you not account him a fool, a felf-deceiver, yea, a mocker of himfelf, who foweth only to the flefh, and yet fondly expects to reap of the Spirit; who flatters himfelf that the ineftimable fruit of life everlafting fhall grow up from the feeble feed of outward fobriety? Take heed left that come upon you, which is written in the Prophets, *Behold, I will plead with thee, becaufe thou fayeft, I have not finned* †.

6. THE heart often ftifles convictions by reprefenting *eternal* concerns as of *little* importance. By far the greateft part of men, although they fee a dying world around them, live as if themfelves alone were to be immortal. Or, one might be apt to imagine from their conduct, that they altogether denied the immortality of their fouls, and believed that they would perifh with their bodies. Whatever be their notional belief, they practically deny the awful doctrine of immortality. How could they otherwife difcover fo anxious a concern about the perifhing trifles of time, about the honours, the pleafures, and the riches of this world; or even about thefe two fimple enjoyments, food and raiment; while deftitute of all concern about death, judgment and eternity; if the belief

* Gal. vi. 3. 7. 8. † Jer. ii. 35.

belief of these things really affected their minds? They discover less wisdom than the beasts of the field, or the fowls of the air, which, if they see one of their number fall, instantly provide for their own safety. But sinners, although they see multitudes of their acquaintance and relations dropping into the grave, are nowise concerned to provide for their safety through eternity. All their anxiety is centred in these inquiries, *What shall we eat, what shall we drink; and wherewithal shall we be clothed?* They barter their souls with Satan, for the temporary and uncertain possession of these things, which are not his to give. They give him the inestimable price of their souls for those mercies that they can receive from God alone. If you talk to them of death and an eternal state, of the certainty and impartiality of the judgment, of the importance of their souls and salvation; they listen as if all these things were spoken to others, as if they had not the least concern in them. They hear these truths as *a tale that hath been often told*, and, perhaps, consider you as officious in bringing such disagreeable subjects to their recollection. This false reckoning, with respect to matters of everlasting moment, undoubtedly discovers the astonishing deceitfulness of the heart. But the bitter consequences of this conduct are expressly declared by the Spirit of God: *Let not him that is deceived trust in vanity, for vanity shall be his recompence. It shall be accomplished before his time, and his branch shall not be green. He shall shake off his unripe grapes like the vine, and shall cast off his flowers as the olive* *. What unspeakable folly and self-deceit is it, for persons who know that it is revealed in God's word that they are formed for immortality, who feel the presages of it within themselves; and who are, at the same time, equally certain that their bodies are mortal, as they receive unquestionable proofs of it every day; and almost every hour, in their own feeble frames, feel the premonitions

* Job xv. 31.—33.

tions of their approaching exit;—to despise all serious consideration of eternity, and to prefer a few transitory comforts to the everlasting possession of God in Christ, perfect conformity to him, and the full enjoyment of him as a Father and Friend? The greater is their folly, as they are assured that *godliness is profitable unto all things, having the promise, not only of the life which is to come, but even of the life that now is;* and that these things, which now engross their attention, would have far greater security, were they interested in those of eternal moment. This is indeed to struggle for pence, and throw away worlds. It is to prefer time to eternity; although there be less proportion between the one and the other, than between a grain of sand and the whole universe. Even in the saints this deceitfulness greatly appears. True, their supreme concern is about the eternal world. But all their attention is little, compared with the weight and importance of the subject. Did they see the business of eternity in its full value and importance, they would deem all their concern about it as but a kind of serious trifling. For it both demands and deserves the greatest attention possible. Every nerve should be strained; every faculty should be exerted to its utmost, every affection should be swallowed up in the work of an unknown eternity.

7. MANY endeavour to fly from a wounded conscience, and so *hold fast deceit by flying* from the *means of grace. For if any be a hearer of the word, and not a doer, he is like unto a man beholding his natural face in a glass; for he beholdeth himself, and goeth his way, and straightway forgetteth what manner of man he was**. These words show that this course is often very effectual. *He forgetteth what manner of man he was.* The unregenerate find that some preachers are more awakening than others. They are better qualified as instruments, for discovering to them their *spiritual* face in the *glass* of the law.

* James i. 23. 24.

law. These they cannot bear. They forsake their ministry, because they cannot enjoy their false peace under it. Like Ahab, they *hate that fellow Micaiah, because he always prophecies evil, and not good.* It was the great sin of Israel, that they became weary of all God's dealings with them: *But my people would not hearken to my voice, and Israel would have none of me* *. The only condition on which such persons will submit to the sound of the Gospel, is that they have nothing but *smooth things prophesied to them.* This course the wicked Cain took to banish convictions. *He went out from the presence of the Lord* †. Not as if he could remove to any place, where God could not see him, or where he could be banished form his essential presence. For he *fills heaven and earth*, and none can *hide himself in secret places, that he should not see him?* But he departed from the Church of God in his father's family, and from the administration of appointed ordinances. Thus are the words of the Prophet accomplished: *Thou hast stricken them, but they have not grieved; thou hast consumed them, but they have refused to receive correction. They have made their faces harder than a rock; they have refused to return* ‡.

8. OTHERS extinguish convictions by *magnifying* the *difficulties* of *religion*. It seems to them a great hardship to perform so many duties, to be *instant in season and out of season.* They reckon God's *commandments grievous*, and the reward scarcely an equivalent for the labour. *It is vain,* say they, *to serve God; and what profit is it that we keep his ordinances, and that we walk mournfully before the Lord of hosts* §. Thus they exclaim, *What a weariness is it?* and they *snuff at it.* They cannot consent to abstain from all sin. What! shall they endure the anguish of plucking out a right eye, or cutting off a right hand? Could they *enter into life whole,* they would do it cheerfully. Like Pharaoh, they think it hard that the only term upon which the Lord can be served, is that *not so much as one hoof must be*

---

* Psal. lxxxi. 11.   † Gen. iv. 16.   ‡ Jer. v. 3.   § Mal. iii. 14.

be left. They terrify themselves with the apprehension of the difficulty of bearing *reproach.* Must they lose their good name, be laughed at by their former friends, and accounted *the offscouring of all things?* Thus, *many of the chief rulers did not confess Christ, because of the Pharisees, lest they should be put out of the synagogue.* They represent to themselves a religious life as a life of continual *melancholy.* They must abandon society, and renounce all innocent mirth. *The slothful man saith, There is a lion without, I shall be slain in the streets.* They must become *poor* in their own eyes, and really *impoverish* themselves by giving to the poor. The young man *went away sorrowful, because he had great possessions.* He could not think of taking up the cross and following Christ.

9. CONVICTIONS are often stifled by the hope of *abundance* of *time*, and the *promise* of a *future* consideration. While some are altogether unconcerned about eternity, there are others, not quite so hardened, who have some kind of seriousness; but delay the due consideration of their eternal interests, because they think it too early. Thousands and ten thousands fall the miserable victims of a false hope. When the concerns of their precious souls intrude themselves on their thoughts, they endeavour to banish them, from the expectation of length of days, and of a continued enjoyment of a merciful dispensation. Such are spiritual sluggards, who solicit conscience for *a little sleep, a little slumber*, or at least *a little folding of the hands to sleep.* This also is a great evidence of the deceitfulness of the heart, for saith the Spirit of God ; *The wicked flattereth himself in his own eyes, until his iniquity be found to be hateful*.* He stifles convictions, resists the ordinary operations of the Spirit, and deludes himself with the hope of life, till hell convince him of that hatefulness of sin, that he refused to learn from the means of grace. This was the case with that fool of whom we read in the parable. Having pulled down his barns, and built larger ones, and filled

* Psal. xxxvi. 2.

led thefe *with fruits and goods*, he faid to his foul; *Soul, thou haft much goods laid up for many years, take thine eafe, eat, drink, and be merry**. *Fool* indeed! to make *fruits and goods*, that could only be ufeful to his body, a portion and fource of confolation to his foul. But fuch is the general folly of mankind. And their fudden and fatal difappointment, like his, often declares its excefs. For that very night, his *foul was required* of him. How foon was the pride of Nebuchadnezzar ftained! How fuddenly were the bloffoms of his felf-complacency and vain-glory blafted; and his capacity of folacing himfelf with thofe delicious fruits, on which his imagination feafted, ravifhed from him by Him who *caufes the arrogancy of the proud to ceafe!* He *walked in the palace of the kingdom; he fpake and faid; Is not this great Babylon that I have built for the houfe of the kingdom, by the might of my power, and for the honour of my majefty? While the word was in the king's mouth, there fell a voice from heaven,—O king Nebuchadnezzar, to thee it is fpoken, The kingdom is departed from thee. And they fhall drive thee from men, and thy dwelling fhall be with the beafts of the field. The fame hour was the thing fulfilled upon Nebuchadnezzar* †. Little did this haughty man imagine that the ample inclofures of his palace, the very gardens of his pleafure, and of his pride, which he had laid out and adorned at fo great expence, were defigned by Providence for a place of pafture to him, in common with his cattle. Could man enfure himfelf, for a certain feries of years, againft the ftroke of death, were he in any degree lord of his time, there would be fome more ground for an apology; though after all, there could be no apology produced of fufficient validity; becaufe man does all in his power to defeat the great end of his being, till brought to obey the command of God, by *believing on him whom he hath fent*. But for man whofe *life is in his lip*, whofe *breath is in his noftrils*, who is *crufhed before the moth*, whofe *days pafs as a fhadow, and are confumed as fmoke*, for man, who is not certain

* Luke xii. 18, 20.   † Dan. iv. 29, 33.

certain of one moment after the prefent, to delay the great concern both of time and eternity, is folly in the extreme, and unfpeakably greater madnefs than it would be for one to amufe himfelf on the brink of a precipice. Therefore, the Spirit of God, in language full of compaffion, thus expreffes the greatnefs of their folly; *Oh! that they were wife, that they underſtood this, that they would confider their latter end!*

LISTEN, then, to the counfel of God, and confider the danger of deceiving yourfelves with refpect to eternal concerns, by thinking them of little moment, or by imagining that you will have abundance of time to attend to them, ere you die. Satan is much indebted to the deceitful heart for performing his work for him. Thus you do his bufinefs, and eftablifh his kingdom. For it is his great aim to perfuade finners to delay the interefts of their fouls. Encouraged from his fuccefs in the firft trial, he ftill manages his old plea with the fons and daughters of Eve; *Ye fhall not furely die:* and with the greateft part he is ftill fuccefsful. From the hope of a delay, at leaft, of the threatened penalty, they are eafily lured to tafte of the forbidden tree of pleafure. The impetuous defire of a prefent practical *knowledge of* fenfual *good*, makes them overlook the certainty of a future experimental knowledge of penal *evil*. Hell is filled with finners who have perifhed before they have *lived half* the *days* that they promifed themfelves. But, O! confider the danger of this conduct. *Hear the word of the Lord, ye fcornful;—becaufe ye have faid, We have made a covenant with death, and with hell are we at agreement; when the overflowing fcourge fhall pafs through, it fhall not come unto us, for we have made lies our refuge, and under falfehood have we hid ourfelves: Therefore, thus faith the Lord God,—Judgment will I lay to the line, and righteoufnefs to the plummet, and the hail fhall fweep away the refuge of lies, and the waters fhall overflow the hiding place. And your covenant with death fhall be difannulled, and your agreement* *with hell shall not stand; when the overflowing scourge shall pass through, then ye shall be trodden down by it**. What would the damned, who are wailing in the bottomless pit, give for such offers of mercy as you now enjoy, as you now despise? Would you take their testimony, if you will not believe that of God? Would you listen to their counsel, if you are determined to reject that of the compassionate Redeemer? How would you be affected, were you addressed by one of these prisoners of despair? Well, the substance of their counsel, whatever may be the supposed motives, you have in the parable of the rich man: *He said to Abraham, I pray thee, Father Abraham, that thou wouldest send Lazarus to my father's house, for I have five brethren, that he may testify to them, lest they also come into this place of torment.* But indeed, if you will not hear *Moses and the Prophets*, if you will not hear Christ and his Apostles and ministers, neither would you *be persuaded, although one rose from the dead.* Consider, therefore, what Wisdom is saying to you, even the Personal Wisdom of God, the Lord Jesus; *He that sinneth against me, wrongeth his own soul: all they that hate me love death* †. You can have no love to eternal death as such, for every creature seeks its own preservation, and every sinner pursues sin under the false notion of good. But while you continue to despise him, you love eternal death in its antecedent, by loving the course that infallibly leads to it. Attend to what the Lord saith to you, even to you, who seem to apprehend, who venture to say by your practice, and perhaps by your very language, that you *have made a covenant with death, and with hell are at agreement; Therefore, thus saith the Lord God, Behold, I lay in Zion for a foundation, a stone, a tried stone, a precious corner-stone, a sure foundation: he that believeth shall not make haste* ‡. He can stand the hail-storm of Justice, he will be in no danger, when it begins to blow. His *house is built on a rock.* Or, *he shall not be confounded.* He shall not be exposed to *shame*

* Isa. xxviii. 14,—18.   † Prov. viii. 36.   ‡ Isa. xxviii. 16.

shame in time, or to that *everlasting contempt*, which shall be the portion of all foolish builders. Even to *you* he declares this. You presumptuous and obstinate sinners he welcomes to build on this *sure foundation*: apply to him, therefore, for faith to embrace and rely on it, both for time, and for eternity.

As this part of the subject is of the utmost moment, we shall improve it more particularly by illustrating the great *danger* of stifling Convictions.

1. THIS conduct is of the most *hardening* nature. All sin is so. He who sins to-day, makes the commission of sin easier to conscience to-morrow. *Evil men wax worse and worse.* There is a progress in sin, as well as in holiness. Is *the path of the just as the shining light, that shineth more and more unto a perfect day?* The path of the wicked resembles it, in the line of opposition: for their *ways go down to death; darkness and destruction are in their paths.* Does he *that hath clean hands wax stronger and stronger?* The wicked also holds on his way. He *strengtheneth himself in his iniquity;* he *strengtheneth himself against the Almighty.* And there is no sin of a more heart-hardening nature than this of quenching convictions. When men make their *neck an iron sinew*, the *brow* becomes *brass*. Obduracy in resisting God is always succeeded by effrontery in sin. They acquire *a whore's forehead.* They *declare their sin as Sodom.* It must be, in the nature of things, that this sin should be very hardening; because he, who stifles convictions, overleaps God's hedges, and does all in his power to destroy those natural restraints that God hath laid on all, even on heathens themselves; he does his utmost to *break* God's *bands asunder, and cast away* his *cords from* him. If a sinner can once resolve to *walk in the imagination of his own heart*, he will soon *add drunkenness to thirst.* The Pharisees, who at first stifled their convictions about the Divine mission of Christ, when *astonished at his doctrine*, not only proceeded, at length, to charge him with being in compact with the Devil, but crucified him as a blasphemer.

2. HE

mere show. Their hearts were never seriously engaged in any duty. They may, like the Pharisees, even *disfigure their faces, that* to others *they may appear* exceedingly devout. But still it is all a solemn farce. There is no truth in their appearances. Whence proceeds this conduct, but from the natural atheism of their hearts? The Apostle gives an account of some *who have a form of godliness, but deny the power thereof**. All, who have nothing more than a form of godliness, do actually deny its power. As they practically deny, they show that they do not really believe with their hearts the reality of religion; because theirs consists in a mere form. And by denying the reality of religion, they materially deny the existence of God. For if a mere form be sufficient, then it cannot be God who is worshipped; for *God is a spirit, and they that worship him must worship him in spirit and in truth.* Those who imagine that mere bodily service will be acceptable to him, deny him to be a spiritual being, and so deny him to be God. When he denounces a wo against his ancient people for their hypocrisy, he traces it up to their atheism. *Wherefore the Lord said, Forasmuch as this people draw near me with their mouth, and with their lips do honour me, but have removed their heart far from me, and their fear towards me is taught by the precept of men: therefore, behold, I will proceed to do a marvellous work,* &c. Then it follows,—*Wo unto them that seek deep to hide their counsel from the Lord, and their works are in the dark, and they say, Who seeth us? and who knoweth us* †? He considers this as the very language of atheism, *Who seeth us? and who knoweth us?* and surely with the greatest justice. For men would never presume to offer such an affront to God if they really considered him as their present witness, and as their future judge. The strict observation that God takes of the whole of our conduct, the certainty of a future judgment, and the awful discovery that will then be made of the secrets of the heart,

* 2 Tim. iii. 5. † Isaiah xxix. 13, 14, 15.

heart, are the arguments ufed by Chrift in diffuading his difciples from imitating the wicked example of the Pharifees in their hypocritical conduct. *Beware ye of the leaven of the Pharifees, which is hypocrify. For there is nothing covered, that shall not be revealed; neither hid, that shall not be known. Therefore, whatsoever ye have spoken in darkness, shall be heard in the light* *. Our Lord reckoned this exhortation of fuch importance to his difciples, both for time and eternity, that as the introduction of a moft memorable difcourfe, and at a very remarkable time, when *there was an innumerable multitude of people gathered together, infomuch that they trode one upon another*, the greateft part of whom he doubtlefs knew to be actuated by unworthy motives, he particularly addreffed thefe words to the twelve: *He began to fay to his difciples, firft of all, beware ye of the leaven of the Pharifees.* As this corrupt leaven is mournfully diffufed through the hearts of believers themfelves, it calls for their peculiar attention to that natural atheifm, which ftill dwells in them, and which is the fource of the other. It is for want of a due impreffion of the being of God on their minds, that with refpect to formality and hypocrify in religious duties, they have fo much reafon to complain that their *hearts are like a bow that shooteth deceitfully*. But in this refpect there is a great difference between real Chriftians and hypocrites. All the fervices of the latter are performed under the influence of an hypocritical fpirit: but with Chriftians this principle prevails only in part; and in as far as it prevails, it is their habitual burden.

3. This corruption of the heart breaks out in the *profanity* and *fenfuality* of the life. The whole labour of many is merely to gratify their fenfual appetites. Carnal pleafure is their higheft aim. They travail with iniquity of every kind, they wallow in every fpecies of debauchery; paying no more regard to their immortal fouls than if they were as vile as their perifhing bodies; nay, far more vile than them. For they treat the foul as if it had been given them

for

---

* Luke xii. 1—3.

was turned to be their enemy; and he is not an inactive enemy; for he *fought against them**. Thus he often did with the Ifraelites. *With many of them God was not well pleafed; for they were overthrown in the wildernefs.* The book of Judges contains many examples of Divine correction, after they were brought into the land of promife. The fea overwhelmed Pharaoh and his hoft, after refifting all convictions, and all the awful warnings received from God, in ten grievous plagues fucceeding one another. Vengeance purfued that wicked prophet Balaam, who acted not only againft his confcience, but againft the miraculous warning of his dumb afs, in doing all in his power to curfe Ifrael, and afterwards enticing them to fin, that God might curfe them. Although he wifhed to *die the death of the righteous,* he had his end with them *who are thruft through with a fword, that go down to the ftones of the pit, as a carcafe trodden under foot.* When *the Spirit of the Lord departed* from Saul, all went wrong with him, and continued to do fo, till at length he was defeated by the Philiftines, and became his own executioner. Pilate fuppreffed and refifted the dictates of confcience in condemning Chrift, while perfuaded of his innocence, left it fhould be concluded that he was *not Cæfar's friend.* But that which he *fo greatly feared came upon him,* in the juft retribution of Providence. For we learn from hiftorical accounts generally credited, that he foon after loft the love of his mafter, and was banifhed to France, where, becaufe of the mifery of his fituation, like Saul, he fell on his own fword.

7. GOD *gives* them *up* to their own *lufts.* He impofes reftraints on the moft wicked. This is abfolutely neceffary, for the prefervation, not only of order in fociety, but of the very being of fociety. When men ftill continue like *bullocks unaccuftomed to the yoke,* and when *full of the fury of the Lord, and of the rebuke of our God,* are only *like a wild bull in a net;* the Lord fometimes takes off all reftraints in fin. *My people would not hearken to my voice*

---

* Ifa. lxiii. 10.

voice—therefore, I gave them up to their own heart's lusts. A man needs no other devil to possess him than these. The name of such a possession is *Legion.* Thus he becomes *exceeding fierce* in sin, and hurries on headlong to destruction, as if it advanced of itself, with too slow a pace. Pharaoh thought he was on the very point of accomplishing the ruin of Israel, when he said; *I will pursue, I will overtake, I will divide the spoil, my lust shall be satisfied upon them*: while God was only *pursuing* him, and about to *satisfy* his offended Justice upon him. Sennacherib was made to flee to his own country, after blaspheming the God of Israel, and losing his army by a supernatural destruction, that he might receive his death from the hands of his sons. If *the house* hath once been *empty, swept and garnished,* by means of convictions and external reformation, and afterwards the *unclean spirit* gets access, he is sure to bring with him *seven other spirits more wicked than himself,* and *the last state of that man is worse than the first* *.

8. In judgment he may lay *occasions* of sin in their way. *God can tempt no man.* He forces no man to sin, because he infinitely hates it. But when he sees sinners determined on iniquity, he sometimes chooses their delusions, as he threatens in his word: *I also will* CHOOSE *their delusions, and will bring their fears upon them.* The reason assigned is their resistance of his calls, and of their own convictions;—*because when I called, none did answer; when I spake, they did not hear; but they did evil before mine eyes, and* CHOSE *that in which I delighted not* †. So the Apostle Paul declares; *Because they received not the love of the truth—God shall send them strong delusions, that they should believe a lie* ‡. It is elsewhere said; *Because Ephraim hath made many altars to sin, altars shall be unto him to sin* §. These occasions of sin are sometimes called *stumbling-blocks. I will lay stumbling-blocks before this people, and the father and the son shall*

* Matt. xii. 43.—45. † Isa. lxvi. 4. ‡ 2 Thess. ii. 10. 11.
§ Hos. viii. 11.

shall fall upon them; the neighbour and his friend shall perish*.

9. GOD may judicially *harden* their hearts. It is one of the inconceivable mysteries of Divine operation, that God should in righteous judgment give up a sinner to obduracy, and yet be at an infinite distance from the sin. But so it is. For the emphatic expressions used on this subject, cannot be restricted to so bare unoperative permission. He seems especially to accomplish this awful work by the means already mentioned, by giving them up to the government of their own lusts; by laying occasions of sin in their way, before which he knows they will fall, although herein they act according to the natural propensity of their hearts; and by delivering them up to the uncontrolled agency of Satan, as a tempter. *The Lord hardened the heart of Pharaoh.* Yea, *the scripture saith unto Pharaoh, Even for this same purpose have I raised thee up, that I might shew my power in thee.* What is the Apostle's inference? *Therefore, Whom he will he hardeneth* †. It is said of the Gentiles, that because *they did not like to retain God in their knowledge, therefore God gave them over to a reprobate mind* ‡. It is declared of the Canaanites, that *it was of the Lord to harden their hearts, that they should come against Israel in battle, that he might destroy them utterly, and that they might have no favour, but that he might destroy them, as the Lord commanded Moses* §. Sinners, in this deplorable situation, are in a manner delivered up to Satan's management. *The God of this world blinds their minds.* So it is said, that the Devil *entered into Judas.* We must not understand this of a literal possession, but of his being given up to his own lusts, under the fearful influence of Satan's temptations.

10. GOD may *refuse* to *hear*, although they should call. He laughs at the sinner, when trying to *break his bands.* But his holy scorn will be far more awful in the end: *Because I called, and ye refused; therefore,*

---

* Jer. vi. 21. † Rom. ix. 17, 18. ‡ Rom. i. 28.
§ Jos. xi. 20.

fore, will I also laugh at your calamity, and mock when your fear cometh *.

11. RESISTANCE of convictions sometimes ends in despair. We have already seen that this was Saul's case. Judas also, although he resisted the different warnings given by his Master, was afterwards affected with such horror of conscience, that he *hanged himself*.

12. THESE abused convictions will, if mercy prevent not, greatly *aggravate* their eternal *condemnation* and *misery*. Sinners, you may now smother conscience, like a spark among ashes; but this is only reserving it as a kindling to *that fire, that shall never be quenched*. You may, in the mean time, trample this worm under foot, or bury it in the earth of your worldly cares; but it *shall never die*. You may *hatch cockatrice eggs*, but you *shall die by eating of them; and that which is crushed, breaketh out into a viper. The law worketh wrath*. The sinner may refuse to hear its voice as *a schoolmaster*, when denouncing the sentence of condemnation, and to *flee from the wrath to come*. But he does not really escape it. He only *treasures up wrath against the day of wrath*. Stifled convictions shall be the great torment of the damned in hell. There, every conscience shall be fully awakened. A despised Gospel will be the most dreadful fewel of that *lake that burneth for ever and ever*. Such sinners will God consume like *briers and thorns*. It is the great aggravation of their misery that they *look upon him whom they have pierced*. For they look only to *wail because of him*. A pierced Christ, in the rejection of his Gospel, and resistance of his Spirit, *heats the furnace* of hell *seven times more*. The *wrath of the Lamb* is represented as the bitterest ingredient in the cup of fury, ministered to unbelievers:
—*Cover us from the face of him that sitteth on the throne, and from the wrath of the Lamb. For the great day of his wrath is come, and who shall be able to stand?* But *kiss the Son, lest he be angry, and ye perish from the way.*

* Prov. i. 24.—31.

SERMON XV.

ON THE DECEITFULNESS OF THE HEART, IN EMBRACING FALSE GROUNDS OF CONFIDENCE.

ISAIAH xliv. 20.

He feedeth of ashes; a deceived heart hath turned him aside, that he cannot deliver his soul, nor say Is there not a lie in my right hand?

THERE is a kind of religion, alas! too generally crept in among professed Protestants, which has no relation to the heart. It entirely overlooks the necessity of a new nature, reduces regeneration to a mere name, or at least renders it a thing impossible, by making it to depend on the will of one who is *led captive by the devil at* HIS *will.* It confines obedience to the letter of the law, and draws a veil over its spirituality and extent; as the Pharisees did, who thought that the law was fulfilled, if the mere letter of it was not transgressed. It knows nothing of the blessedness of purity in heart, without which we cannot *see God.* Not only does it pay little regard to regeneration as the source of all acceptable worship, and to inward holiness as an essential ingredient in it; but it also despises the latter in the relation of an illustrious end appointed by God. For *this is the will of God, even our sanctification.* According to this Pharisaical system, he is fully entitled to the character of a good or virtuous man, who does not positively transgress the literal precept,

Nor

Nor will it greatly detract from his character, though he use considerable freedom with the first table of the law, if he preserve an external respect to the second. If he seem to love his neighbour, he may easily obtain a dispensation from *loving the Lord with all his heart*. But as it is declared in the Word that *the heart is deceitful above all things*, we can scarcely find a greater confirmation of it than this; that many in our time, both teachers and taught, satisfy themselves with a species of religion from which the heart is excluded. They profess to worship God the Spirit; but if it be not *in spirit*, it cannot be *in truth*.

THESE words are a part of that long and beautiful expostulation that God hath with his people, in this and the three preceding chapters, on the subject of idolatry; in consequence of that striking challenge given in chap. xli. 21. not merely to the worshippers of false gods, but to these gods themselves. But as *whatever was written aforetime, was written for our learning*, as every thing is to us a false deity, which receives that place in the heart that belongs only to the true God, and which we embrace as our confidence; they describe the character and situation of all who reject the true salvation, and trust in any lying refuge. In these words we have an account of the conduct of the false worshipper, the cause of this conduct, and the effect proceeding from this cause. His *conduct* is metaphorically represented under the notion of *feeding;* because, as food is the support of the body, whatever a man confides in for eternity is to him the support of his soul. But strange is the food here mentioned. To what the allusion is made, we cannot pretend to determine. Some think, it refers to the custom of penitents under the law, in covering their heads with ashes, or lying among them, in which sense it is used, Psal. cii. 9. *I have eaten ashes like bread*. In this view it expresses the sorry and bitter fruits of idolatry. Probably, there may be a reference to the words immediately preceding. As in verse 19.

the idolater is defcribed as burning part of the tree, of which he makes his idol, as baking bread and roafting flefh with the coals of it; perhaps the Spirit of God means to reprefent his folly in fuch a contemptible point of view, as if he miftook the *afhes* of his fire for the food prepared on it, and ate the one inftead of the other. Or, the words may be defigned to fignify the fhocking ftupidity of confidering *that* as a god, a part of which he hath himfelf already reduced to afhes. At any rate, the expreffion points out a food that is entirely unfuitable to nature, and denotes that a falfe ground of confidence is as unfit for the foul, as afhes would be for food to the body. In much the fame fenfe it is faid, Hof. xii. 1. *Ephraim feedeth on wind.* The *caufe* of this ftrange propenfity and foolifh conduct is next affigned. *A deceived heart hath turned him afide.* This dreadful infatuation proceeds from a heart under the power of deceit. And fo *efficacious* is it, that *he cannot deliver his foul.* The corruption of his heart increafes the blindnefs of his underftanding, and makes it a moral impoffibility for him to fhake himfelf loofe from his vanities:—*Nor fay, Is there not a lie in my right hand?* " Is it not a thing of nought in which " I place my confidence, and which I grafp as eagerly " as if it were my all?" Or, it may be read, *at* my right hand, referring to this as the place of power and dignity.

Having formerly confidered fome of the plans of deceit, which the heart purfues for ftifling convictions altogether; it is our prefent defign to point out fome of thofe falfe grounds of hope for eternity, in embracing which it iffues convictions:

But previoufly, we may obferve more generally,

1. That the heart difcovers its deceitfulnefs by its ftrong propenfity to receive any *error* more *readily* than *truth*. That character of Antichrift is impreffed on the heart of every man by nature;—its working is *with all deceivablenefs of unrighteoufnefs.* That there is no error too grofs for the heart of man to receive,

if

if he be left to the power of his own corruption, is evident not only from the innumerable delusions of those who have no other guide than the light of nature, but especially, from the unspeakable variety of errors and multitude of heresies, many of which are of the most shocking nature, that have been adopted by men who have professed the Christian religion, and pretended to receive the word of God as their only standard. Hell itself could not have been more productive of errors and blasphemies, than the human heart hath been. These are the empoisoned streams that have been issuing from it, in every age of the world, and in every period of the Church. And although the multiplicity of its deceits has almost been expended in so long a course of ages, so that many heresies, which are published as new, are only a revival of those that have been long since antiquated; yet the deceitfulness of the heart, aided by Satan, exerts itself in ushering these into the world, dressed up in a new attire, suited to the taste of the age in which they are produced, and disguised with some greater semblance of truth; like the old and wrinkled Jezebel, who, when she heard of the coming of Jehu, *painted her face, and tired her head*, thinking to soften, if not to captivate the heart of this novice in royalty. It is easier to believe error than truth, because it is agreeable to the deceitfulness of the heart; whereas truth is repugnant to its natural inclination. Every man may be said to be born an heretic; for the seeds of depravity in his heart always dispose him to credit the testimony of Satan rather than that of God. Therefore heresies are mentioned among *the works of the flesh*, because they spring from inward corruption. Some lust, remaining unmortified in the heart, is generally the parent of error in the head. When men *cannot endure sound doctrine*, but *heap to themselves teachers;* it is generally *after*, i. e. *according to their own lusts* *. Even those who have received a religious education, who, from their

---

* 2 Tim. iv. 3.

their childhood, have been trained up in the *wholesome words* of sound doctrine, if their hearts be unaffected by the power of grace, will find a greater propensity to receive error, than to retain the truth in which they have been instructed. The very children of God, who have had the teaching of the Spirit, experience so great deceitfulness of heart, that they are often in danger of questioning the truth, of staggering at the testimony of God, and of apprehending that there is a greater plausibility in error, than in the doctrines of revelation; and were it not for the support of that same Spirit, who hath at first savingly enlightened them, their deceitfulness would carry them so far, and hurry them on so fast, that they would soon *concerning the faith make shipwreck*. So great a propensity is there in the human heart to deceit, that even those, who are in some measure established in the faith, after reasoning on any particular doctrine with adversaries, will at times find somewhat of the fatal influence of error. So keen, so insinuating a poison is this, that the very touch of it is noxious, though it be not tasted. What is fabled of the cockatrice is realized here. This brood of the old Serpent not only conveys fascination, but poison, by a look. Though the arguments, which are urged in defence of any error, be so weak as to bring no conviction to the understanding, yet they will sometimes be so effectual as to leave a dangerous sediment in the heart. Here they make an impression, which truth attended by all the force of the most cogent reasoning, often fails to make. And the reason is obvious. The bowels of the *old man* still yearn on his own kindred.

It is a striking evidence of this inward deceitfulness, that we seldom see a person recovered from error, especially if he has once received the truth and forsaken it: and we as seldom perceive one, who renounces the true faith, stop short at the first error which he embraces. The belief of one error makes way for another, and generally for one grosser than
the

the former. For the farther that men decline from the true foundation, the structure they raise becomes the more hideous, and more immediately threatens the foolish builders with ruin. When men from the malignity of their hearts reject the truth, and against their own convictions propagate error; they are not only successful in deceiving others, but have a miserable success in deceiving themselves into the belief of those damnable doctrines, which at first they received, not so much because they believed them, as because they hated the truth. Hence, it is that error acquires all that *deceivableness of unrighteousness* attributed to the Man of Sin. Men *receive not the love of the truth**. What a person wishes to believe, if contrary to the rule of faith, he will, more easily than could be imagined, persuade himself to believe; because it suits the deceitfulness of his heart, and its fixed opposition to God: and this, notwithstanding the powerful influence of education, the convictions of conscience, and the ordinary operations of the Spirit. Those also, who are assiduous in perverting others, when scarcely confirmed in their own delusions, or when they have not as yet declined far from the truth; by their false zeal, generally not only strengthen their own apostasy, but greatly extend it. Thus the Scripture is fulfilled: *Evil men and seducers wax worse and worse, deceiving and being deceived* †. Does not this illustrate the necessity of still praying, that we may be enabled to *renounce the hidden things of dishonesty*, and preserved from *walking in craftiness, or handling the word of God deceitfully;* and that we may not be *as many, who corrupt the word of God, but as of sincerity, as of God,* that *in the sight of God, we may speak in Christ* ‡ ?

2. THE heart discovers this deceitfulness by its extreme reluctance to the *only way* of salvation, and by its violent *propensity* to every *lying refuge*. We have already considered its attachment to error, *doctrinally*, its inclination to prefer error to truth; and we may now

* 2 Thess. ii. 10.   † 2 Tim. iii. 13.   ‡ 2 Cor. iv. 2. ii. 17.

now attend to this principle as difcovered by its attachment to error, in a *practical* refpect. As we have feen the effects of this deceitfulnefs on the underftanding, we may alfo view its fatal influence on the will. Notwithftanding all the commands and calls of God in the word, to believe in Chrift; the earneft expoftulations and tender intreaties, that God condefcends to ufe with finners on this head; the awful threatenings denounced againft thofe who reject the Son of God; the inward convictions that the finner may have, at times, of the infufficiency of every other foundation of confidence; yet he refolutely leans on his *broken reed*. So averfe is his heart from God's method of falvation, although far more comfortable than obedience to a broken, curfing Law, or toilfome endeavours to attain holinefs without a new nature; that he will rather *weary* himfelf in the greatnefs of *his way*; and *labour in the fire for very vanity*, than accept of the Divine counfel. Many things may incline him to fufpect the fecurity of his fituation. But he will rather *hold faft deceit*, than put the matter to an impartial trial, or put it out of doubt by liftening to him *that fpeaketh from heaven*. Confcience, when deeply wounded, can find no healing from any of his falfe hopes. But he will rather lull it afleep, at the tremendous rifk of its awakening in hell, than make ufe of the *balm of Gilead*, or apply to the omnipotent *Phyfician there*. So violent is his oppofition to the loving Redeemer, and fo vehement is his love to his own devices, that nothing but an *exceeding greatnefs of power* can deliver him. He muft be brought from every falfe fanctuary, and find every treacherous *hiding place* overwhelmed by the ftorm of Juftice, before he be willing to refign them. When driven from one *refuge of lies*, he flies to another, and goes on in this courfe, till by the operation of the Spirit of bondage, he be *fhut up unto the faith**, like a madman, as the metaphor implies, who is confined by his merciful friends from accomplifhing his own

* Gal. iii. 23.

own ruin, on which he is refolutely bent; or, like a prifoner in a ftrong hold, under the condemnatory fentence of the law *. In this fituation he continues, till *the year of* God's *redeemed* be *come*, when *liberty is proclaimed to the captive* by *the Spirit of adoption*, and the rebel is made *willing in the day of power*.

More particularly we obferve,

1. That multitudes betake themfelves to the *general mercy* of God. Perhaps this is the firft lying refuge to which the deceitful heart flies for fhelter, when confcience is alarmed. " I am a fin-" ner indeed," faith the heart, " this I cannot " deny: but God hath no pleafure in the death of " the wicked, for he is a merciful God, and he never " made any of his creatures to damn them." But, alas! this is a treacherous hiding place. God *made man upright, but he hath fought out many inventions*. If any of mankind be damned, the blame lies on themfelves. For they are all *without excufe*. This is efpecially the cafe with the hearers of the gofpel. They are damned, becaufe they *will* not be faved. They perifh, becaufe they defpife the remedy. They inherit eternal death, becaufe they *judge* themfelves *unworthy of everlafting life*, becaufe they *will not come to* Chrift, that they may have it. God indeed is merciful. But his mercy muft be viewed in a twofold light, both with refpect to its *nature* and its *operation*. As to its nature, it is an effential perfection of God. *Unto thee, O. Lord, belongeth mercy*. The object of our worfhip could not be God, unlefs he were infinitely merciful. But it muft alfo be remembered, that mercy is entirely free in all its *operations*. It hath the abfolute choice of its egrefs, of its objects, and of the manner of its manifeftation. *He will have mercy on whom he will have mercy* †. God was under no neceffity of nature to fhew mercy to any of the ruined family of Adam, more than to the angels, who *kept not their firft eftate*. It is a sovereign act of his will, a free *purpofe of grace*. Sinners, you err egregioufly,

* Gal. iii. 23.   † Rom. ix. 15.

egregiously, if you apprehend that God cannot but have mercy on sinful miserable creatures. God cannot *deny himself*. He will never glorify his mercy at the expence of his justice, which is as much an essential perfection of his nature as the former. You altogether confound the attributes of God in your darkened understandings. You make the operation of mercy a necessary act with God, but that of justice arbitrary. You suppose him to be under a necessity of displaying his mercy, but under none with respect to justice. Now, the very contrary is the truth. He acts necessarily in the exercise of Justice, but sovereignly in that of Mercy. He cannot but punish sin, because he cannot but hate it, according to his immutable holiness. And the punishment of sin is just God's operative hatred of it. In the exercise of justice, he looks to the desert of sin. In that of mercy, he can have no such respect; because misery can never have the smallest portion of merit. Can you imagine that God will ever sacrifice an essential perfection of his nature to gratify rebellious worms, *who despise the riches of his mercy?* No. While he proclaims himself to be *the Lord God, merciful and gracious*, he at the same time assures us, that he *will by no means clear the guilty* *. He will not be *merciful to any wicked transgressor* †.

WHAT a lying refuge must this be, since it is *uncovenanted* mercy that you trust in. There is not one promise in the word, which can afford any prospect of mercy, without respect to the everlasting covenant. All the mercy of God to sinners runs in this channel. Therefore these two are joined together. He is the *faithful* God who *keepeth covenant and mercy*, that is covenanted mercy ‡. *The covenant of my peace shall not be removed, saith the Lord, that hath mercy on thee* §. It is mercy confirmed by an oath; *The Lord thy God shall keep the covenant and the mercy, which he sware unto thy fathers* ‖. All the blessings

of

---

* Exod. xxxiv. 6, 7.   † Psal. lix. 5.   ‡ Deut. vii. 9.
§ Isa. liv. 10.   ‖ Deut. vii. 12.

of the covenant are purchased and confirmed by the blood of Christ, and communicated to him, that he may dispense them to us. Therefore, they are *sure mercies*, because not only established by *an everlasting covenant*, but as being *the mercies of David**. But if the general mercy of God be a sufficient ground of confidence, wherein consists the superior blessedness of those *who know the joyful sound?* What necessity was there for the gospel? Wherein are we better than the heathen, who never heard of it? Doth God manifest his mercy out of Christ? Then Christ died in vain. This plan pours the greatest dishonour on the whole work of Redemption, in its contrivance, in its purchase, and in its application. What need for such infinite expence in the display of mercy, if God must necessarily pardon sin? But indeed, there is no mercy with God out of Christ. For *our God is a consuming fire*, who, if *the briers and thorns be* set against him *in battle*, will *pass through them, and burn them up together.* God *keepeth his faithfulness and his mercy only with* him †. It is only in the person and mediation of Jesus, that *mercy and truth have met together* ‡. *With the Lord there is mercy*, only because with him *there is forgiveness*, or *a propitiation* §. Our only hope is in *looking for the mercy of our Lord Jesus Christ unto eternal life* ‖. Nay, Christ himself is *the mercy promised unto the fathers* **. For all other mercies are summed up and concentrated in him, and to be enjoyed only in union to him. He is the *unspeakable gift* of God. We not only have eternal life *through* him, but we have it *in* him. For *this is the true God and eternal life.* But with respect to all who have *no understanding*, who reject this *promised mercy*, this covenanted mercy, who *despise their own mercies*, there is nothing but *a fearful looking for of judgment and fiery indignation, to devour the adversary*; for *he that made them will not have mercy upon them, and he that formed them will shew them no favour* ††.

2. THE

---

* If. lv. 4.   † Pf. lxxxix. 24.   ‡ Pf. lxxxv. 10.
§ Pf. cxxx. 4. 7.   ‖ Jude ver. 21.   ** Luke i. 72.   †† If. xxvii. 11.

2. THE heart often difpofes one to look into itfelf for fomething *good*. Many take this courfe, for a foundation of tranquillity, when any ftorm is raifed in confcience. Perhaps they cannot deny the reafonablenefs of its alarms about their open outward fins: but they fly to the heart. They boaft of its purity. This was the cafe with the Church of Laodicea: *Thou thinkeft that thou art rich, and increafed with goods, and ftanding in need of nothing.* They apprehend, it may be, that they have a confiderable portion of knowledge in the things of God, becaufe they can repeat whole chapters of the Bible; although their learning be like that of a filly bird, which prattles what it does not underftand. They pretend an ardent inclination to good, however much they may err at times. Although they commit grofs fins, they will not allow them to be evidences of wickednefs; becaufe this contains an afperfion on their hearts. Thefe are only evidences of weaknefs. They have been overcome by temptation, while their hearts wifhed to act a very different part. They adopt the language of Abimelech, at leaft in part. If they cannot fay, *In the innocency of my hands,* they will boldly declare,—*in the integrity of my heart have I done this.* Therefore, they perfuade themfelves that God will excufe them, becaufe they defire to do better, however often they fail. But thefe things, inftead of proving that they love God, as they pretend; on the contrary, demonftrate that they are *lovers of their ownfelves,* which is a ftriking evidence of rebellion againft him.

3. OTHERS found their hope on *refolutions* of reformation. They enter into thefe, when *the arrows of the Almighty are within* them, either under Word or Providence. They refolve to do better than they have formerly done, to become *new creatures,* to refift their moft beloved iniquities. This is efpecially the cafe under afflictions. When God's *hand lies heavy upon* them, they try to foothe him into compaffion. They *flatter him with their lips,* promifing

mising an entire change of life, while *their hearts are far from* him. They may, indeed, think themselves sincere. But their sincerity is that of a heart under the dominion of deceit. Their love to sin is still supreme. They seem to love God; but it is only from their dislike to suffering. This conduct we find exemplified by the wicked Pharaoh*.— After the plague of the hail, he *called for Moses and Aaron, and said unto them; I have sinned this time; the Lord is righteous, and I and my people are wicked. Intreat the Lord, that there be no more mighty thunderings and hail; and I will let you go, and ye shall stay no longer.* How vain these promises and resolutions are, the event generally proves, as it did in his case. *When Pharoah saw that the rain and the hail, and the thunders were ceased, he sinned yet more, and hardened his heart—neither would he let the children of Israel go* †. Perhaps, to bind themselves the stronger, they may give their resolutions the solemnity of vows. They may enter into the most solemn engagements before the all-seeing God. But their *goodness is as the morning cloud, and as the early dew.* When sin within them begins to stir, or temptation from without, these strong bonds *are as tow, and the maker of them as a spark, and they both burn together.* Nor is it surprising that they should be of so little avail; because they are made by persons under the dominion of sin, ignorant of the sinfulness and impotency of their situation, and in a dependence on their own strength, without any right sense of the necessity of *a new heart*, of faith in the blood of Christ for justification, or of the communication of new covenant strength from his Mediatory fulness.

4. PARTIAL and outward *reformation* is the confidence of many. Under convictions they proceed so far, as to make some change in their conversation, although they have never been the subjects of a change in the heart. They *escape the grosser pollutions that are in the world, through the knowledge of the Lord*

* Exod. ix. 27, 28. † Ver. 34, 35.

Lord and Saviour Jesus Christ. That they may get rid of the severe admonitions of conscience, they abandon the external commission of some sins. But the love of all sin is as strong as ever. Sin only takes a new channel. Like a river that disappears, it runs more under ground. Ahab, after the Prophet had reproved him, and denounced judgment against his house, not only *lay in sackcloth,* but *walked softly.* In like manner, Herod *feared John, knowing that he was a just man and an holy, and observed him, and when he heard him, he did many things, and he heard him gladly* *. Here we find several circumstances materially good; an esteem for God's messenger, in opposition to that avowed contempt, that is often poured upon his servants by the wicked, he was convinced *that he was a just man and an holy;* a veneration for his person and character, *he feared John;* a concern about his safety, for *he observed,* or rather he *preserved him* †;—

an

---

* Mark vi. 20.

† That this is the proper meaning of the word rendered in our version *observed,* is evident from the constant use of it in this sense in other places, as Matt. ix. 17. Luke ii. 19.; v. 38. It cannot with propriety be alleged that this is not the true sense, because it is added that *he heard him,* which we have no reason to suppose he did, after being rebuked by him: for this expression clearly refers to the past, and not to what succeeded his *keeping* him. Therefore, it is properly translated, *when he heard him.* The Evangelist, according to the manner most ordinarily observed in the gospel-history, without regard to the order of time, takes occasion here to mention Herod's former conduct, before John had given offence. Nor is it any objection to the sense of the word, that *Herod himself had sent forth, and laid hold upon John, and bound him in prison for Herodias' sake,* as we learn from ver. 17. For although Herod might be highly displeased at him, yet it is undeniable that he did not wish to go so far as Herodias; for *when she would have killed him, she could not,* ver. 19. Nay, these words are introduced as the very reason why *she could not* effect her bloody purpose; *For he feared John, and preserved him.* Although he did not reckon it consistent, either with his own honour, or with that of Herodias, whom he had married, ver. 17. to suffer John to preach before him any more, or even to let him at liberty: yet he wished to *preserve* his life. It is indeed said, Matt. xiv. 5. that *when he would have put him to death, he feared the multitude, because*

an attendance on ordinances, inftead of that neglect with which many treat them, or the foolifh inconfideration and indifference of the greateft part, he *heard* him; fome warmth of affections under the word, like that of the ftony-ground-hearers, he heard him *gladly*; a partial reformation, for he not only heard, but *did*; and a reformation of fome confiderable extent, he did *many things*. But ftill his heart remained the fame. For this very Herod afterwards beheaded his faithful preacher. His confcience feems to have been firft awakened by John's miniftry, and afterwards pacified by a partial reformation. But when the Baptift's addreffes became more clofe and particular, when he reproved him explicitly for inceftuous adultery, Herod could not fuffer it. Therefore *he caft him into prifon*. He would be willing to *do many things*, if he might ftill keep *his brother Philip's wife*. He would deny himfelf fome pleafures, and mortify himfelf by fome duties, if his darling fin might be fpared. But when John plainly tells him; *It is not lawful for thee to have her*, when, like Lot in Sodom, he *will needs be a judge*, when he prefumes to define *law* to a fovereign; he renounces his uncourtly chaplain, who had neither a garb*, nor a manner, nor a confcience fit for *kings houfes*, and his partial reformation together.

5. MANY confide in a bare *profeffion* of religion and obfervation of the *form* of duties. We have already fpoken of that difcovery which is given of the deceitfulnefs of the heart, when perfons adopt and maintain

* Matt. xi. 8.

caufe they counted him as a prophet. But we are either to confider this inclination as the immediate effect of his wrath, when recently reproved, which might afterwards fubfide, or be overpowered by his conviction of the Baptift's integrity, and by his remaining veneration for his character; or we muft conclude, that he continued to *preferve* him from the fame political motive which at firft got the better of his bloody inclination, his fear of the multitude. For even after his oath to the daughter of Herodias, to give her whatfoever fhe would afk, he *was exceeding forry*, when fhe demanded the head of John, Mark vi. 26.

a profession of religion hypocritically, with a real intention to impose on others*. We now speak of those who delude themselves, by supposing that they are in a fair way to heaven, because they have *a name to live,* and *a form of godliness.* This is a species of hypocrisy, different from that formerly mentioned, according to the common acceptation of the word; which, although in Scripture used promiscuously in both senses, yet with greater strictness and propriety, applies to him who intentionally deceives others, while he knows his own guile. For the word *hypocrite* denotes one who knowingly plays a false part. For the sake of distinction, the other kind of hypocrite, who deludes himself, may be called a self-deceiver. And indeed, it is a great degree of self-deceit for a man to flatter himself, that his interests are entirely secure, merely because he has a profession of religion, and goes the outward round of duties. The great abounding of such self-deceivers in the Church, may, alas! be too well known from the unprofitableness of their conversation. How unexceptionable soever their external conduct may be, as to positive transgression; yet there is a great want in it. Though their life be not defiled by gross enormities, it is by no means adorned by the fruits of holiness, by a fervour of godliness, by a *labour of love.* Such go no farther in religion, than is barely necessary to maintain their character as professors, and procure admission to the privileges of the Church. Though others may have great apprehensions in regard to them, yet they carry matters so fair, that they could not be justly excluded; as none may presume to determine the state of any to be bad, if they be not ignorant of the truth, or living in the habitual practice of known sin. In a word, they have externally all the *negative* side of a Christian. They are no fornicators, adulterers, drunkards, extortioners or profane persons. Their character is good; they are esteemed by their neighbours; they are regular in the performance of duties:

and

---

* See Serm. xi.

and they conclude that it would be cruel and unjuft to fuch favourable appearances for them to fufpect themfelves.

Persons of this ftamp are defcribed by the Spirit of God: *This people draw near me with their mouth, and with their lips do honour me, but have removed their heart far from me* *. Such felf-deceivers are generally much puffed up with ideas of their own importance and fuperiority to others. Of fuch the wife Agur fpeaks: *There is a generation that are pure in their own eyes, and yet are not wafhed from their filthinefs* †. God expreffes his hatred of this felf-righteous temper: *They fay, Stand by thyfelf, come not near to me, for I am holier than thou. Thefe are a fmoke in my nofe, a fire that burneth all the day* ‡. The fame fpirit Chrift alfo reproved, when he fpake the parable of the Pharifee and Publican *to certain who trufted in themfelves that they were righteous, and defpifed others* §. This felf-deceit the Apoftle James defcribes in a very ftriking manner while he earneftly cautions againft it: *But be ye doers of the word, and not hearers only, deceiving yourfelves* **. When our Lord illuftrates the falfe foundations on which men may reft for falvation, he particularly mentions this as one. *Not every one that faith unto me, Lord, Lord, fhall enter into the kingdom of heaven* ‡‡. Satan who wifhes to keep finners as far from the kingdom as poffible, if he cannot retain them in abfolute profanity, if, in confequence of fome convictions, they adopt a profeffion, will next try to perfuade them to reft here. The heart often falls in with the deceit, becaufe the tranfition from grofs immorality to an outward appearance of ferioufnefs is very confiderable. Therefore there is great danger of relying on it. It is alfo far eafier to make a profeffion, and to obferve ordinances, than to deny one's felf, believe in Chrift, and mortify fin. The Jews found it eafier to keep all the

---

* Ifa. xxix. 13. † Prov. xxx. 12. ‡ Ifa. lxv. 5
§ Luke xviii. 9. ** Ch. i. 22. ‡‡ Mat. vii. 21.

the ceremonial inftitutions which God had appointed, and all the traditions which their fathers had fuper-added, than to *ftain the pride of* their *glory*, by taking up the crofs; becaufe even that burdenfome work was far lefs difagreeable to their corrupt hearts.—The more pure any profeffion is, the greater is the danger. When, on the one fide, one has to encounter the prejudices of education againft found doctrine, to renounce open fins, and to perform a variety of duties unpleafant to corruption; and on the other, to fuftain the reproach of the world, to feparate from former acquaintance, and perhaps to fuffer in temporal refpects; thefe things feem, through the power of deceit, to afford fome ground of confidence and boafting before God.

SERMON XVI.

On the DECEITFULNESS of the HEART, in embracing FALSE GROUNDS of CONFIDENCE.

Isaiah xliv. 20.

A deceived heart hath turned him afide, that he cannot deliver his foul, nor fay, Is there not a lie in my right hand?

IN the preceding difcourfe, we have confidered the deceitfulnefs of the heart as manifefted in fixing on falfe grounds of confidence for terminating convictions,

victions. It hath been observed, that this principle is in general discovered by the strong propensity of the heart to embrace any error more readily than truth, by its extreme reluctance to the only way of salvation, and by its violent propensity to every lying refuge; more particularly, by confidence in the general mercy of God, by disposing a man to look into the heart itself for something good, by depending on resolutions of reformation, and by trusting to reformation of a partial and outward kind.

6. OTHERS deceive themselves into a reliance on their *church-privileges*. This was an ancient error of the Jews. When Jeremiah reproved them for their wicked works, they presumptuously replied, *The temple of the Lord, The temple of the Lord**. They persuaded themselves, that it was impossible that God should reject a people, or any individuals of a people, which was so remarkably distinguished from the nations. Christ found them labouring under the same ruinous deceit. They saw not the necessity of repentance, or of *fruits meet for* it; because they had Abraham for their father †. For the same reason, they had no sense of their need of spiritual freedom, of deliverance from *the bondage of corruption,* from a death *in trespasses and in sins. We be Abraham's seed, and were never in bondage to any man: how sayest thou then, Ye shall be made free?* ‡. During the ministry of Paul, they were trusting to the same sandy foundation. Therefore in his epistle to the Romans, when proving Jews as well as Gentiles to be *under sin*, he sets aside that objection, which the Jews might offer from their outward privileges: *Behold, thou art called a Jew, and restest in the law, and makest thy boast of God* §. They rejoiced in their *name* as distinguishing them from blinded Gentiles. They *rested* in the enjoyment of the law, as committed to them, even while that very law condemned them. They rested in this, instead of coming to Christ, who is the end of the law for righteousness, and

---

* Jer. vii. 4. † Mat. iii. 9. ‡ John viii. 33. § Rom. ii. 17.

and who alone can give *rest to the soul.* They *boasted* in their relation to God as his peculiar and covenant people. Paul himself was once enslaved by this deceit. He had *confidence in the flesh;* because he was *circumcised the eight day, of the stock of Abraham, of the tribe of Benjamin,* one of the two tribes that adhered to the house of David, and to the worship of God, when the other ten revolted from both *; *an Hebrew of the Hebrews, touching the law a Pharisee. These things were gain* to him †. It is much to be feared, that many who are called Christians rest as much on things of the same nature as ever the Jews did. They have been baptised. They are admitted to the Lord's Supper. These are their *circumcision on the eight day,* their *new moons,* and their *solemn feasts.* If this be not the case, why do many of you show so unreasonable an anxiety for baptism to your children; so that nothing will satisfy you, unless all decency and regularity be trampled on, for the more expeditious dispensation of the ordinance; as if the want of it would seal your children under condemnation, or the mere observation of it secure them in salvation? If you confide not in privileges, why are many of you so anxious to receive the Sacrament of the Lord's Supper once a-year, and perhaps, at a particular time, without any desire of celebrating this ordinance more frequently; and so uneasy, if through disease, or by any other unsurmountable obstacle, you be prevented from receiving it at the usual time, or in the ordinary place? How are your minds so serene, after the performance of this duty, without any concern about your meetness for it, or exercise in it? Do not these things indicate, that you rather convert it into a Sacrifice, than receive it as a Sacrament; that you make that day rather a day of expiation, than of commemoration; that you think, with the Papists, that the ordinance confers grace from the *work wrought;* that you make a God of it, give it the room of the blood of

Christ,

---

* 1 Kings xii. 21.   † Phil. iii. 4.—7.

Chrift, and confide in it as an atonement for the fins of the foregoing year, and a fort of difpenfation for thofe of the fucceeding one?

But whatever you may do, God lays no ftrefs on your privileges. Therefore by Jeremiah, he declared to thofe who trufted in them, that he would deal with them, as with the Heathen: *Behold the days come, faith the Lord, that I will punifh all them who are circumcifed with the uncircumcifed: Egypt and Judah, and Edom, and the children of Ammon, and Moab, and all that are in the utmoft corners, that dwell in the wildernefs: for all thefe nations are uncircumcifed, and all the houfe of Ifrael are uncircumcifed in the heart* *. The Baptift told thofe in his time who trufted in their relation to Abraham, that God would rather work a miracle, by raifing up fpiritual children to Abraham from ftones, than acknowledge thefe as his people, who although they had a natural relation to the Patriarch, had *hard and ftony* hearts †. Chrift alfo fhews them, that their connection with Abraham as their natural father, did not preferve them from having the Devil as their fpiritual father; becaufe they did his works ‡. He affures them, that many fhall fay unto him, in the day of judgment, *Lord, Lord, open to us*——*We have eaten and drunk in thy prefence, and thou haft taught in our ftreets;* to whom *he fhall fay, I tell you, I know you not whence you are* §. So Paul informs thofe who *refted in the law*, that if they were *breakers* of it, their circumcifion was *made uncircumcifion.*—For *he is not a Jew, who is one outwardly, neither is that circumcifion, which is outward in the flefh*. But he is a Jew, he is a Chriftian, *who is one inwardly, and circumcifion*, call it baptifm if you will, *is that of the heart, in the fpirit, not in the letter, whofe praife is not of men but of God* **. Thefe things that Paul once counted *gain,* after his converfion, he counted lofs for Chrift. Nay, your external privileges, inftead of juftifying you before

---

* Jer. ix. 25. 26.   † Mat. iii. 9.   ‡ John viii. 34.—44.
§ Luke xiii. 24. 25.   ** Rom. ii. 26.—29.

fore God, will only increase your condemnation, if you trust in them, and reject Christ the *foundation laid in Zion*. Although in respect of privilege, you may be *exalted to heaven*, yet your fall will only be the greater; for you shall be *thrust down to hell.*— It *shall be more tolerable for Sodom and Gomorrah, in the day of judgment, than for you.*

7. Some confide in their *gifts*, or in their *usefulness* by means of them. Those who have formerly been ignorant of the principles of religion, and either by application, or by the common illumination of the Spirit, attain a considerable knowledge of these, are in danger of resting here. The danger is the greater, that knowledge, when unsanctified, *puffeth up*. We see how contemptibly the Pharisees speak of the common people; *This people that knoweth not the law, is cursed*. That this was one of the false confidences of the Jews, is evident from the peculiar notice that Paul takes of it, when enumerating those things on which they rested: *Thou knowest his will, and approvest the things that are more excellent, being instructed out of the law* *. Some may trust in their gifts of utterance in prayer or preaching; or, in their usefulness, either in converting or edifying others: as the Apostle adds; *And art confident, that thou thyself, art a guide of the blind, a light of them who are in darkness, an instructer of the foolish, a teacher of babes, who hast the form of knowledge, and of the truth in the law* †. But gifts of this kind are not confined to saints. They are bestowed for the advantage of others. And although, in general, it be *the lips of the righteous* that *feed many*; yet the common gifts of unholy persons may be useful. For Paul supposes it possible, that he might *preach Christ to others, and be himself a castaway*. Many, perhaps, do not *speculatively*, or in their judgments, rest on gifts, who yet do so *practically*. They find themselves possessed of these. They mistake them for grace, as it is not very easy to distinguish them, without

---

* Rom. ii. 18.   † ver. 19,—20.

without a confiderable degree of fpiritual difcernment. Thus, they do not merely err fo far as to reft on them as evidences of juftification, but as, in fome fenfe, the foundation of it. For the tranfition is very eafy to the deceitful heart, from confidence in a falfe evidence, to confidence in a falfe foundation. And, perhaps, it will be found, that thofe who have no evidences of religion, but fuch as are counterfeit, generally transfer thefe into the room of the foundation : for what is put out of its own place in one refpect, is readily mifplaced in any other. Among the many falfe pretenders to an intereft in him, Chrift particularly mentions thofe, who reft on gifts and ufefulnefs : *I fay unto you, many fhall fay in that day, Lord, Lord, have we not prophefied in thy name, and in thy name caft out devils, and in thy name done many wonderful works?* to whom he fhall fay, *Depart from me, I never knew you, ye workers of iniquity* *. Here they declare the ftrength of their delufive hope, by the manner of their addrefs. It is not only the language of fervency, but of great intimacy. They are introduced as fpeaking to the Judge, as men do to one, with whom they are thoroughly acquainted, although, at the time he may not feem to notice or recollect them ; *Lord, Lord,*—" Thou canft be at no lofs to " know us. We have received many gifts from thee, " and by means of them we have alfo done thee much " fervice !" But he difclaims all knowledge of them, all love to them, all intereft in them. He evidently infinuates alfo, that they might live and die in this felf-deceit. For it is *in that day*, that they are convinced of their falfe confidence. Paul fuppofes that one might have *all knowledge and all faith*, and yet be *as founding brafs, or a tinkling cymbal*.

8. Some may truft to a work of the *Law*, as if it were in itfelf faving. The law may operate on confcience in a twofold manner, either as commanding, or as condemning ; by a difcovery either of duty or of danger. But in neither of thefe ways is it indifpenfably

* Matt. vii. 22, 23.

spensably connected with salvation. For there are many, really interested in Christ, who were never the subjects of a law-work. This is the case with those, who have been united to him in a state of infancy, before they were capable of knowing the operations of the Spirit on their hearts. So it was with Samuel, of whom it is said, that *the child was in favour with the Lord* *; with Jeremiah, to whom he speaks in this manner, *Before I formed thee in the belly I knew thee, and before thou camest forth out of the womb I sanctified thee*†; and with John, the Forerunner of Christ, who *was filled with the Holy Ghost, from his mother's womb* ‡. These persons could not undergo a work of the law before union to Christ. There are others, who have been converted after they were come to years, in whom the operations of the Spirit have been so gradual, that they have scarcely been sensible of this law-work, or sensible of it in so small a degree, that they have been afterwards in danger of doubting the reality of their faith, for this very reason. One of the thieves, who were crucified with Christ, was converted very suddenly; and it does not appear that there was a preparatory work of the Spirit. The convictions of those who were turned to the Lord, by Peter's ministry, on the day of Pentecost, almost instantly terminated in conversion. Those, whose experience corresponds to such examples, have felt little or nothing of terrors, before they were brought into a state of peace, compared with others who have been long in a most deplorable situation, almost driven to despair, ere they obtained a saving discovery of mercy, or who, as the Scripture expresses it, like Ephraim, have *staid long in the place of the breaking forth of children* §. .

On the other hand, there may be some, who for a long time, may be the subjects of a law-work, and that with the greatest severity, who never undergo a saving change, but afterwards give the fullest evidence of their being *in the gall of bitterness*. Esau *found no place for repentance, although he sought it carefully with*

---

* 1 Sam. ii. 26. † Jer. i. 5. ‡ Luke i. 15. § Hos. xiii. 13.

with tears. So severe were the terrors that the traitor felt, when convinced of his guilt in *betraying innocent blood,* that he would rather plunge himself into hell, than bear them any longer on earth. Here it is to be observed, lest any should mistake, that when we speak of some adult persons being the subjects of regeneration, without a discernible law-work, we are far from excluding it entirely. They do not, perhaps, experience any regular, continued, and severe working of the law on their consciences, like that of many others. But they must of necessity be convinced of their sinful and miserable situation by nature, of their absolute inability to deliver themselves, and of their liableness to eternal destruction; before they can embrace Christ as their only refuge. Yet this law-work may be so gentle and gradual, or of so short a duration, as scarcely to deserve the name, and frequently to be almost imperceptible to themselves.

But although it thus appears undeniably, that a regular, formal and continued work of the law on the conscience, is not indispensably connected with salvation, either on the one hand, as marring the evidences of salvation without it, or on the other, as ensuring the reality of a saving change; yet gospel-hearers may through the deceitfulness of their hearts, imagine that all is secure with them for eternity, because of their experience of a work of this nature. Those, who for a considerable part of their lives have been ignorant of the gospel of Christ, or gone on in an unrestrained course of iniquity, are most in danger of falling into this mistake; because the transition from a total indifference about the state of their souls, to some deep, anxious and distressful concern about it, is so great, that they are very apt to conclude they are the subjects of a saving operation of the Spirit. Because they have experienced a legal sorrow for sin, principally arising from the fear of wrath, they flatter themselves that they have felt that sorrow, which is *of a godly sort;* that *repentance which is not to be repented of.* They have been frightened out of their grosser

grosser sins, therefore they presume that they have actually *fled for refuge to lay hold on the hope set before them*. They find some change of course; and they flatter themselves that they have undergone a real change of nature.

9. This principle of deceit is discovered by the sinner's endeavours to obtain justification by *moral duties*. While some depend on a strict observation of appointed ordinances, others go farther, in pretending to obey the whole law. They not only read and pray, and attend divine worship; but they attempt to keep all the commandments, for obtaining life. *They being ignorant of God's righteousness, go about to establish a righteousness of their own;* and thus they do *not submit themselves to the righteousness of God*. We have a very affecting instance of this species of self-deceit, and of the extreme danger of it, in the history of the young man, who applied to Christ, inquiring, *What good thing he should do to inherit eternal life* * *?* He comes to Christ, seeking salvation in a legal way; and Christ answers him *according to his idols. If thou wilt enter into life, keep the commandments* : " if thou art determined to be saved " by thy own doings, then thou must observe the " whole law." As he discovered his self-deceit, in supposing that it was possible for him to *enter into life* in this way; he gave a farther proof of it, in apprehending that he had anticipated the necessity of this injunction. Being ignorant of their spirituality and extent, he replied; *All these things have I kept from my youth up.* And he asks, as if with a secret triumph of heart; *What lack I yet?* " When I have al- " ready done so much for life, is there any thing that can " yet be wanting?" Or, shall we rather suppose, from the modesty and gentleness of his behaviour, that in this inquiry he was influenced by the dictates of his natural conscience, which was not satisfied with all he had hitherto done? Whatever was the case, our Lord gives him one injunction, that fully displays the vanity

* Matt. xix. 16.—22.

vanity of all his pretenfions and endeavours, and the fatal nature of his felt-deceit. *If thou wilt be perfect, go and fell all that thou haft, and give to the poor.* He had formerly mentioned all the precepts of the fecond table, in fo many words, fave that regarding covetoufnefs; and now he tries him on this precept. But whether this was touching him on the tender part, whether this had been his darling fin; as an evidence of the folly of his legal expectations, we are informed that *he went away forrowful, for he had great poffeffions.* It appears, indeed, that he was naturally an amiable perfon. It is alfo faid that Chrift *loved him, (i. e.)* confidered as man. Nay, it is evident, that he came to Chrift, perfuaded that he could teach him the way to eternal life. But notwithftanding thefe things in his favour, the deceitfulnefs of his heart carried him away from the *good Mafter*, and we have no account of his return. It fhows the inconceivable deceitfulnefs of the heart, that fo many are led aftray by this deceit, when it is fo grofs and palpable. For what can be more abfurd, than for fallen man to imagine that he can obey the law for life, a law already broken, a law that fpeaks no comfort to the finner, that only denounces wrath and eternal condemnation againft *every foul of man that doth evil?*

10. MANY truft to their *fincerity* in religion. Rather than renounce the multiplied fubterfuges of legality, they will endeavour to compound with the law, as if they faid to it; " Although we cannot give perfect
" obedience to thy precept, yet, upon condition of
" deliverance from thy penalty, and of being entitled
" to the bleffing promifed, we will make up for the
" want of *perfection* in our obedience by its *finceri-*
" *ty;* and, to amend the whole, wherein we are de-
" ficient, we will truft to the righteoufnefs of Chrift."
This fond imagination of the heart flays its thoufands and ten thoufands of profeffed Proteftants. Nor is it any recommendation to it, that it hath been regularly reduced into form as a doctrine, as if it contained the very effence of the Gofpel, even by men whofe hearts,

it

it is to be hoped, were better than their heads. In vain do you boaſt of your ſincerity as the foundation of your pardon and acceptance with God. Know ye not that the holy law will remit nothing of its demands? It claims the *uttermoſt farthing*. He that *offendeth in one point is guilty of all*. The law as certainly condemns him, as if he had broken every precept. But *in every thing we all offend*. Mere intention will not ſatisfy it. There muſt be action. Therefore, while it reaches to the heart, all its precepts are expreſſed in immediate reference to the outward act. How can it be pleaſed with mere ſincerity, when it hath no knowledge of any one who is under it, but either as perfect, or as condemned by its curſe? For when man was *made under the law*, he was thus ſubjected as an innocent creature. If the laws of an earthly kingdom make no excuſe for a man, becauſe he has become guilty, but on the contrary, for this very reaſon, denounce their vengeance againſt him; how can it be ſuppoſed that the law of a God of infinite purity ſhould thus be trifled with? If you truſt to your ſincerity, you make it your righteouſneſs, and thus reject the righteouſneſs of Jeſus Chriſt. " Oh! no," may you reply, " we " truſt to his righteouſneſs, for it is this that ſupplies " all our defects." Hath Chriſt then become a Saviour to you, only to make you as far as poſſible ſaviours to yourſelves? Muſt his *robe of wrought gold*, his *garment of ſalvation* be degraded and defiled by being joined to the *filthy rags* of your righteouſneſs? Muſt it be rent in pieces to patch up your tattered ſhreds, and make a covering of them? Vain is the attempt. The *new cloth* put into your *old garment*, inſtead of mending it, would only *make the rent worſe*. What *fellowſhip hath righteouſneſs with unrighteouſneſs?* Our Lord's *garment of ſalvation* is like that which he wore, ſeamleſs. It cannot be parted. It muſt either be received wholly, or not at all. Were it poſſible that ſo much as one of your rags, a ſingle work of yours, could be ſeen in it, the all-piercing

cing eye of Juſtice would look through it, and diſcern all your defects. It is only by putting it on completely, that there can be *no ſpot in* you.

But what is this *ſincerity* in which you make your boaſt before God? Do you not confide in it as the ground of your juſtification? If ſo, it muſt be the ſincerity of a perſon who is not yet juſtified; that is, of one ſtill under the curſe of the law. And do you think that the juſt God will accept this? Where is that human law which will accept ſincerity of repentance for any crime, as an atonement for the crime itſelf? It is vain to pretend, that you do not view it as an atonement for your ſins. For if you believe, that your pardon proceeds in any reſpect on this ground, it muſt be your atonement, nay, your only atonement. For you thus make that your righteouſneſs, which is one duty required in the law. And *if righteouſneſs* in the leaſt degree *come by the law, then Chriſt is dead in vain* *. Can there be any true ſincerity in a heart that is *deceitful above all things and deſperately wicked?* Can there be any in a heart, where ſin is enthroned, where it reigns; in a heart divided between God and the world, between God and ſelf, between Chriſt and Belial? Can that man be truly ſincere, who is a ſtranger to ſaving faith, *without* which *it is impoſſible to pleaſe God;* who habitually neglects known duty; who does not *as a new-born babe deſire the ſincere milk of the word*, and *become as a little child?* Can there be any true ſincerity in a heart that *loves* not *our Lord Jeſus Chriſt in ſincerity;* that rejects Jehovah *our righteouſneſs*, that in all things takes to itſelf the pre-eminence? Can that heart be *right with God*, that has ſelf for its great principle, motive, object and end in all actions? Your very confidence in your ſincerity is a certain evidence that it is not genuine. For *curſed be man that truſteth in man.* The ſincerity of the greateſt ſaint that ever lived could not for a moment be the ground of his acceptance. For the greateſt ſincerity we can attain in

* Gal. ii. 21.

in this world is defiled by a corrupt mixture of deceit. But all such evasions clearly manifest the truth of JEHOVAH's declaration in the words of our text, concerning the idolater, which may justly be applied to the legalist: *He feedeth of ashes; a deceived heart hath turned him aside, that he cannot deliver his soul, nor say, Is there not a lie in my right hand?* Every legal worker is indeed an idolater. He worships his own doings. He *sacrifices to* his *net,* and *burns incense to* his *drag.*

11. ANOTHER false confidence, which many fly to, is the *observance* of *superstitious rites.* In some cases, conscience, when awakened, is far more easily satisfied than in others. Its aptness to take peace to itself may be in proportion to the degree of its distress, or correspondent to the circumstances of the person. When the conscience of an ignorant man is roused, it will find rest in the very same confidence, that one more enlightened is shaken out of, in consequence of inward trouble. The same person, in the course of gradual awakenings, may successively embrace a variety of false refuges, still advancing from one kind of deceit to another less obvious, as being more refined than the former. He, who claims merit to himself from obedience, when his conscience is greatly awakened, naturally imagines, through his own deceitfulness, that this obedience will be exceedingly meritorious, if he perform even more than what is commanded. Thus, superstition is the fruit of fear, co-operating with ignorance, and with a mistaken apprehension of pleasing God, in proportion to the difficulty of the sacrifice, and the voluntariness of the offerer. So great is the deceitfulness of man's heart, that he will rather be at any possible expence to pacify conscience, than improve *the blood of sprinkling.* To express the difficulty of those courses, to which men often betake themselves, for procuring a false peace to conscience, they are described under the notion of *labouring in the fire.* And why will men incur such trouble, expence and danger, when the salvation of
God

God is brought so near? The principal reason is, that his plan of salvation is too humiliating to the pride of man. So powerful is the legal principle in the heart, that how much soever conscience may be wounded, if the heart be not broken; it will rather heal these wounds slightly, or bear the smart of them for life, than submit to wash in the fountain of blood. Yea, so proud is the heart, that men would not only be Saviours to themselves, by accomplishing the means of salvation; but Gods, in prescribing the nature of the work itself: and indeed they act so far consistently in usurping both these characters; for none can be a Saviour, but he who is a God. Therefore, they often think God's way too easy, and endeavour to devise one of their own: not to mention the natural folly of the understanding, which is ready to ensure one of success in any enterprise, in proportion to the difficulty attending it; as Naaman thought it impossible, that washing in water should cure him of an inveterate leprosy, and had nearly rejected the Divine prescription, because of its simplicity.

Thus, the poor Heathens imagined that the efficacy of their sacrifices, in expiating their sins, was in proportion to their expence. Therefore they proceeded to the dreadful extremity of offering human sacrifices. But this conduct was far less surprising in them, who had no vision, than in God's peculiar people to whom he had *shewed what is good*. When conscience was alarmed by denunciations of wrath, they proposed this strange question; *Wherewith shall I come before the Lord, or bow myself before the High God?—Will the Lord be pleased with thousands of rams, or with ten thousand rivers of oil*[*]? Sinners will not disturb conscience, if it do not disturb them. We find no inquiries about the method of pardon, till God begins to plead with Israel, as he does in the preceding part of this chapter. But as soon as the arrows of conviction are fixed in the conscience, the sinner cries out, *What shall I do to be saved?*

[*] Mic. vi. 6, 7.

When God declares his controversy; Israel exclaims, as one bewildered in the midst of danger; *Wherewithal shall I come?* The awakened, but unrenewed sinner, rather than embrace the Divine plan, will burst the bonds not only of interest, but even of blood and affection. Here there is a proposal of the most expensive sacrifice, that the human mind strongly actuated by a sense of guilt ever devised. *Shall I give my first-born for my transgression, the fruit of my body for the sin of my soul?*—as if even the unrenewed conscience would so far give its testimony to the justice of the law, as to acknowledge that its natural language is, that the nature that hath sinned must satisfy; as if it would feal the equity of the threatening, *The soul that sinneth, it shall die.* Or, shall we rather suppose that Satan, who has always dared to imitate, yea, to rival God, and who must have known that *the seed of the woman* was to have his heel bruised, that the true *passover* was to be *sacrificed*, first suggested it to men; as wishing to have the appearance of the same honour given to him, that was really to be given to the Judge of all. Be this as it will; he prevailed so far, that this dreadful impiety was not only transacted within his own kingdom among the heathen; but even the *beloved land* was defiled by it. Therefore there is a peculiar propriety in the Prophet's mentioning this kind of expiation; as, at this very time, not only Israel, but Judah was chargeable with so inhuman guilt. These sacrifices they offered in Tophet, or the valley of the son of Hinnom. Ahaz was one of the kings, during whose reign Micah prophesied; and he was one of these barbarous worshippers[*]. Jeremiah also mentions it as one of the great sins both of Israel and Judah in his time[†]. But the merciful God proclaims his abhorrence of such abominable services. He declares that he never *commanded them, neither came they into* his *heart.*

Somewhat in the same manner, do the blinded Papists, in our day, try to pacify a guilty conscience.

---

[*] 2 Kings xvi. 3.   [†] Jer. xxxii. 35.

science. They are taught to believe that they must be saved by the merit of good works. And what are these *good* works? Those are especially meritorious, which have most of will-worship in them; the *vain repetition* of prayers in an unknown tongue; the counting of beads; making the sign of the cross times innumerable; and cruel penances. If they fatigue their bodies by tedious pilgrimages to the tombs of pretended saints; if they pine them by fasting; or mangle them with the scourge; then, in their deluded apprehension, they can not only merit heaven for themselves, but communicate a portion of their merit *to others*, who will not be at so much trouble, if they can purchase it at an easier rate. Nay, may it not be feared, that some Protestants found their hopes of acceptance upon obedience to the commandments of men? They *observe days and months, and times and years:* and many, perhaps, satisfy conscience with these things, even, while they not only despise the sole foundation, but neglect the clearest precepts of the moral law, and thus *make void the commandments of God by* their *traditions.* But the Lord saith; *Who hath required these things at your hands? Bring no more vain oblations unto me.* We see how much he is wroth with professors for resting on such false grounds, from the peculiar energy with which he answers the question of these false worshippers by Micah; *He hath shewed thee, O man, what is good.* As if he had said; " O vain, " foolish and ungrateful people, how can you pro- " pose so ridiculous a question;—a question which " would seem to imply, that I had never called you " to come to me before, that you had never received " any revelation from me? How is it, that you are " so ignorant of the meaning of all the ceremonies " which I have enjoined, as to suppose that they " are required for salvation; when the whole de- " sign of them is only to shadow forth that salvation " contained in the promise of the Messiah? How can " you ever imagine that there can be any proportion

" between

"between ceremonial rites, or even the most costly
"sacrifices of a finite nature, and the evil of sin?
"How can you act so absurdly, as to believe that
"I can accept of human sacrifices, when I have
"often told you, that such a thing never came into
"my heart? Do you think that a practice abhorrent
"to nature, can be agreeable to the God of nature?
"Instead of considering these inquiries, apparently
"so sincere and anxious, as evidences of ignorance,
"and of a cordial desire of instruction; I must
"view them all as vain and shallow pretences to
"cover your aversion from that method of salva-
"tion which I have prescribed. Have I not al-
"ready showed you that way which is good and ac-
"ceptable to me, through the blood of the Lamb,
"typified in all the sacrifices of my appointment?
"Have I not already revealed Him, as the object of
"your faith, who by way of eminence and distinc-
"tion may be called *good*, because of his infinite
"perfections and suitableness as a portion to the im-
"mortal soul, as being God [*];—Him, in whose Me-
"diatory person and work the Divine *goodness* is
"so illustriously displayed;—Him, who deserves this
"appellation, because of his completeness as a Sa-
"viour? Have I not held him up to you as *the good*,
"because he is the only food for the soul [†], the bread
"of life; and as the essential *good* of the new cove-
"nant, the sum and substance of it, in whom all its
"blessings are concentrated, and in union to whom
"all its blessings are to be enjoyed; yea, as the
"*goodness of* Jehovah [‡]? And have I not also fully
"declared the extent of that obedience required, as
"the fruit of an interest in this *good;* that it must be
"of a moral nature, as including not only your duty
"to your neighbour, in acts of justice and mercy to-
"wards him, but your duty to me, in spiritual wor-
"ship, in humility of heart, and in holiness of con-
"versation?"

From these observations we may learn that those
who

---

[*] Matt. xix. 17.   [†] Isa. lv. 2.   [‡] Jer. xxxi. 12.   Hos. iii. 5.

who embrace a false confidence are in the greatest danger from that awful curse denounced by the Spirit of God: *Cursed be the man that trusteth in man, and maketh flesh his arm* *. Although it were supposed, that the curse was originally confined to those who trusted in an arm of flesh, for deliverance from their enemies; this, instead of weakening our conclusion, would give it new strength. If God denounced so dreadful a curse against them, who sought a temporal salvation from an arm of flesh, far heavier must his curse lie on the head of those, who from the same quarter expect a spiritual and eternal salvation. Was he so angry with his people for rejecting him as a temporal deliverer? *Who knoweth the power of* his *anger* against those who reject him as a Saviour from sin and from *the wrath to come*? Were *those* subjected to a curse, who *made haste to go down to Egypt*? Surely, *these* must deserve to feel the effects of his indignation, in a greater degree, in proportion to the unspeakable value of eternal salvation above that which is merely temporal †. If you *trust in man*, if you embrace a false confidence; you not only

* Jer. xvii. 5.

† It is undeniable that this curse extends to all who trust in any thing in or about themselves, whether it respect their performances or privileges. For the term *flesh* is often used to signify any thing pertaining to the law, whether ceremonial or moral. In this sense saith the Apostle of the uncircumcision; *What shall we say then, that Abraham our father, as pertaining to the flesh, hath found?* Rom. iv. 1. In the verse immediately following he shows that by the *flesh* he meant the *works* of the law; *For if Abraham was justified by works, he hath whereof to glory.* Also, when describing true believers, he says; *We are the circumcision which—have no confidence in the flesh,* Phil. iii. 3. Lest any should think that this referred to the literal circumcision only, he repeats the expression once and again in the next verse, and in verse 5, 6, illustrates it in such a manner as to show that he uses it far more extensively. When speaking of that, concerning which any other man might *think that he had whereof he might boast in the flesh,* he not only mentions the privileges of his birth, and his being circumcised; but his connection with the strictest sect among the Jews, his *zeal,* and his *blamelessness touching the righteousness which is in the law.*

only retain yourselves under the curse, which lies on every man by nature, but you subject yourselves to a new and far more tremendous one. The law denounces its curse against every son of Adam, as *a child of wrath;* but it comes in with a new curse against every one, who rejects the blessing, who disbelieves the Gospel. *Take heed, therefore, that ye despise not him that speaketh unto you from heaven.* You may escape the first curse of the law by flying to the blessing of the Gospel. But if you persist in despising this, in *treading under foot the Son of God; there remaineth no more sacrifice for sin, but a fearful looking for of judgment, and of fiery indignation, that shall devour the adversary.*

SERMON XVII,

On the DECEITFULNESS of the HEART, in EMBRACING FALSE GROUNDS of CONFIDENCE.

Isaiah xliv. 20.

He feedeth of ashes; a deceived heart hath turned him aside, that he cannot deliver his soul, nor say, Is there not a lie in my right hand?

IN the two preceding discourses we have illustrated various proofs of the deceitfulness of the heart, in its resting on false grounds of confidence. We now proceed to offer some others.

12. Some

12. Some may rest on their *sufferings* in the cause of Christ. There is nothing that we can either do or suffer, but the deceitfulness and legality of the heart will incline to assume as a ground of confidence before God. Although one may renounce works as the meritorious cause of justification, yet the heart may build on sufferings as some foundation of boasting. One may adopt the language of the disciples with a self-righteous disposition ; *Lord, we have left all, and followed thee : what shall we have therefore ?* As it is not sufficient to constitute a martyr, that a man suffers under a persuasion of the goodness of his cause, unless the cause itself be really good ; as it is not enough that the cause itself be good, unless his principles be correspondent ; one may suffer as a martyr in the eyes of men, while the cause, for which he suffers, may be the only martyr in the estimation of God, because of the impurity of his motives. The approbation of man, or the prospect of having his name embalmed in the annals of the Church, may be his only end, and not the glory of God, or the vindication of injured truth. For a man may not only *give all* his *goods to feed the poor,* but his *body to be burned,* and yet want *charity.* He may be destitute of that genuine love to God, that would make him prefer his glory to every selfish consideration.

13. Others may depend on a *notional faith.*— Some are persuaded of the truth of the Gospel. But they prove that their faith is not *divine,* because it is unfruitful. They may renounce all apprehensions of acceptance before God, through their profession, privileges, or moral duties ; and flatter themselves that they really believe. But their faith reaches no farther than their understandings. It does not really *embrace* that good to which it pretends to *assent.* It makes no appropriation of it in a particular manner. It does not *purify the heart* from sin ; nor does it adorn the life. Besides, they trust in their faith, as the ground of boasting before God. Even the act of
genuine

genuine faith does not juſtify meritoriouſly. This belongs only to the object which faith apprehends, the righteouſneſs of the Redeemer. For, if man were juſtified by faith as his act, boaſting could not be excluded by *the law of faith,* ſalvation would ſtill be by works; and the new covenant would differ from the old in name only. There were ſome in the firſt ages of Chriſtianity, who thought that ſuch a faith might profit them. Theſe are reproved by James, *What doth it profit, my brethren, although a man ſay, he hath faith, and have not works? Can faith ſave him**? Indeed, it may be ſaid, that thoſe, whom James reproved, are not blamed by him for truſting in their faith as the *foundation,* but for truſting in a falſe faith as the *evidence* of juſtification. But though this were granted, yet we ought to remember what hath been formerly obſerved; that generally when men adopt a falſe evidence of juſtification, they do not ſtop here, but inſenſibly build upon it as the foundation. Certain we are, that, in our time, ſome heretics maintain the act of faith to be the only meritorious cauſe of juſtification; while others make it ſo in part, as being what they call the *root* or *beginning* of juſtification. Now, we may not only ſuppoſe, that theſe heretics, as crediting their own doctrine, reſt upon their faith; but there is too much reaſon to apprehend, that others who renounce ſuch falſe doctrine in their judgments, do really embrace it in their hearts.

WHILE ſome ſatisfy themſelves with a mere general hiſtorical faith, others ſeem to go farther. They pretend to appropriate Chriſt to themſelves, to aſſure themſelves of ſalvation through his blood. Yet it is much to be feared, that many ſuch deceive themſelves, both as to the *foundation* of their faith, and as to its *place.* They may deceive themſelves as to the foundation of it. They believe that they ſhall be ſaved, not upon the teſtimony of God in his word; but they take up this perſuaſion at their own hand. They believe that

---

* James ii. 14.

that they do believe. They believe not in the *faithfulness* of God, but in their own *faith*. Themselves are the object of their faith. They also err as to the *place* of this presumptuous faith. For they trust in it. To this they recur for pacifying conscience, and so give it the place of a foundation. When conscience accuses them of want of holiness, they silence its accusations by producing their faith. They tell conscience, that holiness would not justify them before God, that this can only be done by faith in the blood of Christ. This is true indeed. Neither works before, nor after justification, can merit any thing at the hand of God. But let such beware, left they wickedly make the doctrine of grace an apology for their lusts. Can Christ be *the minister of sin?* God forbid. Although faith alone, as an instrument, justifies; yet it does not justify as alone. A solitary faith is not a true faith. *As the body without the spirit is dead, even so faith without works is dead also.* This species of faith, as well as the former, is merely notional. If your own faith be the ground of your comfort under troubles of conscience, if you fly to this as your hiding-place, you *trust in man, and your heart departeth from the Lord.* This also is an evidence of your want of genuine faith. For it is the nature of this grace, in all its actings, entirely to disclaim itself. It is said, *Let a man deny himself.* Now, faith is the greatest act of self-denial. It not only renounces all that a person is, or hath, or hath done, or can do; but it renounces itself, in every acting. Suffer not conscience to be at rest, merely because you have a kind of faith. So had the stony-ground-hearers. So had the rulers, who did not confess Christ. Simon Magus believed. Nay, *the devils also believe* *, and their faith is more firm and operative than that of many professors, for they *tremble.* Nor do they believe in so general a manner as many. For although they cannot apprehend the promise, which was never directed to them; yet, they not only cre-

* James ii. 19.

dit the truth of the threatening, but they appropriate it to themselves. *Art thou come to torment* us *before the time?* Therefore they *tremble*, because from their knowledge of the immutable faithfulness of God, they *believe and are assured* of their own miserable interest in the threatening. The Apostle supposes it possible that a man might have *all faith*, not merely an historical faith, but that which was miraculous, to such a degree, as that he might *remove mountains*, and yet want charity, and so be *nothing*.

14. The deceitfulness of the heart operates in others, by making them rest upon supposed *attainments* in holiness. This is a more refined species of legality than any of these formerly mentioned. Such persons do not rest on the works done by them, like those formerly spoken of, but on the holiness supposed to be evidenced by the performance of these works. In profession, and in their own apprehensions, they altogether renounce salvation by works. But still they some way or other seek for it, as procured by that holiness, which they either consider as the fruit of their works, or as certainly demonstrated by them. They rely not on their profession of religion, on their regularity in attendance on ordinances, or on their performance of moral duties; but on the holy frame and temper of their hearts in the observation of all these. They do not, like the true believer, esteem holiness as the way to heaven, with respect to meetness; as the blessed prelude; and, indeed, an eminent part of it: but view it rather as the foundation of their hopes of enjoying eternal life. Instead of making it the evidence, which is the proper place of evangelical holiness; they rely on it as the foundation. Such hypocritical professors proceed a great deal farther in religion than others. This is, therefore, a deceit, which is far more dangerous, because of its greater depth and subtilty. They are not merely concerned about the outside of duties, but taste of the comforts of them. They have the semblance of all the graces of the
Holy

Holy Spirit, without the reality of one of them.— They have, it may be, an extenſive knowledge of the things of God. They can talk, with the greateſt fluency, of the myſteries of religion ; and have a doctrinal belief of them all. Nay, their knowledge would ſeem to be not merely ſpeculative, but in ſome meaſure practical ; becauſe it is not deſtitute of influence on the converſation. They may appear to be *ſtrong in faith*. Their faith may even ſeem ſtronger than that of thoſe, whoſe hearts are *right with God ;* becauſe, not being ſavingly acquainted with the plague of their own hearts, they have very little jealouſy over themſelves. To appearance their love is very ardent, towards both God and their neighbour.— They may flatter themſelves, that they place all their delight in ordinances, becauſe they fancy that therein they enjoy real communion with God. They may alſo ſuppoſe that they love the brethren *with a pure heart fervently*, becauſe they falſely conſider themſelves as children of the ſame family. Their zeal is ſo keen, that they often go as *he-goats before the flock*, and may even ſeem more concerned about the intereſts of religion than thoſe who are *the children of Zion*. They may give many evidences of repentance, and be *in faſtings often*. Their tears may flow copiouſly in the duties of religion. They may be remarkable for humility, and conſpicuous in liberality. Yet all theſe things may be the mere effects of natural affection, quickened by ſome common operation of the Spirit, without any of his regenerating or ſanctifying efficacy.

It is a ſuppoſable caſe, that thoſe who are entire ſtrangers to ſaving grace, may be *enlightened, and taſte of the heavenly gift, and be made partakers of the Holy Ghoſt, and taſte the good word of God, and the powers of the world to come* *. They may be *enlightened* by a common work of the Spirit on the underſtanding, opening up the doctrines of revelation, and producing an *aſſent* to their truth ; while there is no ſuch

---

* Heb. vi. 4, 5.

such efficacy as is necessary to bring the will cordially to *embrace* them. They may *taste of the heavenly gift*. They may have some affecting discoveries of Christ, who is elsewhere called God's *unspeakable gift*, made to their understandings, so as to operate on their affections; some glowing apprehensions of the grace or glory of Christ, and of the excellency of the way of salvation through him, especially in their imaginations: although they do not really *receive* this *heavenly gift* into their hearts by *faith unfeigned*. They may be *made partakers of the Holy Ghost*, not only in his ordinary operations on the soul, but in his miraculous gifts, as in the first period of Christianity. They may *taste of the good word of God*. They *taste*, although they do not really eat* and feed on it by faith. They may not only have their understandings opened to perceive its *truth*, but some experience of its *power* on conscience, and some feeling of its *sweetness* in their affections, of the *goodness* of this word, so that they persuade themselves, that they not only *assent* to it as *true*, but *embrace* it as *good*. The hearers, who are likened to the stony ground, *received the word with joy*. Those who attended on the ministry of John Baptist were *willing to rejoice in his light for a season*. They may derive an ill-founded comfort from the promises of the word, falsely and presumptuously supposing that they have an actual interest in them. They may also *taste of the powers of the world to come*. As they flatter themselves with the hope of eternal life, they may, through the warmth of their imaginations, and fervour of their affections, in some degree realize, not only the awful doctrines of a resurrection and judgment, but the joys of heaven, by their fancied communion with God, and experience of the love of Christ †. The inspired penman supposes,

---

* Jer. xv. 16.

† Some, who understand *the powers of the world to come* of the different miraculous gifts bestowed on the first Christians, endeavour to confirm their opinion by the use of the same expression, chap. ii. 5. where the penman speaks of the New Testament dispensation

Ser. 17. *as to false grounds of Confidence.* 317

supposes, that all this might be, and yet that the subjects of it might *fall away*, so that it should be *impossible to renew them again to repentance*.

If the heart can proceed so very far in self-deceit, if an unrenewed man can attain so great a resemblance to the true believer; O! how great must the deceitfulness of the heart be! How mournful is it, that through the remains of corruption, the saint himself is at times so much misled by the workings of deceit, somewhat similar to these mentioned. Thou, believer, whose heart hath been opened to God, and opened to thyself, by him who *hath the key of the house of David*, canst tell from thy sad experience, how very prevalent this species of deceit is with thee, which is especially detestable, because so secret, subtile and insinuating; and dangerous, because ever ready to mar the success and comfortable fruits of all thy duties. This is one of these *foxes* that so frequently

---

pensation under the designation of *the world to come*. But it must be observed, that although these expressions are translated in the same way in our version, they are different in the original. The word rendered *world* in chap. ii. 5. (οἰκουμένη) properly signifies the habitable earth; and from its connection, seems to denote the New Testament dispensation. But the word here used is αἰὼν, *age* or *world*. It is acknowledged, that this word is sometimes used to denote the world in its *present* state. But we may safely assert, that not one passage can be pointed out, where it can be understood in this sense, when connected with μέλλων, as in the expression under consideration: whereas, the same phrase is found in other places, where it is granted on all hands, that it signifies the *future* state; as Mat. xii. 32.—*It shall not be forgiven him, neither in this world, neither in the world to come*. Eph. i. 21.—*not only in this world, but also in that which is to come*. Another word of the same meaning, (ἐρχομένος) is joined with αἰὼν, Mark x. 30. and Luke xviii. 30. in both which places, the concluding expression *eternal life*, undeniably explains the meaning of the foregoing, *the world to come*. Those who understand this of miraculous gifts, think their sentiment confirmed by the word δυνάμις, which is generally used to denote these gifts. But, although this be granted, it will by no means amount to a proof. For this very word sometimes refers to the *eternal* state, as in Mat. xxii. 29. and Mark xii. 24. where it is used in reference to the resurrection of the dead, which is one of *the powers of the world to come*;—*Not knowing the power of God*.

quently *spoil* thy *vines, and destroy their tender grapes.* This often robs thee of thy joy and consolation in the very blossom. When thou hast been engaged in a difficult duty, or subjected to a severe trial; when thou hast obtained an eminent degree of communion with thy God; dost thou not often feel a secret but powerful inclination in thy heart, to claim some degree of merit to thyself, in performing the duty, or in sustaining the trial; to admire the lustre of thy own holiness; and to flatter thyself that thou must certainly be *greatly beloved* of the Lord, because thou art so holy and lively in his service? Art thou not ready to think in this manner, as if man could *be profitable to God, as he that is wise is profitable to himself,* as if it had been thine own *sword or arm,* that had *saved* thee, as if holiness had been the produce of thy own heart, or as if God could be a debtor to thee for what thou hast received from himself?

This part of the subject points out to us the great necessity of using all diligence in inquiring into our real *state* before God. In urging this duty, we might enlarge on the fatal consequences of self-deceit, on the impossibility of mending matters in the eternal world, on the indignity offered to God by a false profession, on the holy confidence in duty, which attends a well-grounded persuasion that we do not *run in vain.* But at present we shall only mention one thing, which may be considered as a powerful argument, although only of a secondary nature, enforcing the necessity of the greatest earnestness and diligence in examining our state; and it is this, that he who makes a profession of religion, without knowing its power, gives himself all the fatigue of religion, in an outward respect, while he denies himself all its joys and comforts. Going about a multitude of duties, perhaps many more than God has commanded, he *wearies himself in the fire for very vanity.* Whereas the same duties, if performed from the principle of a renewed heart, in relation to Christ as the only Mediator, through the strength of his grace,

and

and for the glory of God, would be a bringing forth of fruit to life eternal.

You, who are trusting in any of these false grounds, we would earnestly entreat to consider your danger, ere it be too late. The house built on the sand will certainly fall, and if you continue in it, must involve you in its ruin. The further you proceed, if you stop short of true religion, the more hopeless is your case, the more aggravated will be your misery. Your case is the more hopeless, because the more refined your delusions are, conscience is in the greater danger of retaining its false peace. The more near that you *seem* to be to the kingdom of heaven, the farther are you *really* from it, and the greater is the risk, that you may never enter into it. *Publicans and harlots shall enter before you.* Your misery, if you continue in your false confidence, will be the more dreadful. It will receive a double keenness from your fond and flattering hopes. Your superior knowledge, profession, privileges and attainments will greatly aggravate your condemnation. Justice is ready to overtake you. *The hail shall sweep away every lying refuge, the storm shall overflow every* deceitful *hiding place.* Consider what God is saying to you as to the folly of such hopes; *The moth shall eat them up like a garment, and the worm shall consume them as wool; but my righteousness shall be for ever, and my salvation from generation to generation.* Betake yourselves to Christ as your refuge. For *a man shall be an hiding place from the wind, and a covert from the tempest.* These two immutable things, in which it is impossible for God to lie, his *promise,* and his *oath,* afford you *strong consolation* in *fleeing for refuge to lay hold on the hope set before* you.

You, who have been in some measure delivered from the deceitfulness of your hearts, and have seen the blood of Christ to be the only ground of confidence, may be hence entreated to consider the necessity of exercising a godly jealousy over yourselves, and of having your evidences for eternity set in the clearest light; that you may not be

be *ashamed before the Son of man at his coming.*
You see how far false professors may go in religion;
and this should excite you to the greater watchfulness over your hearts. But there is a question, which may here occur to some, a question, the solution of which materially affects every one of us before God. If false professors may have so eminent attainments, and so remarkable a resemblance of true holiness; how may we distinguish between such attainments, as are the fruit of the Spirit's saving work, and those, which only flow from natural affections, or from a common operation? Lest we should *make the heart of the righteous sad, whom God hath not made sad,* we shall endeavour to answer this question; that the Lord's people, through his blessing, may discern the reasonableness of their comfort; and that pretenders may perceive the falseness of their confidence.

1. These attainments, which are saving, have always an *humbling* tendency. They make the subject of them think meanly of himself, perceive much of the hatefulness of sin, and of his own loathsomeness on account of it. Indeed, he thinks always the less of himself, the more he is favoured with these attainments. When Isaiah saw *the Lord high and lifted up;* he cried out, *wo is me! for I am undone; I am a man of unclean lips* *. What was the language of Job, when he obtained a discovery of his God in mercy? *I have heard of thee by the hearing of the ear, but now mine eye seeth thee; wherefore I abhor myself, and repent in dust, and in ashes* †. This is expressly promised, as the fruit of the Spirit's gracious operation and inhabitation. *I will put my Spirit within you,—then shall ye loathe yourselves in your own sight for your iniquities, and for your abominations* ‡. But those attainments, which are merely the result of natural affections, or of a common operation, generally fill the person with pride and self-conceit. *Knowledge puffeth up, but love edifieth.*

2. Saving

---
* Isa. vi. 5.   † Job xlii. 5, 6.   ‡ Ezek. xxxvi. 27. 31.

2. SAVING attainments are confiftent with a godly *jealoufy*. The perfon is anxious till they be brought to the touchftone of the word, till he try them by *the law*, and by *the teftimony*. This temper does the Apoftle Paul, who was fo eminent in godlinefs, difcover: *I therefore fo run, not as uncertainly—left that by any means when I have preached to others, I myfelf fhould be a caft-away.* But the felf-deceiver gives himfelf little anxiety about the reality of his attainments, and efteems it only a lofs of time to bring them to the trial. Thus, he verifies the words of Chrift; *Every one, that doth evil, hateth the light, neither cometh to the light, left his deeds fhould be reproved. But he that doth truth cometh to the light, that his deeds may be made manifeft, that they are wrought in God* *.

3. THE fruit of folid Chriftian attainments is *thankfulnefs* to God. The believer is afraid of *requiting* him *like a foolifh people and unwife*. It is the language of his heart; *Not unto me, not unto me, but unto thy name be the glory.* Like the Pfalmift, he wifhes that his *foul, and all that is within* him, were ftirred up to *blefs his holy name*. But the falfe profeffor is a ftranger to this exercife, what pretences foever he may make to it. For *the* dead *praife not the Lord*.

4. THE Chriftian *difclaims* all his attainments with refpect to *juftification*. He values them, indeed, as the fruit of the Spirit, as the teftimonies of God's love, and as the evidences of the power of religion in his own foul. But he entirely renounces them, in his habitual exercife, as the foundation of acceptance before God, or of any farther degree of favour from him. Whatever gain Paul reckoned upon in his fuppofed attainments before converfion; yet after it, he not only renounces all thefe, but all his real attainments in the exercife of gofpel-holinefs: *What things were gain to me, thefe I counted lofs for Chrift. Yea doubtlefs, and I count all things but lofs for the excellency of the knowledge of Chrift Jefus my Lord, for whom*

---

* John iii. 20. 21.

whom I have suffered the loss of all things, and do count them but dung, that I may win him, and be found in him; not having mine own righteousness, which is of the law, but that which is through the faith of Christ, the righteousness which is of God by faith *. He accounted resting on attainments even in a converted state, on gracious attainments, and those of the highest kind, to be nothing but seeking a legal righteousness. But he, whose attainments are of a different nature, if he rely not entirely upon them, yet considers them as in part his recommendation to God, and as some ground of boasting before him.

5. SAVING attainments leave a *lasting* impression on the *heart*. Even when the affections of the Christian are very languid, *the desire of* his *heart* is to God. Even when overpowered by the unrenewed part, he *delights in the law of the Lord after the inward man*. But the self-deceiver finds the influence of religion only when his affections are enlivened. Strip him of these, and you *take away* his *gods, and what* has he *more?* Although at times he may exceed even the real Christian in fervour, yet, because *the hard and stony heart* remains, when hurried away by corruption, he discovers *the old man* in all his power, he sins with the *full* consent of his will, he *works* iniquity *with greediness*.

6. THE real believer loses not his confidence in God, even under severe *afflictions*. With the Prophet he can say; *Although the fig-tree* shall *not blossom—yet I will rejoice in the Lord, I will joy in the God of my salvation* †. Even where there is a certainty of tribulation, he resolves to keep hold of God as his God. According to the measure of grace he can join with Paul in putting affliction, in all its aspects, at defiance; *Who shall separate us from the love of Christ? Shall tribulation, or distress, or persecution, or famine, or nakedness, or peril, or sword*, &c. ‡. Sometimes he even *glories in tribulation*. But, in general, afflictions

---

* Phil. iii. 7.—9. † Hab. iii. 17, 18. ‡ Rom. viii. 35,—39.

tions discover the vanity of *the hope of the hypocrite.* This is one evidence that Christ gives of a false profession. *He that received the seed into stony places, the same is he that heareth the word, and anon with joy receiveth it. Yet hath he not root in himself, but dureth for a while: for when tribulation or persecution ariseth because of the word, by and by he is offended* *. It is not meant as an invariable test; because it is elsewhere supposed that a man may *give* his *body to be burned,* and not have *charity.* But the nature of Christ's language implies that it will generally hold.

7. THE real Christian does not wish to *stop* short in his attainments. He never thinks he has gone far enough in religion. He still desires to make greater progress in holiness than he has ever made before.— In this we have also the example of Paul; *Not as though I had already attained, or were already perfect: —but this one thing I do, forgetting the things which are behind, and reaching forth unto those things which are before, I press toward the mark for the prize of the high calling of God in Christ Jesus* †. But, on the contrary, the self-deceiver thinks he has gone far enough in religion. Nay, he scarcely imagines that he can make any advancement, for he *counts* himself *to have apprehended.* A great part of his exercise consists in contemplating and admiring the attainments, which, according to his apprehension, he has already made. So, instead of worshipping God, he worships the creature of his own imagination. Instead of considering how far he is behind, he rather inclines to solace himself with his advancement before many around him, and to rest here. This is exemplified in the prayer of the Pharisee: *Lord, I thank thee that I am not as other men.*

8. THE believer is *equal,* or at least *consistent* in his attainments. While he makes progress in duty, in the exercise of grace, in liveliness, and spirituality of affections; he at the same time advances in the mortification

---

* Matt. xiii. 20, 21.   † Phil. iii. 12.—14.

tification of sin. And where the heart is truly sincere, these always go hand in hand. Sin becomes more and more hateful, and is more and more subdued. Therefore, when the Apostle declares, that the life which he lived in the flesh was *by the faith of the Son of God*, with the same breath he says, *I am crucified with Christ* *. Notwithstanding all pretended attainments in religion, all the warmth of affections, and supposed enlargement of heart, which the hypocrite has in duties; his lusts remain as powerful as ever, if not in his life, at least in his heart. Thus he pulls down with one hand, what he pretends to build with the other. While he professes to advance in holiness as to the duties of religion, he advances in sin by the liberty which he gives to his lusts; to those of a more secret kind at least, *the lusts of the mind*, such as pride, self-righteousness, and the like. This is a certain proof of hypocrisy; for *if I build again the things which I have destroyed, I make myself a transgressor* †. The character of Ephraim is applicable to such a professor. *Ephraim is a cake not turned* ‡. He is entirely unequal and inconsistent in his supposed attainments. While he pretends great advancement in spirituality, he is quite a stranger to mortification. Thus he is like a cake that is half roasted, and half raw. View him on the one side, and he seems almost burnt up by the flame of holy affections. But on the other, he is like dough that is scarcely heated by the fire.

In the last place, all true Christians have a real *love* to *holiness*. They love it especially for itself, as being the image of God. The advantages arising from it are not their principal motive. They *give thanks at the remembrance of his holiness*. They *rejoice in the beauty of holiness*. They love God's law, because it is holy; and the holiness of the Divine nature is one great excitement to adoration §. But pretenders,

---

* Gal. ii. 20.   † Gal. ii. 18.   ‡ Hof. vii. 8.
§ Psal. xcix. 5. 9.

pretenders, whatever respect they may profess for holiness, as being necessary to support their present self-deceit, or to secure future happiness, do not really love it as the image of God. They may, in some respect, love it as the supposed fruit of their own heart-purification, or of their own endeavours in one form or other; but they cannot love it as the fruit of the Spirit's gracious efficacy.

SERMON XVIII.

On the DECEITFULNESS of the HEART, with respect to the PERFORMANCE of DUTY.

Psalm lxxviii. 56, 57.

——And kept not his testimonies; but turned back, and dealt unfaithfully like their fathers: they were turned aside like a deceitful bow.

UNDER the law God gave this commandment to his people; *Thou shalt not sow thy field with mingled seed, neither shall a garment mingled of linen and woollen come upon thee.* In unspeakable condescension, he extended his injunctions even to those matters which are in themselves indifferent, and of little moment; that we, for whom *all these things were* especially *written*, might inquire into their spiritual design. This precept might be meant to inform us, how abominable hypocrisy is in the eye of the holy God. He, in a spiritual sense, *sows his field with mingled seed*, who partly serves God, and partly Satan and Mammon; who in duty denies his heart to God; who assumes an appearance of ardent zeal before men, while indifferent before the Searcher of hearts; who maintains *the form of godliness*, but practically *denies the power thereof.* Like the pretended mother, who insisted for dividing the child; our natural deceitfulness pleads for a division of the heart. It will profess to give a part to God; but it must retain the other part for sin.

This

Ser. 18. On the Deceitfulness of the Heart, &c.

This Psalm has been evidently designed for stirring up the church of Israel to confidence in God, and to a strict observation of his law. For this end the inspired penman enumerates her many transgressions in former times, shows the aggravation of her iniquity by rehearsing the mighty works of God, and illustrates the danger of unbelief and disobedience, from the consideration of the various judgments formerly inflicted on account of these sins. In the passage immediately before us, he aggravates the guilt of the Israelites in provoking God, notwithstanding his great mercy in leading them safely through the wilderness to the promised land, and in subduing their enemies. *Yet*, saith he, *they tempted and provoked the Most High God*. In what respect they did so, he shows in the words of our text; they *kept not his testimonies*. This word in general denotes the whole revelation that God hath made of himself in the word. The two tables of the law were particularly called the *testimony* of God; and because these were contained in the ark, it was thence called *the ark of the testimony*.

Here it seems especially to signify the ordinances of his worship; as the *testimonies* of God are directly opposed to the *high places* and *graven images* of false deities, mentioned in the following verse; by which they *provoked him to anger, and moved him to jealousy*. Instead of keeping his testimonies, they *turned back*. They in heart and practice returned to their old lusts and idols, *and dealt unfaithfully like their fathers*. They resembled them in breaking through their solemn engagements to God. *They were turned aside like a deceitful bow*. When they seemed to be directing their feet into *the way of* his *testimonies*, they acted treacherously with God. They were like a bow, which, though the aim be exactly taken, shoots the arrow wide of the mark.

From these words we propose to illustrate the deceitfulness of the heart with respect to duty. We may,

may, *first*, consider some evidences of this principle in the performance of duty. And, *secondly*, in the omission of it.

First, As to the performance of duty, the heart discovers its power of deceit,

1. By diverting a person from those duties, that are most *spiritual* in their nature. The heart, as carnal and unrenewed, is in Scripture often designed *the flesh*, to express its grossness, corruption and opposition to every thing that is truly *spiritual*. Though in itself spiritual, as being immaterial, it is called fleshly, on account of its subjection to sin, and because, in man's state of depravity, the inferior faculties have acquired the ascendant over the superior. In God's sight it has in this respect lost the spirituality of its nature: for in its conformity to the Divine image consists the greatest glory and perfection of the spirituality of the soul. May we not view it as a striking evidence of the carnality of the heart, that it is peculiarly reluctant to all those duties, which are most spiritual in their nature? Indeed, every duty that we owe to God, may in some sense be said to be spiritual; because it can only be acceptable to him, when our spirits, as renewed, are engaged in it. But some duties are more especially spiritual, as more immediately relating to God himself, who *is a Spirit, and will be worshipped in spirit;* and as demanding a closer engagement of the soul than others, which are more of an outward kind.

Thus, the heart will often submit to those duties which a man owes to his neighbour, while it spurns at those, of which God is the immediate object. Nay, it may bear with a regular attendance on public or private worship. But it is very averse from secret duties. It is extremely unfond of secret prayer, because in this ordinance the worshipper has *to do with God* only. When one has ill will to another, he may pass the time tolerably in his company while others are present; but he feels very disagreeably,

when

when left alone with him. Self-examination and personal fasting are duties to which the carnal heart makes the keenest opposition, because it is their tendency to give a fuller view of sin, of the emptiness of self, of its own deceitfulness, and of the necessity of renewed supplies of grace; and because these are, in the experience of believers, made eminently useful in increasing hatred of sin, and the *desire of the soul to the name* of Christ, and *to the remembrance* of him. It may bear with a careless, unaffected reading of the word; but meditation on it, in a dependence on the Spirit as the great interpreter, is an exercise to which it discovers great backwardness? because the word, thus accompanied, is *a lamp to the feet, and a light to the path;* because it is profitable in so many respects,— *for doctrine, for reproof, for correction and instruction in righteousness.* It will plead that these duties are of too difficult a nature; that they require too close an attention; that it is very provoking to God to perform them carelessly; and therefore insist for the neglect of them, and for giving a preference to those of a more general nature. The Pharisees were very willing to *tithe mint, and anise, and cummin*, but they omitted *faith and the love of God*, as well as *the weightier matters of the law* with regard to man [*]. But the great reason of this aversion of the heart, as unrenewed, from more secret duties, is that it is afraid of a close dealing with God, lest its own iniquities be discovered; and is apt in such a situation to say to him, as the wicked king to the faithful Prophet, *Hast thou found me, O mine enemy?* This leads us to observe,

2. THAT it endeavours to prevent any real *communion* with God, and to distract the mind by *wanderings* in duty. We have seen that the heart, as deceitful, always discovers great aversion from those duties that are most spiritual in their nature. But it discovers a still greater reluctance to *spirituality* in these, and in every other. If it prevail not with the professor, so far as to divert him entirely from engagement in

[*] Mat. xxiii. 23.; Luke xi. 42.

Christian exercise, especially of a spiritual nature; it will struggle hard to hinder him from engaging in it in a spiritual manner. It will argue from the great fatigue to which the mind is subjected, when constantly on the stretch, when still exerted to its utmost in Divine service. It may even, at times, submit to the exertion of all our natural abilities for the discharge of a duty, of some constant exercise of rational endeavours, of some intenseness of the mind; but it strives with violence against a spiritual engagement of heart, consisting in an entire dependence on the grace of Christ, and present improvement of it, by deriving supplies from his inexhaustible fulness. This is a stroke against corruption, which it will use every effort to parry. When it finds that God demands the heart in every duty, it will consent to give him the rational understanding, if it cannot make a better of it; or some degree of affections working in a natural way: but it cannot accede to the proposal of giving the whole heart, as implying not only the exercise of every faculty, but of every one in a spiritual manner. At the thought of devoting the whole heart to God in every service, it trembles for its beloved lusts; because it is impossible that there can be a real, spiritual engagement of soul in any duty, but it must directly tend to the crucifixion of these. For every advancement which the Christian makes in communion with his God, leads him farther into himself, and quickens him in carrying on the war against his spiritual enemies. Every act of spiritual worship, that ascends from the renewed soul to God, may be said to descend again, and to rebound on the head of some one corruption, in advancing its gradual destruction: as every considerable breach made in the wall of a besieged city, not only gives opportunity to the assailants to enter in, and brings them nearer to possession; but exposes the besieged to destruction: as they are in the greatest danger of being buried in the ruins.

To prevent thefe confequences, the heart incites to *wandering and diftraction* in religious worfhip. This is the cafe both with faints and finners. The greateft part of gofpel-hearers *honour* God *with the lip,* while the *heart is far from* him. They feem to liften, and it may be, attentively, to what is fpoken to them in the name of the Lord; yet they fcarcely attend to a fingle fentence. Inftead of hearing his word, as thofe who muft give account, their hearts are often following their eyes; they are making their obfervations on the appearance and deportment of thofe around them; or perhaps, their hearts are ftill farther removed. They are forming worldly fchemes, and meditating on their ordinary employments. To many profeffors, the Sabbath, and even the time of Divine fervice, is a feafon for recollecting all that they have done, or fhould have done through the foregoing week, and for planning the operations of the following. Then they confider what bufinefs they fhall do, what promifes they fhall fulfil, what vifits they fhall make, probably, what mifchief they fhall execute, on the fix enfuing days; even when they profefs to be worfhipping God the Spirit; or, if they hear what is faid, it is only with the bodily ear. They give themfelves no trouble to attend with the heart. *They come unto thee as the people cometh, and they fit before thee as my people, and they hear thy words, but they will not do them: for with their mouth they fhew much love, but their heart goeth after their covetoufnefs.* Can any fruit be expected from fuch profeffors? Surely No. For the gofpel is a mere found to them; *and lo! thou art unto them as a very lovely fong of one that hath a pleafant voice, and can play well on an inftrument: for they hear thy words, but they do them not* *? Inftability is mentioned by the Apoftle James, as an evidence of deceitfulnefs. *A double-minded man is unftable in all his ways* †. *The wicked is like the troubled fea, when it cannot reft, whofe waters caft up mire and dirt* ‡. This evil is to be found, in a great degree,

---

* Ezek. xxxiii. 31, 32.   † Jam. i. 8.   ‡ Ifa. lvii. 20.

gree, with many real Christians, and in some degree with all. They experience instability of heart in every duty. In public worship they are often harassed by this. When ready to think that their hearts are *fixed, trusting in the Lord;* ere they are aware, they find them *wandering to the ends of the earth.* When they endeavour to pour them out in prayer to the God of their life, and have, perhaps, attained some enlargement in his service; they find that, in a moment, the merest trifle will distract their minds, and carry them away from him. That, which they would scorn to take notice of in the presence of an earthly superior, or even of an equal, will steal away their attention from God, and make them offer *the sacrifice of fools.* When they read his blessed word, their minds are often so unsettled, as not to observe the literal meaning of the expressions. When they sit down at his holy table, and make the most solemn approach that man can make to God, before he stand at his judgment-seat; even there, they find it impossible to restrain their hearts from wandering. When they would view the Redeemer as set forth crucified, a very small matter will so divert the attention, as to make them forget the very duty in which they are engaged. When the Christian would, in any duty, try the exercise of faith in Christ, as his Lord and Saviour, he finds many temptations arising from his own deceitfulness, that in a moment turn away his eyes from Christ, and fix it on that which profiteth not. This instability, as far as it prevails, prevents his present comfort, mars the duty in which he is engaged, and hinders his progress in grace. When, like Reuben, he is *unstable as water,* how can he *prevail?*

3. By inciting to *hypocrisy.* The most eminent Christians will be sensible of the great prevalence of this corruption in religious worship. It discovers itself by a secret desire *to be seen of men.* There is no duty that the saint can perform, if it be liable to outward observation, wherein he is wholly abstracted from this sinister motive. Although he habitually

prefers

prefers *the praise of God* to that of man; yet the natural inclination which every one has to support his own character, and gain the esteem of others, will always in some measure prevail. Can we deny, that it is frequently a sense of the eye of man being on us, which influences us to some fervour in duty, more than a desire of the glory of God; or, at least, that the one is greatly blended with the other, often obscures the evidences of its sincerity, and checks its fervour? That real Christians are in great danger of assuming appearances of religion, and of making professions, from which their hearts are presently estranged, is very evident from the example of so eminent a saint as Peter. Before the arrival of the messengers from Cornelius, he had received a revelation from God, informing him that the Gentiles were to be made partakers of the same privileges with the Jews, and had afterwards the most satisfying evidence, that *on the Gentiles also was poured out the gift of the Holy Ghost;* yet, when at Antioch, he acted with duplicity. For after he had eaten for some time with the Gentiles, he withdrew himself from them, when some Jews came down from Jerusalem; and not only lived after the manner of the Jews, but compelled the Gentile converts to live in the same manner. On this account Paul *withstood him to the face, because he was to be blamed,* and charged him with dissimulation, (Gal. ii. 11,—14.) or, as the word may be rendered *hypocrisy.* For the literal translation of ver. 13. is, *and the other Jews* hypocrised *likewise with him; insomuch that Barnabas also was carried away with their* hypocrisy. The enemies of holiness often call the people of God hypocrites, because they perform duties which themselves neglect; while it is the greatest presumption in them to judge the heart, without the most undeniable external evidences. But every real Christian, although he can appeal to God his habitual sincerity, and constant desire of it, will be ready to acknowledge, that often could they look into his heart during the performance of duty, they would find far

more

more reason for the charge. Were they his witnesses in secret, they might often hear him complaining, that his heart is as *a bow that shooteth deceitfully;* and confessing, that amidst all his outward appearances and inward struggles, he is *carnal and sold under sin.*— Hypocrisy discovers itself in the exercise of believers, not only by their desire *to be seen of men,* but even in their secret duties, when there is no opportunity of outward observation, by an hypocritical desire to be seen of God. Our meaning is, that the people of God are sometimes disposed to appear to him more fervent in duty than they really are, to make professions of love to him which they do not presently feel, to express a hatred of sin and desire of his favour, without the immediate sense of either in their hearts.

4. By prompting the professor to *retain sin* in his heart, even when he draws near to God. At all times it is our duty to endeavour the destruction of this irreconcileable enemy of God, and of our souls. But it is more especially incumbent, when we are about to sist ourselves immediately before the Searcher of Hearts in any ordinance of his appointment. For the indulgence of any sin will deprive us of holy confidence. *If our heart condemn us,* much more will *God,* who *is greater than our heart, and knoweth all things.* It is the greatest insult to him, to come into his presence with a heart locking sin in its embraces. And if we *regard iniquity* in our hearts, we may be assured that he *will not hear* us. Therefore our Lord exhorts us, when we are to offer a gift, if our *brother has ought against* us, *first* to *go and be reconciled* to him, and then to *come and offer* our *gift.* To the same purpose are the words of his servant Paul, when speaking particularly of the greatest external act of religion; *Therefore let us keep the feast, not with old leaven, neither with the leaven of malice and wickedness, but with the unleavened bread of sincerity and truth* *. By an allusion to the ordinance of God with respect to the observation of the passover,

---

* 1 Cor. v. 8.

passover, sin in general is called *leaven;* because when suffered either in a collective body, or in an individual, it pervades and sours *the whole lump*, and sincerity is opposed to this *leaven*; because wherever it is suffered, the heart is acting under the influence of deceit. Now, in the prospect, or in the performance of any instituted duty, the heart often insinuates, that there is no necessity for all this strictness. It either hides its leaven as much as possible from the eye of conscience, and pretends that it is all purged out already; or pleads that it is so little that it cannot affect the lump, that it cannot spoil the duty; or, without attempting to diminish it, boldly avows that there is no danger in retaining it. Thus the person may be prevailed with, perhaps, to *eat and drink unworthily*, and so *to eat and drink judgment to himself*, and to venture on that awful denunciation; *Cursed be he that doth the work of the Lord deceitfully, and cursed be he that keepeth back his sword from blood**. He does so by *keeping back his sword from* the *blood* of his spiritual enemies, that *war against the soul*. He *brings that which was torn, and the lame, and the sick;* although God hath said, *Cursed be the deceiver, who voweth and sacrificeth unto the Lord a corrupt thing* †.

5. BY exciting a person to *rely* on his *own strength.* This attempt the heart, as deceitful, often makes, well knowing that if it can be successful in producing so false a dependence, it will effectually prevent all the blessed fruits which would spring from duty, if performed in the strength of the Lord. For he, who engages in it in his own ability, deliberately procures the inheritance of the curse, instead of observing the appointed means of inheriting the blessing. For it is declared, *Cursed be man that trusteth in man, and maketh flesh his arm, and whose heart departeth from the Lord* ‡. The legal observation of duty, instead of bringing one nearer to God, drives one farther away from him, and is a voluntary renunciation of him. Therefore, in this respect, is the heart

---

* Jer. xlviii. 10.   † Mal. i. 13, 14.   ‡ Jer. xvii. 5.

heart said to *depart from the Lord*. Although the Holy Spirit pronounces this sentence on the man who rejects Divine strength; yet the false heart maintains its doctrine, and recommends its own as the surest ground of confidence. It insinuates that it is a very uncertain method of performing duty, to rely on help, which is altogether invisible; and that it is therefore preferable to depend on that strength which man is more assured of, as belonging to himself, and being ever present with him. It particularly employs the natural principle of self-gloriation as an argument against, at least, a total dependence on the Lord; because then a person, let him perform duty ever so well, must disclaim all, and confess himself to be entirely a debtor to free grace. With this the heart cannot be satisfied. It always presents its claim for some share of the glory. If it seem to consent that God should have a part, still it inclines to reserve the principal part to itself. Believers often discover this self-confidence; though, in general, they feel the consequences of it with severity. We have an instance of this also in the history of Peter. When our Lord foretold that all his disciples should leave him in the hour of his bitterest sufferings, Peter contradicted him, and asserted, that although all men should deny him, yet he would not; nay, that although he should die with him, he would not deny him. The warm declaration of love and attachment to his Master, was in itself commendable. But he grievously erred in forming and expressing his resolution entirely in his own strength. And as a chastisement for his self-confidence, the Lord suffered him awfully to display and feel his own weakness, by leaving him without the present influences of his grace, the assistance of which he had despised, and giving him up to the power of his own corruptions; in consequence of which he not only denied his Lord, but *cursed and swore* that he knew him not.

6. It pleads the uprightness of its *intention* as an apology for a multitude of defects. As it is declared, with

with respect to the duty of contributing to the necessities of others, that *if there be first a willing mind, it is accepted according to that a man hath, and not according to that he hath not* *: the heart lays hold of this, and converts it into an excuse for many sins. Is a duty abridged or carelesly performed, from the prevalence of a worldly spirit? The deceitful heart suggests, that God will overlook this, because the person wished to do well. Hath the mind been filled with distracting thoughts during the performance? Comfort shall be drawn from the compassionate declaration of our Lord; *The spirit indeed is willing, but the flesh is weak*: while the defect hath chiefly proceeded from carnality of spirit. Or, perhaps, one duty is maimed, under the pretence of performing another, not presently required. Thus Saul excused himself for disobedience with respect to the Amalekites, under the pretence that the people had *spared the best of the sheep, and of the oxen, to sacrifice unto the Lord God* †. Indeed this deceit of the heart is the source of all that corrupt doctrine of sincerity as the ground of acceptance, by which the covenant of grace is converted into a legal covenant, or *new law*, unknown both to God, and to those who are the subjects of *godly sincerity*.

7. THERE are many, on the other hand, who please themselves with the form of duty, without any regard to the *intention*. To such professors it appears in the highest degree unreasonable, injurious, and absurd to deny that they can perform good works; while they present many prayers, regularly attend public ordinances, and do so many actions of kindness to their brethren of mankind. Can these be evil works, which God expressly commands? Or can they be bad men, when they can do such works? All this would do very well, could these servants ensure themselves, that he, whom they call their master, would look on their performances just as they do, or that he would view them with the eye of man. But

* 2 Cor. viii. 12. † 1 Sam. xv. 15.

But as this is one of the most common, it is also one of the most ruinous deceits that the heart of man is subject to: *for the Lord seeth not as man seeth; for man looketh on the outward appearance, but the Lord looketh on the heart.* These actions are, indeed, good as to the matter of them; and at least for the order of society, and for the advantage of others, it were to be wished that men abounded more in them. But the mere external form of duty is comparatively of so little account with God, that, when this is all, even those duties that he hath himself required are rejected by him with detestation. *Your incense is an abomination unto me.* Why so? Because the right principle is wanting. The duty is performed without proper motives and ends. It is to the secret principle of the heart that the Lord looks. For it is this especially that denominates an action to be good or evil. This doctrine is admitted by you in the ordinary transactions of life. Therefore, in making trial as to facts, do you not, as far as possible, endeavour to discover the motive? What is it that constitutes the difference between a mistake and a lie, or between lawful killing and murder, but the intention of the agent? Now, what is your leading principle in performing these actions, which you boast of as good? Is it not to appease God? And do you not therefore give him the lie; by still considering him as an enemy, while he declares that *fury is not in* him? Is it not to avoid hell? And do you not therefore want that *love* which *casteth out fear?* Is it not to procure heaven? And do you not therefore labour as mere hirelings, not as sons? Is it not to establish your own righteousness? And do you not thus refuse to *submit* yourselves *to the righteousness of God?* Is it not often merely to recommend yourselves to others? And is not this to *love the praise of men more than the praise of God?* In a word, is not Self the great principle, motive, and end of all your religious actions? And can you think that God will accept them as truly good; when you neither *love* Him *with all your heart,* nor propose his glory as your

your highest end? Is not this the great reason why God rejected the fasts of his ancient people, when they inquired of him with respect to their continuance; the want of a proper principle in their pretended acts of humiliation? *When ye fasted and mourned in the fifth and seventh month, even those seventy years, did ye at all fast unto me, even to me? And when ye did eat, and when ye did drink, did ye not eat for yourselves, and drink for yourselves* * ?

8. By stirring up the believer to spiritual *pride* after enjoying the Divine presence in duty. Into this snare he is very apt to fall. All the gracious discoveries which God makes of himself have an humbling tendency, because they at the same time manifest the Christian's unworthiness. The more that one really sees of the glory, holiness, and love of God, the more must one's own meanness, impurity, and enmity appear. Although this is the native tendency of such gracious manifestations, the deceitful heart improves them in a way directly contrary. The more we receive from God, the less reason have we for boasting; because we run the deeper in arrears to sovereign grace. We have, therefore, as little reason for gloriation on this ground, as, in secular concerns, a debtor has on account of the multiplication of his engagements to his creditors. The corrupt heart insinuates the very reverse. It would persuade us, that the more we receive from God in his service, the more he is indebted to us. God denies that man can be *profitable to his Maker*. The proud heart avers it, and boldly asserts that he is obliged to us for the tribute of spiritual worship which we render to him; although this can only be paid out of his own treasury, by the influences of his grace. Pride makes a foolish appearance in any part of the conduct of man, because it suits one so ill, who is not only dust, but polluted dust. But its folly and extravagance especially appear, when it operates with regard to God. For thus man, by the most dreadful presumption, virtually runs a parallel between God and himself.

---

* Zech. vii. 5, 6.

Of every species of pride this is the most deceitful, detestable, and dangerous. It is the most *deceitful*, because it shelters itself under the garb of humility. It is a poison extracted from the sweetest flowers; a weed, which grows up under the covert of the most pleasant plants. It derives its existence, and its strength from the abuse of gracious manifestations on the part of God, and of gracious exercise on that of the Christian. Spiritual pride often arises in the soul, after it has been endeavouring to renounce itself, and professing to be indebted to God for all. Perhaps, it imposes itself on the saint, under the semblance of godly joy, or of the consolations of the Spirit, or of unfeigned gratitude. It is the most *detestable* kind of pride. For it has less foundation than any other. Pride can never have a true foundation. But whatever shadow of reason there may be for it in the conduct of one man towards another, there can be none with respect to God. For before him *the nations are as the drop of a bucket, and as the small dust of the balance;* yea, with him, *all the nations are counted as less than nothing, and vanity*. It is also the most *dangerous*. Being so deceitful, it is the more difficult to discover it. This kind of pride diffuses its contagion before it is perceived. It also eminently exposes the Christian to the tokens of the Lord's displeasure.

If pride is such an abomination to him in any, that he is said to *see the proud afar off*, as if he abhorred to take a look of him at hand; how much more abominable and provoking must it be in his own children, who are unspeakably more indebted to him than others. He expresses his indignation, by immediately withdrawing his gracious presence, when it is thus abused. David said in his prosperity, *I shall never be moved. Lord, by thy favour thou hast made my mountain to stand strong*. But he soon saw his folly; *Thou didst hide thy face, and I was troubled* *. These words might literally refer to his confidence in the outward prosperity of his reign,

---

* Psal. xxx. 6, 7.

as mountains often metaphorically fignify kingdoms; and to the difcovery of the vanity of this confidence by fome fevere chaftifement. But it is more than probable that they refer to his religious exercife. At any rate, as *thefe things were written for our learning;* as many things, fpoken and done literally, contain fpiritual inftruction, as engroffed in the facred canon for the ufe of the Church ; and as the exercife of the deceitful heart is the fame, in like circumftances, although the fubjects be different; the words may be viewed in a fpiritual fenfe. This kind of pride, of which the Pfalmift's language may be underftood, feems to be the moft fubtile and refined. It does not appear that he claimed any merit to himfelf, or that he confided in any fpiritual ftrength, as arifing from the exercife of his own powers. He afcribes both the caufe and the effect to God. He mentions his favour, good will, or grace as the caufe; *By* THY *favour,*—and his own ftanding as the effect of God's operation ;—THOU *haft* MADE *my mountain to ftand ftrong.* " Wherein then lay his error ?" may you fay. " Perhaps, we are not to conclude that God " hid his face from him, as a teftimony of difpleafure " with any part of his conduct ; but only for the trial " of his faith. Nay, his exercife feems to be commend-" able, as expreffive of the higheft gratitude." But this agrees not with the tenor of the Pfalm, the defign of which is evidently to extol God, becaufe of the fhort duration of his anger. For verfe 5th, he makes this declaration ; *His anger endureth but a moment;* and while he acknowledges his offence, he mentions God's gracious return as an evidence of this, verfe 11th. Wherein then confifted his fin ? He not only feems to have thought that he was henceforth ftill to enjoy the *profperity* of fenfible manifeftations ; *I fhall never be moved;* but to have preferred the gift to the giver, the difplays of Divine grace to the gracious God himfelf, the ftream to the ever-living fountain, grace already received to that grace contained in the promife. He exalts himfelf in his own heart, n the enjoyment

enjoyment and evidences of this favour. He speaks, as if former manifestations of Divine love would supply him to the end, without any constant, or even additional supply : *Thou hast made my mountain to stand strong,* or as it may be read, *Thou hast made strength to stand in my mountain;* as if he, either in temporal or spiritual respects, could stand in his own strength. This apprehension would naturally make him neglect the use of means, become remiss in prayer, relax the exercise of faith, and lay aside his watchfulness. Wherefore, he was brought to see the necessity of a continued dependence on the Lord as his helper, verse 10th. We find him in many other places expressing his confidence in the very same language ; *I shall never be moved,* yet without any token of the Lord's anger. But then, he builds his confidence on another foundation ; upon the Lord's being *at* his *right hand* * ; not on that grace, which was already given him, but on that which remained with God †. Or, he expresses his confidence in this language, only as presently claiming God for his *rock and salvation* ‡. It was better for Paul, after his great manifestations, to be buffeted by the Devil, most probably by some bodily affliction, than by the pride of his own heart : *Lest I should be exalted above measure, there was given to me a thorn in the flesh, the messenger of Satan to buffet me.* And the very answer that was made to his prayers, under the temptation, taught him this important lesson;—that his dependence was not to be on any former communications, but on the grace treasured up in Christ, the Head of the covenant : My *grace is sufficient for thee; for* my *strength is made perfect in weakness* §. To illustrate the danger of spiritual pride, and to deter us from it, the example of Satan is held up as a beacon by the Spirit of God : *Lest being lifted up with pride, he fall into the condemnation of the Devil* **.

9. By

---

* Psal. xvi. 8.   † Psal. xxi. 7.   ‡ Psal. lxii. 2,—6.
§ 2 Cor. xii. 6,—9.   ** 1 Tim. iii. 6.

SER. 18.   *as to the Performance of Duty.*   343

9. By *diſſuading* the Chriſtian from duty, when the obſervation of it is attended with *no comfort*. We have ſeen that the heart as deceitful, ſubmits to duty with reluctance, at any rate. But if it fail in this reſpect, if he be determined to make a trial of duty, in obedience to the Divine command; it will next endeavour, either to mar the ſuccefs of the exerciſe, or to drive away the perſon from it altogether, becauſe he experiences no comfort at all, or a great deal leſs than he expected. We have in the word of God both precept and example to encourage us to continuance in duty, as the way to comfort. We are commanded to *pray without ceaſing, always to pray, and not to faint,* to *pray always with all prayer and ſupplication, and watch thereunto with all perſeverance.* Chriſt ſpake the parable of the importunate widow and unjuſt judge, to inculcate the neceſſity of importunity in religious duties, and improved it by propoſing this queſtion; *Shall not God avenge his own elect, who cry day and night unto him, though he bear long with them?* This queſtion he reſolves by the following gracious anſwer: *I tell you, that he ſhall avenge them ſpeedily*.* Not *ſpeedily*, it may be, according to their limited expectations; but *ſpeedily*, in anſwer to their importunate and unremitted ſupplications. We have many examples in the ſacred hiſtory, confirming the neceſſity and efficacy of perſeverance in duty, as the way to comfort. Jacob wreſtled with the Angel of the covenant till daybreak, and ſaid to him; *I will not let thee go except thou bleſs me*; and *he bleſſed him there.* Ere Paul obtained a gracious anſwer, he *beſought the Lord thrice.* The Syrophenician woman took all the reproofs of Chriſt in good part, and continued to urge her requeſt, till at length he ſaid to her; *Be it unto thee even as thou wilt.* But the deceitful heart would have the believer to make a god of his comforts, by giving up with God, when theſe are withheld. It ſpeaks in this manner; *It is vain to ſerve God, and
what*

* Luke xviii. 1.—8.

what profit is it, that we have kept his ordinance, and that we have walked mournfully before the Lord of Hosts *? *Wherefore have we fasted, and thou seest not? Wherefore have we afflicted our soul, and thou takest no knowledge* ‡? The great end of religious worship is the glory of God. But this the deceitful heart rejects, pleads comfort in the duty itself, together with its agreeable consequences, as the highest end.

10. By making the person seek *comfort* from the mere *performance* of duty. In what way soever the duty has been observed, the heart persuades us to draw consolation from the mere observation of it: as the poor deluded Papist flatters himself, that there is real merit in counting over his beads, or in repeating his prayers, although in an unknown tongue. Even the Christian is in danger of being thus ensnared, by resting on the duty, in which he is engaged with a view to any particular blessing, as if the performance of the duty itself infallibly secured the blessing. As, on the one hand, he is in danger of neglecting the means that God hath appointed; so, on the other, of confiding in them, as if there were an indispensable connection between them and the end. Through his inward deceit, he may be at times ready to apprehend, either that the duty will be accepted of God for the work performed, or that his person will be accepted because of the duty. We ought to be as diligent and fervent in duty, as if our all depended upon it, as if this were really the foundation of our acceptance; and, at the same time, to be as much denied to it, as if the observation thereof were nowise necessary. We must *work out our salvation with fear and trembling;* but only as assuring ourselves that *it is God who worketh in us both to will and to do.* We must study to *observe all things whatsoever* Christ hath *commanded, and when we have* done all in our power, acknowledge that we are *unprofitable servants*, and that we have done

far

---

* Mal. iii. 14. † Isa. lviii. 3.

far lefs than what was *our duty to do* *. It is evident that the Pharifee juftified himfelf before God, becaufe of the performance of fome kind of duty. But, becaufe of this falfe confidence, he *went down to his houfe* condemned of God : for this is clearly implied in the contraft ftated between him and the Publican. Nehemiah pleads with God for the remembrance of his fervices in fuch a manner, that at firft view we might be apt to imagine, thefe were the ground of his hope : *Remember me, O my God, concerning this, and wipe not out my good deeds that I have done for the houfe of my God*. But we find that he afterwards adds, when urging the fame requeft ; *Remember me, O my God, concerning this alfo,—and fpare me according to the greatnefs of thy mercy* †. Even while he feems to plead his duties, he entirely difclaims them as meritorious ; and relies only on the riches of Divine mercy difcovered in the revelation of grace. This fhows that when he afks the remembrance of his good deeds, he wifhes them to be remembered only as evidences of the fincerity of his love to God, and to his kingdom. The children of God may be earneft with him for the acceptance of their fervices, even while they renounce them as in any degree meritorious ; *Hear my prayer, O Lord*, faith the Pfalmift, *give ear to my fupplications ; in thy faithfulnefs anfwer me, and in thy righteoufnefs. And enter not into judgment with thy fervant : for in thy fight fhall no man living be juftified* ‡.

11. By infpiring one with greater *boldnefs* in duty, becaufe of *former comfort* in the obfervation of it. This difpofition is extremely natural, and to the moft of profeffors it may appear perfectly innocent. " May " not he, who has received many former affurances " of his welcome in approaching a friend, come with " greater confidence afterwards ?" But, *My thoughts are not your thoughts, neither are your ways my ways*, *faith the Lord*. This is nothing but a more fecret working of legality. For the only foundation of our

approach

---

* Luke xvii. 10. † Neh. xiii. 14. 22. ‡ Pfal. cxliii. 1.

approach to God as a Father, in any duty, is the perfect righteousness, the finished work of him who *engaged his heart to approach* unto God as a Judge. Therefore, the choicest comforts, the most precious and inestimable tokens of Divine love to us, must never be assumed into an equality with the Son of his love, or that righteousness with which, and on account of which alone, he is *well pleased*. For Christ hath said; *I am the way:—no man cometh to the Father but by me*. He is *the way*, as excluding every other. He is the *consecrated way;* and therefore, it is sacrilege to think of any other, or to think of altering this by any additions of our own. It is in him only that *we have boldness and access with confidence by the faith of him. Without faith it is impossible*, in any duty, *to please God**. Now, the object of faith is always *without* us, and never any thing *within* us. It is not Christ in our *hearts*, or any evidence of this; but Christ in the *promise*. Former comforts are not matter of faith, but of experience. Therefore, they cannot be the ground of confidence in drawing near to God. The foundation of the believer's access to God in every duty, through the whole course of the Christian life, is the very same as at first,—nothing but the blood of Jesus. He can have no renewed access to God, but on the self-same ground on which he had his access in the act of justifying faith. Therefore, every right approach to God is just *doing* this *first work* over again. He does not come as a saint, that is, on the foot of his saintship; but as still a guilty creature, in himself considered, improving the blood of Christ anew, as *the way into the holiest of all*. For Christ is not only *the door*, by which the believer at first *enters in*, but by which *he goes in and out* in the constant progress of a life of faith †. Under the law, every renewed approach to God, in public worship, was with blood. Because of the perfection of the one sacrifice of Jesus Christ, there is now no occasion

* Heb. xi. 6. † John x. 9.

casion for any other. But we must not presume to come to God, but by offering this anew in the exercise of faith. Therefore, every believer is a priest, not in the absurd and irrational sense of the Papists, in their idolatrous sacrifice of the mass; but because he still holds up to God, in every duty, the one perfect sacrifice of Jesus Christ our Passover. The former enjoyment of communion with God may be admitted, as an encouragement to the renewed observation of duty; as a mean for enlivening us in the performance of it; and as a collateral confirmation to weak faith. So the Psalmist improved it; *I will remember thee from the land of Jordan**. But it is abused, it is idolised; if assumed as in any respect the foundation of faith, or ground of boldness in coming to the throne.—It might in the same manner be proved, that if a person approach God with *less* boldness after apparent repulses, under the hiding of his countenance, or while conscious of the Prevalence of iniquity; it proceeds from unbelief and legality. For it demonstrates, that he does not sufficiently improve the blood of Christ as his *only* way, and as a way that is constantly open even to the chief of sinners.

The Apostle John, indeed, makes an observation in his first Epistle, chap. iii. 21. which may seem, at first view, to overturn this doctrine; that *if our heart condemn us not, we have confidence towards God*. But he does not say that this consciousness of integrity is the foundation of our confidence. He only asserts the matter of fact, which no reasonable person can deny;—that a sense of integrity is attended with boldness in duty. He is not there treating of the foundation of our access to God, but of that of assurance with respect to our state, as derived from scriptural evidences. For it is expressly said, ver. 19. *Hereby know we that we are of the truth, and shall assure our hearts before him.* How do we know this? *If our heart*

* Psal. xlii. 6.

heart condemn us not, if we are conscious of indulging no known sin, of neglecting no known duty.—Now, what is the result of this consciousness? We approach God in duty with a good conscience, as opposed to one that condemns a person for habitual hypocrisy in religion. But he by no means makes this consciousness the ground of boldness with respect to access and acceptance; nor does he declare that the conscience can become good, can be pacified, or be kept in peace by any of our doings. He asserts nothing more here than what we find elsewhere, that in order to our drawing near *with a true heart*, we must have *our hearts sprinkled from an evil conscience* *; and that the *conscience* must be *purged from dead works, to serve the living God* †. *If our heart*, saith he, *condemn us not, we have confidence towards God;* i. e. " If our consciences be really sprinkled " with the blood of Jesus, delivered from a sense of " guilt, and attest our justification before *God the* " *Judge of all*, through *Jesus the Mediator of the* " *new covenant;* then we with holy confidence draw " near to God as a Father." But it may be said, that this explanation does not agree with the following words; *And whatsoever we ask, we receive of him, because we keep his commandments.* But *because* must not be here understood, as denoting the ground of our success in prayer, but only as expressing an evidence. As *God heareth not sinners*, but *heareth the righteous;* when, after proper trial, we have a consciousness of sincerity towards him, we may be assured that he heareth us: not on account of our sincerity as the meritorious cause; but because this sincerity is an evidence of genuine faith in Christ, as our way to the Father. In the same sense he adduces our obedience to God's commandments as a reason why we may be certain that he will hear us; because obedience is the evidence, as being the fruit of faith. The particle *because*, is used in the same sense here, as in verse 14. about the meaning of
which

---

* Heb. x. 22. † Heb. ix. 14.

which there can be no doubt; *We know that we are paſſed from death to life, becauſe we love the brethren.* No one will ſay, that our love to the brethren is the *cauſe* of our regeneration. It is only mentioned as the *evidence*. Is the queſtion then aſked; "On "what account doth God give us *whatſoever we* "*aſk?*" The anſwer is; It is only for the ſake of Chriſt. But is it inquired; "How may we be aſ- "ſured, that we are ſuch whom God heareth?" The anſwer is very different. We may be aſſured of this, becauſe our conſciences, after the moſt accurate examination, teſtify that we have an unfeigned regard to all God's commandments; whence we may conclude that we are true believers.

From what has now been offered, you may be exhorted to watch over your inward deceitfulneſs, as it diſpoſes you to formality and deadneſs in the performance of duty. If your hearts can ſo far prevail with you, as to ſuffer religion to dwindle down to a mere form, a ſtated round of duties; you can expect no progreſs in grace, no comfortable fruits from this lifeleſs worſhip. You will become *like the door upon its hinges*, which regularly moves backward and forward, but ſtill continues in its old place. Endeavour to *walk with God* in every duty. This was the attainment of Enoch; and *he had this teſtimony, that he pleaſed God.* Preſs after fellowſhip with him in every act of worſhip, follow hard after him, pant after his preſence, *as the hart panteth after the water-brooks.* One great reaſon why the people of God enjoy ſo little communion with him, is that they have this ſo little for their ſupreme deſire. When conſcience ſummons them to duty, they obey; but how often indifferent whether or not they *ſee the king's face?*

Implore deliverance from *diſtraction* in his ſervice. This is highly diſhonouring to *God*, and it robs you of both the comfort and the profit of duty. God doth not reprove his ancient people for want of frequency, but for want of uprightneſs and fervour in worſhip. He blames them not for neglecting the form,

form, but for withholding the heart; *Ye said, Behold, what a weariness is it, and ye have snuffed at it, saith the Lord of hosts, and ye brought that which was torn, and the lame, and the sick: thus ye brought an offering. Should I accept this of your hands? saith the Lord.* And this he charges against them as an evidence of the deceitfulness of their hearts in the observation of commanded duty, for it immediately follows: *But cursed be the deceiver, who has in his flock a male, and voweth, and sacrificeth unto the Lord a corrupt thing; for I am a great king, saith the Lord of hosts**. As distraction in duty is a frequent complaint of the people of God, we may suggest to you the following considerations, which, through the divine blessing, will be useful in accomplishing your victory over this operation of deceitfulness.—Beware of rushing into duty, *as the horse into the battle.* Endeavour to compose your minds for it by serious *meditation*, either on the solemnity of the duty, or on some spiritual subject, which may tend to fix your attention. And while you thus *muse*, the *fire* of holy affection may *burn*.— Let your minds be constantly impressed with an awful sense of the *Divine* perfections, and especially when you are about to engage in worship. Seek to have your hearts affected with a deep conviction of God's omniscience. This is his command; *Be still, and know that I am God.* Remember that he *looketh to the heart,* that he *will be worshipped in spirit and in truth.* Consider his unspeakable Majesty. He is *the High and Holy One who inhabiteth eternity, whose name is holy.* It is an act of infinite condescension in him to receive the adoration either of men, or of angels. *He humbleth himself to behold the things which are done in heaven, and in earth.* Consider that he is a *jealous God,* and that *ye cannot serve him.* For *his jealousy burns like fire.*—Endeavour to attain a constant sense of your own *vileness* before him. The consciousness of your inferiority will make you very attentive, and respectful in the presence of an earthly superior.

* Mal. i. 13, 14.

superior. How much more reason is there for this in the presence of him, who is *King of kings*. Let your minds be filled with a conviction of the inestimable value of your privilege in having access to his throne. Formality and distraction in duty are greatly owing to the want of a just impression of the importance of our liberty of access.—Study an affecting sense of the greatness and urgency of your *necessities*. He who supplicates life or any eminent mercy from another, will not readily forget the intention of his approach to him, or wander from the principal subject. It absorbs his whole attention, because he knows his necessity. You have eternal life, and many other important blessings to ask of God: and may not the magnitude of these arrest your attention?—Habituate your *affections* to the contemplation of *heavenly* things. *Set your affections on things above.* This will greatly prevent distraction in worship; because spiritual contemplation will become, in some measure, your natural element. It is the ordinary carnality of the affections, that so easily steals away the heart in duty.—Try to restrain them in their *first* wanderings. It is far more easy to stop a chink, than to resist the violence of a torrent. *Keep the heart above all keeping.*—Avoid those objects that ordinarily distract your attention. Make *a covenant with* your *eyes.* Keep a watch over all your senses; restrain your imagination.—Depend not on your *own* natural or spiritual *powers. Trust in the Lord with all thy heart, and lean not to thine own understanding.* Put your hearts into his hand. *Commit thy way to God, trust him; and he will bring it to pass.* While engaged in other duties, often look to the Lord in ejaculatory prayer. Even a look may *lighten* you. Intreat that he may *unite* your hearts to *fear his name.*—Improve every duty, as if assured that it were to be your *last.* You cannot say of any duty, that this may not be the case. Therefore *whatsoever thy hand findeth to do, do it with all thy might.*—Ponder the great *advantages* resulting from stability in Divine worship. It is often

ten attended or succeeded by a comfortable sense of upholding grace, as the Psalmist testifies; *My soul followeth hard after thee, and thy right hand upholdeth me.* Peace is its concomitant. *Great peace have they who love thy law.* In this way the Lord most ordinarily gives the gracious answer. *Ye shall seek me, and find me, when you shall search for me with all your heart.* On the contrary, by indulging vanity in God's service, you mock him, and expose yourselves to the tokens of his displeasure. You *take his name in vain,* and he will *not hold* you *guiltless*.

AGAIN, when you obtain nearness to the Lord, seek to be *clothed with humility.* For God *resisteth the proud, but he giveth* more *grace to the humble.* Arm against spiritual pride. *Learn of* Christ, who *is meek and lowly in heart.* When you have enjoyed enlargement in duty, be concerned to renounce self, to ascribe all to God, and to wrestle with him, that he may *cast down every imagination and high thing that exalteth itself,* in your hearts. Instead of fixing your eye upon the comfort you have received, try to fix it on *the God of all comfort,* and to turn it inward to the wickedness that lodgeth in you, as a mean of self-abasement.

IN a word, depend only on the strength of Divine grace in every duty. Claim an interest in it, saying, *Surely in the Lord, have I strength.* Pray for the Spirit. As it is through Christ, so it is by this one Spirit, that *we all have access to the Father.* Without his influence, you can neither have comfort in duty, nor advantage from it. For, *saith the Lord, upon the land of the daughter of my people will come up nothing but briers and thorns, until the Holy Ghost be poured down from on high.* Amidst all your professions and performances, you will be as *dry bones* in *the valley of vision,* without his breathing on you. Let us therefore cry with the Prophet; *Come from the four winds, O breath, and breathe upon us slain, that we may live.*

SER-

SERMON XIX.

ON THE DECEITFULNESS OF THE HEART, WITH RESPECT TO THE OMISSION OF DUTY.

PSALM lxxviii. 56, 57.

————*And kept not his testimonies; but turned back, and dealt unfaithfully like their fathers; they were turned aside like a deceitful bow.*

WHEN the heart of Pharaoh in some degree relented, under the weight of the judgments which God brought on him for his obduracy, he called Moses, and said to him; *Go ye, and serve the Lord; only let your flocks and your herds be stayed.* But Moses replied; *Our cattle also shall go with us; there shall not an hoof be left behind; for thereof must we take to serve the Lord our God* *. The deceitful heart, when it pretends to comply with the call to duties, is always for abridging them, for limiting them in this or that manner, or for a substitution of one in the place of another; and cannot consent to a full and entire service of God. If we engage in one duty, it suggests that we may easily pass over another; if we perform one part of a duty, that we may rest satisfied with this, and omit the other parts of it. But, depending on divine strength, we must reply to the deceits of the heart, as Moses did to Pharaoh; *There shall*

* Exod. x. 24,—26.

shall not an hoof be left behind, for thus *must we serve the Lord our God.*

In the foregoing discourse we have considered the deceitfulness of the heart in regard to the performance of duty; we are now,

Secondly, To take a view of it with respect to omission.

1. The heart urges the *delay* of duty, and thus discovers its deceitfulness, by promising a *future* opportunity. Many a sinner is altogether ruined, and many a saint loses much progress and comfort in religion, through delays. When a person discovers by Word or Providence, that he is called to a particular duty; when conscience, or the motions of the Holy Spirit powerfully second this call, and illustrate the urgency of it; the great aim of Satan, and of the corrupt heart, working in concert, is to procure a delay. Often when the call is loud and urgent, they endeavour to avert its force, and to turn aside the current of conviction, by insinuating that another time will be more proper. Thus, when God commanded those who had returned from captivity, to rebuild the temple, they said; *The time is not come, the time that the Lord's house should be built* *. But we may be assured, that when the heart, in opposition to the calls of Word or Providence, to the testimony of conscience, or the Spirit of God, urges the delay of duty, it is with a secret design to neglect it altogether. In this case, many objections will be made to the seasonableness of the present opportunity. Obstacles will be powerfully pleaded as of the greatest importance, when opposing the service of God, which would be treated with indifference or contempt, did they oppose the fulfilment of any temporal engagement. Those things will appear as insurmountable difficulties, which are unworthy of the smallest consideration. The spiritual, as well as the natural sluggard, still saith; *There is a lion without, I shall be slain in the streets* †. There are two things with regard to duty,

* Hag. i. 2. † Prov. xxii. 13.

duty, which ought always to be viewed in connection. There is the duty itself, and its season. We are not to rest satisfied in the mere performance.— We ought also duly to consider the proper time.— There are some things of perpetual obligation, without regard to time or circumstances. Others are only incumbent, if observed in their proper place and season. They cease to be duties, and may rather be viewed as sins, if we engage in them without regard to the appointed order. The observation of the Sabbath is a duty incumbent on all; but it is limited to the first day of the week. Were we to remove it from this, and pretend to observe it on any other day; instead of being an acceptable service, it would be a sin aggravated by the most dreadful presumption. Reproof is an unquestionable duty; *Thou shalt not hate thy brother in thy heart, thou shalt in any wise reprove thy brother, thou shalt not suffer sin upon him.* But to give it in such a manner, or at such a time, as that it could only tend to exasperate, would be to *cast pearls before swine.*

There are duties of another kind, which though they still retain their nature, and are always necessary, are most suitable when the proper season is considered. Thus, fasting, thanksgiving and solemn vowing, are more peculiarly incumbent in some seasons than in others. Now, it is exceedingly necessary to consider the proper place of every duty, that one may not interfere with another; that one less immediately necessary may not justle out another; to which there is an immediate call, and that all may be observed in their proper order and connection. *God hath made every thing beautiful in his time* *. Many duties, though they do not lose their obligation, lose much of their beauty, and of their usefulness also, when the proper time is neglected. The treacherous heart, if it cannot get them altogether avoided, is still for misplacing them. Thus, it often prevents their blessed fruits. It still wishes to invert God's order. The Israelites

* Eccl. iii. 11.

Israelites would not enter into the promised land, when God commanded them: but afterwards, when he had assured them that they should *fall in the wilderness*, they said; *We will go up unto the place which the Lord hath promised* *. Saul would not wait till Samuel came, but *offered a burnt-offering* at his own hand †. The Lord's people will frequently find, that when they have delayed duty beyond the proper time, he withdraws his presence, and suffers them to drag through it with little or no comfort; as a chastisement for their negligence, and to teach them to be more conscientious, and more attentive to the proper season. But the neglect of the proper season, is by no means to be improved as an excuse for the total omission of duty; if it be of such a nature as to be incumbent at all times. For it is far better to observe it, although the best opportunity has been slipped, than to neglect both the season and the duty. In order to evade the call of God, the heart often urges a commutation of duties. It pleads the expediency of performing one instead of another. It was for a sacrilegious act of this kind, that Saul was rejected of God. Although he had received an express command to destroy every thing belonging to the Amalekites, he *spared the best of the sheep, and of the oxen, to sacrifice unto the Lord.* But Samuel said; *Hath the Lord as great delight in burnt-offerings and sacrifices, as in obeying the voice of the Lord? Behold, to obey is better than sacrifice; and to hearken, than the fat of rams* ‡.

2. It persuades us to omit duty by calling in the *world* to its aid. This is a faithful ally to the corrupt heart, and is always willing to lend its aid in turning us away from God. That love to this world, which is to be found even in believers, is a great hinderance to them in many duties, we may say indeed, in all. For the world will either so far prevail, as entirely to prevent the observation of duty; or by its influence in distracting the heart, will be in some degree successful

---

* Num. xiv. 40.—45.   † 1 Sam. xiii. 9.   ‡ 1 Sam. xv. 15.—22.

cefsful in hindering the Chriſtian from performing it aright. When God and conſcience call to duty, the heart will reply; "Is this the way in which we are to provide for our families? Muſt we ſuffer them to ſtarve, and call this religion? Can we ſuppoſe, that God requires men to neglect their natural ſupport, under the pretence of ſerving him? Shall we imagine that, as the object of worſhip, he can act inconſiſtently with himſelf, as the Creator and Preſerver of men? We allow that he is juſtly entitled to our adoration; but can we think that he requires it, when it interferes with our natural ſubſiſtence?" The deceitful heart will alſo apply the injunction of the Spirit of God; *Be—not ſlothful in buſineſs*, as if it were not to be underſtood in connection with the preceding command with reſpect to *fervency in ſpirit*. This is always one of the ſtratagems of the heart, to darken the mind as to the proper medium which God has pointed out in every thing relating to his ſervice. At one time, it will inſinuate to a profeſſor that he ought to devote himſelf to religion altogether, and to leave his own ſupport, or that of his family entirely to Providence: that it may bring a ſcandal on the ways of God; convert the profeſſor into a buſy body; make way for its own operations under the maſk of zeal; wean him gradually from thoſe duties in which the life of godlineſs eminently conſiſts; or perhaps, by and by, give him a thorough diſtaſte at the whole of religion. Thus, it contradicts the command of the inſpired Apoſtle; *Now, them that are ſuch,—who walk among you diſorderly, working not at all, but are buſy-bodies,—we command, and exhort by our Lord Jeſus Chriſt, that with quietneſs they work, and eat their own bread**. At another time, as we have ſeen, it will attempt to divert a perſon from commanded duty, by alleging that the calls of the world ought rather to be obeyed, and that we are only to attend to religion, when we have nothing elſe to employ us. This
is

---

* 2 Theſſ. iii. 11, 12.

is a great difcovery of its deceitfulnefs and oppofition to God; for he requires us to keep every thing in its proper place. While he teacheth us, that we are not fo to neglect our callings, as to diftrefs our families; he, at the fame time, reprefents attention to bufinefs only as a fecondary duty. While he declares, that *he who provideth not for his own, and fpecially for thofe of his own houfe, hath denied the faith, and is worfe than an infidel* *; he alfo commands us to *feek firft the kingdom of God and his righteoufnefs*; promifing, and calling us to believe, that *all other things fhall be added*. He enjoins us to *fet* our *affections on the things that are above*, to *labour for the meat that perifheth not*, to *glorify* him, *whatfoever* we *do*; and thus to carry religion into the whole of our conduct; by the union of diligence in bufinefs and fervency of fpirit, to *ferve the Lord*; and by the finglenefs of our eye, and fpirituality of our affections, to fanctify and ennoble even the common actions of life.

The deceitful heart will find no difficulty from the world, no obftacle arifing from bufinefs, when there is a call to agreeable company, or to a favourite amufement. It will fuffer you to confume as much time as you pleafe in eating and drinking, in converfation or recreation. But it can find none for God, for fecret or family religion, for prayer or fpiritual conference with fellow-chriftians. How is it that your worldly concerns are always in danger, when God calls for your fervice; but you fee none, when your companions call you, though you fpend not only your time, but your fubftance with them; though you are not only relaxed from work, but have the cup of temptation in your hand? Whence does this proceed, but from the deceitfulnefs of your heart, that always wifhes to keep at a diftance from the fervice of God? Does not this conduct difcover the great prevalence of unbelief? You will not truft him with your temporal interefts; though he hath declared, that *they, who truly feek* him, *fhall want no good thing*.

---

* 1 Tim. v. 8.

thing. You tremble for every moment that you spend in his service through the week, lest it hurt your business, lest it ruin you and bring you to bankruptcy; although he hath assured you, that his *blessing maketh rich*, and that *therewith he addeth no sorrow.* Do you not believe, that the blessing of God can amply reimburse your small expence of time in serving him; and that his curse can entirely defeat the success of your business, when you make it a plea for resisting his call? You have good reason, at least, for believing this. For the curse of the Lord shall enter into the house of the wicked, *and it shall remain in the midst of his house, and shall consume it with the timber thereof, and the stones thereof**. What can you expect, but that his curse should attend your temporal mercies, and blast the fruit of your labours; when you wilfully neglect duty on this account? Know you not that the time, which ought to be devoted to God, in every stated duty, and which you sacrilegiously refuse, is not yours, but his? It is claimed by the Lord of your time. If you, therefore, refuse it to him, you are chargeable with robbing God. A most dreadful crime indeed! You do not deny him what is yours, but what is his own. Listen to his declaration to this purpose; *Will a man rob God?* Alas! It is no uncommon thing to see men robbing one another, carrying away the property of others by oppression or extortion, nay, by open rapine and violence. But bad as human nature is, can we really suppose that it has proceeded to such a pitch of wickedness, as that violence should be done to God himself? Yes; even this is a species of violence no less common than the other, though far less wondered at:—*yet ye have robbed me: but ye say, Wherein have we robbed thee? In tithes and in offerings. Ye are cursed with a curse; for ye have robbed me, even this whole nation**. You rob God, when you deny him those duties which he hath commanded, and that time which he hath

---

* Zech. v. 4.   † Mal. iii. 8, 9.

hath allotted for the performance of them, and which he juftly claims as his *tithes and offerings.*

3. It prefents *evil* in oppofition to prefent duty. Every believer has a divifion in all the powers of his foul. There is in each faculty one principle for God, and another for fin. The underftanding is partly *light in the Lord,* and partly in darknefs. The will is in part fubjected to the law of God, and in part to that of fin. The affections are only partially renewed. Sin hath ftill a powerful intereft in them. Therefore, the Chriftian would fometimes appear to have two faculties of the fame kind, oppofite to each other; to have one mind warring againft another, one will ftruggling againft a contrary will; becaufe of the war carried on between the oppofite principles of grace and corruption, in every faculty of the foul. His heart, as renewed, is indeed inclined to God in a fupreme degree; yet viewed as deceitful, it is ftill inclined to fin. There is a principle of grace implanted in every power. But it nowife alters the nature of remaining corruption. Sin, as far as it dwells in him, is as much inclined to break forth as ever. Therefore, although he *delights in the law of the Lord after the inward man,* and loves God with the heart, and *with all the heart,* with refpect to the fuperlative nature of his affection; yet his heart, as far as it is unrenewed, ftill continues to work in the way of deceit. So, when he has a call to duty, and finds a fpiritual inclination to it; his heart, according to the ftrength of its deceitfulnefs, prefents evil in oppofition to the good which he wifhes to do. Thus, Paul, fpeaking of his experience as a converted perfon, declares; *I find then a law, that when I would do good, evil is prefent with me* *. He teftifies that evil was prefent with him. It lay near him; not like an object, naturally at a diftance, brought in upon him; but as denoting fomething in union with himfelf. He calls this a law, not as if he meant that *evil* or fin had an abfolute

---

* Rom. vii. 21.

folute dominion over him ; but as fignifying that the remaining corruption of his heart acted after the manner of a law, by prefcribing a rule for his conduct ; by enforcing this with motives fuited to his corruption, propofing carnal pleafures as its rewards, and a privation of thefe, with worldly fufferings, as its punifhments; a law being fometimes recommended by the former, and always fenced by the latter ; nay, by often compelling him to a prefent fubmiffion,— *leading into captivity.* The Apoftle found this law, that when he *would* DO GOOD, *evil* was *prefent*. Every believer will find the fame. His heart may give him fome reft, when he has no immediate call to duty; but when he hath, and is about to obey it, he may expect a renewed affault. The *evil* of the heart always appears with greateft violence, when there is an operative inclination in the renewed part to the fervice of God. When God' prefents an opportunity of ferving him, to which the renewed will confents, the deceitfulnefs of the heart offers a temptation to evil ; and by the artfulnefs or force of the temptation, endeavours to divert the believer from the *good* that he defigns. It may alfo be obferved, that very frequently it attempts to turn him afide from duty, by prefenting *evil* in its nature directly oppofite to the *good* intended. If he fees the neceffity of godly *forrow*, it will entice to carnal *mirth ;* and try to turn him afide from the one, by engaging him in the other. If he finds the neceffity of the mortification of any particular luft, if he is inclined to it by the motions of the Holy Spirit ; the heart fteps in with its corrupt propofals, and perhaps feizes an opportunity of indulging the very luft that he wifhed to mortify. Does he aim at *humility*, and endeavour through grace to deny himfelf? Even then his perfidious heart excites him to fpiritual *pride*. Does he endeavour to attain *fpirituality* of affections, to have them fixed on God as his *exceeding joy?* Then the *flefh* is brought in with its corrupt motions and affections ; and he is inftigated

ftigated to *make provifion for* it, *to fulfil the lufts thereof.*

4. It diffuades from duty, becaufe of *infufficiency* for performing it aright. The deceitful heart will often contradict itfelf, rather than fail of its intention, to baffle all the attempts of the believer in the fervice of his God. If engaged in duty, it perfuades him to depend on his own ftrength. If he be convinced of the folly of this propofal, it will try to hinder him from duty, becaufe of felt inability. It fpeaks the truth indeed, when afferting his utter infufficiency of himfelf. But if it affume the appearance of an advocate for God, if it *transform* itfelf *into an angel of light ;* it is only to ferve the interefts of the kingdom of darknefs, by altogether difcouraging the Chriftian from obedience. While it endeavours to deprefs him with a fenfe of his emptinefs, it conceals from his view the fulnefs that is in Jefus his Covenant-head, for qualifying him for every work to which he is called ; or ftrives to prevent his application to this inexhauftible treafury. He is, in a fpiritual fenfe, in the fame fituation with the fervant of that man of God, Elifhah, who could only perceive the hofts that compaffed the city with horfes and chariots, and is ready to fay with him ; *Alas ! how fhall we do ?* while he cannot fee that there are more with him *than all that are againft* him*. Even when he hath fome conviction of that all-fufficiency which is in Chrift, his own deceitfulnefs fo far prevails, as to make him diftruft the communication of it to him. He views himfelf as fo unworthy, that he can lay no claim to it. Or, he confiders the exercife of faith in deriving fupplies from this quarter, as fo difficult, that rather than engage in it, he will neglect the duty. He finds that his heart is nowife difpofed to appropriate this fulnefs; and he makes this an excufe for omitting the duty required: as the young man David caft off the armour of Saul, becaufe it did not fit him. But this may eafily be known to the Lord's people as a device of

---

* 2 Kings vi. 15. 16.

of their corrupt hearts, or of Satan, to turn them aside from duty. It is, indeed, the work of God to convince his people of their inability to perform any duty; but he never does so with a design to make them resist the call; but, on the contrary, to increase their spiritual diligence in coming to him for all that strength which they need, and which he hath graciously promised. The Psalmist had a deep sense of his own weakness. But faith was his support. *I had fainted, unless I had believed to see the goodness of the Lord in the land of the living.* From his own experience, therefore, and by the Spirit of inspiration, he calls others to the same exercise of dependence on the Lord, amidst the greatest sense of weakness, and the most violent temptations to despondency. *Wait on the Lord: be of good courage, and he shall strengthen thine heart; wait, I say, upon the Lord* *. Against this evil our Lord prescribes the same antidote; *Let not your heart be troubled: ye believe in God, believe also in me* †. It is matter of praise, that while sensible that *we are not sufficient of ourselves to think any thing as of ourselves,* we have the most abundant warrant to add;— *but our sufficiency is of God.* Here self-denial appears in its greatest beauty and loveliness; when, in consequence of a conviction of our own emptiness, it leads us to that superabundant fulness which is in Christ; when, from a deep conviction of our own inability, we are made to acknowledge that *without* Christ, *we can do nothing,* and enabled in the exercise of faith to say, *We can do all things through Christ that strengtheneth us.* Let none therefore despond under a sense of unfitness for the performance of duty, and neglect it on this account; but rather imitate the exercise of David, when he was in danger of being overcome by sinful dejection: *Why art thou cast down, O my soul? and why art thou disquieted within me? Hope thou in God; for I shall yet praise him, who is the health of my countenance, and my God* ‡.

5. It

* Psal. xxvii. 13, 14.   † John xiv. 1.   ‡ Psal. xlii. 11.

5. It prompts the Christian to resist the present call to duty, for want of a proper *temper*. By this is meant a right disposition of heart, liveliness of affections, a present feeling of the comforts of religion. Many excuse their neglect of duty, by pretending that they do not think it incumbent on them, save when they feel their hearts disposed to it; because they would otherwise dishonour God, and receive no comfort in his service. But it is to be feared, that those who habitually neglect Divine worship, when destitute of this pleasant warmth of affections, and who attempt to vindicate their conduct; only present an apology for the reluctance of their hearts to duty itself, and are in a most unlikely way to attain that temper which they expect, or at least, a real disposition of soul for the service of God. To neglect duty, because we do not feel a present glow of affection, discovers the greatest legality, and the grossest ignorance. This is a certain evidence of legality. For such conduct necessarily supposes, that they consider their fervour in duties as the ground of their acceptance. A comfortable warmth of affections, is most desirable, indeed, in the service of the Lord. But it is not essential to acceptable worship. A duty may be performed in the exercise of faith, while no sensible comfort is attained. But wilfully to omit any one for want of this, is to renounce the true foundation of our access to God, which is only through Christ, the *Highpriest of our profession*, our New Testament altar, that alone can *sanctify the gift*; and to embrace something in ourselves, either as our warrant for the performance, or as the ground of our hope in regard to the acceptance of our services. This also discovers the greatest *ignorance*. For it supposes,—either that our disposition for duty proceeds from ourselves, and not from God, that it must be wrought by us, and not in us by his Spirit;—or, that we are to expect his gracious consolations, while we obstinately resist the calls of word and providence.

WE cannot take a more effectual way to prevent the attainment of a suitable disposition for duty, than to neglect the call for want of it: as, on the other hand, the most direct way to obtain liveliness of affection, and *the joy of* God's *salvation* in his service, is depending on promised grace, to obey his call. Indeed it is very commendable exercise for persons before they engage in duty, to seek access to the Lord therein; to endeavour to remove their affections from carnal objects, and to set them *on the things that are above;* and to call to their recollection those considerations, which most naturally tend to fill the soul with spiritual desires. But the omission, or even the delay of present duty, because we find the inefficacy of our endeavours to attain a right temper of mind, is the device of Satan, and of the corrupt heart, to deprive us of all comfort and edification in the way of the Lord. If your hearts be languid and unaffected, to whom should you apply but to God, that he may *touch* them with *a live coal taken from off his altar?* If you have no present comfort, can you reasonably look for it in keeping at a distance from the God of all grace, and of all consolation? How can you more reasonably expect his presence than in the exercise of obedience to his commands, amidst all felt inability? When the Church complains of the Lord's absence, and thus earnestly supplicates his return; *Oh that thou wouldst rent the heavens, and come down;*—she comforts herself by this consideration: *Thou meetest him that rejoiceth, and worketh righteousness; those that remember thee in thy ways**. The Lord in mercy meeteth or preventeth them who *work righteousness*, who endeavour obedience to his commandments, who *remember him in his ways;* not those who forget him, who omit duty, because they do not experience his gracious presence, who will only remember him in their own ways. Of the same nature is her language elsewhere: *Yea, in the way of thy judgments, O Lord, have we waited for thee; the desire of*

our

---

* Isa. lxiv. 1. 5.

our soul is to thy name, and to the remembrance of thee *. It is in the path of obedience alone, that the Lord's people may expect their necessary supplies from him; and it is not surprising that these should be denied, when they *turn the back, and not the face.* It is more glorifying to God, and more edifying to the saints, that they should perform many duties without a sense of his presence, than omit one, because of the want of this.

6. It dissuades from duty, by representing that an *eminent* measure of *holiness* is not *necessary* to salvation. This is an objection made by the deceitfulness of the heart to frequency in religious services, and especially in those which are extraordinary and occasional. It is extremely averse to intimate communion with God, and to a strict course of holiness. Therefore, when there is a call from God, or an inclination in the renewed part to any exercise, especially if it be out of the ordinary line, it suggests this reflection; " That a man may be a real Christian without the " performance of such a duty; that he may be as " sure of heaven, though he neglect it." Thus it attempts to impede the Christian's progress in holiness, by raising obstacles to a life of dependence on the Lord. It reasons with him against a life of faith, as if his own salvation, and not the glory of God, were his highest end; as if his greatest concern were to get heaven to himself, and he were under no obligation to glorify God on earth. But this objection, as it arises from deceitfulness, is itself very false and delusory. For, though it were true, as the heart falsely represents, that our own salvation were our highest concern; still, it would be our duty to aim at the highest degree of holiness we could by any means attain, because thus we should have the highest evidence of the certainty of our salvation; holiness being the clearest proof of a justified state. It is, therefore, our duty, even for making sure our justification, to aim at an eminent measure of holiness.

* Isa. xxvi. 8.

nefs. But as the principle on which it proceeds is falfe, becaufe the glory of God is our higheft end ; its reafoning from this principle is doubly deceitful. For holinefs is the only way to glorify God, and to attain our own happinefs. We can never glorify God, but by a fpiritual life; and the greater our progrefs, the more inftrumental are we in glorifying him. Nay, our very heaven muft efpecially confift in conformity to God; and if we defire a heaven upon earth, we can only attain it by *following holinefs, without which no man can fee the Lord*. It is, therefore, our indifpenfable duty to *prefs forward towards the mark for the prize*, to *leave the things that are behind, and reach forth unto thofe that are before*. It is not enough that we, in regeneration, *enter in at the ftrait gate*. We muft all our life long be engaged in the fame exercife. Therefore, faith Chrift to his hearers ; *Strive to enter in at the ftrait gate ; for many fhall feek to enter in, and fhall not be able* *. It is worthy of attention, that the word here ufed is of the fame import with that which denotes the agony of our Lord in the garden †. It fignifies fuch a ftriving as implies the greateft ardour and engagement of foul, a contending againft the greateft oppofition, a ftriving *in an agony*. We are to ftrive in the fame manner, and with fuch a holy agony of foul in *working out our falvation*, and in *preffing into the kingdom of heaven*, as Chrift fubmitted to in the purchafe of it. And there is the greateft neceffity for this ; becaufe we have the fame enemies to oppofe us; Sin, Satan, the World, and Death: though, bleffed be God! if we be in Chrift, we have not like him to ftruggle with divine and infinite wrath, or with thefe enemies in their full power.—If we liften to this objection of the deceitful heart ; if we neglect any duty, to which we are called or moved by the holy Spirit ; we not only make no advancement in holinefs, but we have no prefent evidence of its reality : becaufe we are deftitute of one of its moft certain characters. For it operates in a cheerful obedience

* Luke xiii. 24 † Luke xxii. 44.

obedience to the will of our Father. It is alfo of an univerfal nature, producing a *refpect to all* his *commandments.*

7. It inclines to the neglect of duty, left others fhould conftrue it as *prefumption* or *hypocrify*. Often, when confcience calls the Lord's people to his fervice, and their hearts as renewed are difpofed to it, their inward deceitfulnefs prevents them, by awakening a fear of propofing or performing it, left their conduct be liable to mifapprehenfion. The Chriftian knows fo much of his own wickednefs, that he is apt to think every one around fhould know it as well as himfelf. He perceives fo much hypocrify in every act of worfhip, that he would not be furprifed, though others fhould conclude him to be an arrant hypocrite. Therefore, when he finds a call, and fomething like an inclination to duty, he is frequently prevented by a fear, left others imagine that he is affuming appearances of religion, to the reality of which he is a ftranger. Now, what is this but his deceit, endeavouring to turn him afide from God? Does not this difplay a greater love to his own character, and to the opinion of others, than to the honour and approbation of the Searcher of hearts? When this is of weight enough to deter from duty, is it not a proof, that the fear of man hath, in the mean time, more influence than that of God? That modefty which would hinder us from propofing or performing duty, when there is a prefent call, is of a baftard kind. It is not Chriftian humility. Our Lord accounts it an evidence of our being afhamed of him. It is utterly inconfiftent with that holy boldnefs which would make us overlook every confideration in comparifon of the glory of God, and be willing rather to have our own reputation trampled in the duft, than that it fhould be preferved at the expence of one duty that we owe to him. This is a modefty, for which God may be provoked fo to chaften his people, as to give them juft caufe of fhame, and to cover their faces with deferved confufion.

WE

We shall conclude with the following directions,

1. Beware of neglecting the *seafon* of duty. God's time is always the fittest for his own service. You can be at no loss to know the seafon of those duties which are of a stated nature. That of others, which are occasional, is to be learned from the word of God, from the calls of providence, from the testimony of conscience, and from the motions of the Spirit in you who are his children. Consider the danger of neglecting any duty in its proper seafon. At any rate, when you perform it afterwards, it will very probably be at the expence of some other which is more immediately requisite. Perhaps, the Lord may, in just displeasure, deny you the opportunity that you have promised to yourselves: or, if this be not the case, he may deny you the power, or the inclination to embrace it; or, if neither of these be with-held, he may refuse you his gracious presence, in that duty which you have delayed beyond its proper time: as we have seen with respect to the Israelites. For as they would not enter into the promised land, when God commanded them; afterwards, when they would have entered, he refused his permission.

2. Do not plead the *world* as an excuse for the omission of duty. God hath given you abundance of time to yourselves. *To every thing there is a seafon, and a time to every purpose under the heaven.* You may easily accomplish all your worldly business, and yet devote that time to God which he requires. Were you more diligent in *redeeming the time,* you might consecrate much of it to him, that is spent to no purpose at all, or to the worst of purposes. If you find your hearts habitually or frequently excusing you from duty, because of the cares of the world; you have great reason to fear, that the love of the world is predominant in you, and that *the deceitfulness of riches* will *choke the word, and make it unfruitful.* Our Lord represents this as the very excuse that those offered, who were altogether averse to the Gospel-feast. *One said I have bought five yoke of oxen,* &c. The consequence

sequence was, that *one went to his farm, and another to his merchandise.* And what doth he assign as the reason of this conduct? *They made light of it.*

3. Be extremely suspicious of every *excuse* that your heart offers for the neglect of duty. You have great reason to dread, that such excuses proceed from deceitfulness or carnality. Never admit of one without trying it to the utmost. If you are willing to find or admit an excuse, it is a certain evidence of your aversion to the service of God. Sustain no apology, that conscience cannot approve, when it is tried by the word of God. Sustain none, but what you are assured, God will sustain at his impartial tribunal.

4. *Quench not the Spirit,* when exciting you to duty. This is *grieving* to *the Holy Ghost, by whom you are sealed to the day of redemption.* It discovers the highest ingratitude to him, when, notwithstanding all your unworthiness, he doth not cease to be *a reprover.* It is extremely prejudicial to the interests of religion in your souls. You, who are the subjects of his common operations, may provoke him to depart from you altogether. For it is written: *They rebelled, and vexed his holy Spirit, and he was turned to be their enemy.* And O! what a dreadful thing is it, to have the Spirit of all grace, the giver of all consolation, the fountain of all true peace, for your enemy? You, who are his own people, his temples, his peculiar charge, may by continuing to grieve him, provoke him to depart for a long time, with respect to sensible manifestations; and in such a manner, that you may never again in this world, enjoy so great a measure of his comforts as you have formerly enjoyed.

5. Carry on, in the strength of promised grace, a constant *war* against the *carnality* of your hearts, against that opposition, which is in them to duty. Be not discouraged, because, when you *would do good, evil is present with* you. Is there any one who says, that he never found *evil present* with him in opposition to good; that his heart, with the greatest, and with universal

universal alacrity, still complies with the service of God? This is a certain evidence of *reigning* deceit, and of gross ignorance of his state before God. Sin will not always oppose in the same manner, or with the same violence; but it will always in some degree oppose *good*. If you are strangers to this opposition, it testifies that your corruption takes another channel; that you have taken up your rest in the duties performed, or that nothing but mere natural affection is at work with you; which is the reason that matters go so smoothly on. It is against the Lord's anointed that the wickedness of Saul especially appears. Cain might have lived peaceably, had not his brother been righteous. If sin get a full vent in the channel of self-righteousness, it will make little opposition to duty: for this is a course as natural to it as any other. If religion go no farther than the affections, while the throne of the heart is still reserved for sin; it may seem an easy matter for a man to do *the good that* he *would*. While the assault is only made on the outworks, the *strong man* may seem to be at rest, because he can still *keep his goods in peace.*

Finally, press after an eminent measure of holiness. It is not enough that you are believers. You must seek to *apprehend that for which also* you are *apprehended of Christ;* and to *grow up into him in all things. Be ye therefore perfect, even as your Father who is in heaven is perfect.*

SERMON XX.

On the DECEITFULNESS of the HEART, as influencing the CONDUCT in LIFE.

James i. 22.

But be ye doers of the word, and not hearers only, deceiving your ownselves.

FEW are disposed to learn, from the general wickedness of the world, the knowledge of their own hearts. When we suffer from others, when we are ensnared by their devices, and injured in our own characters, or property; we naturally entertain ideas to the prejudice of those from whom we suffer. We suppose them to be worse than others, and resolve, if possible, to avoid them for the future. But alas! we do not improve these evidences of deceitfulness in others, by viewing their conduct as a picture of our own hearts, by comparing their deceitful actions with those to which we ourselves have still a great propensity, and which we would certainly perpetrate, were we not restrained by some means or other. We do not resolve more carefully to avoid ourselves. We hate the same things in them, which we love and indulge in ourselves, at least in the principle. Whereas, did we think justly, we would consider their conduct as consonant to our own secret inclinations, and interpret their actions as expressive of the character of our

our own hearts: for *as in water face anfwereth to face, fo the heart of man to man.*

In the firſt part of this chapter, the Apoſtle exhorts thoſe to whom he writes to a right improvement of the day of trial, and to a proper deportment, whether their circumſtances be proſperous or adverſe. From verſe 13. to 18. he ſhows that all evil proceeds from ourſelves, and all real good from God. Then, (ver. 19, 20.) he exhorts to meekneſs of ſpirit, and to a ſincere and humble reception of the word. In verſe 22. he ſhows that it is not enough that we profeſs to receive the word with our hearts, but that we muſt diſcover its influence in our whole converſation: *But be ye doers of the word.* This expreſſion is of the ſame meaning with that uſed verſe 25. where he who *looketh into the perfect law of liberty, and continueth therein,* is ſaid to be *not a forgetful hearer, but a doer of the work,* and so *bleſſed in his deeds.* In both, this character is oppoſed to mere hearing;—*and not hearers only.* That which we at firſt only *hear,* we muſt afterwards *do.* What comes to us as a *word,* muſt go from us as a *work.* He declares briefly, but very emphatically, the folly of being ſatisfied with mere hearing;—*deceiving your ownſelves.* Others may not be deceived by this conduct; for it affords none of thoſe proofs of ſincerity which are requiſite. But it is often productive of a fatal ſelf-deceit. Theſe words evidently contain this doctrine; That when the practice is not correſpondent with the profeſſion, it diſcovers the power of ſelf-deceit.

Having already illuſtrated ſome of the operations of deceitfulneſs, with reſpect to the performance and omiſſion of thoſe duties, which more immediately relate to God, we now propoſe to conſider it a little, as influencing the *Conduct* in *Life.*

1. It appears in general, by a ſtrong propenſity to *abuſe* thoſe precious *truths,* which men profeſs to believe. Many ſeem to receive the truths of God, only to trample them under foot. This practical error is, perhaps, the moſt ſhocking that can be imagined, and

the moſt dangerous alſo. For men ſolace themſelves with the apprehenſion of being found in the faith, while they only uſe the word as the inſtrument of their iniquity, as a tool for the gratification of their abominable luſts. We might mention various evidences of this mournful abuſe of divine truth, which appear in the conduct of many profeſſors. They may all be comprehended in one, which is of great importance,—the abuſe of the doctrine of the free grace of God manifeſted in the whole of our ſalvation, or as the ſcripture expreſſes it, *turning the grace of God into laſciviouſneſs.* Some, it may be feared, if they profeſs to believe the abſolute ſovereignty of Divine grace, in chuſing a certain number of mankind loſt to eternal life, without any foreſight of faith or good works, as meritorious cauſes, will improve their boaſted faith in this doctrine, by concluding that they may live as they pleaſe, and indulge themſelves in every iniquity: becauſe if God hath decreed their ſalvation, they cannot fail of attaining it; but if otherwiſe, whatever they do, they ſhall be damned. But they do not conſider, that God in his decree hath fixed faith and holineſs as *means,* no leſs abſolutely than ſalvation as the *end;* that men are *choſen to ſalvation, only through ſanctification of the Spirit, and belief of the truth;* nay, that in the decree, he views holineſs not merely as a mean, but as an illuſtrious part of the end, having *choſen us that we ſhould be holy and without blame before him in love.*—If they profeſs to believe juſtification without works, through the imputed righteouſneſs of Chriſt, they will wickedly conclude that there is no neceſſity for holineſs or good works, becauſe they have no merit before God; while he hath abſolutely declared that *without holineſs no man ſhall ſee the Lord,* and that this freedom from condemnation belongs only to thoſe *who walk not after the fleſh, but after the Spirit.* They overlook the indiſpenſable neceſſity of evangelical holineſs, as the only proper evidence of the reality of juſtification, as *adorning the Goſpel,* glorifying to God, attractive

tive to others; as the image of him who is *the first-born among many brethren;* the evidence of our title to the heavenly inheritance, and our meetness for the full possession of it. If they deny the doctrine of free-will, and assert the necessity of the Spirit to *work all our works in us;* hence will they impiously infer, that they may be entirely regardless of those very means which God himself hath appointed, and in the due observation of which we are alone warranted to expect the promised blessing. For we are commanded to *seek the Lord while he may be found.* They will, perhaps, presume to resist, as far as possible, the operations of the holy Spirit, or at least, give themselves no trouble to cherish and improve them; because they know that, when these are saving, they cannot fail of success. The doctrine of the perseverance of the saints will also be abused as an encouragement to the commission of iniquity, because they know that none, who are Christ's, shall eternally perish; though we are assured that they are only *kept through faith,* and that they are *preserved blameless to his heavenly kingdom.*

This conduct is by the Spirit of God esteemed to be an express denial of the faith. And it is the more base and detestable, because it is sheltered under a profession of it. It is accounted a denial of Christ, nay, of the very being of God. Of such speaks the Apostle Jude: *There are certain men crept in unawares, who were of old ordained to this condemnation, ungodly men, turning the grace of our God into lasciviousness, and denying the only Lord God, and our Lord Jesus Christ* *. To reason, and to act in this manner, is really to *deny the Lord that bought us* †, and to make *Christ the minister of sin* ‡. Of this abuse of the doctrine of truth, Paul speaks with the greatest abhorrence; *Shall we continue in sin, that grace may abound? God forbid. How shall we that are dead to sin, live any longer therein* § *?*

But

---

* Jude ver 4. † 2 Pet. ii. 1. ‡ Gal. ii. 17.
§ Rom. vi. 1, 2.

But as the deceit of the heart inftigates fome to abufe thefe precious doctrines in this manner, the fame principle takes another courfe with others. It makes them ftagger at the faith, and even reject it, becaufe thus abufed. When they fee its profeffed friends fell it at fo low a price, it proves to them a ftumbling-block, hardens them in their iniquity, and makes them conclude that this accurfed conduct is the native refult of the doctrines they profefs to believe. This the Apoftle Peter mentions as a certain effect of the corruption of the truth, which is *after godlinefs. Many fhall follow their pernicious ways, by reafon of whom the way of truth fhall be evil fpoken of*.* Under the influence of this temptation, many have interpreted the word of God in direct oppofition to the plain meaning of language; and when confcious that their forced expofitions would not ftand the teft, have dared impioufly to declare, that if the penmen of fcripture had known how much their modes of expreffion would have been abufed, they would never have employed them. But no one could fpeak in this ftrain, did he not fecretly difbelieve that thefe *men of God fpake as they were moved by the Holy Ghoft*. Nor need men be ftaggered at the abufe of Divine truth in our time; when they know that it was abufed in the very fame manner, even in the days of the Apoftles. They have no more reafon for rejecting the doctrine of grace, becaufe fome abufe it, than for denying themfelves meat and drink, becaufe fome are gluttons, and others drunkards. The bee can fuck honey from the fame flower from which the wafp diftils poifon. Men abufe thefe precious doctrines, only becaufe they do not cordially believe them. Were this the cafe, they would prove the life of their fpirits. The fame truths, which to fome are *the favour of life unto life*, are to others *the favour of death unto death;* not merely in the end, but even in the mean time; becaufe their deceitful hearts ufe them as ftumbling-blocks, and through the power of their

---

* 2 Pet. ii. 2.

their lufts, they thence take occafion to harden themfelves more and more in iniquity. *Unto the pure all things are pure; but unto them that are defiled, and unbelieving, is nothing pure: but even their mind and confcience is defiled.* And indeed this inward defilement is the reafon that nothing is pure to them. For it communicates its infection to every thing that approaches it. The natural effect of this defilement of mind and confcience is immediately mentioned: *They profefs that they know God; but in works they deny him; being abominable and difobedient, and unto every good work reprobate* *.

2. It appears by an attempt to reconcile *religion* and the *world*. Many profeffors try to love God and the world at the fame time, to pleafe both the one and the other, to make fure of heaven without quitting their hold of earth, to ferve both JEHOVAH and Baal. This charge God exhibits againft Ifrael, in his inftructions to the Prophet Ezekiel: *They come unto thee as the people cometh, and they fit before thee as my people, and they hear thy words, but they will not do them: for with their mouth they fhow much love, but their heart goeth after their covetoufnefs* †. But this attempt is vain, and a ftriking evidence of the power of deceit. For it is exprefsly declared, that if we *love the world, or the things of the world, the love of the Father is not in* us. Do not flatter yourfelves that you can grafp the true riches in the one hand, and retain the *mammon of unrighteoufnefs* in the other, by dividing your heart between both. The love of the world in its corrupt opinions, in its childifh vanities, in its evil cuftoms, in its unfatisfying honours, pleafures, and profits, is reprefented as a fpiritual adultery in profeffors; becaufe it is a direct apoftafy from that God, whom in profeffion they have chofen as the fupreme object of their affections. *Ye adulterers and adultereffes, know ye not that the friendfhip of this world is enmity with God? Whofoever therefore will be a friend of the world is the*

VOL. I.   B b b   enemy

---

* Tit. i. 15, 16.   † Ezek. xxxiii. 31.

enemy of God.[*] The world itfelf is an enemy to God; and can you be his friends, while you love his implacable enemy? The world is God's rival. It claims the dominion of the heart. Now, God will be fatisfied with nothing lefs. He commands you to love him *with all the heart, and with all the foul.* But *no man can ferve two mafters, for either he will hate the one, and love the other, or he will hold to the one and defpife the other. Ye cannot ferve God and Mammon*[†]. Hath not Chrift given himfelf for us, *that he might deliver us from this prefent evil world?* And can we be interefted in his death, without renouncing the love of the world? Is it not the work of the Spirit, by means of the crofs, to *crucify us to the world?* Is it not exprefsly required of the profeffed difciples of Chrift, as an evidence of their being *rifen with* him, that they *feek the things that are above?* We have a ftriking example of the fatal confequences of this vain attempt in the hiftory of Ananias and Sapphira, who, for a warning to profeffors in all fucceeding ages, to beware of the rock on which they were wrecked, were immediately deftroyed by the hand of God. Peter, by Divine infpiration, accufes them of having *their hearts filled by Satan* with deceitfulnefs againft the Holy Ghoft. *He faid unto Ananias; Why hath Satan filled thine heart to lie unto the Holy Ghoft;* or, as the words may be rendered, *to deceive the Holy Ghoft,* to endeavour fo impious and fruitlefs a deceit [‡]? They pretended to fell all their property for the behoof of the Church, and to give the whole of the price to God; while they retained part of it to themfelves. Their conduct, amidft all the blaze of their profeffion, declared that their hearts were ftill wedded to the world; and not only fo, but contained a moft daring denial of Divine Omnifcience.

3. The liberty of the *tongue* in *backbiting* others, is a farther evidence of the deceitfulnefs of the heart. This is a fin extremely prevalent among profeffed Chriftians.

[*] James iv. 4.   [†] Matt. vi. 24.   [‡] Acts v. 3.

Christians. What is the bulk of the conversation of many, but a continued detraction from the character of their neighbours? This base practice is directly opposite to all the comforts of society. But, from its prevalence, one would almost be in danger of apprehending, that it was considered as one of the chief pillars of society, and of mutual intercourse among its members. Did we take a just and impartial view of the world around us, we would be apt to think, that men in general had combined to keep no faith one with another; but on the contrary, to surpass even the beasts of prey, by devouring each other, without regard to the sameness of kind. There are always two ingredients in this detestable practice,— Malice and Dishonesty. Backbiting evidently discovers a *malicious* spirit. For it is ever meant to expose the person, against whom it is directed. His faults, either real or supposed, are the mark at which it constantly aims. His good qualities are either passed over in silence; or if they be mentioned, it is but very slightly, or only in such a way, as to detract from them and infuse a doubt of their reality.— Though the good qualities of a person should be far more conspicuous than his failings; yet those are generally considered as less worthy of praise or imitation, than these of reprehension. Often, indeed, it is a secret unpleasant conviction of superior worth, that prompts persons to indulge themselves in the language of backbiting; that thus, if possible, they may bring those, who are the objects of their envy, and perhaps of their fear, more on a level with themselves. For many a one is there, whose *eye* is *evil*, because his brother's *eye is good*. It always implies *dishonesty*. For if there be any thing in the conduct of another, that gives us offence, that appears dishonouring to God and prejudicial to him, or that includes others in its evil consequences; we ought to make himself acquainted with it, and in meekness and love to deal with him as a brother. The dishonesty of this conduct is a farther evidence of its malicious nature;

for

for it shows that professors, in publishing the faults of others, do not wish themselves reclaimed, but only their faults propagated. This practice is also a great inlet to lying. For we generally find, that those who delight to dwell on the failings of their neighbours, will invent a falsehood, rather than cease from the language of calumny, or deny themselves the barbarous pleasure of assassinating others in their good name. And slander, when once propalled, is like a stone rolled in snow, which always gathers by its motion. It is seldom or never repeated without aggravation. This is one of those spots that defile Church-members, the origin of which, as being of a more secret nature than many other offences, often in particular instances cannot be discovered by the most diligent inquiry, and therefore cannot be so easily managed as a foundation of censure. To say the truth; and can we say it without sorrow? it is so general, at least in some degree, that we would be at a loss where to begin. It stains the conversation of many, who in other respects walk as becometh saints. Who can wash his hands, and say, in regard to this iniquity, I am clean?

DID we for a moment consider it merely in a *rational* point of view, we would not hesitate to declare its unreasonableness, or be at any loss to discover its folly. For when we hear those, with whom we have intercourse, indulging themselves in backbiting others, who, perhaps, have but newly left our company, and who have been treated with every mark of friendship; what can we expect, but that we shall be the next butts for the shafts of their malice? Or, when we take a liberty to ourselves in this despicable gratification, is it not natural to suppose that others will retaliate, and use the same freedom with us, that we have used with them? But if we bring this unchristian practice to the unerring standard of God's *Word*, we shall have a far more striking discovery of its evil and folly. There we find that backbiting is represented as the fruit of *a reprobate mind*,

and

and that *backbiters and whisperers* are classed with *haters of God*. And no wonder, for they are haters of man, who is the image of God. Envy and malignity are joined with murder. Indeed, they are the murders of the heart: *Being full of envy, murder, debate, deceit, malignity* *. It is given as a negative character of the man who shall dwell in God's tabernacle, that *he backbiteth not with his tongue, nor doth evil to his neighbour, nor taketh up a reproach against his neighbour* †. On the contrary, the character, conduct, and danger of the wicked are described in the following address: *Thou givest thy mouth to evil, and thy tongue frameth deceit; thou sittest and speakest against thy brother, thou slanderest thine own mother's son.—Now, consider this, ye that forget God, lest I tear you in pieces, and there be none to deliver* ‡. Backbiting is also produced in scripture as an evidence of the deceitfulness of the heart; and the habitual commission of this sin, as an undeniable proof of hypocrisy in religion. For it is declared that *deceit is in the heart of them that imagine evil* § ; and that *the wicked is snared by the transgression of his lips* ∥.— It is also said, that *an hypocrite with his mouth destroyeth his neighbour*. So cruel is calumny, that it carries destruction in it. This is the murder of the tongue, as malice is that of the heart. When men's *teeth are spears and arrows, and their tongue a sharp sword*, there is every reason to fear that their right hand would also be *a right hand of cruelty*, did not the Lord *restrain the remainder of their wrath*. An habit of this kind, is, in the context, mentioned by our Apostle, as an unquestionable evidence of the falsity of a profession: *If any man among you seem to be religious, and bridleth not his tongue, but deceiveth his own heart, this man's religion is vain* **.

4. THE deceitfulness of the heart is manifested by the prevalence of *dissimulation* and *falsehood*. A great part of conversation, especially among those in higher ranks

* Rom. i. 28,—30. † Psal. xv. 1,—3. ‡ Psal. l. 19,—22.
§ Prov. xii. 20. ∥ Prov. xii. 13. ** James i. 26.

ranks in life, confifts of profeffions which are entirely infincere. Men, for eftablifhing their characters, or ferving their interefts, often pretend the greateft efteem and affection, where there is naught but difguft and alienation. It can never be inconfiftent with the character of a Chriftian to endeavour a kind and gentle demeanour towards all, while that injunction of the Spirit is contained in his word ; *Be courteous.* But this is the great error. Men often make profeffions to which they are altogether ftrangers, nay, even while actuated by feelings directly contrary, and while regardlefs of that important command ; *Let love be without diffimulation.* If men view it only in a natural refpect, there can be nothing more mean and defpicable, than, merely for accomplifhing their own purpofes, to pretend affections which they never felt, and to utter expreffions which their inward feelings belie. This is entirely inconfiftent with the character of a child of God, of whom it is faid, that *he fpeaketh the truth in his heart ;* and who is bound conftantly to imitate the example of Jefus, in whofe *lips* there was *no guile.* The deceitfulnefs of the heart often feeks a vent to itfelf in the language of *flattery.* This confifts in beftowing falfe praife, or in afcribing perfections to others, which we do not believe they poffefs. This is always an evidence of a double heart. Therefore faith the wife man ; *He that goeth about as a talebearer revealeth fecrets ; therefore meddle not with him that flattereth with his lips* *. The plain meaning of this injunction is ;—" A talebearer tries
" to ingratiate himfelf with you, by telling you the
" fecrets of another, that he may lay your heart open :
" while difcommending him he praifes you, that he
" may gain your confidence. But he is to be avoid-
" ed, for he feeks your confidence, only that he may
" have it in his power to treat you in the fame man-
" ner. He will as readily reveal your fecrets as thofe
" of another." *A man that flattereth his neighbour, fpreadeth a net for his feet.—He that hateth, diffem-*
bleth

---

* Prov. xx. 19.

bleth with his lips, and layeth up deceit within him. When he speaketh fair, believe him not: for there are seven abominations in his heart. *Whose hatred is covered by deceit, his wickedness shall be shewed before the whole congregation.—A lying tongue hateth those that are afflicted by it, and a flattering mouth worketh ruin* *.

Lying is a vice mournfully prevalent, and a striking evidence of the deceit of the heart. It is too common for men to cover one sin by another; to tell a lie that they may conceal some other transgression. Their temptation to this, is a sense of shame, arising from the commission of sin, or a fear of suffering from men like themselves. But it is a dreadful aggravation of their guilt, and a confirming proof of the hardness of their hearts under sin. Besides, it generally defeats its own intention. For few are so obdurate, as not to discover their guilt, one way or another, by the very means which they take to conceal it; either by their want of ingenuity, or by their confusion. This also declares that they are presently destitute of a sense of the omniscience of God, as all their concern is, how they may hide their guilt from man; and that they are impenitent under the load of iniquity; for there can be no true repentance before God, while persons endeavour to conceal their guilt from others, by *adding sin to sin*. This iniquity is extremely dishonouring to God. For it is a denial of his nature, as *the only true God*, the God *who cannot lie*; and particularly of his attribute of omniscience, as the Searcher of hearts. It is extremely dangerous to souls. For, as we have seen, when persisted in, it precludes the possibility of repentance, and hardens the sinner in the commission of iniquity. For *whoso covereth his sin shall not prosper*. It is exceedingly prejudicial to society; because it looses the bonds of union by which men are knit to each other, one of the most powerful of which is mutual faith. It is directly opposite to the character of God's people; for *they are children that will*

* Prov. xxvi. 24,—28.

will not lie *. The Apostle Paul uses a very strong argument against this detestable practice, taken from its inconsistency with the renewed nature of believers: *Lie not one to another, seeing that ye have put off the old man with his deeds, and have put on the new man* †. With respect to persons of this character, there is no exception as to their exclusion from the kingdom of God. For *all liars shall have their part in the lake, that burneth with fire and brimstone, which is the second death* ‡. All who go on in a course of this kind, in a peculiar manner claim their relation to Satan; for *he is a liar, and the father of it* §.

5. This corrupt principle breaks out in the life by *dishonesty* in civil transactions. It were scarcely necessary to speak of the literal transgression of the eighth precept of the Divine law, because it is so obvious as to require little illustration; did not many discover the power of their deceit, by supposing that the crime is proportioned to the magnitude of the injury done to others. They judge of the degree of sin, according to the value of what is stolen. But this is altogether a false rule. He is as truly a thief in God's account, who steals a penny, as he who steals a pound. And why so? Because the one is no more his property than the other. Perhaps, it may be said, that it is baser to steal a trifle than a great matter. For the temptation is less, and the baseness or wickedness of heart, manifested in the commission of any crime, is certainly greater in proportion to the weakness of the temptation. He, who steals a mere trifle, is surely possessed of a very dishonest mind; because the thing stolen can do him very little service. So deceitful is the heart, that many imagine there is little harm in a petty theft. But if the thing be the property of another, it does not signify what it is. Thou art not only forbidden to covet thy neighbour's house or wife, ox or ass, but *any thing that is thy neighbour's*. God hath not said; Thou shalt not steal this or that; but absolutely,

---

* Isa. lxiii. 8.   † Col. iii. 9, 10.   ‡ Rev. xxi. 8.   § John viii. 44.

folutely, *Thou shalt not steal.* Neceffity is no plea. For every thief will plead fome kind of neceffity. No man would fteal, if he did not think that he had occafion for what he covets. Work more diligently, and you will find no need for difhoneft courfes. The time fpent in devifing and executing your plans of petty theft, would very probably bring you in as much by lawful induftry. *Let him that ftole, steal no more ; but rather let him labour, working with his hands the thing which is good, that he may have to give to him that needeth* *. This is the way not only to fupply your own neceffities, but to be able to relieve thofe of others. Befides, you cannot get the good of what you have by difhonefty. You can neither confidently afk, nor expect the bleffing to attend it. *The curfe of the Lord shall enter into the houfe of the thief, and it shall remain in the midst of his houfe, and shall confume it, with the timber thereof, and the ftones thereof* †. It is indeed faid, *Men do not defpife a thief, if he steal to fatisfy his foul when he is hungry* ‡. Hence fome may urge the plea of neceffity. But there can be no neceffity for ftealing, when a man is able to work, or when he can beg. Begging is far more honourable than ftealing. But it muft be obferved, that thefe words do not relate to theft in the eftimation of God, but only in that of man. It is not faid, that a man is not a thief, that God doth not account him fo; or even that men do not form this judgment of him ; but only, that in the cafe fuppofed, they *do not defpife* him. That is, he is rather pitied, when his ftraits are fo great, that he is overcome by a temptation to theft, merely to fatisfy the refiftlefs cravings of nature. Nor is it faid, that he does not merit punifhment. For, it is added, *If he be found, he shall reftore feven-fold, he shall give all the fubftance of his houfe.* Thefe words are not fpoken to extenuate the guilt of theft, but to aggravate that of adultery ; as fhewing that it is a more heinous fin than theft ; becaufe the man, who fteals to fatisfy his hunger,

* Eph. iv. 28. † Zech. v. 4. ‡ Prov. vi. 30.

hunger, yields to a temptation for the gratification of a natural, finless appetite; but he who commits adultery, invades the property of his neighbour to satisfy a brutish, abominable lust.

But in how many different ways does the deceitfulness of the heart appear, even while men do not absolutely put forth the hand to steal? How many, in trade, use false weights and measures, to defraud their neighbours, and procure wealth; and yet flatter themselves, as if they were innocent before God? *Ephraim is a merchant, the balances of deceit are in his hand: he loveth to oppress. And Ephraim said, Yet I am become rich, I have found me out substance: in all my labours they shall find none iniquity in me, that were sin* *. But *the false balance, or, the balance of deceit, is abomination to the Lord.* Many, in buying and selling, take the advantage of those who are ignorant. *It is naught, it is naught, saith the buyer,* it is a thing of no value; *but when he goeth his way he boasteth. As a cage is full of birds, so are their houses full of deceit; therefore they are become great, and waxen rich* †. Often are the poor and fatherless the prey of the deceitful, who *grind their faces,* and rob them of their substance. *The people of the land have used oppression,* or, as it may be read, *deceit,—they have vexed the poor and needy; yea, they have oppressed the stranger wrongfully* ‡. Many instances of the same kind might be mentioned;—not restoring what has been lost, or using proper means to discover the rightful owner;—borrowing without an intention to pay, retaining what has been borrowed, when it may be thought that the owner has forgot, or refusing to repay, when one has ability; all which are actions of dishonesty, and fruits of inward deceitfulness. But these we cannot now particularly illustrate.

6. In a word, what is the *history* of *mankind* but a history of the deceitfulness of the heart in its unspeakable variety of forms? Whether we view it on a larger, or on a smaller scale, it in general presents the same

---

* Hos. xii. 7.   † Jer. v. 27.   ‡ Ezek. xxii. 29.

fame mournful picture. The conduct of individuals is just a miniature of that of greater bodies. Here, we see private persons deceiving, *biting and devouring one another:* There, we see whole communities mutually devising the most habile schemes of deceit, for infringing the most sacred obligations, for depriving each other of property, of credit, or of that idol honour, that *Moloch* which hath so often had its altars drenched with human blood. Here, we see individuals professing the greatest friendship and affection, while they eagerly wait an opportunity of blasting the characters of others. *If he comes to see me,* saith David of an enemy under the mask of friendship, *he speaketh vanity; his heart gathereth iniquity to itself, when he goeth abroad he telleth it* *: and again; *The words of his mouth were smoother than butter, but war was in his heart: his words were softer than oil, yet they were drawn swords* †. There, we see nations, again and again, making the warmest protestations of peace, while secretly straining all the sinews of war. Often is a credulous nation reduced to the same situation with Edom: *All the men of thy confederacy have brought thee to the border: the men that were at peace with thee, have deceived thee, and prevailed against thee: they that eat thy bread have laid a wound under thee* ‡. You may hear individuals vindicating themselves in the most solemn manner before God and the world, while they only *lie in wait privily to slay the innocent;* and, in like manner, collective bodies making the most awful appeals with respect to the uprightness of their intentions, to the Judge of all, as well as to the nations around; and specifying instances, almost innumerable, of injurious treatment which they pretend to have received; while their sole intentions are to blind others, whom it is their interest to retain in a state of amity, and to destroy or subdue those, who, perhaps, so far from being the aggressors, have been the only sufferers. On the one hand, you may perceive a cruel and insidious

Joab

* Psal. xli. 6.   † Psal. lv. 21.   ‡ Obad. ver. 7.

Joab taking an unsuspicious Amasa by the beard, saluting him, and saying, *Art thou in health, my brother?* while he smites him to the heart *: on the other, a deceitful prince *entering peaceably even upon the fattest places of the province, and scattering the prey, and spoil, and riches; and forecasting his devices against the strong holds* †. Indeed, when the heart is *full of debate and deceit*, it is no wonder that it should also be *full of envy and murder* ‡. As *wars and fightings* in general proceed *from lust*, the most of those between different powers more immediately originate from that of deceit. It is because the greatest part of princes, like him mentioned in Daniel, *after the league work deceitfully*, that the blood of their unhappy people is made to *run* like water on the *streets*. Of this corruption it may be said, as of mystical Babylon, that *in her skirts is found all the blood shed upon the earth:* and as this base principle naturally issues in blood, God, in righteous judgment, punishes it in this way. Thus he threatens concerning the treacherous king of Judah, who broke covenant with the king of Babylon; *As I live, surely mine oath that he hath despised, and my covenant that he hath broken, even it will I recompense upon his own head:—and all his fugitives, with all his bands, shall fall by the sword, and they that remain shall be scattered towards all winds* §.

We shall only improve this branch of our subject by warning you all against *backbiting*. It is a mournful truth that this evil greatly prevails among professors. Nay, there is too just ground to assert, that it prevails more generally among them, than even among the profane. Now, it may not be altogether improper to enquire, what may be some of the reasons of a fact apparently so incredible?—Sin, in professors, often takes a more *secret* channel, than what it occupies in those who are without, or that in which it flowed in themselves, while they made no profession. Regard to character or interest lays them

under

* Sam. xx. 9, 10. † Dan. xi. 24. ‡ Rom. i. 29.
§ Ezek. xvii. 19. 21.

under a necessity of guarding against the grosser pollutions of the world. Perhaps, they confide in their profession and external reformation. But sin, like a torrent confined in one place, must break out in another. It still retains the dominion in their hearts: and if it find no vent by *the lusts of the flesh*, it withdraws into the more secret channel of *the lusts of the mind*, such as pride, malice, envy, and the like. Now, malice and envy break out in evil-speaking and backbiting. But the profane person hath not his lusts so hemmed in ; and his manner of life most naturally leads him to an indulgence of the lusts of the flesh, rather than of those of the mind. At any rate, the fountain of sin in the heart is more divided.—This iniquity may be found greatly to prevail even with real Christians. They *mortify the deeds of the body*. But their attention is often too much confined to those sins that tend most to defile the conversation; especially when languid in the exercise of grace. Undoubtedly, as far as this sin prevails, as far as it remains unmortified, they are defective in the evidences of true religion : and wherever it is habitual, as really as any other sin, it will prevent admission into the kingdom of God *.

PROFESSORS pacify their consciences by supposing that backbiting is comparatively a *little* sin. They in their minds run the parallel between this and their former iniquities: and are at no loss to conclude that this is scarcely worth the mentioning. When a man *sits and speaks against his brother*, he thinks that God will *approve his sin* †. But the comparison of sins is a very delicate subject. All sin is infinitely evil, objectively considered. And perhaps, some of the lusts of the mind, though reckoned far less heinous than those of the flesh, may be no less so in the estimation of that God, whose *thoughts are not our thoughts*. This we know, that *whosoever hateth his brother is a murderer, and abideth in death;* and that the sins proceeding from the lusts of the mind are,

* Gal. v. 21. † Psal. l. 20, 21.

are, by the Spirit, marked down in the same criminal list with those of the flesh, as *worthy of death.**

Again, from the peculiar obligations that professing Christians lie under to the exercise of *brotherly love*, the *want* of this grace may occasion a greater prevalence of backbiting. Wherever this prevails, indeed, it must be owing to the want of love. But in those situations in life, wherein any duty is peculiarly requisite, if it be neglected, the contrary sin generally occupies its place. For example, in the married life, if love subsist not between the parties, there is commonly aversion. Now, love to one another is more especially incumbent on fellow Christians than others. They are bound by the strongest ties. In profession they are members of one body; they *all eat the same spiritual meat, and drink the same spiritual drink.* And if there be a defect in regard to this holy affection, there is every reason to apprehend, that the contrary will fill up its room. The law hath an irritating power on the lusts of men, and if their hearts are not really subjected to its authority in any precept, their enmity breaks out by a peculiar opposition to it. For *sin, taking occasion by the commandment, works* in them *all manner of concupiscence:* and the less that the authority of the law is felt in any article, the more does sin seem to be *dead* †. Matters must necessarily take this course, according to the frame of the heart, and according to the nature of sin and duty. There can be no vacuity in the soul. All that room, which is not occupied by grace, must be possessed by sin. All in the heart, that is not love, is really enmity.

Farther, the uncommon prevalence of this sin among professors may be partly owing to the *abuse* of *gifts*. These, as far as they are unsanctified, minister fuel to the natural pride of the heart. *Knowledge puffeth up.* As pride in every shape is attended with great meanness, the pride of superior gifts may

dispose

* Rom. i. 27.—31.   † Rom. vii. 8.

dispose a person tacitly to compare himself with others, to show his own imagined superiority by the liberal use of his tongue in defaming their characters. To a conduct somewhat like this the Apostle refers, when he saith; *For we dare not make ourselves of the number, or compare ourselves with some that commend themselves; but they, measuring themselves by themselves, and comparing themselves amongst themselves, are not wise**. Nay, a consciousness of inferiority to others may produce this conduct. Thus they wish to bring others more to an equality.

Besides, *false zeal* may have the same effect. This often creates a spirit of censure and severity. Those who know the necessity of purity of communion, sometimes suffer their zeal to degenerate into bitterness. They discover that it is false; for instead of directing it toward *the beam* in their *own eye*, they are principally concerned about *the mote in their brother's*. They farther manifest its hypocritical nature; because it does not excite them to use proper means for reforming what is pretended to be offensive. For they do not *rebuke* their *brother*. They *suffer sin upon him*. All the means used by them tend to the destruction of his character, and not to the reformation of his practice. When there is nothing more than a mere profession, or when religion is at a very low ebb; both the heart and practice are apt to speak the same language with that of the carnal Jews; *Stand by thyself, come not near to me, for I am holier than thou.*

In a word, this sin is indulged rather than those that are more gross, because it is often more *difficult* of *discovery*. Many things are spoken in hints and whispers, which are not easily traced; though they frequently wound more deeply than the heaviest charges of a direct kind, because they leave ground to suspect, that the matter may be worse than it is represented, nay, that it may be a great deal worse than it really is. Thus professors, while indulging this sin, are less afraid of church-discipline. And perhaps, the

* 2 Cor. x. 12.

the relaxation of this, in too many inftances, with regard to evil-fpeaking, gives too much encouragement to it ; as profeffors, being fuffered to pafs with impunity, are apt to conclude that the offence is trivial. But let us be concerned, under a deep fenfe of the higheft authority, and depending on the ftrength of divine grace, to lay afide all malice, and all guile, and all hypocrifies, and envies, and all evil-fpeakings ; to fpeak evil of no man without a proper call ; and to obey that great commandment, *Thou fhalt love thy neighbour as thyfelf.*

SERMON XXI.

ON THE DECEITFULNESS OF THE HEART, IN THE ABUSE OF PROSPERITY.

JEREMIAH xlix. 16.

Thy terriblenefs hath deceived thee, and the pride of thine heart.

THE providence of God is a bleffed, and a divine commentary on the Word, which all his people, according to the meafure of grace given to them, will be concerned to read, fearch into and underftand by the light of the holy Spirit, who alone can *lead into all truth.* It is efpecially a commentary on the promifes, whether they relate to the profperity or adverfity of God's children. From an attentive obfervation of providential difpenfations, a comparifon of thefe with the promifes and declarations of fcripture, and a diligent confideration of the work of the Spirit in their hearts, as concurring with both; they receive the moft convincing, fatisfying and irrefragable demonftration of the truth of religion,—a demonftration, to which unbelievers are entire ftrangers; and little known even to many Chriftians, who are inattentive to the ways of the Lord. The heart employs various methods of deceit, to deprive the children of God of the comfortable and edifying fruits of a proper improvement of divine difpenfations; whether thefe be profperous or adverfe.

THE charge contained in the words of our text is exhibited againft Bofrah, the chief city of the land

land of Edom. According to a common figure, a part of the country is put for the whole. There is a confiderable difference among interpreters as to the meaning of the word rendered *terriblenefs*, as it no where elfe occurs. But the fenfe given in our Verfion feems moft agreeable to the context. It denotes the natural ftrength, the power, and the profperity of Edom, all in one point of view. Deception is the effect afcribed to this. *Thy terriblenefs hath deceived thee.* It produced fuch a vain confidence, that the Edomites thought they were fecure from all danger. But the greatnefs of Edom's power was not properly the caufe of her deceit. It was only the occafion. The caufe follows in the words;—*and the pride of thine heart.* The meaning plainly is, that from outward ftrength and apparent fecurity, the pride of her heart took occafion to deceive her into falfe confidence. The words themfelves may be rendered, *By thy terriblenefs thy proud heart hath deceived thee.* They exprefs the natural effect of riches, power, abundance, or profperity of any kind on the carnal heart. Thefe excite its pride, and tend to carry it away from God the only refuge.

The words afford us the following doctrine,

That worldly profperity is often abufed by the heart, as the occafion of felf-deceit; or, that the heart often difcover its deceit in the abufe of profperity.

All that is intended here, is to illuftrate the actings of this corrupt principle in abufing profperity. It does fo,

1. By *ingratitude*. Sinners receive all God's mercies with an unthankful heart. All that he gracioufly confers, they confider as juftly belonging to them; and were it withheld, they would accufe him of denying what they can claim as their own. *She did not know,* faith the Lord, concerning the Church of Ifrael, *that I gave her corn, and wine, and oil, and multiplied her filver and gold**. Although it is from God that finners receive their food and raiment, their prefervation

* Hof. ii. 8.

preservation from day to day, their health, strength and many deliverances; yet they acknowledge not the Giver. Multitudes, who live on Divine bounty, live as unthankfully as the beasts of the field. They sit down to their table and rise from it, they eat and drink like the *brutes that perish;* without considering, that *whether* they *eat or drink, or whatsoever* they *do, they should do all to the glory of God.* Yea, they are more unthankful than the beasts of the field. Even these discover a sense of gratitude to their benefactors. The savage lion will be tamed by the kindness of his keeper. Therefore, the Lord, by a beautiful figure, summons in the brute creatures as witnesses against his professing people, with respect to their ignorance, ingratitude and rebellion; and the inanimate creatures, as judges of his controversy with them. *Hear O heavens, and give ear, O earth: for the Lord hath spoken: I have nourished and brought up children, and they have rebelled against me. The ox knoweth his owner, and the ass his master's crib: but Israel doth not know, my people doth not consider* *. Perhaps, it was such an abuse of mercies as this, that holy Job feared his children might be chargeable with, in the days of their feasting; when *he offered burnt-offerings according to the number of them* all. For *Job said, It may be that my sons have sinned, and cursed God in their hearts* *. He does not imagine that they had openly blasphemed God. But he fears that their festivity might have proved a temptation to them to think lightly of God, to forget their obligations to him, and thus in effect to *curse* him *in their hearts.* For he well knew, that through the corruption of human nature, feasting and cursing, prosperity and irreligion, often go hand in hand.

Many are the spiritual mercies, which the unregenerate receive from God. He gives them his word and ordinances, wherein *the bread of life* is exhibited. He warns them by his servants. He strives with them by his Spirit. They reject and despise the heavenly manna. Their *souls lothe this light food.*
O !

---

* Isa. i. 2, 3.   † Job i. 5.

O! what infinite patience doth he exercise toward them! What a wonder of longsuffering is it, that he doth not consume them in a moment; that he so often *turns away his anger, and stirs not up against them all his wrath;* that he suffers his earth to bear them, even while it groans under the load of their wickedness; that he doth not *command the deep to swallow them up, and the pit to shut her mouth upon them**. But herein he discovers that he is *God and not man*, that he is justly entitled to the appellation of *the Highest*, because he *is kind unto the unthankful, and the evil* †.

INGRATITUDE is a sin eminently chargeable even against the children of God. It is far less surprising that this should be the character of those who acknowledge such a father as Satan, who, instead of eternally glorifying God for the honour of being made an angel of light, by his ingratitude and ambition transformed himself into an angel of darkness; than that they, who are children of the Father of mercies, and themselves the children of so many mercies, should so often *requite him like a foolish people, and unwise*. When they are anxious for any mercy, they resolve, and perhaps solemnly vow, that if God will be pleased to bestow it, they will ever retain a grateful sense of his kindness. He condescends to grant their request. But often they *remember not the multitude of his mercies, but provoke him*, like his ancient people, *at the sea, even at the Red Sea* ‡. This was the great aggravation of the sin of the Israelites, that it was committed *even at the Red Sea*. These words refer to the signal evidence of their unbelief, not after they had passed through the sea, but before they had entered it. For *when Pharaoh drew nigh— the children of Israel cried unto the Lord. And they said unto Moses, Because there were no graves in Egypt, hast thou taken us away to die in the wilderness* §. But a day or two before, the Lord had delivered them from their bondage, by a multitude of miracles.

---

* Psal. lxix. 15.   † Luke vi. 35.   ‡ Psal. cvi. 7.
§ Exod. xiv. 10,—12.

miracles. Yet, instead of remembering his mercies for a long time after, they immediately provoked him by their unbelief. Thus, his people, even when asking renewed deliverances, often forget those that they have formerly, and perhaps recently received. We have a striking example of the natural ingratitude of the heart towards God, in the history of the ten lepers whom Christ cleansed. He improves their conduct for the instruction of those that were present, by proposing a question; and alas! is there not too much reason to propose the same to the bulk of Christians? *Were there not ten cleansed; but where are the nine* *? Such conduct displays the great treachery of the heart, both with respect to God and ourselves. The heart deceives itself. When we earnestly desire any mercy, we flatter ourselves that we will receive and improve it with thanksgiving. The heart also deals deceitfully with God; for it forgets him, as soon as the mercy is received. Therefore, he proclaims ingratitude to be an evidence of the basest treachery: *I said, How shall I put thee among the children, and give thee the pleasant land, the goodly heritage of the hosts*, or multitude *of nations? And I said, Thou shalt call me, My Father, and shalt not turn away from me.* Then it follows: *Surely, as a wife treacherously departeth from her husband, so have ye dealt treacherously with me, O house of Israel* †. This conduct towards our gracious Benefactor is productive of bitter consequences. Our ingratitude for mercies received often provokes him to deny us others, which he would otherwise bestow, sometimes to recal those already given, and frequently to blast them in the enjoyment. *Therefore*, saith the Lord to his unthankful people, *I will return, and take away my corn in the time thereof, and my wine in the season thereof* ‡. And again; *But this people hath a revolting, and a rebellious heart, they are revolted and gone. Neither say they in their heart, Let us now fear the Lord our God, who giveth rain, both the former and the latter in his season: he reserveth unto us the appointed*

---

* Luke xvii. 17.   † Jer. iii. 19, 20.   ‡ Hos. ii 9.

pointed weeks of the harvest. Your iniquities have turned away these things, and your sins have withholden good things from you.

2. By disposing us to make a *God* of our mercies. The deceitfulness of the heart, so violent is its opposition to the living God, works by contraries, and often by extremes. If it do not tempt us to despise his mercies altogether, it will excite us to put them out of their proper place. By either of these methods, although directly opposite, it gains its wicked purpose, in making us forget the *God of* our *mercy*. Often do Christians give that room in their hearts to the gift, whether spiritual or temporal, which they ought to reserve for the great Giver. The mercy itself is more the object of their desire and delight, than the sanctified use of it. The perfidious heart easily makes the transition from a supposed thankfulness to the Benefactor, to an overvalue for the benefit. We are apt to suffer this adoration of Divine mercies to steal in upon us, by falsely viewing it as an evidence of our gratitude †. We perceive that the

---

* Jer. v. 23,—25.

† THAT idolatry, which seems to have a just, though inglorious claim to the highest antiquity, originated in all probability from an abuse of Divine mercies, proceeding from a false notion of gratitude. Men, whose wandering life required attention to the ordinances of heaven, at the same time affording abundance of time for it, and whose unclouded sky invited them to this agreeable employment; impressed with a sense of the unspeakable utility of the heavenly bodies, and especially of the sun, might at first flatter themselves that they only testified their gratitude to God, when they darted a look of veneration to this glorious creature. Hence the transition was extremely easy to some external token of respect, such as that which Job speaks of ; *If I beheld the sun when it shined, or the moon walking in brightness, and my heart hath been secretly enticed, or my mouth hath kissed my hand*. Chap. xxxi. 26.—28. Yet after all, they might not think with him, that if they had done so, they had *denied the God that is above*. By habituating themselves to this practice, which seems to have been one of the earliest modes of adoration, and from which, indeed, the very word is borrowed, they would soon avowedly *worship the creature more than the Creator*, address the sun as itself the proper object of worship, and even transfer their worship to fire as its most natural emblem.

the one extreme of undervaluing the tokens of God's love, is highly dishonouring to him; and, from an anxiety to avoid it, rush into the other, and immoderately set our hearts upon them. Endeavouring to avoid one evil, we plunge into another, equally dangerous to ourselves and offensive to God. For he is so provoked by his own people, that he often takes away the mercy altogether, or turns it into a cross; so that its continuance gives them more pain than ever the prospect, or the enjoyment of it gave them pleasure. Though he withdraw not the mercy, he frequently changes its nature. He will suffer no rival in thy heart, O Christian, for it all belongs to h:m; and when thy love to worldly comforts ceases to be secondary and subordinate, it is an encroachment on his prerogative. Therefore, must the usurper of the throne of God be cast down, that *in all things he may have the pre-eminence.* When precious comforts are thus converted into severe crosses, how great is the trial! There is a double bitterness attending it; not only that of the distress presently felt, but the painful recollection of the happiness formerly enjoyed. The history of Rachel, the beloved wife of Jacob, affords us an instance of the danger of an overweaning attachment to any temporal blessing, whether desired or received. So anxious was she for children, that she said to her husband; *Give me children, else I die;* as if he had been to her, *in God's stead, who had withheld from her the fruit of the womb.* But the greatness of her sin was declared by the severity of her suffering. For that very event which she so ardently desired as her chief mercy, and on which she so unlawfully set her heart, proved, in the righteous dispensation of God, the occasion of her bitter affliction and untimely death. She fell a sacrifice to that temporal mercy which she idolised*. Agreeably to her experience, the comfort, which the Christian immoderately values, often becomes his *Benoni,* the son of his sorrow, and the cause of his suffering.

* Gen. xxx. 1, xxxv. 16.—18.

WE have given an example of a mercy sinfully desired; and we may add another with respect to one received, but abused. Eli was a saint of God; but his great sin seems to have been an inordinate love to his children, which carried him so far, that rather than be severe to them, he would openly neglect his duty to God. Although his sons were *men of Belial*, yet he only rebuked them gently for their enormous wickedness, saying; *Why do ye such things* *? But the Lord who had anointed him to the priesthood, smote him in this very mercy, that was the occasion of unfaithfulness in his service. He said to him, *Wherefore kick ye at my sacrifice, and at mine offering, which I have commanded in my habitation, and honourest thy sons above me, to make yourselves fat with the chiefest of all the offerings of Israel my people?—Behold! the days come, that I will cut off thine arm, and the arm of thy father's house, that there shall not be an old man in thine house.—And this shall be a sign unto thee, that shall come upon thy two sons, upon Hophni and Phinehas: in one day they shall die both of them* †. In the word, God often reveals himself under the character of a jealous God. He is very jealous of his honour, and will discover it by the severe chastisement of his own children, when they turn their hearts away from him, and fix them on any thing else. Therefore, he saith; *Behold I have refined thee, but not with silver; I have chosen thee in the furnace of affliction. For mine own sake, even for mine own sake will I do it. For how should my name be polluted? and I will not give my glory unto another* ‡.

3. BY *consuming* Divine mercies on *lust*. *The wicked ask, that they may consume it on their lusts* §. They neither desire mercies, nor improve those which are bestowed, for the glory of God; but only as making provision for their inordinate or unlawful affections. This iniquity God charges against the Israelites. That *corn and wine, and oil, and silver, and gold*, which he gave

---

* 1 Sam. ii. 12. 23.   † Ver. 31. 34.   ‡ Isa. xlviii. 10, 11.
§ Jam. iv. 3.

gave them, they *prepared for Baal**. The blessings, which he hath bountifully bestowed, are often devoted to the pride of our own hearts. We find ourselves in possession of these, and we forget the God who gave them. Like Jeshurun when we have *waxed fat* with mercies, we are ready to *kick*, to *forsake God that made* us, and *lightly to esteem the Rock of our Salvation. Of the Rock that begat* us we are *unmindful, and we forget God that formed* us †. This iniquity is especially dishonouring to God, when chargeable against those, who in profession are his children: as Moses adds in that song, of which the preceding words are a part; *When the Lord saw it, he abhorred them, because of the provoking of his sons, and of his daughters.* This conduct he ascribes to their unfaithfulness and deceit. *For they are a very froward generation, children in whom is no faith;* that is, in whom is no truth, persons who cannot be depended on, who are full of perfidy. The same thing is asserted in the words of our text; *The pride of thine heart hath deceived thee.* By reason of outward prosperity, the deceitfulness of the heart wrought by the lust of pride. How often is it seen, that those who showed a great regard for the duties of religion, when in mean or narrow circumstances as to the world, seem to think them unworthy of their attention when they attain to greatness or affluence. *The ax boasts itself against him that heweth therewith; the saw magnifies itself against him that shaketh it; the rod shakes itself against him that lifteth it up; and the staff lifts up itself, as if it were no wood* ‡. When men discover such ingratitude towards the God of their mercies, and make him the butt of their pride, it is nowise surprising that they should extend it towards their fellow-men. *Their strength is firm. They are not in trouble as other men: neither are they plagued like other men. Therefore pride compasseth them about as a chain: violence covereth them as a garment* §. We are in dan-

Vol. I.   E e e   ger

* Hof. ii. 8. † Deut. xxxii. 15. 18. ‡ Isa. x. 15. § Ps. lxxiii. 4.—6.

ger of confuming the mercies of God on our carnal appetite, like the Ifraelites in another inftance: *They did eat, and were filled ;—they were not eftranged from their luft.* When men continue to confume his benefits in this manner, he is fometimes provoked to confume them in his anger: *Therefore their days he did confume in vanity, and their years in trouble* *.

4. By afcribing their profperity to fome other caufe than *God.* His ancient people took that corn, and wine, and oil, which he had given them, and not only *prepared* them *for Baal,* but afcribed them to him. So far were they from improving them to his glory, that they did not even acknowledge him as the Giver. It is the language of the finner; *I will go after my lovers, that give me my bread and my water, my wool and my flax, mine oil and my drink* †. When the Lord fmiles on the work of his hands, and gives him abundance of the good things of this life, he afcribes all to his own induftry. He *fays in* his *heart, My power and the might of my hand have gotten me all this wealth* ‡. Perhaps he attributes the bleffings received to his very lufts, to the fuccefs of his covetoufnefs, or of his ambition. Thus did the vain-glorious Sennacherib. He was only *the rod of* God's *anger,* and *the ftaff in* his *hand* was God's indignation; yet we find him uttering this prefumptuous language: *By the ftrength of my hand I have done it, and by my wifdom; for I am prudent: and I have removed the bounds of the people, and have robbed their treafures, and I have put down the inhabitants like a valiant man* §. Even the Lord's people, from the prevalence of deceit, are in great danger of afcribing their mercies to fome other caufe than God, or to fomething befides him. They will not wholly deny the praife to the God of their Salvation; but they do not afcribe it entirely to him. When they receive fignal mercies from him, they are apt to imagine that thefe are in fome degree deferved by their holinefs and integrity of converfation; that

he

---

* Pf. lxxviii. 29.—33.   † Hof. ii. 5.   ‡ Deut. viii. 17.
§ Ifa. x. 5. 13. 15.

he could not juftly deny them fuch tokens of his favour, when they are fo faithful and diligent in his fervice. He often, indeed, confers their mercies in fuch a manner, as to exclude every appearance of any hand but his own; as altogether to *caft out boafting:* but legality fhuts its eye againft all thefe evidences, and claims a fhare of the praife with God. His language to a profeffing people, applies, alas! too frequently to his own children: *I have even from the beginning declared it unto thee; before it came to pafs I fhewed it thee; left thou fhouldeft fay, Mine idol hath done them, and my graven image and my molten image hath commanded them.—Yea, thou heardeft not, yea, thou kneweft not, yea, from that time that thine ear was not opened: for I knew that thou wouldeft deal very treacheroufly, and waft called a tranfgreffor from the womb* *.

5. By *denying* God the ufe of thofe mercies which he hath himfelf beftowed. When, in the courfe of his providence, he confers on one a greater portion of common bleffings than on another; it is for this end, that he may ufe them for his glory, and in the manner of laying them out, return them to the Lord. No talent is to be *laid up in a napkin*. According to the meafure of temporal benefits received from God, we are ftewards for him. He allows us to take the lawful ufe of them; but forbids us to confine them to ourfelves. It is ftill his command, with refpect to all the mercies he confers; *Occupy till I come;—Caft thy bread upon the waters*. The good things of this life, which flow from his liberal hand, muft be devoted to God himfelf. Therefore, it is promifed; *I will confecrate their gain to the Lord, and their fubftance unto the Lord of the whole earth* †. But why *to the Lord of the whole earth?* This very character would feem to fet afide the force of the declaration. *Although* he *were hungry* he *would not tell* us, *for the world is* his, *and the fulnefs thereof.* Yet thofe things which we poffefs, however unworthy in themfelves, from the ftate of the Church,
and

* Ifa. xlviii. 5. 8.   † Mic. iv. 13.

and from the ordinary course of Providence, have such an importance conferred on them, that in infinite condescension the Lord declares, that he *hath need of them*. Not absolutely, for the reason already mentioned; but relatively, and according to circumstances; because it is his pleasure that the necessities of his Church should be supplied in this manner. To limit and regulate us in our expectations, the omnipotent God, in the general tenor of his conduct, deigns to make use of the intervention of means. To those who are rich in this world he gives the same commission as to the clouds, to distil their abundance more equally on those who are below them. He could easily at once disperse his treasures without their assistance. But it secures a greater return of gratitude, when in this way *the bowels of the saints are refreshed*, and when they are retained in constant dependence on him for their daily supplies.

WE are also to remember, that while in the good Providence of God we are blessed with fulness, many of our brethren of mankind are in danger of perishing for want. According to our ability we ought to supply them: and this, if done in faith, the Lord considers as done to himself. *He that giveth to the poor, lendeth to the Lord.* The poor of his people especially call for our love and sympathy. How earnest was the great Apostle of the Gentiles, in stirring up the Church to make liberal contributions for the poor saints at Jerusalem! By what a powerful argument does Christ enforce this duty! *Inasmuch as ye have done it unto the least of these my disciples, ye have done it unto me.* To this purpose is his injunction; *Make to yourselves friends of the mammon of unrighteousness, that when ye fail, they may receive you into everlasting habitations* *. He calls his hearers to lay out the riches of this world in acts of beneficence to the poor, and especially his poor; as in this manner the saints, who have been refreshed by them in their state of pilgrimage, will joyfully welcome them,

* Luke xvi. 9.

them, as their generous benefactors, into the manfions above. Not as if this liberality were meritorious of *everlafting habitations:* but when it proceeds from a fincere and believing heart, it is a certain evidence of a *right to enter in through the gates into the city.* He calls the good things of this life *the mammon of unrighteoufnefs,* not only becaufe they are often unjuftly acquired, but becaufe they are laid out in the fame manner, if we confider not God's end in giving them. But many deny thofe things to God, which his own bounty hath beftowed. Though they *have all things and abound,* they would efteem it prodigality to contribute any thing for the Church of Chrift, or for the poor of his people. But this is the way to provoke him to curfe their bleffings, or to remove them altogether. *There is that fcattereth and yet increafeth; and there is that withholdeth more than is meet, but it tendeth to poverty* *. David was convinced that his own liberality, and that of his fubjects, in contributing for building the temple, was only reftoring to God a fmall portion of what they had received from him. *O Lord our God, all this ftore, that we have prepared to build thee an houfe for thy holy name, cometh of thine own hand, and is all thy own* †.

6. By unfatisfied *defires* and immoderate *longings* for a *greater* degree of temporal profperity. When the heart hath tafted of mercies of this nature, it is not fatisfied; it craves more. If its defires be fulfilled, inftead of being content with thefe, it flatters itfelf, that if fuch another mercy were beftowed, it would afk nothing further. But this only argues its deceit; for even though this be granted, it is ftill as importunate as ever. The more it receives, its defires are enlivened and enlarged the more. The pleafures, the honours, and the riches of this world, which are all that it contains, are totally unfatisfying. The foul feels a want and emptinefs attending all fublunary pleafures, which renewed enjoyment can never fupply. The Ifraelites firft murmured for

---

* Prov. xi. 24.   † 1 Chron. xxix. 16.

for water. When they found this, they could not drink of it, becaufe it was bitter. When the bitter water was miraculoufly fweetened, they complained that they had no bread. When manna was rained from heaven about their tents, they lufted for flefh, and ardently longed to return to the pots of Egypt. So unfatisfying is worldly honour, that as we learn from profane hiftory, that Macedonian prince, who had no better right to be diftinguifhed from others by the flattering furname of *the Great*, than his bearing a greater refemblance to *the Deftroyer*, when he had over-run almoft all the kingdoms of the earth, like a torrent, fat down and wept, becaufe he had not another world to conquer. In regard to riches, we have the eftimate of Solomon. Defcribing the avaricious man, he fays; *There is no end of all his labour, neither is his eye fatisfied with riches; neither faith he, For whom do I labour, and bereave my foul of good* * *? He that loveth filver fhall not be fatisfied with filver, nor he that loveth abundance with increafe* †.

7. By *hardening* itfelf under profperity. No mercy whatfoever can leave us as it finds us. It muft either prove a bleffing or a curfe. It will either have a mollifying, or a hardening influence on our hearts. *The goodnefs of God*, manifefted in profperous difpenfations, will either be a mean of *leading* us *to repentance;* or by *defpifing the riches* thereof, *after our hardnefs and impenitent heart*, we will *treafure up to* ourfelves *wrath againft the day of wrath* ‡. The former, indeed, is the natural and direct tendency of all the mercies which we receive from our liberal Benefactor: but accidentally, through the depravity of human nature, the latter is alas! by far the moft ordinary confequence. Thofe mercies that the wicked receive from God are attended by his curfe, which deprives them of the very nature of mercies: and inftead of being improved as means of repentance, they prove to them occafions of hardening. Becaufe Providence fmiles on them, they either deny a Providence

* Ecclef. iv. 8. † Ecclef. v. 10. ‡ Rom. ii. 4, 5.

vidence altogether, or perfuade themfelves that God is by no means difpleafed with their iniquities. *Becaufe judgment is not executed againft* their *evil works fpeedily*, their *hearts are fully fet in them to do evil*. Even this may be in part verified as to the children of God, when in a ftate of declenfion. They cannot, indeed, by the abufe of mercies, *treafure up* to themfelves vindictive *wrath;* but they often fubject themfelves to fatherly anger. Often, as a fevere chaftifement for their fins, he fuffers them to be greatly hardened under mercies.— Thofe of a *temporal* nature prove occafions of partial obduracy. The mercies and deliverances, which the Lord granted to that godly king Jehofaphat, feem to have hardened his heart in fome meafure: for he joined himfelf with Ahaziah king of Ifrael, who *did very wickedly*. Therefore God fent a prophet to inform him, that he had *broken his works**. Spiritual mercies are alfo fometimes abufed as an occafion of obduracy. Their gofpel-privileges and enjoyments, nay, their higheft fpiritual attainments may be proftituted by the corruption within them, for turning away their hearts from God. Peter had not only received many diftinguifhing evidences of his Mafter's approbation in the commendation of his faith, but had recently been admitted to participate of the fymbols of his body and blood; and had his feet wafhed by his condefcending Lord: yet thefe very pledges of love the deceitfulnefs of his heart abufed, as an occafion of awakening pride and felf-confidence. Therefore, he infifted, that though all the difciples, and even *all men fhould deny* Chrift, yet he would not deny him; nay, that though he fhould die with him, he would not deny him.

THEREFORE, ye carelefs ones, ye *who are at eafe in Zion*, confider that you do not, you cannot receive God's mercies in vain. To you they muft either prove a real bleffing or a dreadful curfe.— While you continue eftranged from Chrift, all your bleffings

---

* 2 Chron. xx. 36, 37.

blessings are curses to you. They are so in the mean time. For you receive no mercy from God as a Father. To this you have forfeited all your title by sin. All the temporal kindnesses bestowed proceed from him as a judge, who sustains the condemned criminal till the sentence be either executed or relaxed. They come not to you under the banner of the Covenant of Grace, but under the maledictory sentence of the Covenant of Works. You are *cursed in your basket, and in your store ; in your lying down, and in your rising up.* They also prove curses to you eventually. Instead of tracing up the streams of creature-comforts to the only fountain of true and lasting blessedness ; you convert them into *the bitter water that causeth the curse,* by suffering yourselves to be hurried away by them towards *the lake that burneth for ever and ever.* For you abuse them as the instruments of fulfilling your wicked desires, as occasions of turning you farther away from God. So dreadfully do you pervert common mercies from their original design, that *the whole creation* is represented as *groaning and travailing in pain* under the load of your iniquity. That curse, which springs out of the blessing, by the abuse of it, is of all the most bitter ; as by this conduct you offer the highest insult to him, who *supplieth the wants of every thing that liveth.* Be assured, that all these mercies shall rise up in judgment against you, and, if you continue in this miserable state, greatly aggravate your condemnation. Embrace God, therefore, while he *waiteth to be gracious.* Embrace him as *the God of* your *mercy* through his beloved Son, as he offers himself to you in the gospel. Then all your mercies will be sanctified, and come to you as tokens of his parental love, and preludes of the eternal fruits of it.

As for you, my brethren, who have chosen God to be your portion ; it is your incumbent duty to retain his mercies fresh in your memories, to have them engraved on your hearts. There is no merit in your gratitude. It cannot entitle you to future mercies. But this is the path of duty, in which, by the moſt indiſpenſable obligations, you are bound to walk. Give him all the glory of what mercies ſoever you receive: ſaying, *Bleſs the Lord, O my ſoul, and all that is within me, be ſtirred up to bleſs his holy name.* Put them not in the place of God to you, elſe you will *provoke him to jealouſy.* Depending on his grace, let it be your conſtant aim to improve your time, your health, your riches, your abilities, your goſpel-privileges, your all for his glory. *Bleſſed is that ſervant, whom, when his maſter cometh, he ſhall find ſo doing.* He will ſay unto him, *Well done, good and faithful ſervant, enter thou into the joy of thy Lord.* Let your deſires be regulated according to God's word, with reſpect to temporal enjoyments. You have no title to aſk more than what Chriſt hath pointed out in that form of prayer which he taught his diſciples: *Give us this day our daily bread.*— Labour, eſpecially *for that meat which periſheth not*, for the *daily bread* of your ſouls. Let it be your continual deſire to feed by faith on *the bread of life.* Here it is warrantable for you to have enlarged and unſatisfied deſires; and the boundleſs capacity of the ſoul in this reſpect was given it for no other purpoſe. It was framed with this faculty of unlimited craving, juſt that it might be filled with an infinite God. Nor will he fruſtrate ſuch deſires. For *he filleth the hungry with good things. The liberal ſoul deviſeth liberally, and by liberal things ſhall he ſtand. Bleſſed are they that hunger and thirſt after righteouſneſs; for they ſhall be filled.*

SERMON XXII.

On the DECEITFULNESS of the HEART, with respect to ADVERSITY.

ISAIAH lvii. 17.

——*I smote him: I hid me and was wroth; and he went on frowardly in the way of his own heart.*

IN this verse we have an account of God's displeasure with Israel. To denote the greatness of it, the same expression is twice used;—*I was wroth.* The cause is also assigned, which was *the iniquity of his covetousness.* With this sin God's ancient people were eminently chargeable. We have one instance mentioned in the context. With respect to the watchmen of Israel, it is said, chap. lvi. 11. *They are greedy dogs which can never have enough.* The effect of Divine indignation is likewise declared; *I smote him; I hid me.* While these words express the manner in which God deals with his own children, by withdrawing his gracious presence from them; as respecting his professing people in general, they seem literally to refer to some severe temporal calamity. He *smote* them by *hiding* his face. He withdrew his protection from them, and they became a prey to their enemies. But what was the consequence?
Did

Did Israel return to the Lord? Far from it. Afflictions, of themselves, will never produce this effect. *He went on frowardly in the way of his own heart.* He persisted obstinately, perversely, or rebelliously. Literally, *he went on like a vagabond,* in courses of error and self-deceit; the very curse of Cain. He continued under an evil counsellor, and in a wicked way;—*after the way of his own heart.*

Having formerly illustrated the deceitfulness of the heart in the abuse of prosperity, all that we propose from these words is, to consider it with respect to adversity.

1. This sometimes appears by *despising* afflictions. Many attempt to outbrave calamity, as if they were stronger than God. Therefore saith the Apostle; *Ye have forgotten the exhortation which speaketh unto you as unto children, My son, despise not thou the chastening of the Lord**. Those may be said to *despise* his *chastening,* who account it a small matter, who from a principle of pride and presumption think it unworthy of them to seem affected with it, or refuse to *turn to the hand that smiteth.* Many, when they feel affliction taking hold of their spirits, as well as of their bodies, and awakening them to a concern about their state, deem it entirely inconsistent with the dignity of their characters to suffer this to appear, or even to indulge it within themselves; and are affronted at the idea of being in any degree afraid to make their appearance before the awful and impartial tribunal. We despise affliction, when we ascribe it merely to natural causes. In bodily distress, or any outward adversity, whether affecting our persons, our characters, or our substance, we may generally allow the concurrence of these. But if our views extend no farther, we undoubtedly *despise the chastening of the Lord.* For whatever may be the instrumentality of natural causes, we may be assured that there is a superior, a divine agency.— Though God may employ these as the immediate means of affliction; yet these very means are under his

* Heb. xii. 5. Prov. iii. 11.

his direction, and only accomplish his purposes. In all the adversities that befal us, he hath still a supreme and over-ruling hand. *Affliction cometh not forth of the dust, neither doth trouble spring out of the ground**. These figurative expressions are used to represent, in a striking manner, the absurdity of viewing affliction as if it proceeded solely from natural causes, as if it grew up like an herb of the field, a spontaneous production of nature, without any care of the husbandman. Elsewhere the Spirit of God exhibits the same conduct, in viewing adversity as if it were entirely accidental, in a ridiculous point of light, by comparing it with other things, which either to do, or to imagine, would argue the greatest folly. *Will a lion roar in the forest, when he hath no prey? Will a young lion cry out of his den, if he hath taken nothing? Can a bird fall in a snare upon the earth, where no gin is for him? Shall one take up a snare from the earth, and have taken nothing at all? Shall a trumpet be blown in the city, and the people not be afraid? Shall there be evil in a city, and the Lord hath not done it* †? The evil of affliction or punishment is here meant: and these questions proposed by God himself, declare, not only that where this natural evil is, it always proceeds from him; but also, that those despise it who perceive not, or *consider not the operation of his hand.* He either evidently employs means in laying on affliction, or sends it without any obvious intervention of means, or directly counteracts them altogether. We may give you an undeniable illustration of this, which will be confirmed by the observation of almost every thinking person. Have you not often seen that those, who, especially when afraid of an infectious disorder, have taken every possible precaution to avoid it, and have gone so far as to throw off natural affection, by leaving their nearest and dearest relations while in affliction, have eventually found that all their labour and anxiety were in vain? While flying from their

indispensable

---

* Job v. 6. † Amos iii. 4,—6.

indispensable duty to others, they have themselves been arrested by affliction: whereas those, on the other hand, who in obedience to the call of Providence, have put their lives in God's hand, endeavoured to discharge their duty, and discovered no undue anxiety, have been preserved in a surprising manner from any injury whatever. Is not this an evidence, that whatever be the instrumentality of natural means, it is all derived from the over-ruling hand of God; and that they are so far from being absolutely necessary as the immediate occasions of affliction, that he can at pleasure directly counteract their operation?

AGAIN, we despise affliction, if we consider not its origin, which is the corruption of our whole nature by sin. Hence it is that all adversity primarily springs: for without sin there could be no suffering. The words formerly mentioned may in their connection be considered as an illustration of this: *Although affliction cometh not forth of the dust, neither doth trouble spring out of the ground; yet man is born unto trouble, as the sparks fly upwards**: that is, "Though "man himself be indeed a creature of the dust, "formed out of the ground, and possessed of a mor- "tal body; yet we are not to apprehend that his "origin as a creature is the cause of his suffering, "that *affliction* hath *come forth of the dust* with him- "self, or that the troubles to which he is exposed, "arise, as some heretics maintain, from the natural "weakness of his frame, because his body is com- "posed of gross matter; but to view these as occa- "sioned by that corruption diffused through his na- "ture, by disobedience to God and breach of cove- "nant with him. Man is indeed *born unto trouble;* "but this proceeds not from any necessary or in- "herent infirmity in his original constitution, but "from his being born a sinner." For without sin, the body of man, though material, and so corruptible, would have been preserved by the hand of Omnipotence

* Job v. 6, 7.

tence from affliction and death, from every symptom of actual corruption. This interpretation is confirmed by a review of the context, and by connecting this passage with what is declared in the close of the preceding chapter; where men are said to *dwell in houses of clay,* to have their *foundation* also in *the dust,* and to be so feeble as to be *crushed before the moth* *. Now, the words formerly mentioned may be viewed as illustrating these. "Though his founda-
" tion be in the dust, yet it is not on account of this
" that he is subject to trouble; but because his founda-
" tion hath been weakened and destroyed by the
" entrance of sin." It is therefore highly necessary that we should trace up affliction to its source, and humbly confess that we were *shapen in iniquity and conceived in sin.*

Adversity is also despised, when the subjects of it do not consider the more immediate cause of it, which is the anger of God because of sin, and confess with Moses *the man of God; We are consumed by thine anger, and by thy wrath are we troubled* †. The Lord may, indeed, in sovereignty visit his own children with the rod, without any immediate procuring cause on their part. But it is still the safest course for us to view our iniquities as the reason of his contending; because there is always too much ground for it: and it is only *of the Lord's mercies that we are not consumed.* It is, therefore, our duty under affliction, of what nature soever, to review our hearts and lives, to search out our sins, and particularly to make a diligent inquiry about those which may be the immediate causes of provocation.

Further, affliction is despised, if we do not consider the design of it. The end which God proposes in his word, is thereby to discover to us our sins, and turn us from them to himself. *If they be bound in fetters, and holden in the cords of affliction; then he sheweth them their work, and their transgressions that they have exceeded. He openeth also their ear to discipline, and com-*
mandeth

* Job iv. 19. † Psal. xc. 7.

mandeth that they return from iniquity *. In a word, *the chastening of the Lord* is despised, when those who are under it seek not unto him. Many are so careless and obdurate under affliction, that they will not even apply to him for deliverance : and this contempt of the rod, especially as discovered by unwillingness to call upon God, is pointed out as a fruit and evidence of the hypocrisy or deceitfulness of the heart ; *The hypocrites in heart heap up wrath ; they cry not when God bindeth them* †.

2. By *repining* under adversity. In the exhortation mentioned by the Apostle, it is not merely said ; *My son, despise not thou the chastening of the Lord ;* but added ; *Neither faint when thou art rebuked of him ;* or as it is in the Old Testament, *Neither be weary of his correction.* Persons repine under affliction, if they spurn at it ; if, like Ephraim, they are *as a bullock unaccustomed to the yoke* ; if they kick and throw at providential dispensations, like an untamed bullock that has not been used to labour.—A fretful spirit is discovered, when we are apt to account God unjust in afflicting us. Often men make no other improvement of a discovery of affliction as proceeding from God, than to accuse him of severity ; as if *the Judge of the whole earth* would not *do right.* They are ready to say, like the wicked Cain ; *My punishment is greater than I can bear.* They compare their sins and sufferings together, and instead of acknowledging that *after all that is come upon them, for* their *evil deeds and for* their *great trespass,* God hath *punished* them *less than* their *iniquities deserve* ‡ ; they see their sins in so diminishing a light, that they are in danger of apprehending that their punishment exceeds their desert. Indeed, we may be assured that we are never delivered from a fretful disposition under adverse dispensations, unless we are not only preserved from reckoning God unjust, but enabled positively to justify him in the whole of his conduct towards us ; unless we cordially join with Daniel in his confession ; *O Lord, righteousness belongeth*

unto

---

* Job xxxvi. 8.—10.   † Job xxxvi. 13.   ‡ Ezra ix. 13.

unto thee, but unto us confusion of faces, as at this day*. Till we cheerfully exculpate God, and charge all the blame to our own iniquity, we are never properly delivered from repining. You may not absolutely proceed so far in presumption, as in words to accuse God; but it is undeniable that you still do so in heart, till you be brought expressly to justify the whole of his conduct, and to say in sincerity of soul; *He is the rock, his work is perfect; for all his ways are judgment; a God of truth, and without iniquity; just and right is he* †. *The Lord is righteous in all his ways, and holy in all his works* ‡.—Under adversity we also faint and repine, unless we exercise faith with respect to God's wise and holy ends, and as to a blessed termination of it. If we yield to dejection and unbelief, it is a certain evidence that we are fretful under his chastening hand.—The case is the same, if we be not brought to resignation, and made to say; *Good is the will of the Lord.* If we do not commit ourselves into his hand, and resign ourselves wholly to his disposal, we assuredly fret at his dispensations.— The same thing may be observed with respect to patience. This differs from resignation; as the latter denotes a present submission of ourselves to the divine will, and the former, a waiting God's time. Resignation respects our present exercise under the rod; patience—our expectation of deliverance from it in such a season and manner as shall be for the glory of God. Now, a fretful spirit under adversity is a sad discovery of inward deceitfulness; for it shows, that our hearts would lead us to renounce God and refuse subjection to him. Can any thing be a greater evidence of deceit, than for vain man to imagine that he hath a right boldly to inquire of God the reasons of his conduct? *Shall the clay say to him that fashioneth it, What makest thou? or thy work, He hath no hands?*

3. By keeping *death* at a *distance*, if the affliction be of a bodily kind. The corrupt heart still presents the same deceit to us, wherewith Satan at first entangled

* Dan. ix. 7. † Deut. xxxii. 4. ‡ Psal. cxlv. 17.

tangled our firſt parents: *Ye ſhall not ſurely die.* And this is a ſuggeſtion to which we are extremely willing to liſten. Though death is the end of all afflictions, though every affliction, nay, every infirmity, every pang, however tranſient, is a prelude of our approaching exit, and a warning to prepare for it; yet men are ſtill difpoſed to flatter themſelves with hopes of life, how little ground ſoever there be for ſuch expectations from the nature or courſe of the difeaſe. You will often ſee a man in the very graſp of *the king of terrors*, when phyſicians and friends have renounced all hope, ſtill deluding himſelf with the pleaſing expectation of overcoming the power of his malady. Can this be accounted for, without reſolving it into the ſuperlative deceitfulneſs of the heart? But on this we enlarge not, as we have ſpoken a little of it already, on a former branch of this ſubject.

4. By forming empty *reſolutions* of *repentance* and *reformation,* while under affliction. Many in trouble aſſume an air of penitence, of whom it may be ſaid in the days of proſperity, that *God is not in all their thoughts.* When *the valley of the ſhadow of death* begins to open, in its unſpeakable terrors, on the ſinner's view, when he hath the proſpect of making an immediate appearance before the Judge of the univerſe, while at the ſame time his ſins ſtare him in the face, and he is *made to poſſeſs the iniquities of* his *youth;* he promiſes to himſelf, to God, and to others, that if his life be mercifully ſpared, he will become quite a new man, renounce the wicked courſes to which he hath been addicted, and ſet his heart on the ways of God. But the removal of the rod ſo frequently demonſtrates the vanity of theſe reſolutions, that death-bed repentance is become a proverbial phraſe, for expreſſing any thing on which there can be very little dependence. No ſooner are many ſuch penitents reſtored to health and ſtrength, than they forget all the reſolutions, vows and engagements made in the time

of affliction; nay, perhaps blush at the recollection of them, and are affronted that their acquaintance should know such instances of their weakness: and to remove from their minds, as far as possible, every injurious idea of their being serious in these, they will afford them the most certain evidence of the contrary, by plunging deeper than ever into the mire of iniquity. If these resolutions at any time hang heavy on their minds, they strive to lighten the burden by using every mean to harden conscience, obliterate the memory of the past, and debar any apprehensions of the future. In a word, they do all in their power to fly from themselves. As for the ministers or christians, whose instructions, exhortations and prayers they have earnestly solicited when in affliction, after their recovery they know them not. Perhaps, the very sight of them gives an edge to conscience and memory, which they wish eternally blunted.

Now, whence is it that these resolutions, made in the time of trouble, appear so transitory and ineffectual? The reason is, that they have proceeded from a deceived, and a self-deceiving heart. They have all been made in a dependence on their own strength. The work has been by no means thorough; and therefore it has no duration. Though in some measure convinced of sin, as to its dangerous consequences; they have had no discovery of its evil nature; of its abominable impurity, as committed against a God of infinite holiness; or unspeakable wickedness, as opposed to a God of infinite love. They have never seen the necessity of being *born again of the Spirit*, of being really *renewed in the Spirit of* their *mind*. They have not been *in an agony to enter in at the strait gate;* and there is little wonder though they be afterwards nowise concerned to walk in *the narrow way* of evangelical holiness. Notwithstanding all their bustle about eternal life, they have been satisfied to retain *the old man*, with all his lusts. Therefore, he breaks out in their conversation, with all his deeds.

5. By

5. By exciting men to *make lies their refuge*. The deceitful heart prompts them to truſt in earthly means for deliverance from affliction, in the power of medicine and human aſſiſtance. But alas! this is a falſe confidence; for *vain is the help of man*. All means muſt be ineffectual, unleſs the Lord be pleaſed to bleſs them. But many entirely depend on the means, and vainly flatter themſelves with hopes, becauſe of their efficacy in other caſes. Alluding to ſuch conduct as this, the Lord deſcribes the folly of his ancient people in the following manner; *When Ephraim ſaw his ſickneſs, and Judah ſaw his wound, then went Ephraim to the Aſſyrian, and ſent to king Jareb: yet could he not heal you, nor cure you of your wound**. Even that good king, Aſa, provoked the Lord by his falſe confidence in adverſity, in two different inſtances. With reſpect to the firſt, we are told that Hanani the ſeer came to him and ſaid; *Becauſe thou haſt relied on the king of Syria, and not relied on the Lord thy God, therefore is the hoſt of the king of Syria eſcaped out of thine hand*. And afterwards, when under bodily affliction, *in his diſeaſe he ſought not to the Lord, but to the phyſicians* †. If the affliction which perſons are under is not of a bodily kind, or does not immediately affect their health and ſtrength: they often fly to their wicked companions, that they may drown their cares in drunkenneſs and debauchery. *Let us eat and drink, for to-morrow we die.* Or they betake themſelves to diverſions; like Saul, who, when the evil ſpirit came upon him, called upon David to play on the harp, that he might chaſe him away. This courſe many take to lull or chaſe away convictions, or diſpel their grief for worldly loſſes. This evil ſpirit that haunts them, they try to baniſh by amuſements.—We do not here ſpeak of the many lying refuges of a ſpiritual kind, to which ſinners reſort under adverſity, becauſe we have conſidered ſeveral of theſe already. Only in general it may be obſerved, that when they find the vanity of all human applications,

---

* Hoſ. v. 13.   † 2 Chron. xvi. 7.—12.

tions, and all their earthly hopes to be *as the giving up of the ghost*, they will even apply to God for deliverance. Nay, through the force of education, instruction, or an awakened conscience, they may pretend to fly to Christ. But this is by no means matter of choice with them, but of dire necessity. They see, perhaps, that they have no time left for performing good works, for doing as much as in their apprehension might entitle them to eternal life. Therefore, rather than perish altogether, they prefer that way which alone seems to afford them any distant prospect of safety. They are on a bed of affliction, *tossed like a wild bull in a net*, being *full of the fury of the Lord, and of the rebuke of God* *. Therefore, from the constraining influence of terror, they will pretend to rely on Christ, though with far greater reluctance than one accustomed to *fare sumptuously every day*, would submit to feed on the husks of swine, merely to preserve himself from perishing. But though this be the only true refuge of the soul, it proves a false one to them; because they do not embrace it with the heart. Perhaps, they secretly despise Christ and his righteousness, and are so unwilling to be eternally indebted to sovereign grace for salvation, that nothing but the overwhelming fear of hell would make them yield for a moment to so humiliating a claim.

OTHERS, it may be, are rationally convinced of the necessity of his all-perfect righteousness, for answering the demands of law and justice; but they cannot submit to him as a complete Saviour. They would joyfully embrace him as a Priest, to save them from *the wrath to come*; but they cannot acknowledge him as a King, to deliver them from sin the cause of it, and from *this present evil world*. The Christ, whom they pretend to receive, is indeed a false refuge. He is not that *deliverer come out of Sion, to turn away ungodliness*. He is not that all-sufficient Redeemer, *who of God is made unto us wisdom, righteousness, sanctification and redemption*.—It is with regard to such false supplicants

* Isa. li. 20.

plicants that the Lord declares; *They have not cried unto me with their heart, when they howled upon their beds* *. Perhaps, they have cried loud enough with the voice. But in all their crying he difcerns not the voice of children, but compares it to the howling of wild beafts; becaufe the exercife of the heart is wanting. And indeed, what important difference is there between the cry of a rational, and that of a brute creature, if the rational part be not engaged. As long as he is in this fituation, like Nebuchadnezzar when driven from his kingdom, *his heart is changed from man's, and a beaft's heart is given unto him* †. But the great want in this religion of neceffity, is not only perceived by the Searcher of hearts alone. It foon appears to all around. How aptly does the language of infpiration defcribe the fuddennefs of the finner's tranfition from hypocritical prayers to cordial debauchery : *They have not cried unto me with the heart, when they howled on their beds ; they affemble themfelves for corn and wine, and they rebel againft me.* The howlings of diftrefs are quickly overpowered by the howlings of drunkennefs. And the whole of this is afcribed to the deceitfulnefs of the heart ; *They return*— in their prayers they have profeffed and promifed to return ; and they do fo in their conduct ;—*but not to the Moft High.* It is only to their former wickednefs. *They are like a deceitful bow.* However much the bow may feem bent, how fair foever the aim may appear, they ftill fhoot wide of the pretended mark.

6. By making them *defpife means*. We have feen again and again, how the deceitfulnefs of the heart works by contraries, in its oppofition to God. If it prevail not with thofe under affliction to depend abfolutely on means, it will ftrenuoufly urge the total neglect of them. Many, when in trouble, reafon in this manner; " If my time be come; if it be
" determined that I am to die by this diftrefs ;
" then I may be certain that no means can pre-
" vent death : and if more time be allotted to me,
" I

* Hof. vii. 14.—16. † Dan. iv. 16.

"I shall recover whether I use them or not." But this discovers the greatest folly. With equal propriety might one in health reason thus ; " Since my days " are determined, I can neither die before my time " nor outlive it; therefore, I need neither eat, nor " drink, nor do any thing for the preservation of " life." But you ought to remember, that, in the decree, the means are appointed as certainly as the end ; and that the end can only be accomplished in connection with the appointed means. Therefore, they must not be separated, even in our apprehension, for a single moment. The use of means, in affliction, is often as necessary as the use of natural support, when we are in health. No means, indeed, can be of any efficacy, without the blessing of God. He often works without means, and sometimes in opposition to them. But it is still our duty to use them, humbly depending on his gracious influence. This is implied in the sixth precept of the moral law ; *Thou shalt not kill.* For it virtually requires of us the use of all lawful means for the preservation of life ; and prohibits the neglect of them, under the pain of being accounted by God chargeable with self-murder. When Hezekiah was in a dangerous disease, though the Lord had assured him of recovery, yet afterwards he commanded the use of certain means, in subserviency to the determined end. For *Isaiah said*, and undoubtedly it was by God's command ; *Let them take a lump of figs, and lay it for a plaister upon the boil ; and he shall recover* *. Though Paul had himself been assured by a Divine revelation, and had communicated this assurance to all who were in the ship, that not one of them should be lost ; yet when the mariners were about to take to the boat, he said to the centurion and soldiers ; *Except these abide in the ship, ye cannot be saved* †. Many, when they meet with worldly losses, are apt to be so overwhelmed, as to sit down listless and inactive, as if they were to use no means for obtaining redress. They are disposed

---

* Isa. xxxviii. 21.   † Acts xxvii. 22. 31.

posed to say; *Behold! this evil is of the Lord: why should I wait for the Lord any longer?*—Or, if they be in affliction about the state of their souls, under terrors of conscience, Satan and their own deceitfulness prompt them to despise the means which God hath appointed. " We have often used them," may they say, " and are none the better: and why should " we give ourselves any more trouble about them?" But, surely, there is no situation in which we can be, but it is still the safest course to *wait on the Lord*. We ought to wait on him, even *in the way of his judgments*.

7. By seeking *deliverance* from the affliction itself, rather than the *sanctified* use of it. This is a natural fruit of deceitfulness. For it wishes always to divert our eye from God's declared design in affliction, which is, *to take away sin*. We often find those who are strangers to prayer, crying to God in distress; but it is only for deliverance from this as an evil, without any sense of the necessity of deliverance from the evil of sin, or of the sanctification of the rod. *In their affliction*, saith the Lord, *they will seek me early**. But this exercise arises only from the severity of distress, or from the force of conviction. We have many instances of it in the history of the Israelites; *When he slew them, then they sought him, and they returned and enquired early after God.—Nevertheless, they did flatter him with their mouth, and they lied unto him with their tongues: For their heart was not right with him, neither were they stedfast in his covenant* †. Never, till the heart be affected by the gracious influence of the Spirit, will it sincerely pour forth that prayer; *Turn thou me, and I shall be turned; for thou art the Lord my God* ‡. The children of God themselves are too often, indeed, more concerned about deliverance from the rod, than about a blessing with it. The severity of the stroke, or rather the impatience of their hearts, makes them neglect the consideration of the Lord's love in afflicting them. Though he hath declared, that

---
* Hos. v. 15. † Ps. lxxviii. 34.—37. ‡ Jer. xxxi. 19.

that whom he *loveth he chafteneth, and fcourgeth every fon that he receiveth;* and that if we be *without chaftifement,* then are we *baftards and not fons;* yet the perfidious heart often dares to give God the lie, and infinuates that fevere affliction is a far more likely evidence of baftardy than of fonfhip. Thus, the gracious end which God hath always in view in afflicting them, that they may be *made meet to be partakers of his inheritance,* is often obfcured, if not wholly caft out of fight.

In the laft place, the heart difcovers its deceitfulnefs, by abufing adverfity, as an occafion of *hardening* itfelf againft God. Every afflictive difpenfation, in itfelf confidered, contains the language of mercy, even to finners. For it is *the Lord's voice,* calling them to repentance; and feconding his commands, invitations, entreaties and expoftulations, to this purpofe, in the Word. The greateft finner, under affliction, is welcome to claim the benefit of God's gracious promife; *By this fhall the iniquity of Jacob be purged, and this is all the fruit to take away his fin.* But by reafon of the lufts of men, this merciful tendency of the rod is often counteracted. God, in fovereignty, is pleafed to withhold his renewing grace, without which no means whatever will be profitable to falvation. The confequence is, that they continue in fin. Perhaps, he even withholds reftraining grace: and they being left to their own counfels, abufe affliction as an occafion of hardening. This was the cafe with Pharaoh. The more that God afflicted him, the more was his heart hardened. When he *faw that there was refpite, he hardened his heart, and hearkened* not unto Mofes and Aaron*. Similar to this, was the conduct of that very people whom God had delivered, at the expence of Pharaoh and all his hoft, according to the confeffion of Nehemiah: *Thou lefteft them in the hand of their enemies, fo that they had the dominion over them; and teftifiedft againft them, that thou mighteft bring them again unto thy law; yet they dealt proudly, and hearkened*

---

* Exod. viii. 15.—19.

hearkened not unto thy commandments, but sinned against thy judgments ;—and withdrew the shoulder, and hardened their neck, and would not hear*.

ADVERSITY, at times, hath in some measure this effect, even as to the children of God. When he visits them with judicial strokes, because of their iniquities, instead of being humbled under them, they are sometimes rather hardened. Or, if they seem affected in the mean time, as soon as the affliction is removed, they return to sin. Thus, in the words of our text, we have an account of Ephraim's conduct, under God's smiting hand; *He went on frowardly, in the way of his own heart.* These words may not only express the conduct of a backsliding people in general, but that even of real saints among them, when affliction is not attended with the Spirit's gracious influence. That they may be thus far extended, would seem from the gracious promise that follows; *I have seen his ways, and will heal him: I will lead him also, and restore comforts unto him, and to his mourners* †. We have a particular example of this in the conduct of good Asa. When reproved by Hanani the Prophet, for *not relying on the Lord,* and informed of his displeasure with him on this account, and of the evidence of it; so far was he from being humbled, that he *was wroth with the Seer, and put him in a prison-house; for he was in a rage with him, because of this thing. And he oppressed some of the people the same time.* Nay, he so far abused this testimony of the Divine displeasure, that he hardened himself still more. For it was after this, that in his disease he *sought not unto the Lord, but to the physicians* ‡. The Lord describes obduracy under judgments, as a fruit and evidence of the treachery of the heart: for when Israel abused his mercies, he tried them with judgments, and these also they abused. Therefore he gives this command to the Prophet; *Go ye up upon her walls, and destroy; but make not a full end: take away her battlements, for they are not*

* Neh. ix. 28. 29. † Isa. lvii. 18. ‡ 2 Chron. xvi. 7.—12.

the Lord's. *For the house of Israel and the house of Judah have dealt very treacherously against me, saith the Lord. They have belied the Lord, and said, It is not he, neither shall evil come upon us, neither shall we see sword nor famine* *.

From this subject, you, who are under adversity of any kind, may be exhorted to endeavour the discovery of the sin or sins, which may be the procuring causes of God's displeasure. In order to this, earnestly apply to him by prayer, that he may be pleased to let you know the reason of his indignation. Imitate the conduct of Job, while in a most deplorable situation; *I will say unto God, Do not condemn me; show me wherefore thou contendest with me* †. This was the course that David also observed under a severe public affliction. When there was a famine in the land, he *enquired of the Lord; and the Lord answered, It is for Saul, and for his bloody house, because he slew the Gibeonites* ‡.—Attend to the voice of conscience, and hearken to its testimony, in regard to the cause of adversity. This is God's deputy within you, a witness, nay, a judge appointed by him to take cognifance, not only of your actions, but of your thoughts. Therefore, it is your duty to give it a fair hearing. *The spirit of man is the candle of the Lord, searching all the inward parts of the belly.* Conscience is thus described, because it is its proper work to investigate the heart, and to discover what is lurking there. *Commune with your own heart.* What sin doth conscience most readily charge you with? This, very probably, is the cause of God's anger. The consciences of Joseph's brethren, in the day of their calamity, suggested the reason of it without the least hesitation; *They said one to another, We are verily guilty concerning our brother, in that we saw the anguish of his soul, when he besought us; and we would not hear: therefore is this distress come upon us* §. They are not satisfied with a confession of their guilt, merely in reference to the time

---

* Jer. v. 10,—12.   † Job. x. 2.   ‡ 2 Sam. xxi. 1.
§ Gen. xlii. 21.

time when the crime was committed; they fay not, *We were guilty.* Their fevere unmerited treatment from a ftranger, brought all the cruelty of their conduct towards the innocent Jofeph frefh on their hearts. They perceive the unpurged guilt of their old fin ftaring them in the face, from under the dark brow of the prefent threatening difpenfation. *We are verily guilty concerning our brother.*—Diligently confider the nature, manner, and circumftances of the affliction. The fin may be often read in its punifhment. In this refpect, the nature of the caufe appears in the effect. Jacob was deceived by Laban in his marriage. Thus the Lord chaftifed him for his finful conduct in the way which he took to obtain the bleffing, by deceiving his good old father Ifaac. He was himfelf enfnared by means of the darknefs of the night, as he had over-reached his father by reafon of the darknefs of old age. Rachel, his beloved wife, impatiently faid unto him; *Give me children, elfe I die.* And the gratifying of her inordinate defire was indeed the caufe of her death. Adonibezek was a fignal inftance of the juftice of providential retribution. So ftrong was his conviction of this, that he was obliged to confefs it, although to his fhame: *Threefcore and ten kings, with their thumbs and great toes cut off, did gather their meat under my table. As I have done, fo God hath requited me* *.

FARTHER, reflect on the temper of your minds, when the affliction was brought on you. Were you languid in the exercife of grace. Then, it was probably fuch a call as that, *How long wilt thou fleep, O fluggard? When wilt thou arife out of thy fleep?* The procuring caufe of an affliction may be often difcovered by a confideration of one's temper, when it was fent. This was remarkably exemplified in the cafe of Nebuchadnezzar. *He walked in the palace of the kingdom of Babylon, and faid; Is not this great Babylon that I have built for the houfe of my kingdom, by the might*

---

* Judges i. 7.

might of my power, and for the honour of my majesty. While the word was in the king's mouth, *there fell a voice from heaven, saying, O king Nebuchadnezzar, to thee it is spoken, the kingdom is departed from thee?* In the very paroxysm of his vain-glory he was arrested by the messenger from God. And he was afterwards made to acknowledge, that *those who walk in pride he is able to abase* *.—Compare your situation with that of those who in former times have been afflicted in the same manner, especially if your adversity be of a peculiar nature. If you are guilty of the sins which procured the rod to them, you may with great probability conclude, that it is for these very sins that God afflicts you. *For whatsoever things were written aforetime, were written for our learning.* So Paul addressing the Corinthians, with respect to the judgments inflicted on the Church of Israel, observes; *These things were our examples, to the intent we should not lust after evil things, as they also lusted* †. Try what is your beloved sin : and, in a word, examine what are these sins for which you are most frequently reproved under the ministry of the gospel. As of old, the Lord did nothing without revealing it to his servants, the Prophets, *so the secret of the Lord is* still *with them that fear him.* By his Spirit he still makes his word *quick and powerful.* What is the sin for which conscience most frequently reproves you under the word, the sin with regard to which you find the word *as a burning fire shut up in* your *bones?* You have great reason to view this as the reason of God's controversy.

Again, we exhort you to seek the sanctified use of your afflictions. If they be not sanctified, as you have seen, they will turn out to your hardening in the mean time, and to your greater condemnation in the end. Be earnest in prayer that the Lord would bless them to you, either as means of *bringing* you *within the bond of* his *covenant*, or of *building* you *up in your most holy faith ;* that he would make them instrumental for the mortification of sin, for strengthening

---

* Dan. iv. 29,—31. 37. † 1 Cor. x. 6.

ening grace, and for preparing you to be partakers of his inheritance. You may inquire, how you shall know if afflictions be really sanctified to you? This you may know, by applying to your hearts in the exercise of self-examination some of the observations made in the doctrinal part of this discourse. Do you patiently submit to the will of God, are you preserved from repining under the rod, and in some measure enabled to say; *Good is the will of the Lord?* Are you made to justify him in all his dispensations, to *ascribe righteousness to* your *Maker, who giveth songs in the night?* Are you engaged in self-abasement and self-condemnation? Are you, under affliction, disposed to flee to God in Christ as your only refuge, saying; *God is my refuge and my strength, a very present help in time of trouble?* Are you more concerned to get adversity sanctified than removed? Can you view affliction as coming out of the hand of a kind and compassionate Father, who doth not *afflict willingly, nor grieve the children of men?* Do your trials increase your hatred of sin? Are you more afraid of the evil of sin, than of that of affliction? Do they increase your love to the Redeemer? Do they influence you to walk more closely with God? Do they stir up the exercise of faith, so that your conduct in some measure corresponds to that of Job; *Though he should slay me, yet will I trust in him?* Do you reckon your severest trials preferable to a life of sin, like Moses, who *chose rather to suffer affliction with the people of God, than to enjoy the pleasures of sin for a season?* Do you find rest to your soul in God's word? Does your experience keep pace with the Psalmist's; *Thy word is all my comfort in mine affliction, and in all my straits I am revived by this thy word alone?* If such be your real attainments, however weak the degree, it is a certain evidence that your adversity is among those *all things* that *work together for* your *good*, and that in the end you shall have this song put into your mouth; *We went through fire, and through water, but thou broughtest us out at length unto a wealthy place.*

SER.

SERMON XXIII.

On the DECEITFULNESS of the HEART, in disregarding PROVIDENTIAL DISPENSATIONS in general.

Psalm lxxviii. 7, 8.

—And not forget the works of God ;—and might not be as their fathers ;—a generation that set not their heart aright, and whose spirit was not stedfast with God.

GOD addresses men, whether renewed or unrenewed, in a twofold way; by Word, and by Providence. These often go hand in hand. He gives a commission to his dispensations to confirm his word. With respect to both, the unrenewed are obstinate, and refuse to hearken. This sin is often eminently chargeable against his own children. Therefore he complains of his Church, not only that she would not listen to his voice, but that she did *not regard the operation of his hands.* It is, then, of the greatest consequence for us to attend to the deceitfulness of our hearts, as it impedes this necessary exercise.

The Inscription of this Psalm does not absolutely determine whether it was written by Asaph, or only committed to him as one of those *set over the service of song in the house of the Lord.* But whether he or any

any other was the inspired penman, he could only speak as a type of Christ. For the introduction of the Psalm, in its proper extent, could only refer to the great Prophet. He alone could justly say; *Give ear, O my people, to my law.* That Christ is properly the speaker here is evident from the following words; *I will open my mouth in a parable, I will utter dark sayings of old:* for these are expressly applied to him in the New Testament*. We learn the reason that these *sayings* were to be uttered not to that generation only, but to *the generation to come.* They were given with this design. For *he established a testimony in Jacob, and appointed a law in Israel, which he commanded our fathers to make known to their children.* And for what end?—*That the generation to come might know them.* And this was to be done in their successive generations,—*that they might set their hope in God, and not forget the works of God, but keep his commandments.* Remembering in scripture often signifies, not merely a simple recollection of any thing in the memory, but the desire of the heart; as in Heb. xi. 15. *And truly, if they had been mindful of that country from whence they came out, they might have had opportunity to have returned. But now they desire a better country.* The latter expression, *desire,* explains the meaning of the former, *mindful.* Remembering God often signifies true faith and religion; Isa. xlii. 21. *Remember these things, O Jacob,* &c. Remembrance sometimes denotes the engagement of the whole heart with any object; as in Song i. 4. *We will remember thy love more than wine.* On the other hand, to *forget* God metaphorically signifies unbelief and opposition to him in general, Hos. iv. 6. *Thou hast forgotten the law of thy God.* The *forgetfulness* here meant does not denote a mere neglect, but a positive rejection: for this declaration is thus prefaced, *Thou hast rejected knowledge.* Forgetting the *works* of God seems especially to signify, either first, a contempt or disregard of them in the mean time.

---

* Matt. xiii. 34, 35.

time; thus *confideration* is directly oppofed to forgetfulnefs, Pfal. l. 22.—or, fecondly, a fuffering them to flip out of the mind, whatever impreffions they have made at firft. And fometimes it includes both. That it is not the firft merely that is meant here is evident from this, that *not forgetting* the *works* of God, and *keeping his commandments*, are joined together. They were fo to remember his works as thereby to ftir themfelves up to obedience. They were to remember the works of God, that they *might not be like their fathers a ftiffnecked and rebellious race.* We have the great reafon of a contempt of God's operations in the mean time, or forgetfulnefs of them afterwards, in the words that follow;—*a generation that fet not their heart aright, and whofe fpirit was not ftedfaft with God.* Their heart was not *fet aright*, it was not *prepared*, as the word may be read. It was not renewed by a work of grace. Therefore it was that all the works of Providence made fo little impreffion. Their *fpirit* was *not ftedfaft*. They often feemed to look well, and they *fpoke well;* but there was not *fuch a heart in them.* They dealt deceitfully with God; for as their character is more fully delineated, verfe 34.—37. when they feemed to be anxioufly *feeking* after God, they only *flattered him with their mouth, and lied unto him with their tongues: for their heart was not right with him, neither were they ftedfaft in his covenant.*

These words afford the following propofition, That the want of a right heart, or to exprefs it otherwife, the deceit of the heart is the great reafon that men do not obferve the works of God.

As this part of the fubject is of great importance, and little attended to by the generality, even of real Chriftians, it may not be improper to view it with confiderable extent. We may,

I. Show

I. Show what is implied in a diligent obfervation of providential difpenfations.

II. Illustrate fome of the deceits employed by the heart for preventing this exercife.

III. Consider its defigns in diffuading us from it.

IV. Offer fome encouragements to this neceffary work.

V. Subjoin fome cautions as to the interpretation of the language of Providence.

I. Such a diligent obfervation implies,

1. A close *invefligation* of the various *fteps* of Providence towards us. The Providence of God may be viewed either as common or fpecial. His common Providence extends to all creatures, the wicked not excepted. *The Lord is good to all, and his tender mercies are over all his works**. But there is a fpecial Providence exercifed toward his people. *The angel of the Lord encampeth round about them that fear him, and delivereth them* †. His *eyes run to and fro throughout the whole earth, to fhow himfelf ftrong in behalf of them whofe heart is perfect towards him* ‡. This fpecial care extends in fome meafure to elect veffels, even while they are in the ftate of nature; in their merciful prefervation from death, and from the unpardonable fin, till the time of the accomplifhment of his purpofe of love concerning them. The Providence of God, though exercifed in a common manner towards the unregenerate, is by them habitually difregarded. It is, therefore, his fpecial Providence with refpect to the Saints which we have principally in our eye; as they alone will be concerned to attend to his difpenfations. Now, it is neceffary that they fhould carefully obferve the whole of his procedure, not as if they could clearly perceive his gracious hand in every particular event which befals

---

* Pfal. cxlv. 9. † Pfal. xxxiv. 7. ‡ 2 Chron. xvi. 9.

befals them, but becaufe they muſt in this Chriſtian exerciſe expreſs their deſire of diſcovering his hand, and wait for the diſplay of it. That preſervation, protection, leading or ſupport which others receive from God as the common Preſerver of men, comes to them from their own God and Father, dealing with them according to the Covenant of Grace, and making *all things work together for good.* There are many events, indeed, which are ſo trivial, that Chriſtians cannot immediately diſcern the hand of God in them: but there are others not more important in themſelves, which, in their connection, diſcover not only Divine co-operation, but infinite wiſdom and diſtinguiſhing love. It is their duty ſtill to look for a diſplay of his merciful operation, and in this exerciſe they will learn to ſee it more and more. We may ſpeak more fully on this head afterwards. At preſent we ſhall only mention the following things, which may be uſeful to the believer in his endeavours to diſcover a gracious Providence in particular diſpenſations. He ought to be firmly and conſtantly perſuaded that the Lord is dealing with him in a way of love, and that all things which befal him, though he cannot preſently diſcern the deſign of them, do actually proceed from his God and Father, and concur in preparing him for *the inheritance of the ſaints in light.* A conſtant belief of this great and delightful truth will ſharpen his deſire for a diſcovery of the Divine procedure in the whole of life. Again, thoſe diſpenſations that reſpect natural life, health, ſickneſs, or the exerciſe of his rational faculties, he can be in no danger of miſinterpreting, when he views them as having a peculiar concurrence of love attending them. Thoſe alſo which tend to diſcover ſin, to reprove for it, to quicken grace, to alienate our hearts from the world, may ſafely and without exception be viewed as diſpenſations of Providence which we are called eſpecially to obſerve. To theſe may be added all ſuch as contain evident anſwers of prayer.

2. *Attention*

2. *Attention* to the *temper* of our *hearts*, to the *dictates* of *conscience*, and to the *motions* of the *Holy Spirit*, which concur with these dispensations, are also necessary. It is not enough that we view any particular providence as coming out of the hand of God, or that we believe his love in it. We must compare the outward dispensation with the temper of the heart while it befals us, that we may obtain a just view of it. When, for example, an event takes place which hath a tendency to humble us in our own apprehensions, and to lay us in the dust before God; we should turn our eyes inward, and carefully examine whether we have in any respect been indulging pride; because the dispensation evidently seems to contain this language. Are we deeply wounded by a discovery of the coolness, instability, or perfidy of an earthly friend? Let us diligently inquire, if we have not been placing too much confidence in man, expecting more solace from the creature than it can afford, and thus provoking the Lord, by *making flesh our arm?* For this is undoubtedly the voice of such a heart-corroding trial. Nor is it sufficient that we try the secret workings of the heart. We must also listen to the voice of conscience, summon it impartially to give in its testimony against us, and hear what it has to accuse us of before God. If we lay a restraint upon conscience, if we stifle its suggestions; we take the most effectual way to prevent a proper discovery of the design of the dispensation. Nor ought we to satisfy ourselves with receiving the testimony of conscience. It is necessary that we attend to the motions of the Holy Spirit in us. It is the privilege of all true Christians to be *led by the Spirit.* He not only leads them externally by a gracious Providence, but internally by correspondent suggestions, pointing out the design of the outward dispensations; and all these are correspondent to his standing testimony in the Word. We must, therefore, be exceedingly careful not to *quench the Spirit, by whom we are sealed to the day of redemption.* These precious inward influences

concur

concur with the outward methods of Providence, by discovering the design of them, as levelled at some particular sin, the knowledge or mortification of which is necessary; or as requiring the more vigorous exercise of some grace. To recur to an example formerly mentioned;—do the motions of the Spirit tend to humble us before God, as abominable by reason of any one sin, or of our sins viewed collectively, in correspondence with an outward dispensation of an humbling nature? Then we may be assured that the intention of God in this method of procedure is really to increase our self-abasement.

3. An accurate *trial* of the meaning of all dispensations by the infallible standard of *revelation*. We have already observed, that Providence is a commentary on the Word. But we must still remember that the Word is the text. As *no scripture is of any private interpretation;* as little is any providence. We must not interpret the Divine procedure according to our own fancies or humours, but according *to the law and the testimony*. When the Church meets with severe dispensations, we are not thence in unbelief to conclude that *the Lord hath forsaken* her; but to bring his providence to the light of such a gracious promise; *By this shall the iniquity of Jacob be purged; and this is all the fruit, to take away his sin:* even although the dispensation should be so severe, that he should *make all the stones of the altar as chalk-stones that are beaten in sunder* *. When we wish to learn the *reason* of public afflictions, we will receive light from such a declaration as this; *Your iniquities have separated between you and your God.* We are to apply the same rule, as to those dispensations that immediately regard ourselves. In the cxi. Psalm, which especially respects the works of God, we find the Psalmist observing this method. He traces up the gracious preservation of the Saints to the stability of the covenant: *He hath given meat to them that fear him: he will ever be mindful of his covenant* †. He compares the faithfulness

and

---

* Isa. xxvii. 9. † Verse 5.

and equity of his providential conduct with the truth and stedfastness of his Word: *The works of his hands are verity and judgment: all his commandments are sure: they stand fast for ever and ever, and are done in truth and uprightness* *.

4. AN earnest desire of perceiving God's *design* as of a *loving* nature. We should not be merely concerned to discover his design as in itself, or as respecting any particular object, any sin, grace or duty; nor should we rest satisfied with believing his love in the general tenor of Providence; but we should labour to *know the love that God hath to us* in every dispensation. It ought to be our constant aim, in observing the course of his procedure with us, to receive confirming evidences of his love. We have the Divine authority for believing that the diligent observation of Providence is one principal way of obtaining such gracious discoveries. *For as many as are led by the Spirit of God, they are the sons of God* †. This leading not only includes the work of the Spirit in the heart in mortifying sin, mentioned in the preceding verse; but all the means which the Spirit employs for accomplishing this work, among which we may justly reckon Providence. Now, those who are thus *led by the Spirit*, who experience his conduct in outward dispensations, as all working for their good, have the most comfortable evidence of their near relation to God. In this way doth the Spirit eminently bear witness with our spirits that we are the sons of God; by discovering love in all events, and making them subservient for quickening us in the delightful exercise of crying, *Abba, Father*, whatever be his course with us in the world. When, by the operation of the Spirit, along with the Word, in our hearts, we see every providence impressed with Divine love to us, and promoting our sanctification, it is a testimony of sonship which is certain and infallible.

5. A FAITHFUL *recording* of these dispensations. It is

---

* Psal. cxi. 7, 8.   † Rom. viii. 14.

is not enough that we obferve them in the mean time. We muft fo treafure them up in our hearts or memories, as to be able to bring them forth, when there is occafion for them afterwards. It is beft to have them engraved on the heart; for when they are thus deeply impreffed by the power of the Spirit, they will never be forgotten. But it may be very ufeful to Chriftians to keep what is called a *diary*, and regularly to commit to writing what they experience of the love of God to them, not merely in their own exercife, but in his providential difpenfations. As we are in great danger of forgetting them, we need to ufe every proper help. While this plan may be obferved for their own advantage in future, they ought to exercife great prudence in keeping thefe memorials to themfelves, unlefs there be a very clear call to the contrary; left any improprieties in them fhould afford ground of ridicule to an irreligious world. So much was Job concerned to obferve and remember the Divine difpenfations towards him that he breaks out in this vehement exclamation; *O! that my words were now written; O! that they were printed in a book; that they were engraven with an iron pen and lead in the rock for ever* *. If Samuel was fo much interefted in the external management of the kingdom of Ifrael, that he *told the people the manner of the kingdom, and wrote it in a book, and laid it up before the Lord* †, how much more fhould we be concerned to record the manner of God's fpiritual kingdom, of that kingdom which is *within* us, and his various methods of managing it, and to *lay up before the Lord* this memorial of his wifdom, power, and love. If this method be obferved, it is moft proper to record thefe things when they are frefh in the memory, and when we are impreffed, not only with the providences themfelves, but with all their concurrent circumftances, and with a clear view of God's gracious defign in meafuring them out to us. Thus did the Ifraelites, when recently delivered at the Red Sea, of which we have an account, Exod. xiv. The chapter immediately

---

* Job. xix. 23.   † 1 Sam. x. 25.

diately following begins with thefe words : *Then fang Mofes and the children of Ifrael this fong unto the Lord, and fpake, faying, I will fing unto the Lord, for he hath triumphed glorioufly.* Why are we fo often told that the ancient worthies fet up pillars in commemoration of particular events ? Thefe things were undoubtedly *written for our learning*, and teach us that we ought to record the mighty acts of the Lord. When he delivered the children of Ifrael from the Philiftines, *Samuel took a ftone and fet it between Mizpeh and Shen, and called the name of it Ebenezer,* that is, a ftone of remembrance, *faying, Hitherto hath the Lord helped us**. The fame example we have in the conduct of Jacob, Jofhua, and others. In a word, Mofes delivered one charge to the Ifraelites, with refpect to their tedious, dangerous, and perplexed fojourning in the wildernefs, which is ftrongly defcriptive of the duty of every fpiritual Ifraelite : *Thou fhalt remember all the way which the Lord thy God led thee thefe forty years in the wildernefs* †.

We now proceed, II. to illuftrate fome of the deceits practifed by the heart, in order to prevent a diligent obfervation of providential difpenfations.

1. It entices us to *indifference* about *practical* religion. Always when men are carelefs about the power of godlinefs in their hearts, they are negligent with refpect to the Divine procedure towards them : for it requires fome conftant meafure of livelinefs in the fervice of God to difpofe one to a diligent obfervation of his providential conduct. The languid Chriftian will never be an attentive Chriftian. It is as vain to expect this as to fuppofe that a watchman, while afleep on his tower, fhould anxioufly guard againft danger, and narrowly infpect every paffing object. A man fpiritually afleep, as to the exercife of grace in his own foul, cannot have his eyes open on the methods which God obferves with refpect to him in his Providence. He will either altogether difregard his operations, or interpret them falfely. It

is

---

* 1 Sam. vii. 12.   † Deut. viii. 2.

is the lively, the vigorous Christian alone, who will not only observe outward dispensations, but compare them with the present situation of his heart, with the testimony of his conscience, with the rule of the Word, and with the motions of the Holy Spirit within him; and trace the footsteps of Divine love in all the paths of the Lord his God. While the grace of faith was asleep as to its exercise in the heart of Peter, he could neither observe nor understand the meaning of Providence. He knew not that the inquiries of the servants in the judgment-hall had all their direction from God himself, and were designed for proving his attachment to Christ. He did not perceive that this trial was sent to humble him in his own apprehension, and to discover to him the folly of his presumptuous imaginations and vain-glorious declarations. Never till his injured Master looked on him in love and compassion, and dispelled the languor of grace in his soul, did he understand his design in suffering him to be so closely questioned and so firmly accused by the officious servants of the High-priest, to deny his Lord, and even to go the dreadful length of cursing and swearing that he *knew not the man*. Then he not only considered the meaning of this dispensation, but compared it with what Jesus had formerly spoken. *He remembered the words of the Lord, and went out and wept bitterly* *. If the deceitful heart once prevail with us to become negligent in the exercise of grace, the neglect of Divine dispensations is the unavoidable consequence.

2. It represents them as *uncertain*. There is so much atheism in the heart of man, that he is prone to attribute many things to mere chance or accident. This is a nonentity, which receives almost universal homage. For, inquire at those who believe in the doctrine of mere Chance, what they mean by it? And they will honestly tell you, they mean nothing at all. Any thing that cannot be accounted for on natural principles, or according to the common course

of

---

* Luke xxii. 61, 62.

of events, is afcribed to this phantom of the imagination. But we muft either deny the immenfity and univerfal influence of God, or confefs that there can be no fuch thing as Chance in the world; becaufe there cannot be two ruling principles of action, both pofleffed of univerfal influence, and efpecially, oppofed to each other in nature and operations. Either Chance prefides over all the actions and circumftances of human life, and Providence over none of them; or Providence over all, and Chance over none. There are, indeed, many things which are contingent to us, as nowife refulting from the intervention of fecondary caufes, or not influenced by thefe, in any way difcernible by us. But whatever is accidental to us, muft be refolved into a fupreme and all-wife Providence, which over-rules all actions and events; and actually concurs, either by employing fecondary caufes, though we cannot obferve them, or by working without their agency. It muft, therefore, be faid of Chance, that idol to which fo many oblations are made, as the Apoftle declares with refpect to all falfe deities, that it *is nothing in the world*. For, indeed, this very Chance, which is fuppofed to have fo great an influence in human affairs, was one of the falfe deities that the heathens worfhipped. They acknowledged it by the name of Fortune. And it muft be confeffed, that herein they were more rational than many, who call themfelves Chriftians: for though they could not account for thofe operations which they afcribed to it, confcience feems to have declared that they muft owe their exiftence to a firft caufe, to a God, however much unknown. May we not add, that their faith bears a greater refemblance to the Apoftle's, than that of the believers in Chance, when he declares concerning God; *In him we live, and move, and have our being?* This, indeed, was originally the language of one of their own poets. It muft be granted, that fome of their Philofophers went to the fhocking extreme of deifying every part of matter. But this ridiculous idea evidently originated from the corruption of a most important doctrine, the universality of Providence. And it is very questionable, whether this opinion, gross as it is, exceeds in absurdity the doctrine of mere Chance. Did not men live *without God in the world*, they would not blindly deny his universal superintendence, and ascribe to a mere chimæra the influence which proceeds from that Being who is every where present. So blind, so atheistical and deceitful is the heart, that even those who not only believe a Providence, and disbelieve Chance, but who endeavour to observe the workings of Providence, are often ready to reject them, from the idea of uncertainty. They find it difficult to allow the Divine concurrence in particular actions, because they cannot discern it. But as this proceeds from no other principle, than that natural blindness in the mind which tends to absolute atheism; it acknowledges no better reason than that which disposes man to disbelieve the being of God altogether; even his invisible nature. But, if we credit the testimony of Scripture, why should we be at a loss to believe his concurrence in particular events, when it assures us, not only of his superintendence over all, but of his agency with respect to all, in one way or another? *From the place of his habitation he looketh upon all the inhabitants of the earth. He fashioneth their hearts alike: he considereth all their works* *.—*A man's heart deviseth his way, but the Lord directeth his steps* †.

3. The heart represents many events as *trifling* and unworthy of attention. Many, who believe in general, that all things which befal them are over-ruled by God, are notwithstanding ready to apprehend that it is derogatory to his dignity, to suppose that he should have a particular design in those events, which are in themselves of little consequence. But shall we not believe that his Providence extends even to the smallest matters; when he hath declared, that the grass of the field, which is trodden under foot of man and beast, which *to-day is, and to-morrow is cast into the oven,*

---

* Pf. xxxiii. 14.   † Prov. xvi. 9.

oven, is clothed by God; that *the very hairs of* our *heads are all numbered*, however infignificant and innumerable to us; that fo trifling a creature as *a fparrow*, does *not fall on the ground without* our *Father*, without his knowledge, concourfe, and immediate agency*; and when the fmalleft and vileft of his creatures are made the minifters of his will, and the executioners of his judgments, as in the fatal experience of the Egyptians †? Indeed, we cannot form any juft apprehenfion of Providence, without thinking of it as in every refpect particular. To fuppofe that God pays no regard to thofe actions that are comparatively trivial, is to deny his Providence entirely. For, as by his omniprefence, he muft fill every part of the univerfe at the fame moment, in every part his influence muft be exerted. The eye of Omnifcience muft neceffarily include every object, even the minuteft; elfe it could not deferve the name. The hand of Omnipotence muft comprehend in its grafp the moft defpicable atom floating in the air, as really as *the ftars in their courfes;* elfe it would be limited in power and operation: as the fame bright luminary, which enlightens the palace, darts its rays through the crevices of the dungeon, and equally exhales the naufeous fteams of the dunghill with the fragrant fluids of the garden. And if Divine Providence extends to the fmalleft matters, fhall we fuppofe that it does fo without defign? This, indeed, would be to derogate from the infinite wifdom of God, as the Governor of the world: for we cannot afcribe infinite wifdom to a Being, who does any thing without defign, or without relation to an end. If it is not difhonouring to God to believe that he fuperintends the minuteft objects; furely it cannot be anywife inconfiftent with thofe apprehenfions that we ought to entertain of his greatnefs, to believe that he hath a fpecial intention in all the actions performed under his influence. Do we not often fee that thofe things which are trivial in themfelves, lead to the greateft events,

---

* Mat. x. 29. † Exod. viii. 16.—17.

events, and are neceſſarily connected with them? Chriſtians, by an attentive obſervation of things, which others paſs over without the ſmalleſt notice, will often perceive the moſt inſignificant means directly leading to the moſt important ends.

Who could have thought, that ſuch a rich cluſter of illuſtrious providences would have been ſuſpended on ſo trifling a circumſtance, as that of Joſeph's being the favourite child of his father;—providences big with the fate, not only of the whole family of Jacob, but of the moſt conſiderable portion of the Church of God then in the world;—neceſſary, according to the Divine purpoſe, to the very exiſtence of that people who were afterwards to be conſecrated as peculiar to himſelf, and to the accompliſhment of that one promiſe, in which all revelation concentred, the birth of that ſeed in whom all the families of the earth ſhould be bleſſed? Who could have imagined that an event, apparently ſo accidental, as that of the Iſhmaelites paſſing by, while Joſeph was in the pit, which ſuggeſted to Judah the more gentle idea of ſelling him, ſhould have been indiſpenſably connected with all thoſe great events, that were requiſite for the ſalvation of the Church of God in every age? Every minute circumſtance of the treatment of Joſeph, was neceſſary to form a link in that glorious chain, which led to the completion of God's purpoſes and promiſes. Had he not been the favourite of his father, he would not have been hated of his brethren; had he not been hated, they would not have caſt him into a pit; had not the Iſhmaelites paſſed by at this very time, he might have periſhed there; had he not been ſold to them, he would not have been carried into Egypt and ſold there; had he not been ſold to the captain of Pharaoh's guard, he would not, through the revenge of his baffled miſtreſs, have been caſt into that priſon *where the king's priſoners were bound;* had he not been caſt into that very priſon, he would not have been acquainted with the king's butler; had not the king's butler dreamed, Joſeph would not have been known to him as

an

an interpreter of dreams ; had he not been thus known to him, such a mean person must have remained a stranger to Pharaoh ; had not Pharaoh known and believed him, he could not have provided against the famine, he could not have saved his father's house, he could not have given them a place in Egypt, the Church of God could not have been tried in that *iron furnace*, and delivered from it by an astonishing display of Almighty power. There was a collateral link in this chain, which must not be forgotten. What is more despised, and in general more despicable than a dream? Yet had not Pharaoh had a dream which troubled him, the butler would not have remembered Joseph ; had he not remembered him, Pharaoh would not have applied to him for the interpretation of his dream, Joseph might have rotted in prison, Egypt would most likely have been consumed by the famine, and the seed of the Church would have perished. So striking are all these circumstances, and so closely connected, that it is difficult to believe that any rational person should read this history, and yet retain a doubt of a particular Providence. We are sure there was none in the mind of Joseph. He considered all these things as taking place under the direction of infinite wisdom. This very consideration did he use, for comforting the troubled hearts of his brethren, after he had revealed himself to them ; *Be not grieved, nor angry with yourselves, for——God sent me before you, to preserve you a posterity in the earth, and to save your lives by a great deliverance. So, now, it was not you that sent me hither, but God* *. And, afterwards ; *As for you, you thought evil against me, but God meant it unto good, to bring to pass, as at this day, to save much people alive* †. It would scarcely seem worth the observing, that even a king should lose his rest for a single night. Yet this circumstance with respect to Ahasuerus, immediately led to the preservation of Mordecai, and to the disappointment and disgrace of the haughty and revengeful Haman ; nay, concurred

with

* Gen. xlv. 8. † Gen. l. 20.

with other circumstances, in accomplishing the destruction of this *adversary*, and the deliverance and enlargement of the people of God *.

4. It opposes this exercise, as if it unavoidably tended to *enthusiasm*. In this light will the *children of this world*, at any rate, consider it, because *God is not in all* their *thoughts*. Need it then appear surprising, that they should never think of observing him in their lives? But as the wickedness of the heart is essentially the same in all, even the *children of light* are often prompted, by their corruption, to disregard the operations of the Lord, under the pretence of its tendency to Enthusiasm. The greatest Christians, through the prevailing weakness and ignorance of their minds, or perhaps from present fear, arising from a sense of guilt, may be ready at times to put a construction on particular events that they will not justly bear, a construction very remote from the intention of God. But this is no argument against the thing itself. There is no Enthusiasm in *setting the Lord before* us, and in a diligent observation of the whole tenor of his conduct. Some degree of Enthusiasm may steal into the best duties of believers, and be very prejudicial to them. But bad and dangerous as this extreme is, it is preferable to that of indifference. It is safer to be in some instances *righteous overmuch*, than to disregard religion altogether. One had much better mistake God's language in any particular dispensation, than entirely neglect the designs of Providence. That is a cloud which may obscure his way for a moment; but this is a path of darkness in which he gropes and stumbles continually. Who would not rather chuse to suffer a temporary glimmering of his eyes from the lustre of the sun, than to be totally deprived of the use of them by a perpetual midnight darkness? There can be no Enthusiasm in a strict observation of the ways of the Lord, unless it be Enthusiasm to believe a particular Providence, influencing and over-ruling all events. For, if we believe this,

instead

* Est. vi. 1.

instead of being Enthusiasts in endeavouring to trace it, we are practical Infidels, if we act otherwise. If in the one case, we do not believe too much, which has been formerly proved; in the other, we act as if we believed nothing at all. That sort of religion only is Enthusiasm, which hath no foundation in the Scriptures. But if the belief of a particular Providence, and of the necessity of observing it, is to be rejected under this notion; we at once throw reject the whole of religion, refuse the authority of the Word of God, and virtually deny his very being. For if any of his works are excluded from his observation, *his kingdom ruleth* not over all. And if we deny the universality of his kingdom, we must necessarily deny his Immensity. If all things, even the most minute and insignificant, were created by God with infinite wisdom and power; if all his creatures were *very good*, in reference to the end proposed; the same wisdom, power, and design, must we attribute to God, in the preservation and government of them all.

5. This constant observation of Providence, is represented as a great *bondage* to ourselves. Well knows the deceitful heart, that if Christians were more diligent in the observation, and faithful in the remembrance of providential dispensations, it would greatly tend to the further discovery and mortification of its own deceitfulness: therefore, it opposes this course with the greatest ardour. It makes not a single objection to the expence of time and labour in its own service; but it has a thousand to the smallest expence of either in the service of God. When the Christian is disposed to this vigilant attention, it proposes the same question with Judas; *Wherefore is all this waste?* And for the same reason too. For as Judas was a thief, and wanted to have the money for his own purposes; the design of the treacherous heart, in complaining of this waste of time and trouble in observing Providence, is, that both may be solely devoted to itself. It wishes to deprive the Christian of that

precious

precious spikenard, that *excellent oil* of the holy Spirit, which would often be poured upon him in the exercise of this spiritual diligence, and diffuse its fragrance all around. It complains of this as a bondage, because it really views the whole of God's service in this light, and especially every thing that tends to excite the Christian to fervency and watchfulness: for it vehemently wishes to *break* God's *bands asunder, and cast away* his *cords.* It dreads the careful observation of Providence, and of Divine love attending it, as a bond that would often restrain the violence of iniquity. But it is entirely false that this is a bondage. Indeed, it requires a strict and minute attention, a careful investigation of circumstances. But the concurrence between the Providence of God, and the operations of the Spirit on the heart, is often so clear and distinct, that it strikes our eye whether we will or not; and is observed by us, even when, from reluctance to be reproved, we wish to overlook it; or to have our heart averted from any purpose agreeable to its inclinations, though evidently opposed by God. The language of Providence is frequently so loud, as to make the most deaf to hear. Its operations are at times so perspicuous, that *he who runs may read* them. This commandment, instead of being grievous, is in the course of obedience attended with the greatest delight. Can any thing be more pleasing to the saint of God, than by a diligent inspection of his providential management, to see all his *ways* to be *truth and mercy; all things working together for* his own *good;* and every dispensation proceeding from God as a merciful and compassionate Father? Shall we suppose a dutiful and grateful child, to esteem it a bondage to recollect and ponder in his mind the many instances of his parent's affection; to consider the love that is in his frowns, as well as in his endearments; and to survey the whole of his conduct, as conducive to his own real interest and happiness? And shall the children of an heavenly Father, deem it burdensome to reflect on that pity and tenderness

tenderness that he manifests to them, when they know that he loves them infinitely more than the most tender earthly parent, and that all his dispensations are just the proofs which he gives, that *as far as the east is from the west, so far hath he removed* their *transgressions from* them*? Though this exercise should at first be attended with some difficulty; yet by means of prayer, vigilance and perseverance, their spiritual discernment and experience will be so increased, as to render the work far more easy and delightful. There is a progress in this as in every other part of the Christian exercise. *The path of the just is as the shining light that shineth more and more unto a perfect day.* And we know that all *the ways of wisdom are pleasantness.*

6. The heart may perhaps plead that this course is *neglected* by *many* who are as *good* Christians as we. It is the ruin of many, that they take their fellow-professors as an example, especially if they are esteemed saints. They think that if they go as far in religion as they do, they may rest satisfied: and they generally propose them as patterns in those things wherein they are most deficient. They look at the worst things about them, and consider these as warrants for their practice. The deceitfulness of the heart thus seeks to shield itself under the pretence of *walking by the footsteps of the flock.* Those who are led astray by it, in this instance, consider not in how many things such Christians exceed them. They only attend to these circumstances, in which, through prevailing infirmity, or perhaps, from the power of temptations to which themselves are strangers, they are on a level with them. But this is a false rule of conduct; for we are only to follow Christians as far as they follow Christ. Paul, though an eminent saint, and not *behind the chief of the Apostles,* could only propose himself as an example as far as his conduct was consistent with that of the great pattern: *Be ye followers of me, as I also am of Christ.* In following others

* Psal. ciii. 12.

others we are also to carry this direction along with us; that instead of viewing their infirmities as a warrant for indulging the like in ourselves, we ought to improve them as means for exciting us to greater diligence and watchfulness; because sin or folly never appears in so striking a light as in the most exalted characters. *Dead flies cause the ointment of the apothecary to send forth a stinking savour; so doth a little folly him that is in reputation for wisdom and honour**. Instead of viewing their superior worth as a reason why we should copy their faults, we should consider it as an excitement to follow them in those things only that are most worthy of imitation. Besides, this is a dangerous rule, because we have not the spirit of discernment. We may form an opinion with respect to the state of fellow-professors; but we have no test that is absolutely certain. The only perfect pattern is Christ himself. He hath *left us an example that we should follow his steps*. While we are to follow others only as they follow him; we are to follow him without any limitation. And without the smallest reserve he could say; *I have set the Lord always before me*. Hence it was, that his holy human soul had the continual comfort of observing that the Lord *maintained* his *lot*, that amidst all his adversities the *lines* had *fallen happily to* him *in pleasant places*, and that the Lord was *always at* his *right hand* †. What unspeakable delight must he have had in viewing all the lines of that extraordinary providence that environed him, as terminating in the completion of those illustrious prophecies which acknowledged him as their subject?—As the conduct of the great Head is the only perfect example, the Word of God is the only infallible rule. Neither the opinions, nor the practices of the best of saints are to be our Bible. We ought to respect the one, and imitate the other, in subordination to this unerring standard. This is that *sure word of prophecy to which we do well to take heed*.

* Eccl. x. 1. † Psal. xvi. 5. 6. 8.

SERMON XXIV.

On the DECEITFULNESS of the HEART, in disregarding PROVIDENTIAL DISPENSATIONS in general.

Psalm lxxviii. 7, 8.

—And not forget the works of God;—and might not be as their fathers;—a generation that set not their heart aright, and whose spirit was not stedfast with God.

III. WE are now to advert to the designs of the deceitful heart in dissuading us from observing divine dispensations.

First, It wishes to deprive God of the glory resulting from this exercise. His great object in all dispensations, as in all his works without exception, is to glorify his own name. *All men shall fear, and shall declare the work of God; for they shall wisely consider of his doings. The righteous shall be glad in the Lord, and shall trust in him; and all the upright in heart shall glory* *. The heart still wishes to arrogate praise to itself. Therefore, it labours to deprive God of the glory of his wisdom in directing and managing these dispensations. Where they are not observed and recorded, that infinite wisdom which often appears in them, passes unnoticed. Men see nothing more in the most striking events, than in the most ordinary actions or occurrences of life. The glory of his power is also disregarded. Though particular providences

* Psal. lxiv. 9. 10.

providences be accomplished in so illustrious a manner, as to declare that they proceed from no other than that God who *worketh all things according to the counsel of his will*, and who *doth according to his will in the army of heaven, and among the inhabitants of the earth;* yet the children of men, by neglecting them, pour contempt on that *excellence in working*. The revenue of glory, which is due to the love of God, is also refused. Though he be following his people with tokens of his mercy, surrounding them with loving kindness, and making all his *paths to drop down fatness;* yet by disregarding his work, they ungratefully deny him the praise.

SECONDLY, By this inexcusable negligence the delusive heart designs to deprive believers of much real comfort. There are two channels in which the Lord communicates consolation to his people. These are his Word and Providence. But we lose much of our comfort, if we keep these separate. When the one is made to pour its abundance into the other, the peace of believers is *like a river, and* their *glory like a flowing stream* * The dispensations of Providence confirm the truth of the Word; while the Word discovers the meaning, and regulates us as to the improvement of these. There is an awful threatening pronounced against such as pay no attention to these things: *Because they regard not the works of the Lord, nor the operation of his hands, he shall destroy them, and not build them up* †. This, indeed, has a principal reference to the wicked. But it frequently obtains a partial completion even with respect to the children of God, because of their shameful negligence: and its efficacy is visible in their mournful deadness and want of comfort in the ways of God. Again it is said; *They regard not the work of the Lord, neither consider the operation of his hands. Therefore, my people are gone into captivity, because they have no knowledge; and their honourable men are famished, and their multitude dried up with thirst* ‡. This is one great cause of the

* Isa. lxvi. 12.   † Psal. xxviii. 5.   ‡ Isa. v. 12, 13.

the spiritual captivity, languor and barrenness of many true Christians. On this account is their *moisture turned into the drought of summer.* We shall mention some of the comforts which they would derive from this exercise. of which the deceitfulness of the heart deprives them by lulling them into habitual negligence.

1. DILIGENT observation would eminently open up the *mystery* of Providence. Here there is a great and unknown depth. Many dispensations befal us and others which we cannot fathom. But though the mystery of Providence in its full extent, even as to any individual, is in the present state incomprehensible to us; yet we might attain a far greater knowledge of it, were we sufficiently diligent. For *the secret of the Lord is with them that fear him.* By discovering the secret of Providence in one dispensation, we might have a key that would be useful in unlocking others. Therefore it is said ; *Who is wise, and he shall understand these things? prudent, and he shall know them? for the ways of the Lord are right, and the just shall walk in them: but the transgressors shall fall therein* *. It is evident that these words refer not only to the commandments and ordinances of God, but to his dispensations. In another place he puts a question nearly of the same import with this, which clearly implies that the spiritually wise will know the meaning of his judgments : *Who is the wise man that may understand this,—for what the land perisheth, and is burnt up like a wilderness, that none passeth through* †. With respect to these events that are to take place in the latter days, it is declared to Daniel ; *None of the wicked shall understand, but the wise shall understand* ‡? For want of a due observation of former dispensations, we are often at a loss in regard to those that afterwards take place, and in danger of stumbling ; as was the case with the disciples, when in the absence of Christ they were ready to perish in a storm. *He went up unto them into the ship, and the wind*

---

* Hos. xiv. 9. † Jer. ix. 12. ‡ Dan. xii. 10.

wind ceafed; and they were fore amazed in themfelves beyond meafure, and wondered. For they confidered not the miracle of the loaves, for their hearts were hardened *.

2. It tends to increafe a holy *fear* of God. When his judgments are vifibly written, according to the threatenings of the word, in the deftruction of thofe who are his open enemies, they often produce this effect. When *God fhoots at* the wicked *with an arrow*, fo that they *make their own tongue to fall upon themfelves;* it is declared, that *all men fhall fear, and fhall declare the work of God* †. When he gives remarkable deliverance to his people, *fends* fuch *redemption to his folk*, that it is thence undeniable that *he hath commanded his covenant for ever;* they are at no lofs to draw this inference; *Holy and reverend is his name* ‡. Even the heathen mariners *feared* Jehovah *exceedingly*, when they faw his wonderful works with refpect to his rebellious prophet §.

This is an illuftrious mean of difcovering Divine *love*. In the cvii. Pfalm, we have a particular enumeration of many of the methods of Providence with refpect to the children of men. It contains a ftriking account of various afflictive difpenfations, whether temporal or fpiritual, of the conduct of thofe who are exercifed with them, and of the manner in which God is pleafed to grant deliverance. At the clofe of each defcription, there is a repetition of this pathetic wifh; *Oh that men would praife the Lord for his goodnefs, and for his wonderful works to the children of men.* This is very far from being a *vain repetition*. There is a peculiar beauty and propriety in it, as undoubtedly declaring that the great defign of God, in thefe varied operations, is to illuftrate his goodnefs, compaffion and long-fuffering, and to fecure a revenue of glory to himfelf. To encourage his people to an attentive obfervation of the whole of his conduct, as peculiarly tending to illuftrate his covenant-love, this
defcriptive

---

* Mark vi. 51. 52.   † Pfal. lxiv. 7.—9.   ‡ Pfal. cxi. 9.
§ Jonah i. 16.

descriptive and eucharistic song is concluded with these remarkable words; *Whoso is wise, and will observe* * *these things, even they shall understand the loving kindness of the Lord.*

4. This exercise tends greatly to strengthen *faith*. This grace, indeed, in all its actings rests on the Word of God as its foundation. But it does not reject assistance from other quarters. Particularly, it derives much confirmation from an experience of divine love in the dispensations of Providence. While it adheres closely to the Word as its proper foundation, with this it compares these dispensations, views them as illustrations of its truth, and thus draws in support to itself. Nay, we may say that it belongs to the direct and proper exercise of faith, to compare Providence with Revelation; and from the correspondent operations of the one, to assure itself of the unchangeable faithfulness of the other. It is just by bringing the ways of the Lord to the rule of his word, and observing the perfect conformity between them, that faith discovers the equity of them all. Hence it is, that the Church can sing this song; *He is the Rock, his work is perfect; all his ways are judgment; a God of truth and without iniquity; just and right is he* †. Thus the believer is persuaded of the infinite *justice* of all God's proceedings, not merely from the testimony of his word viewed by itself, but as confirmed by his works. In the same sense, the Prophet Habakkuk, when considering the conduct of God towards his Church, cries out; *His ways are everlasting* ‡: because, how various soever they be, and though they may seem even to cross each other, they all directly lead to the accomplishment of one eternal and immutable purpose

---

* This word does not merely denote attention in the mean time, but such an observation of any thing, as conveys the idea of treasuring it up in the memory, and of pondering it often in the mind. In this sense, it seems to be used Genesis xxxvii. 11. with respect to Joseph's dream; "His father *observed* the saying." It frequently signifies the careful preservation or observation of any thing as sacred. Thus it is often used with respect to a solemn oath, and to the covenant of God.

† Deut. xxxii. 4.   ‡ Hab. iii. 6.

purpose of love, as their happy end. To this agrees the testimony of the Psalmist; *All the paths of the Lord are mercy and truth to such as keep his covenant and his testimonies* *. They are not only *mercy*, as leading to their complete salvation; but *truth* as directly confirming his word. Not one step of his conduct with respect to them, is inconsistent with one promise in the Bible. *Not one good word of all that he hath spoken can fail.* When the Christian sees one mercy, one deliverance, whether of a temporal or spiritual nature, coming from God as *love*, in confirmation of his promise, and in answer to the expectation and prayer of faith; it hath a wonderful and most delightful influence, in encouraging him to the renewed and continued exercise of faith. Then he can more cheerfully join with David; *Into thine hand I commit my spirit.* And what is the present excitement? *Thou hast redeemed me, O God of truth* †. " Thou hast already " discovered thy faithfulness in the accomplishment of " the promise; thou hast never hitherto disappointed " my faith." Sinners themselves are sometimes made to know the *justice* of God from his providential dispensations. The hearts of the sons of Jacob, when they had sold Joseph, were so obdurate, that they seem to have used every mean to aggravate their father's affliction. They sent him his coat of many colours, dipped in blood; as if they meant by this very circumstance to reproach him for his partiality. For a long course of years, they appear to have no compunctions with respect to their conduct. But at length they see their sin, and the justice of God, in the peculiarity of their punishment. They had dealt roughly with a brother. A stranger, as they suppose, is raised up to avenge his quarrel, and *speaks roughly to them*. They had cast their brother into a pit, because they looked on him as a spy on their conduct; for *he brought unto his father their evil report*. They are themselves cast into prison, under the pretence of their being spies. By their wickedness they had bereaved their father of

one

---

* Psal. xxv. 10.   † Psal. xxxi. 5.

one beloved fon: now they fee him in danger of lofing another, who filled the place of the former in his affections, and was indeed his only temporal confolation for the lofs of Jofeph. They had fpoken lies to their father about him: and now they are accufed of falfehood by one, who, as they imagine, knows nothing of their crime. They had fent their brother into Egypt: and Egypt is the fcene of their fufferings. They had caft off the fear of God in their conduct towards Jofeph: and the words of this ftranger, who, as they would be apt to conclude, knew not the God of Jacob, cut them to the heart; becaufe amidft all the feverity of his conduct, he profeffes a ftrict regard to juftice: for faith he, *I fear God.* Therefore *they said one to another, we are verily guilty concerning our brother, in that we saw the anguish of his soul when he besought us, and we would not hear: therefore is this distress come upon us* *.

THE *holiness* of God alfo appears with peculiar luftre and majefty in the glafs of providential difpenfations. When Nadab and Abihu were ftruck dead by fire from the Lord, Mofes confoles his brother Aaron from a confideration of the Divine holinefs: *This is it that the Lord spake, saying, I will be sanctified in them that come nigh me, and before all the people I will be glorified: and Aaron held his peace.*— The *wisdom* of God alfo appears to greater advantage. How ftriking muft have been the difplay of this perfection to Jofeph, when he looked back on all the fteps of the Divine procedure towards him, and on all the finful inftrumentality that men had in his fufferings, and faid; *As for you, ye thought evil against me, but God meant it unto good!* By this means alfo he *shows his people the power of his works* †. Nay, he confirms their faith in his very *being*. A delay of judgments has often proved to his children, occafionally, a temptation to unbelief. But when the hand of God is ftretched out, faith returns to its proper exercife; *so that a man shall say, when he seeth the vengeance,*

VOL. I.   M m m

* Gen. xlii. 21.   † Pfal. cxi. 6.

vengeance, Verily, there is a reward for the righteous; verily, he is a God that judgeth in the earth *.

5. This is also a great excitement to *live closely* with *God*. Nothing, surely, can more directly tend to endear communion with Him, than a daily unwearied observation of all dispensations, as proceeding from him as a reconciled God, a loving Father, and a compassionate Redeemer; and an unvaried endeavour to trace his love in these dispensations. We are informed that Enoch *walked with God:* and certainly it is an eminent part of this acceptable exercise and exalted attainment, constantly to aim at seeing God walking with us, and, in every step of our pilgrimage, *conducting* us, by his *good Spirit, to the land of uprightness.* When one, either from faith or experience, or from the happy union of both, can appeal to the Searcher of hearts, in the words of Asaph; *Nevertheless, I am continually with thee; thou hast holden me by my right hand;* it must have great influence in stirring him up to the study of universal holiness; and incite him, according to the natural operations of the new creature, to express himself in such language as this; *Whom have I in heaven but thee? and there is none upon earth that I desire besides thee* †.

6. This practice must throw great light on the *evil* of sin, by discovering providential frowns and chastisements for those parts of our conduct that might otherwise appear trivial. Many of the Lord's people have, by the course of his gracious providence, been convinced of the iniquity of those practices that have formerly appeared innocent. They have seen Providence contending with them; and being thence led to inquire into the reason of the controversy, have found it occasioned by some part of their conduct, which, till then, they reckoned *void of offence.* Jehosaphat, it would seem, did not see his error in contracting so great an intimacy with Ahaziah king of Israel, who *did very wickedly,* till the Lord had *broken his*

---

* Psal. lviii. 11.   † Psal. lxxiii. 23,—25.

his works*. He not only reproved him by the mouth of a Prophet for this confederacy, but previously engaged the winds in his quarrel, by destroying the fleet that he had built for trading to Tarshish.

FINALLY, this is an eminent mean of *humbling* the Christian. When he attends to all the providential reproofs for sin that he meets with, or recollects all the dark, perplexed, and dangerous steps in his pilgrimage, through which he hath been conducted, and considers the *casting down* which has invariably succeeded a *lifting up;* it tends greatly to abase him in his own apprehension. Thus the Lord spoke to his ancient people: *Thou shalt remember all the way which the Lord thy God led thee these forty years in the wilderness, to humble thee, and to prove thee, to know what was in thine heart.* As he kept them so long in the wilderness, and led them so often hither and thither, for the purpose of humbling them; the very remembrance of their tedious course, and of the great variety of afflictive dispensations which were measured out to them, would, through the Divine blessing, be productive of the same happy effect. So will it be with all true Israelites. When they review the tenor of Providence towards them; and especially when they consider the many murmurings, accusations, and rebellions that their stubborn unbelieving hearts have been chargeable with under trials, they will *know what was in* their *hearts,* and thence be humbled before the omniscient God. But they will also see, that although he hath tried them in this way, it was that he might *do* them *good at* their *latter end* †.

IV. WE are now to suggest some motives for encouraging Christians to this exercise.

1. THE first thing that demands our attention is the *command* of God. Thus did he address his Church in the wilderness; *Only take heed to thyself, and keep thy*

---

* 2 Chron. xx. 35,—37.   † Deut. viii. 2,—16.

thy soul diligently, lest thou forget the things which thine eyes have seen, and lest they depart from thy heart all the days of thy life; but teach them thy sons, and thy sons sons *. And shall we make it a question, whether the command of God ought to have influence on our consciences? This is undoubtedly a most *reasonable service;* as, by obeying this precept, we observe that course which is most intimately connected with our own comfort.

2. We might also urge the *promise, Whoso is wise and will observe,* &c. The immutable God hath pledged his faithfulness for the success of this work; *Even they shall understand the loving kindness of the Lord:* There is absolute certainty here; for there is a conveyance of Divine power in the promise to all who believe it, and shew their faith by obedience. Whatever testimonies of the love of God may be afforded to others who are less attentive, there are peculiar and striking manifestations secured to those who excel in diligence; *Even they shall understand, &c.* But on this topic we enlarge not, having glanced it already.

3. The *example* of the saints is another excitement. Jacob did not forget the Lord's mercies towards him. He acknowledges them with gratitude, humility and wonder; and to express his sense of their greatness and distinguishing nature, he contrasts them with his own unworthiness and with his former destitute situation; *I am not worthy of the least of all the mercies, and of all the truth which thou hast shewed unto thy servant: for with my staff I passed over this Jordan, and now I am become two bands* †. When he afterwards obtained a deliverance from the rage of his brother Esau, he acknowledged it as immediately coming from God. Therefore, when he met with him in peace, he said to him, *I have seen thy face as though I had seen the face of God* ‡. He was sensible that in this tender meeting with his brother, wherein he found nothing but love, after he was assured that he had come

---

* Deut. iv. 9.   † Gen. xxxii. 10.   ‡ Gen. xxxiii. 10.

come out against him with an hostile intention and preparation, he had a gracious discovery of Divine love to him, and an evident seal of his reconciliation to God. He declares himself as fully persuaded of fatherly love in this merciful dispensation, as if he had received a renewed intimation of it from the mouth of God. Therefore, he speaks in language similar to that which he used, when God declared that *as a prince* he had *power with* him, *and* had *prevailed;* and as alluding to that unparalleled interview. For then he said; *I have seen God face to face* *: and now he says to his brother; *I have seen thy face as though I had seen the face of God.* Thus he was as really assured of the love of God to him, by his providential dispensation in the one case, as he had been assured of it by an immediate revelation in the other. One, careless about the operations of God, would have ascribed the kindness of Esau to some sudden change in the temper of his mind, arising from natural inconstancy; or to the mollifying influence of the valuable present which Jacob sent before him; or passed it over as one of the unaccountable accidents of life; without losing time in searching for the cause. But Jacob attributes it entirely to Divine power, restraining the wrath of his formerly implacable foe; and converting his bitter enmity into the most tender affection.—The same attentive conduct is discovered by David; *I remember the days of old, I meditate on all thy works: I muse on the works of thy hands* †. It was eminently exemplified in his deportment, when the Lord testified his approbation of David's design of building him an house, by informing him that he had reserved this work for his son, and declaring that he would *build him a sure house.—Then went king David in, and he sat before the Lord, and he said, Who am I, O Lord God? and what is my house, that thou hast brought me hitherto* ‡?

4. THE consideration of God's constant and tender *remembrance* of *you* may encourage you to this exercise. Have I not graven thee, saith the Lord,

* Gen. xxxii. 30. † Psal. cxliii. 5. ‡ 2 Sam. vii. 18.

on the palms of my hands? and thy walls are continually before me. He that toucheth you, *toucheth the apple of mine eye.* If you are in truth his people, he hath set you *as a seal upon* his *heart, and as a seal upon* his *arm.* He hath practically shewed you that his *love* was stronger than *death,* and his *jealousy* more *cruel* than *the grave;* for the *many waters* of affliction could *not quench* this *love,* nor could all *the floods* of indignation *drown it.* He not only remembers your persons, but all your works. For *God is not unrighteous to forget your work and labour of love, which ye have shewed towards his name.* There is indeed no merit on your part. You are *unprofitable servants.* Yet God would deem it unworthy of his essential justice, to forget this; because he hath bound himself to you by gracious promises. He is now treasuring up, in his everlasting remembrance, all those little services of love that you perform for his name's sake: and those actions, which you scarcely think worth remembering, shall be all rehearsed before assembled worlds. The book of his remembrance shall be opened, and he will in infinite love and condescension say to you; *I was an hungred, and ye gave me meat,* &c. Those things that you cannot remember, or are almost ashamed to acknowledge, because of their littleness and imperfection, he will not be ashamed to confess before his holy angels. The little that you speak for Christ, in commending him to others, your conversation about the affairs of his kingdom, is carefully listened to and remembred by him. The Prophet Malachi informs us that, in an evil time, *they that feared the Lord spake often one to another.* Well, did he disregard their exercise? No; for *the Lord hearkned and heard it.* The expression is doubled, to express his accurate observation of such work, the satisfaction that he hath in it, and the impossibility of its being forgotten. Your very *thoughts* about his name, his perfections, his glory and kingdom, are so precious in his estimation, that they are all registered in his presence. Though you

you should have no proper opportunity of expressing them to others, though they should be expressed only in feeble wishes and desires; as these proceed from love to him, they shall by no means be overlooked. For *a book of remembrance was written before him for them that feared the Lord, and that thought upon his name* *. Even your *tears* are precious to him; the tears that you shed for your own sins, and for those of the world around you, that *lieth in the wicked one*. He keeps a cistern for them. He preserves a faithful memorial of them. Therefore saith the Psalmist, *Put thou my tears into thy bottle: are they not in thy book* ‡? And if he remembers your works, your words, your thoughts, and your very tears; can you indulge yourselves in forgetting his mercies? If he remembers your *work of love*, which is so very insignificant, can you forget the operation of his hand, which is one uninterrupted dispensation of love to you? If he records the words that you speak for him; can you bury in oblivion his words of grace and manifestations of mercy to you? Doth he treasure up your unworthy thoughts; and will you not account his *thoughts precious?* Doth he register your very tears; and will you not shed them more abundantly, when you reflect on your own unspeakable ingratitude?

5. The recollection of former mercies will afford you an *argument* with God for *renewed* instances of his love. By rehearsing these and pleading his unchangeableness in love; you frame a most powerful argument. It was with this view that Jacob acknowledged *all the mercies, and all the truth*, that the Lord had shewed him; that he might have a plea for a new interposition. This is not *the manner of man* indeed. But *as the heavens are higher than the earth, so are* the Lord's *ways higher than* our *ways*. The more that a sinful worm hath run in arrears to God, the more, if possible, is he welcome to draw upon him: for nothing is so pleasing to him as to *devise liberally* at his hand. Therefore, Jacob infolds his petition between

---

* Mal. iii. 16.   ‡ Psal. lvi. 8.

a declaration of former deliverance, and a promise of future good ; *I am not worthy of the least of all the mercies, &c. Deliver me, I pray thee, from the hand of my brother, from the hand of Esau.—And thou saidst, I will surely do thee good* *. When the Psalmist had this prayer to present, *Remember, Lord, the reproach of thy servants*; he prefaces it in the following manner, *Lord, where are thy former loving kindnesses* †? In the same way does the Apostle comfort himself ; *Who delivered us from so great a death, and doth deliver ; in whom we trust that he will yet deliver* ‡. In this manner did our great Pattern pray for deliverance from his awful desertion. He not only referred to the confidence and success of his fathers according to the flesh, who *trusted in God, and were delivered ;* but he recounted the former evidences of a peculiar Divine care about himself ; *But thou art he that took me out of the womb ; thou didst make me hope when I was upon my mother's breasts.* And he issues all in this supplication ; *Be not far from me, for trouble is near* §. Let us then *be followers of God as dear children* ; for herein, undoubtedly, he hath left us *an example that we should follow his steps.*

In a word, God considers you as *contemners* of his operations, unless you bestow your attention on them. He concludes that you account them unworthy of your observation, and find no delight in this exercise. *The works of the Lord are great, sought out of all them that have pleasure therein* **.

But as this exercise, however comfortable and necessary, is, through the infirmity of man, liable to great abuse ; we shall conclude by offering a few CAUTIONS with respect to the proper management of it.

1. Beware of making Providence the *rule* of your conduct. This would be to put it in the place of the word, which is not merely the principal, but the only rule. Sometimes, indeed, the Lord's people, when in darkness, are assisted in forming a judgment as to their

---

* Gen. xxxii. 10.—12.   † Psal. lxxxix. 49, 50.   ‡ 2 Cor. i. 10.
§ Psal. xxii. 4.—11.   ** Psal. cxi. 2.

their duty, by something that occurs in the course of Providence. Perhaps, he *hedges up their way with thorns*, and *makes a wall, so that they cannot find their paths*, those which they incline to take. But merely from this to infer the sinfulness of that course, which they proposed, is to follow a dangerous line of conduct. Such motions of Providence are not to influence us, unless we perceive that the way, which seems to be pointed out, is in itself agreeable to God's revealed will, and more glorifying to him than the other. For we must remember that there is a most important distinction between the will of God as to our duty, and his will as to the event in Providence. Nothing but what is lawful is the will of God, in the first sense, as enjoined in the word. Sin itself, the greatest of evils, is his will as to providential dispensation. It is his will to permit it; else we may be assured it could never have had a being in the world. Therefore, by using the motions of Providence as a rule of duty, we may directly oppose God's revealed will, and not only plunge into enthusiasm, but provoke God by great iniquity. David's men tried to persuade him to interpret Providence in this manner. When Saul came into the cave, they said; *Behold the day of which the Lord said unto thee, Behold I will deliver thine enemy into thine hand, that thou mayest do unto him as it shall seem good unto thee.* But David rejected the proposal with detestation, because Saul was the Lord's anointed *.

2. JUDGE not of providential dispensations by their outward *aspect*. This is often very threatening, while the Lord hath nothing but love in his heart. It was Jacob's error that he judged in this manner. *All these things*, said he, *are against me*. And many of the seed of Jacob have, in their successive generations, been caught in the same snare. Were we to form any judgment of the design of such dispensations by their external appearance, it should rather be the reverse of that which would seem at first view most natural.

* 1 Sam. xxiv. 4.—6.

natural. It would be nearest the truth to conclude, that those who are most severely chastised are most dear to God; and that those who enjoy the greatest share of prosperity are the objects of his aversion.— For *whom the Lord loveth he chasteneth. The wicked have no bands in their death, but their strength is firm. They are not in trouble as other men; neither are they plagued like other men.* And in general, as is said of Lazarus, the righteous have, in this life, their *evil things;* while the wicked have their *good things.* But the Holy Spirit expressly forbids us to pretend to judge of the love or hatred of God, by the course of his Providence. Therefore, saith the Preacher; *When I applied mine heart to know wisdom, and to see the business that is done upon the earth: then I beheld all the work of God, that a man cannot find out the work that is done under the sun: because though a man labour to seek it out, yet he shall not find it: yea, farther, though a wise man think to know it, yet shall he not be able to find it. For all this I considered in mine heart, even to declare all this, that the righteous, and the wise, and their works, are in the hand of God; no man knoweth either love or hatred, by all that is before them. All things come alike to all: there is one event to the righteous, and to the wicked: to the good, and to the clean, and to the unclean: to him that sacrificeth, and to him that sacrificeth not: as is the good, so is the sinner; and he that sweareth, as he that feareth an oath* *.

3. In all your observation of Divine Providence, still remember that the ways of God are *unsearchable.* His judgments are *a great deep.* Paul, when writing of the wonderful dispensations of Providence, in the rejection of the Jews and calling of the Gentiles, after he had said a great deal on the subject, starts back, like a man that had gone beyond his depth, crying out; *O the depth of the riches both of the wisdom and knowledge of God! how unsearchable are his judgments, and his ways past finding out! For who hath known*

the

---

* Eccl. viii. 17. ix. 1, 2.

the mind of the Lord? or who hath been his counsellor* ? Think not that you can ever comprehend the *extent* of God's dispensations. There are many circumstances which far surpass your reach. For we *know* but *parts of his ways.* Often it will be equally difficult to understand their *design.* It is your duty, especially with respect to yourselves, humbly to endeavour to discover this. But the event will often show, how dangerous it is positively to determine. Who could have thought that the crucifixion of Christ, *through weakness,* was absolutely necessary to his living, as our Head, *by the power of God?* Often you cannot trace the *chain* of Providence. The connection between one link and another is not apparent. God leaves no mark of his course behind him. Therefore, faith the Church ; *Thy way is in the sea, and thy path in the great waters ; and thy footsteps are not known* †. At other times, there are such intricacies in his conduct, that our weak eye cannot follow him. *Clouds and darkness are round about him.* One event is, to our apprehension, so warped with another, that we cannot distinguish them. There is *a wheel within a wheel:* and these are *high and lifted up;* often *so high, that they are dreadful.* In a word, the *reasons* of providential dispensations are often very mysterious. Therefore, they must be observed with the greatest caution. Sometimes, they are the very contrary of those that would most naturally occur. The reasons of many parts of the Divine procedure shall remain unknown to the children of God, till the whole mystery of Providence be revealed in the kingdom of their Father. What they *know not now,* they shall *know hereafter. Then shall we know, if we follow on to know the Lord.* Whatever darkness is now on his paths, then shall we see that his *going forth,* in every instance, hath been *prepared as the morning.*

4. BEWARE of forming a *rash* judgment with respect to God's *designs. He that believeth shall not make*

---

* Rom. xi. 33, 34. † Psal. lxxvii. 19.

make haste. One motion of Providence may be intimately connected with another, which is either not discernible, or at a great distance. In consequence of hasty conclusions, the children of God have often plunged into practical errors. Moses *supposed his brethren would have understood, how that God by his hand would deliver them* *. And thus, he, who was to deliver Israel, had to flee for his own life; because he only considered outward circumstances, without waiting for the express call of God. Jacob did not rashly judge of the event, from Joseph's dream; but he *observed the saying.—Blessed is he that waiteth.*

5. Be especially on your guard against *harsh* and *uncharitable* judgment. Many turn and twist Divine Providence, as if it were meant for a toy to their own peevish humours. It smiles or frowns, just as they feel love or dislike to their neighbour. They talk as confidently, as if they were of God's counsel. But all such daringly *intrude into those things which* they have *not seen, vainly puffed up by* their *fleshly mind.* If any evil befal a man, with whom perhaps they are displeased; " I foresaw this," will they vauntingly say, " I knew he could not pros-" per; I always expected something of this kind." Or, perhaps they will interpret the dispensation as an infallible token, that God is provoked by some secret wickedness committed by that person, and that he takes this way to reveal it. Our Lord guards his hearers against this uncharitable interpretation of Divine procedure. When *some told him of the Galileans, whose blood Pilate had mingled with their sacrifices; Suppose ye,* said he, *that these Galileans were sinners above all the Galileans, because they suffered such things?—or those eighteen, upon whom the tower in Siloam fell, and slew them; think ye that they were sinners, above all men that dwelt in Jerusalem?* He expressly denies it; *I tell you, Nay:* and gives a severe check to such a spirit, by warning those, who seem to have been actuated by it, of their own danger:

* Acts vii. 25.

ger: *But except ye repent, ye shall all likewise perish* *.

But it may be said; "To what purpose observe the motions of Providence, or consider the operations of God's hand; if we be not permitted to form a judgment as to the reasons or intentions?" Be more assiduous in endeavouring to discover the designs of Providence with respect to yourselves, than others. Thus you will be far less in danger of forming an erroneous judgment. In judging as to others, you are apt to be misled by appearances, or by secret prejudice and the envious wish of the heart. But in judging with respect to yourselves, you are most in danger of erring on the side of partiality. Besides, here you have conscience as your assistant, which, if left to itself, will generally, in some measure, speak the truth. The children of God have also the motions of his Spirit, accompanying the word, to direct them. Some dispensations, indeed, are so distinctly written, that *he who runneth may read*. When there is a striking similarity between the sin and the punishment; when *the wicked is* evidently *driven away* IN *his wickedness*; there is little danger of misinterpretation. The consciences, even of wicked men, in such cases, suggest the meaning of the Providence. But where there is no previous or present discovery of remarkable iniquity, it is presumptuous to conclude, from adverse events, that this is the reason. The friends of Job formed a false judgment in this respect. His uncommon afflictions were the sole ground on which they rested their charge of hypocrisy. Not only did Job accuse them of speaking *wickedly for God;* but God himself testified his great displeasure with them. He said to Eliphaz the Temanite; *My wrath is kindled against thee, and against thy two friends: for ye have not spoken of me the thing that is right, as my servant Job hath*. Therefore he directed them to bring a sacrifice, and to apply to Job, that he might pray for them; *lest*, saith he, *I deal with you after your folly* †.

The

---

* Luke xiii. 1.—5. † Job xlii. 7. 8.

The Jews seem to have formed the same opinion of those who perished by the cruelty of Pilate, and by the fall of the tower of Siloam, which Job's friends did of him. They had no other evidence than this; yet they concluded that they were *sinners above others*. Nay, it appears to have been at that time an error common among them, to judge from the outward afflictions of individuals, that God was contending because of some atrocious sin. The disciples proposed this question to Jesus, concerning the man who was blind from his birth; *Who did sin; this man, or his parents, that he was born blind**? On this account also, the Jews said to the man himself; *Thou wast altogether born in sin* †.

While, therefore, you attend to the works of God, seek *wisdom from above*. Thus that which is written shall be fulfilled as to you; *They shall wisely consider of his doings*. Let it be more your concern to be stirred up to duty already known, and to attain further acquaintance with it, by means of providential instruction, than to indulge a vain curiosity. This improvement of Providence is represented as the fruit of a *wise* consideration thereof. For it immediately follows the promise recently mentioned; *The righteous shall be glad in the Lord, and shall trust in him; and all the upright in heart shall glory*. If you rightly observe Providence, this exercise will have the same effect in your experience, as it had in that of the Psalmist: *I meditate of all thy works. I muse on the work of thy hands. I lift up my soul unto thee: my soul thirsteth after thee as a thirsty land* ‡.

---

* John ix. 1, 2.   † John ix. 34.   ‡ Psal. cxliii. 5, 6.

END OF THE FIRST VOLUME.

Lately Published,
By the same AUTHOR,

In a handsome crown Octavo, price 1s. 6d.

THE

SORROWS OF SLAVERY,

A POEM:

CONTAINING A

FAITHFUL STATEMENT OF FACTS,

RESPECTING THE

AFRICAN SLAVE TRADE.

LONDON:
Printed for J. Murray, No. 32, Fleet-street; C. Elliot, Edin.; J. Duncan, and Dunlop and Wilson, Glasgow.

Also Lately Published, Price one Shilling,

The Second Edition of the

FORCE OF TRUTH;

An AUTHENTIC NARRATIVE:

By the Rev. THOMAS SCOTT,
Morning Preacher at the Lock-chapel.

Printed for Bellamy and Robarts, No. 202. Strand, London, who are also publishing by subscription, in weekly numbers, price six-pence each,

The Rev. Mr SCOTT's FAMILY BIBLE,
With entire orginal Notes and Practical Observations, at the end of every chapter; to be completed in 120 numbers, with an elegant plate to each, and such maps as may be necessary.

www.ingramcontent.com/pod-product-compliance
Lightning Source LLC
Chambersburg PA
CBHW051855300426
44117CB00006B/398